MENTAL HEALTH LAW

MENTAL HEALTH LAW

by

BRENDA HOGGETT
*Formerly Professor of Law
at the University of Manchester,
Law Commissioner,*

Now THE HON. MRS JUSTICE HALE, DBE
*High Court Judge,
Visiting Professor,
King's College, London*

LONDON
SWEET & MAXWELL
1996

First Edition 1984
Second Edition 1987
Third Edition 1990
Fourth Edition 1996

Published in 1996 by Sweet and Maxwell Limited of
100 Avenue Road, Swiss Cottage, London NW3 3PF
Computerset by Interactive Sciences, Gloucester
Printed by Butler and Tanner, Frome, Somerset

*No natural forests were destroyed to make this product; only farmed timber was
used and replanted*

ISBN: 0421522100

A CIP catalogue record for this book is available from the British
Library

FOREWORD

SIR LOUIS
BLOM-COOPER Q.C.

This book needs no exordium. In its subject-matter there can be no cavilling with the view that mental health, within the framework of well-constructed and not too prescriptive legalism, is an increasingly vital segment of public law and administration. The fact that Brenda Hoggett's seminal work has gone into a fourth edition within two decades speaks volumes for the compelling need for an authoritative, up-to-date work, not just for legal practitioners but for social workers, doctors, hospital managers and administrators. Its author likewise needs no introduction. Her name, not too artfully disguised by her recent, merited translation to judicial heights, has long been linked to the subject-matter. Her leadership at the Law Commission on producing a final report on Mental Incapacity was outstanding, drawing plaudits from a wide range of professionals and administrators not usually given to lavishing praise on members of the legal profession.

The subject matter, its author and a new edition at a time of incremental interest and practice in mental health law suffice for commendation. If the book is to be commended, what more can, or should the foreworder say than simply commend it? If it is less than commendable, nothing can be said that should rescue the work from the fate of being unobtrusively shelved. But I trust that the honour which Brenda does in inviting me to write, knowing full well the maverick quality of this foreworder, is an invitation to say something profound or provocative. As to the former, I confess not to be a thinker, let alone someone whose thoughts are ever more than superficial. But provocative—I prefer the epithet, challenging—I am capable of being.

Brenda Hoggett wrote in *Public Law* in the Summer of 1983 that it remained to be seen whether anyone (other than lawyers and the members of the Mental Health Act Commission) will actually gain from the provisions of the 1983 Act which enlarged, without substantially deviating from, the precepts of the 1959 Act. Apart from a weak obligation on health and social services authorities to provide "after-care" for patients discharged from long-term detention—she was alluding to the beguiling and often, since then, unfulfilled section 117—and the weakening and infrequently used Guardianship Order, there was nothing in the legislation to develop the *rights* of patients to receive services in the community, or to encourage a genuine community concern for the mentally afflicted. Now that since 1991 we have been pitchforked into care in the community, where is the legislative response to the protection of incapacitated and vulnerable people living in the community? The Law Commission's proposals on *Mental Incapacity* awaits a governmental endorsement and promise for legislation. Ministers have consistently told the Mental Health Act Commission, which has campaigned for a review of mental health law, that the 1983 Act will have to be reviewed "sooner or later", while demonstrating by their inactivism a desire to postpone the day of review. The 1983 Act, as Brenda states in her conclusion to this edition of her work, is beginning to look decidedly old-fashioned. The 1983 Act is not just out of date and out of step with the times; it presents entirely the wrong image to practitioners in the mental health system. Any legislation in this field must, of course, provide for safeguarding the rights of patients detained for treatment for psychotic disorders. But if the shift of care and treatment from hospital to community is to be a reality, the legal framework must reflect the primacy of rights and duties of community care, with infringements of liberty taking on a supportive, hospitalising role. Society's values relating to mental health cannot go legislatively unacknowledged.

Legislation is a time-consuming activity. To be soundly based it is necessary that legislators should be authoritatively briefed. The 1983 Act itself went through a gestation period of at least four years, starting with a consultation document in the dying days of the Labour administration. A new Mental Health Act is unlikely to emerge much before the end of the millennium. The review should be put in train now—in early 1996. What form should the review take? It would be tempting to take as a model the preparatory work for the Children Act 1989. The Department of Health and Social Security (as it then was) set up a working party, in that mental health year of 1983, of department officials, with support from Lord Chancellor's Department and the Law Commission, on which Brenda Hoggett was such a notable contributor. That was, quintessentially, a specialist body to pronounce upon a specialist subject. While Government eschewed the tradition of Royal Commissions of the past, and the only post-1979 Royal Commission has been on Criminal Justice, my view is that there is real benefit in excluding from membership of a body reviewing the mental health system, anybody connected with psychiatry, social work, sociology or mental hospital administration or management (I do not seek to be prescriptive; the idea is to keep off the reviewing body those who know the system and come to the topic with pre-conceived notions, however well-founded). I envisage an independent body composed of men and women of experience, achievement and measured judgment, indifferent completely to party-political advantage and unallied to the vested interests in psychiatry and law, so often at odds with each other. The body would necessarily be addressed with vigour by a range of interest and reform groups (all readily identified) as well as the principal professional bodies involved in mental health. Its deliberations will be the stronger for maintaining a deliberately lay outlook. By "lay" I mean unconnected with any of the actors in the mental health system. It should insist on the rendering in lay language of all opinions and data submitted to it. The jargon of psychiatry and the law should not be allowed to blind the public and legislators to the dictates of social policy. It would require a strong secretariat which had access to all relevant material and other subject-matter, and it may need to commission some research, although the wealth of contemporary knowledge suggests that research would be more by way of compilation, digestion, analysis and assessment of existing research findings.

Entered into a genuine spirit of inquiry, such a body could sketch the broad principles of mental health policy for the twenty-first century. Not all of its report could conceivably be conclusive, or, for that matter, make firm recommendations. Reflection, deliberation and a description of choices would greatly inform both public and political debate in the shaping of policy. The task should be conducted in a European setting. How do our neighbours in the European Union order these matters? Mental ill-health knows no territorial boundaries. Human beings suffer in much the same ways in modern industrial societies of western civilisation.

PREFACE

This book was first written in 1975, because there was then no book to recommend to my student psychiatrists and social workers at the University of Manchester to help them with their statutory functions under the Mental Health Act 1959. My thanks then were mainly due to those students, and to other tutors on those courses, who helped me to understand what their problems were. The law was still dominated by the professional model, although the rumblings from the lawyers and others were beginning to be heard. The second edition followed the Mental Health Act 1983, and so it is not surprising that my thanks then were also due to the members and staff of the Mental Health Review Tribunals and to the Council on Tribunals on which I had served, as well as to colleagues in the law who were now conducting serious research in the subject which I was simply trying to understand and explain. By the time that the third edition appeared in 1990, the focus was again beginning to shift, towards the problems raised by the growing numbers of mentally disabled adults living in the community. My thanks then were due to my colleagues at the Law Commission, who had already begun the work which culminated in the Report on Mental Incapacity published this year. I still owe them all, and everyone who helped the Commission with that project, a great debt of gratitude for all that they have taught me. From time to time I even have the opportunity of putting some of it into practice in the courts.

For this edition my thanks must go above all to my clerk, Barbara Cojeen, who is fast qualifying herself for a new career as a research assistant and has tracked down many a reference for me, with the able assistance of the Supreme Court Library; to Adina Halpern, Nightingale Fellow-Commoner at Trinity Hall, Cambridge, and Claire Johnston at the Law Commission, for their penetrating comments on the manuscript; and to Sir Louis Blom-Cooper Q.C. for contributing such a sparkling foreword.

As usual, I have only myself to blame if I have missed anything or got it wrong. One deliberate mistake is to anticipate the coming into force of the Mental Health (Patients in the Community) Act 1995 and the Health Authorities Act 1995 on April 1, 1996 (but not the consequent rules and regulations, which are not yet available). Otherwise I have tried to state the law as it is today.

December 13, 1995   *Brenda Hale*

CONTENTS

TABLE OF CASES

xi

xiv

xvii

TABLE OF STATUTES

xix

TABLE OF STATUTORY INSTRUMENTS

xxix

TABLE OF CIRCULARS

xxxiii

TABLE OF EUROPEAN MATERIAL

INTRODUCTION

Mental health law serves a shifting mass of conflicting interests and ideologies. The general public are no doubt suspicious that mental disorder may too readily be used as an excuse for criminal behaviour. But they forget that (at least since the abolition of the death penalty) the consequences may be just as severe for the patient and sometimes more so. One reason for this is the public outcry which greets any mistaken decision to set a mentally disordered offender free. We can all perceive the benefits in keeping mental patients in an institution out of harm's way, especially if this holds out some comforting hope of eventual improvement or cure. This probably explains why the Victorians were prepared to spend more public money on keeping patients in asylums than on keeping paupers in the workhouse. But it also explains why they wanted watertight guarantees against confinement of the wrong people. The fit pauper did not deserve it and the sane man did not want it. The resulting legalism was seen as a disaster for those who genuinely needed treatment.

Given the public attitudes which still surface from time to time, the Mental Health Act 1959 was little short of revolutionary. There had been such advances in treatment and in psychiatry that the medical profession were able to argue that both they and their patients should be set free from the straitjacket of the past. Henceforward, mental patients should be treated no differently from any others. They should be admitted to hospital without special formalities. It should still be possible to compel them to accept treatment if they refused to accept their doctors' advice, but this should be done with the minimum of formality and only when strictly necessary. Mentally disordered people who committed crimes should be able to be admitted to hospital for treatment in much the same circumstances as other patients who needed it. Once there, they should be treated just like those other patients, unless they were so dangerous that special safeguards were needed to protect the public. That apart, the length of time patients would spend in hospital, and the treatment they would receive while there, could safely be left in the hands of the medical profession. The patients undoubtedly benefited from the new psychiatry. But the new law was just as liberating for the psychiatrists as it was for their patients. Freed from their duty to guard society's misfits and rejects in isolated barracks in the countryside, they could concentrate on their new-found power to cure the sick. Although accompanied by a policy of transferring as many patients as possible into the community, this was an almost wholly medical and therapeutic approach to patient treatment and care.

In the 20 years which followed, it became clear that many of the patients formerly given asylum did not fit the new system. The 1959 Act assimilated the law relating to mental handicap with that relating to mental illness, but was mental handicap—now generally known as learning disability—a medical problem at all? What was to happen to the chronic or psychogeriatric patients who took up so many psychiatric beds? Above all, should hospitals have to take offenders with inadequate, aggressive or irresponsible personalities whom society did not want but whom the courts wanted to send to hospital rather than to prison? As ordinary hospitals became more open, special hospitals filled up with patients who in the past would have easily been managed in an asylum, until eventually there was nowhere prepared to have them.

As the medical model showed itself more and more reluctant to provide for many whose needs society and the courts wanted it to address, the model itself was increasingly challenged both in theory and in practice. Some of that challenge came from the "anti-psychiatrists" within the profession itself. They argued that mental illness was not an objective fact, but a label applied to behaviour which the psychiatrist regards as abnormal because of his own ideas about what is appropriate in any given situation. The mythical label, it was said, places the patient in complete subjection to the doctor, ruling out effective communication between them. Instead of helping the patient, it manipulates him for its own ends. Other challenges came from other professions which claimed an increasing role in under-standing and treating the patient. These added to the distrust of institutional solutions and stressed the importance of social factors in the causation and identification of mental illness.

Lawyers in this country played little part in all this ferment. On the other side of the Atlantic, however, they had woken up to the possibilities of the Constitution in controlling the activities of the "therapeutic state". A mass of research and litigation attempted to lay down acceptable criteria for the psychiatric deprivation of liberty, the procedural safeguards required, and the right to a minimum standard of treatment in return. The United Kingdom was still mainly concerned with the protection of society from the dangerous offender. This was the impetus for the Butler Committee on Mentally Abnormal Offenders which reported in 1975. But a series of scandals in mental hospitals had revealed that many patients were not dangerous at all, rather a chronically underprivileged group who were particularly vulnerable to exploitation both in and out of hospital.

The National Association for Mental Health (MIND) began to subject the comfortable assumptions in the 1959 Act to an increasingly uncomfort-able scrutiny. This was largely the work of Larry Gostin, an American lawyer, who produced two influential studies of the Act in practice, with suggestions for reform in line with principles being developed in the United States (Gostin, 1975 and 1977). The DHSS set about reviewing the Act (DHSS, 1976 and DHSS et al., 1978) and attempted to reconcile the irreconcilable views of all the different professions and interests involved. The resulting Mental Health Act 1983 improved the procedural safeguards and introduced some independent control over what went on in hospital. But it changed the underlying substance and purpose very little. The purpose is still to ensure that people suffering from mental disorder of almost any description can be given the medical treatment and care which the doctors think that they need.

Since implementation of the 1983 Act there has certainly been a greater involvement of lawyers and a developing body of case law interpreting the Act's provisions, which was almost non-existent under the 1959 Act. The nettle of diverting as many mentally disordered offenders as possible away from the criminal justice system has been firmly grasped (Reed, 1992). Mental illness is no longer the Cinderella of the National Health Service (Department of Health, 1992). The major development, however, has been a shift of professional and public attention away from the issues of detention and treatment in hospital and towards the problems of providing good quality health and social services in the community for the increasing numbers of people who need them. With that go the legal questions posed

2

by those who are unable to take some or all of the necessary decisions for themselves or to protect themselves against abuse or exploitation (Law Commission, 1995).

Such has been the pace of change, in the health and social services, in attitudes of and towards the patients themselves, and in the legal culture, that the 1983 Act is beginning to look very old-fashioned. Already, powerful voices are calling for another review (Mental Health Act Commission, 1993). There are also transatlantic signs of the pendulum swinging back towards co-operation rather than confrontation between psychiatry and the law in the pursuit of "therapeutic jurisprudence" (Carson and Wexler, 1994). But public documents here already reveal substantial agreement on the principles which might underpin a new Mental Health Act:

——People should be looked on as individuals, with proper regard to their sex, race, social and cultural background and other characteristics; they should be treated in such a way as to promote and enhance their own self-determination and personal responsibility; even if they are unable to decide for themselves, or matters have to be taken out of their hands for their own sake or that of others, they should still be consulted and their views given proper weight.

——Care and treatment in the community is to be preferred to care and treatment in institutions; institutional care should be provided under conditions of no greater control, segregation or security than is justified by the degree of danger to self or others; there should be a comprehensive multi-disciplinary approach to providing care and treatment in the community; the views of family and carers should also be taken into account.

——Legal procedures should be available to protect those who are unable to protect themselves from ill-treatment, neglect or exploitation; but whenever power is assumed over an individual, there must be proper substantive and procedural safeguards, in line with the requirements of the European Convention on Human Rights; and the assumption of power carries with it the obligation to provide the services which the individual needs.

What follows is a textbook designed for all who have anything to do with mentally disabled or disordered people in or out of hospital, for social workers and others who care for them in the community but who may have to use compulsory powers, for doctors, nurses and other professionals concerned with their medical treatment and therapy, and for lawyers, advocates and advice workers who try to protect their interests. It tries to explain the arguments which lie behind the present state of the law and which may go on in the future. But it is not a work of philosophy committed to any particular point of view, except to the proper recognition of the status and needs of all concerned.

1 THE MENTAL HEALTH ACT 1983: THE BASIC SCHEME

The present law relating to the care and treatment of mentally disordered people in England and Wales is contained in the Mental Health Act 1983. This consolidated the Mental Health Act 1959 with the substantial amendments made by the Mental Health (Amendment) Act 1982. The 1959 Act followed the deliberations of the Royal Commission on the Law relating to Mental Illness and Mental Deficiency of 1954 to 1957 (Percy, 1957). At the time, it constituted a revolutionary break with the traditions of the past. To appreciate why this was so, it is necessary to take a brief look at the earlier attitude of the law.

1. OUT OF MIND AND OUT OF SIGHT

In the early days, the only forms of mental disorder generally recognised were "lunacy" or "madness" and "idiocy". The common law allowed the confinement of the dangerously insane, those who seemed disposed to do mischief to themselves or others (Lanham, 1974; see also Chapter 4), but not the harmlessly eccentric or weak-witted. The insane might be kept in conditions which are now thought appalling, and often subject to individual "mechanical restraint" (a euphemism for shackles, manacles, cages and the like). By the turn of the eighteenth and nineteenth centuries, a growing body of opinion was inspired by the more humane system of "moral treatment" pioneered by places such as the Retreat, the Quaker institution in York. Reformers pressed for control and supervision over the private madhouses run for profit (beginning with the Act for regulating Madhouses of 1774) and later over the charitable hospitals funded by public subscription then being set up. They also persuaded the county authorities to set up rate-funded asylums (first permitted in the County Asylums Act of 1808). These were started for pauper and criminal lunatics, but were soon allowed to take paying patients. The culmination of these efforts came in 1845, when the Lunatic Asylums Act obliged all county and borough authorities to set up asylums, and the Lunatics Act established the Lunacy Commissioners. This was an independent body with powers to supervise standards and protect patients in all the hospitals, asylums and licensed houses in the country (apart from the oldest charitable hospital, Bethlem, which escaped control until 1854). Reconstituted as the Board of Control in 1913, this body continued, with some modifications, until the 1959 Act.

These reformers thought that the answer to the bad institutions of the past lay in the good institutions of the future. Their measures reinforced the assumption that mental patients were to be segregated and imprisoned, whether or not they could be treated or made better. Demand for places in asylums grew and grew, as workhouses and families recognised the opportunity of providing for some people who did not readily fit into the harsh assumptions underlying the new Poor Law of 1834, not only the conventionally insane but also the aged mentally infirm. In 1807, there were only 2,248 people (or 2.26 per 10,000 of the population) officially recognised as insane, both in and out of institutions. By 1890, there were

86,167 (or 29.26 per 10,000). Ninety per cent of these were paupers and all but a small proportion, particularly in the county and borough asylums, were acknowledged to be incurable (Scull, 1979). Not surprisingly, considerations of economy had turned these huge and isolated "warehouses for the insane" into very different places from those which the early reformers had envisaged.

The other concern of the legislators (often bitterly opposed by the pioneers of reform, such as Lord Shaftesbury) was with the procedures for commitment. Ordinary members of the public could perceive the benefit in removing the disordered out of harm's way but only if there was no risk that they themselves might be confined. Well-publicised mistakes fuelled the demand for much more elaborate commitment procedures, particularly for private patients, which culminated in the Lunacy Act of 1890. This provided for formal certification by a judicial order, following a petition by relatives or poor law officials and supported by medical evidence. The same approach was adopted when publicly-financed institutions for the mentally handicapped were established under the Mental Deficiency Act of 1913, following the Report of the Royal Commission on the Care and Control of the Feeble-minded of 1908 (Radnor, 1908). The most severely handicapped "idiots" had previously been included in the definition of "lunatics", but this Act extended the concept of segregation to a much wider class of socially inadequate or inconvenient, as well as intellectually disabled, people.

These reform movements had two results which were unpopular with medical opinion from at least the end of the nineteenth century. First, because of the original desire to improve standards in institutions, patients who were certified under the Acts could only be admitted to the specialised institutions controlled under them. Mentally ill patients could only be committed to asylums, mental hospitals and madhouses, although these became known as "designated" public mental hospitals, "registered" hospitals, or "licensed" private nursing homes. Mental "defectives" could only be committed to "directed" public institutions or "certified" private ones. A mental "defective" could not be admitted to a mental illness hospital, although the personality disorders which were included as "defects" are now treated (if at all) as part of psychiatry rather than the care of people with learning disabilities. Nor could a mentally ill patient be admitted to a mental handicap institution. There was a growing number of other hospitals prepared to treat patients outside the ambit of the Acts altogether (some of them in "de-designated" parts of mental hospitals), but these could only take patients informally and could never use the compulsory measures.

Secondly, although private "licensed" houses had long been allowed to take "voluntary boarders" who could afford to pay, the asylums and institutions maintained at public expense were at first only permitted to take certified patients. The impecunious, who constituted the great majority, could not be treated in hospital on a voluntary basis. Formal certification involved a stigma which many doctors shrank from imposing upon their patients until, it was said, it was too late for treatment to have any chance of success. The medical profession were also identifying new forms of mental disorder falling far short of obvious "madness" or "lunacy" and for which certification and confinement were thought neither necessary nor appropriate. The "shell shock" cases of the First World War increased public awareness of these. The first step towards freely available treatment without certification was taken when the Maudsley Hospital was founded in 1915, with a special statutory dispensation to admit voluntary non-paying patients.

For most mentally ill patients, however, the major change came with the Mental Treatment Act 1930. This began the break away from the legalism, procedural formality and institutional domination of the late nineteenth century, towards the professionalisation, informality and integration with general medicine which were the hallmarks of the mid twentieth century (Unsworth, 1987). It followed the Royal Commission on Lunacy and Mental Disorders of 1924 to 1926 (MacMillan, 1926). "Asylums" were renamed "mental hospitals" and "lunatics" became "persons of unsound mind". A "temporary" status was introduced for non-volitional patients who required treatment for no more than a year, and a "voluntary" status for those who were able to make a written application to be treated in hospital.

Until the 1959 Act, then, there were three different types of patient in mental illness hospitals—voluntary and temporary patients under the 1930 Act and patients certified under the various procedures in the 1890 Act. For mental "defectives" there was a totally different, if rather less complex, set of procedures under the Mental Deficiency Acts of 1913 and 1927. These did not include a voluntary status, but the institutions were not expressly prohibited from taking patients without formality. After 1952, this was officially encouraged for short stays, and the Percy Commission recommended that it could be extended to long-stay patients without waiting for legislation. In the Commission's Report, and in the 1959 Act which implemented it, a determined effort was made to break down the rigid legal boundaries and integrate the separate legal systems relating to "lunacy" and "mental deficiency".

Two developments lay behind much of the Percy Commission's thinking. First was the introduction of the National Health Service in 1948. This had led to most hospitals of any type being vested in the then Ministry of Health, and to some rearrangement of the functions of the Board of Control, but nothing had been done to remove the rigid and antiquated categorisation of mental hospitals. The Commission believed that there was no longer any need for strict legal control over public hospitals. Further, as improvements depend upon the availability of resources, full responsibility should rest with the government department which controlled the allocation of resources within the health service as a whole. The Board of Control could safely be abolished, and with it the legal segregation of mental hospitals from the main stream of hospital development.

Second was the great optimism about the advances in medical treatment for the major mental illnesses, through psycho-surgery, electro-convulsive therapy and above all the new breed of psycho-tropic drugs, the major tranquillisers. These made it possible for increasing numbers of seriously disordered patients to be discharged into the community or treated on open wards in ordinary hospital conditions. It no longer seemed necessary for the law to assume that these patients were inevitably different from the physically sick or injured. For the most part, they could be admitted to hospital in just the same way. Compulsory procedures could be kept only for those for whom they were absolutely necessary. Once in hospital, their treatment and care could be left in the hands of the medical profession. As many as possible would be discharged back into the community just like other patients.

Hence, removing the legal controls over mental patients was inextricably linked with removing the legal controls over their doctors. The 1983 Act was mainly concerned to reimpose some of the latter.

2. INFORMAL ADMISSION TO HOSPITAL

The basic principle introduced by the 1959 Act is now contained in section 131(1) of the 1983 Act:

> "Nothing in this Act shall be construed as preventing a patient who requires treatment for mental disorder from being admitted to any hospital or mental nursing home in pursuance of arrangements made in that behalf and without any application, order or direction rendering him liable to be detained under this Act, or from remaining in any hospital or mental nursing home in pursuance of such arrangements after he has ceased to be so liable to be detained."

This means that patients may enter hospital for treatment for mental disorder in just the same way that they would enter hospital for a physical disorder, without any special formalities. The trend away from compulsory admission to mental illness hospitals was established before the 1959 Act. Even in 1955, they were only 27 per cent; by 1970, this had fallen to 17.5 per cent, and by 1986 to 8.1 per cent of all admissions. The decline in compulsory admissions to mental handicap hospitals was even more dramatic, largely because there was previously no statutory voluntary status; by 1986, they had fallen to only 0.65 per cent. Since then, official figures have covered all types of unit. The proportion of compulsory admissions still hovers around 8 per cent of all admissions; but this masks a considerable increase in numbers during the early 1990s, from around 16,300 in 1987/88 to around 21,400 in 1992/93; and in some inner city hospitals pressure on beds is so acute that a very high proportion of admissions is compulsory.

More significant still was the decline in the proportion of patients in hospital at any one time who were liable to be detained. In 1955, 70.4 per cent of those in mental illness hospitals were certified, because most voluntary patients stayed for only a short time and compulsion was still used for the long-stay chronically ill; and virtually all mentally handicapped patients were detained. By 1986, fewer than 5 per cent of all resident patients in NHS mental illness or mental handicap hospitals were detained. Figures for resident patients are no longer published, perhaps because the aim is to phase out the use of hospital as a place of permanent residence, and so the turnover is such that it would be misleading to give a snapshot on one particular day. The total number of detained residents is now thought to be around 11,500.

Theoretically, at least, informal patients enjoy two legal rights which detained patients do not. They may leave hospital whenever they like (see Chapter 7) and they may refuse to accept any form of trea ment which they do not want (see Chapter 6). Their mail is not censored in any way, they may be registered to vote, and they have unimpeded access to the courts. In practice, however, there are several different types of informal patient. Only those who appreciate the need to be in hospital and are generally content to accept their doctors' advice can be classed as completely "voluntary". There are three other categories to whom that description cannot be applied and for whom the benefits of being "informal" rather than "compulsory" are harder to assess.

First, there are many who lack any real understanding of their situation, whether because of brain damage, senile dementia or severe learning disability. A major conclusion of the Percy Commission was that such patients need no longer automatically be certified. The non-objecting could be equated with the consenting rather than the dissenting. That does not mean that the law permits the hospitals to restrain or treat them as it sees fit. The precise extent to which it may do so depends upon principles of the common law which are discussed in detail in Chapter 6. Whenever it is proposed to exceed the limits of the common law, in particular where the patient has evinced a definite desire to leave the hospital or to refuse a specific form of treatment, the hospital can only proceed if it is both able and willing to invoke the compulsory procedures in the 1983 Act.

These procedures can be seen as a protection of, rather than a threat to, the patient's integrity (DHSS *et al.*, 1978). They should ensure that active and precise attention is given to the patient's case by medical staff. Thereafter the case must periodically be reconsidered by the consultant. The hospital has a positive duty to ensure that the patient understands his position. The patient has the right to apply to a Mental Health Review Tribunal for his discharge and to the protection of the Mental Health Act Commission while he remains subject to detention. There are safeguards over the use of electro-convulsive therapy and long-term drug treatments. Indeed, Carson (1983) has suggested that some informal patients would do well to get themselves detained in order to obtain a second opinion on their treatment, while the Law Commission (1995) has proposed that the same safeguards should be extended to informal patients who are unable to give a valid consent.

There is no English body comparable to the Mental Welfare Commission in Scotland, which has a legal duty to protect *all* people who may, because of mental disorder, be incapable of protecting themselves, whether or not they are detained in hospital. The Mental Health Act Commission (see Chapter 6) was set up under the 1983 Act, principally in order to safeguard the interests of detained patients. But it has repeatedly asked for its remit to be extended to the *de facto* detained, in practice those elderly or severely disabled patients, who are unable to exercise any genuine choice, but who do not exhibit the active dissent which provokes professionals to invoke the compulsory procedures.

Secondly, there are children who are "volunteered" for admission by their parents or others, including local social services authorities, who have parental responsibility for them. The number of mentally handicapped children resident in hospital declined by about 80 per cent from 1976 to 1986, compared with a decline of 30 per cent in mental handicap hospital residents as a whole. There have never been so many mentally ill child residents, but they also fell by 24 per cent over the same period. Nevertheless, it is a matter of great concern that *any* child should be living in hospital unless he needs constant medical and nursing care. There are still some short-term admissions of severely disabled children for respite purposes. Of much greater concern are the growing numbers of children who are admitted to psychiatric facilities, or to other units where they may be given treatment which they do not want, because of their emotional or behavioural problems. They constitute another group who do not have the safeguards attached to the compulsory procedures but who cannot be described as genuine volunteers. Their legal position, which is discussed in Chapter 3, is complex and unsatisfactory.

Finally, there are those informal patients who are reluctant to accept their doctors' advice and wish either to leave the hospital or to refuse a suggested course of treatment. They may however stay and accept treatment, because they know or believe that they could otherwise be forced to do so, by being what is colloquially termed "sectioned" under the Act. This is done by a formal process of applying to the hospital managers for admission either for assessment or for treatment. To prevent their leaving before this can be done, they may be detained for a short period under section 5.

3. DETENTION OF "IN-PATIENTS" UNDER SECTION 5

Section 5(1) makes it clear that an application for compulsory "admission" may be made in respect of a patient who has already been informally admitted to hospital. Indeed, a substantial proportion of applications relate to patients in hospital, most of them informal (Barnes, Bowl and Fisher, 1990; Department of Health, 1995a). An application cannot be made in respect of a patient already detained under an application, except that an application for long-term admission for treatment may be made while a patient is detained short-term for assessment (s. 5(1) and (6)). But if the authorities are not immediately able to complete an application, perhaps because a relative or social worker is not available, section 5 provides two procedures for keeping an informal patient in the hospital for a short time. Neither can be used to prolong the detention of a patient whose "section" is about to expire (s. 5(6)) and neither gives any statutory power to impose treatment without consent (s. 56(1)(b)).

Both powers apply only to someone who is already an "in-patient," a term which is not defined. In ordinary language, it is usual to distinguish between an out-patient, who attends for an appointment with a specialist or for emergency treatment in casualty, and an in-patient, who has been allocated a bed in a ward. The Code of Practice (Department of Health and Welsh Office, 1993) defines an informal in-patient as someone "who has understood and accepted the offer of a bed, who has freely appeared on the ward and who has co-operated in the admission procedure" (para. 8.4). Thus these powers should not be used as a way of preventing a would-be suicide from leaving casualty when he comes round after having been "washed out", or to convert a day patient into an in-patient.

Under section 5(2), the doctor in charge of an in-patient's treatment may furnish the hospital managers with a report which authorises the patient's detention in the hospital for 72 hours from the time when the report is "furnished". Presumably, this means the time when it reaches the administration. The section is not specific about who may do the detaining (compare s. 6(2), p. 83, later)). For example, could the doctor authorise the staff to detain the patient even though the hospital managers wished to release him? The doctor "in charge" is thought to mean the consultant (or other) on whose list the patient is; but he may nominate *one* other doctor on the hospital staff to act for him in his absence (s. 5(3); that delegate cannot himself delegate to another, for "*delegatus non potest delegare*").

The criterion for making these reports is simply that "it appears to" the doctor concerned "that an application ought to be made" for compulsory admission under the Act. This is not as wide as at first it appears. The words

do not suggest that a purely speculative detention of a patient who *might* be
liable to compulsion is allowed, still less of a patient whom the doctor does not genuinely believe to be sectionable. The form prescribed (Mental Health (Hospital, Guardianship and Consent to Treatment) Regulations 1983, Form 12) requires him to explain the reasons for his opinion, including why informal treatment is not or is no longer appropriate. Nevertheless, the power does apply to *any* doctor in charge of *any* patient in *any* hospital. It certainly allows, for example, an obstetrician to detain a woman whom he believes has become "sectionable" after childbirth; but the Code advises that he should contact a psychiatrist immediately (para. 8.5) and if a patient is under the care of both a psychiatrist and a non-psychiatrist, the former should be "in charge" for this purpose (para. 8.6).

Section 5(4) permits even swifter action by a registered first-level nurse trained in nursing the mentally ill or the mentally handicapped (see the Mental Health (Nurses) Order 1983). The in-patient must already be "receiving treatment for mental disorder". The nurse must believe: "(a) that the patient is suffering from mental disorder to such a degree that it is necessary for his health or safety or for the protection of others for him to be immediately restrained from leaving the hospital; and (b) that it is not practicable to secure the immediate attendance" of the doctor who could act under section 5(2). The power is clearly aimed at patients who are threatening to leave the hospital at any minute. It should not be used to restrain or seclude patients during an episode of disturbed behaviour.

The nurse must record his belief on the prescribed form (Form 13). The *form* does not require reasons, but the Code (para. 9.4) states that these should be recorded in the patient's notes; and (para. 9.2) that before acting the nurse should assess: the likely arrival time of the doctor as against the likely intention of the patient to leave; the harm to the patient or others if he did leave immediately, taking account of what he says he will do, the likelihood of suicide, his current behaviour especially if unusual for him, the likelihood of violence, recent messages from relatives or friends, recent disturbance on the ward, and relevant involvement of other patients; and finally the patient's known unpredictability and "any other relevant information from other members of the interdisciplinary team."

There is then immediate authority to detain the patient in the hospital for six hours or until the earlier arrival of the doctor (the time of lapse must be recorded on Form 16 by the same nurse or by an authorised nurse of the same class: reg. 4(5)). The initial record must be delivered to the managers, either by the nurse or someone authorised by him, as soon as possible after it is made. Once again, it is not clear what would happen if they disagreed. When the doctor arrives, he may invoke the power under section 5(2), although in theory the patient might disappear while he is doing so; the 72 hours are then calculated from the time when the nurse made the record (s. 5(5)). If the doctor does nothing, the patient is free to go.

Both powers envisage a decision by a doctor or nurse who is on the spot (see, for example, reference to the "attendance" of the doctor in section 5(4)). It is clearly unlawful to leave blank forms ready signed to be used by other staff as and when needed (see Code, para. 8.10). The Act does not specify (as it does elsewhere) that the doctor must have examined the patient, but the Code does require this (para. 8.10) and it is probably unlawful for him to rely on information given over the telephone. There have been allegations of such tactics (Miller, 1975) and, more seriously, of using the power as a handy substitute for the full compulsory procedures, for example by persuading a patient to enter hospital informally and making a report the same day (Bean, 1980), or as a periodic means of persuading long-stay patients to co-operate in their treatment.

More worrying still is the practice of using section 5 to detain patients in order to transfer them to another hospital. As the Mental Health Act Commission (Practice Note 3, 1994) point out, the usual transfer powers under section 19 (p. 161, later) do not apply, so patients may only lawfully be transferred with their consent or under the common law doctrine of necessity, perhaps where urgent treatment is essential or the patient is unable to decide for himself (see further in Chapter 6); but transferring an acutely disturbed patient can be dangerous, disruptive and frightening for him and so the practice is undesirable.

Official figures formerly implied that the use of section 5 was very rare, but now that changes in status are recorded, they confirm the Commission's experience that "considerable use" is made of it in some hospitals: there were over 1,000 uses of section 5(4) and nearly 8,000 uses of section 5(2) (950 of these conversions from section 5(4)) in England in the year ending March 31, 1993 (Department of Health, 1995a). No doubt doctors and nurses are reluctant to jeopardise their relationships with informal patients by holding this sort of threat over them, although the patient who knows that the power exists may not appreciate this. The existence of compulsory powers casts an inevitable shadow over all hospital admissions for mental disorder, even if most informal patients are less affected by it than might be supposed (Cavadino, 1988).

4. AN OUTLINE OF THE COMPULSORY POWERS

Although the great majority of patients are admitted informally, the numbers of psychiatric admissions are such that compulsion is still a relatively common event. The downward trend of the 1960s and 1970s was not so marked during the 1980s, perhaps because hospital admission is reserved for the more acute cases where compulsion is more likely to be needed, but perhaps also because of a greater "rights orientation" among patients and professionals alike. During the 1990s the numbers of informal and formal admissions have risen again. There were nearly 270,000 admissions in England in 1992/3, almost 22,000 of them compulsory. Before the details are examined in later chapters, it may be helpful to summarise all the various compulsory powers to admit patients to hospital, or to a place of safety, or to place them under guardianship or supervision in the community.

(a) Applications under Part II of the 1983 Act

Most compulsory patients are committed to hospital by means of an application made by the patient's nearest relative or an approved social worker (ASW) and supported by one or two doctors. If accepted by the hospital to which it is addressed, the application is sufficient authority to detain and usually to treat the patient against his will. There are three types of application for admission to hospital, colloquially known as "sections" or even "orders", and two for care in the community. All are subject to review by an independent mental health review tribunal.

(i) Under section 2, an application for admission for assessment authorises the patient's detention for up to 28 days. Most forms of treatment for his mental disorder may be given without his consent during that time. The application must be supported by recommendations from two doctors, one an approved specialist in mental disorder, to the effect that:

(a) the patient "is suffering from mental disorder of a nature or degree which warrants the detention of the patient in a hospital for assessment (or for assessment followed by medical treatment) for at least a limited period; and
(b) he ought to be so detained in the interests of his own health or safety or with a view to the protection of other persons."

(ii) Under section 4, an application for admission for assessment may be made in an emergency with the support of only one medical recommendation. The doctor need not be an approved specialist, although he should, if possible, have previous acquaintance with the patient. The grounds are the same as for a section 2 admission, but both the applicant and the doctor must also state that "it is of urgent necessity for the patient to be admitted and detained under section 2" and that "compliance with the provisions . . . relating to applications under that section would involve undesirable delay." The application authorises detention for up to 72 hours, but the admission may be converted into an ordinary section 2 admission by the provision of a second medical recommendation within that time. Unless and until that is given, however, there is no statutory power to impose treatment without consent.

(iii) Under section 3, an application for admission for treatment may again be made either by the nearest relative or by a social worker. However, if the nearest relative objects to the admission, the social worker must seek authority from a county court. The patient may be detained in the first instance for up to six months. Then the detention may be renewed, on the advice of the responsible medical officer (RMO), for a second six months and thereafter for a year at a time. Most forms of treatment for the patient's mental disorder may be given without his consent. The initial application must be supported by recommendations from two doctors, one an approved specialist, to the effect that:

(a) the patient "is suffering from mental illness, severe mental impairment, psychopathic disorder or mental impairment and his mental disorder is of a nature or degree which makes it appropriate for him to receive medical treatment in a hospital; and
(b) in the case of psychopathic disorder or mental impairment, such treatment is likely to alleviate or prevent a deterioration of his condition; and
(c) it is necessary for the health or safety of the patient or for the protection of other persons that he should receive such treatment and it cannot be provided unless he is detained under this section."

(iv) Under section 7, an application for the reception of a patient aged 16 or over into the guardianship of a local social services authority or private individual may be made in the same way as an application for admission for hospital treatment but to the local authority rather than the hospital. The disorders covered are the same but the "treatability" test (b) does not apply. Instead of (c), it must be "necessary in the interests of the welfare of the patient or for the protection of other persons that the patient should be so received." The guardian can dictate where the patient is to live, how he is to spend his time and who must be allowed to see him, but cannot insist that he accepts treatment for his disorder.

(v) Under section 25A, introduced as from April 1996 by the Mental Health (Patients in the Community) Act 1995, an application, supported by an ASW and one other doctor, can be made by the RMO of a patient aged 16 or over who is detained in hospital for treatment for the patient to be supervised after he leaves hospital. The disorders covered are again the same but the other grounds are:

> "(b) there would be a substantial risk of serious harm to the health or safety of the patient or the safety of other persons, or of the patient being seriously exploited, if he were not to receive the after-care services [to be provided under s.117]; and
> (c) his being subject to after-care under supervision is likely to help to secure that he receives [those services]."

The powers and other details are equivalent to those of guardianship but under the control of the health rather than social services.

(b) Powers relating to people accused of crime

A much smaller number of patients are admitted as a result of the orders of a court or the directions of the Home Secretary, after they have been accused or found guilty of criminal offences. These powers are mostly contained in Part III of the 1983 Act, although some derive from other statutes.

(i) Under section 37 of the 1983 Act, all courts may make ordinary hospital orders over certain criminal offenders. The effect is almost identical to that of an admission for treatment under section 3 of the 1983 Act, so that the patient's fate is controlled by the medical authorities rather than the court. The grounds are that:

> "(a) the court is satisfied, on the written or oral evidence of two registered medical practitioners, that the offender is suffering from mental illness, psychopathic disorder, severe mental impairment or mental impairment and that ... (i) the mental disorder from which the offender is suffering is of a nature or degree which makes it appropriate for him to be detained in a hospital for medical treatment and, in the case of psychopathic disorder or mental impairment, that such treatment is likely to alleviate or prevent a deterioration of his condition ... and
> (b) the court is of the opinion, having regard to all the circumstances including the nature of the offence and the character and antecedents of the offender, and to the other available methods of dealing with him, that the most suitable method of disposing of the case is by means of an order under this section."

(ii) Under section 41 of the 1983 Act, the Crown Court may make a restriction order if, in addition to the grounds for making an ordinary hospital order, it "appears to the court having regard to the nature of the offence, the antecedents of the offender and the risk of his committing further offences if set at large, that it is necessary for the protection of the public from serious harm."

A restriction order removes the usual power of the medical authorities to decide whether a patient may move or leave: the former is the exclusive province of the Home Secretary and the latter is decided either by the Home Secretary or by specially constituted mental health review tribunals: either may grant an absolute or conditional discharge, but a conditionally discharged patient remains liable to be recalled to hospital by the Home Secretary. Under section 43, a magistrates' court which has the evidence required for a hospital order may commit an offender to the Crown Court with a view to a restriction order being made; under section 44, the committal may be to hospital if a bed is available.

(iii) Under section 48 of the 1983 Act, the Home Secretary may direct the transfer to hospital of remand and civil prisoners and people detained under the Immigration Act 1971, if they are suffering from mental illness or severe mental impairment of the appropriate nature or degree and in urgent need of medical treatment. Under section 47, he may direct the transfer of people serving custodial sentences, if they are suffering from mental illness, psychopathic disorder, severe mental impairment or mental impairment where the other medical criteria for a hospital order are fulfilled. Under section 46, he may direct the detention in hospital of people detained during Her Majesty's Pleasure under the armed forces legislation. These last, and transferred remand prisoners, must be made subject to restrictions, but with ordinary prisoners the Home Secretary may choose between a transfer with or without restrictions. Any restrictions must end when the imprisonment would have ended, but even after that a patient who was transferred during a prison sentence (*i.e.* under s. 47) may remain subject to an ordinary hospital order. Patients transferred with restrictions may be returned to the prison system if the transfer is no longer warranted on medical grounds.

(iv) Under section 36 of the 1983 Act, the Crown Court may remand an accused person to hospital for treatment where it has evidence from two doctors, one an approved specialist, that the accused is suffering from mental illness or severe mental impairment of the appropriate nature or degree. Under section 35, all courts may remand an accused to hospital simply for reports, where they have evidence from one specialist doctor that there is reason to suspect that the accused is suffering from mental illness, psychopathic disorder, severe mental impairment or mental impairment, and the court believes that it would be impracticable to make such a report if he were remanded on bail. Finally, under section 38, all courts may make an interim hospital order, for up to six months in all, over a convicted offender, if they have evidence from two doctors, one approved, that he is suffering from mental illness, psychopathic disorder, severe mental impairment or mental impairment and that there is reason to suppose that his condition is such that a hospital order may be appropriate.

(v) The Crown Court may find an accused unfit to plead because of mental disorder, or not guilty by reason of insanity of what would otherwise be a crime. Under the Criminal Procedure (Insanity) Act 1964 and the Criminal Procedure (Insanity and Unfitness to Plead) Act 1991, the court can choose between ordering admission to hospital, with or without restrictions, guardianship, supervision and treatment, or an absolute discharge. People found unfit to plead who are placed under restrictions may have to return to face trial if they become fit to do so.

(vi) All courts have power to make probation or supervision orders with a condition that the offender undergo some psychiatric treatment. Section 3 of the Powers of Criminal Courts Act 1973 permits this for most offenders aged 16 or over and the Children and Young Persons Act 1969 for juveniles. There must be evidence from one specialist doctor that the person is suffering from mental disorder which requires and may be susceptible to medical treatment but which does not warrant a hospital order. If the patient is admitted to hospital, however, he is an informal patient unless other compulsory powers are taken and thus there is no statutory power to impose treatment without his consent, although his failure to co-operate may sometimes be a breach of the order.

(vii) Under section 37 of the 1983 Act, the courts also have power to place offenders aged 16 or more under the guardianship of a local social services authority or private individual. The grounds are the same as for a hospital order, except that instead of (a) (i) they read "(ii) in the case of an offender who has attained the age of 16 years, the mental disorder is of a nature or degree which warrants his reception into guardianship under this Act."

(c) Detention in a "place of safety"

Apart from the power to hold for a short time those who are already in-patients in a hospital (see section 3 earlier), there are two provisions under which a person may be taken to and detained for up to 72 hours in a "place of safety". This includes (among other places) both a hospital and a police station. These give no authority to treat the patient without his consent.

(i) Under section 136 of the 1983 Act, if a police officer finds in a place to which the public have access a person who appears to him to be suffering from mental disorder and to be in immediate need of care or control, he may, if he thinks it necessary in the interests of that person or for the protection of other persons, remove the person to a place of safety.

(ii) Under section 135(1) of the 1983 Act, a social worker may apply to a magistrate for a warrant which will permit a police officer to enter premises by force if need be. The social worker must swear that there is reasonable cause to suspect that a person believed to be suffering from mental disorder (a) has been, or is being, ill-treated, neglected or kept otherwise than under proper control, or (b) being unable to care for himself, is living alone. The police officer must be accompanied by a social worker and a doctor, but once entry has been gained, the person may, if thought fit, be removed to a place of safety without being formally "sectioned".

(d) Powers under other legislation

Some people who are suffering from mental disorder may find themselves detained in hospital, or elsewhere, under quite different legislation. The two major examples relate to the young and the old respectively.

(i) Under the Children Act 1989, children who are being looked after by local authorities, whether under a care order or other compulsory powers or by arrangement with their parents, may be placed for treatment or assessment in psychiatric facilities; provided that certain conditions and procedures are fulfilled, these may include secure facilities.

(ii) Under section 47 of the National Assistance Act 1948, a local authority may apply to a magistrates' court for the removal to hospital or other suitable place of a person who, according to the certificate of the community physician, (a) is suffering from grave chronic disease or being aged, infirm or physically incapacitated, is living in insanitary conditions;

16

and (b) is unable to devote to himself, and is not receiving from other persons, proper care and attention. The initial order is for up to three months, but it may be renewed for further periods of up to three months at a time. If the evidence of two doctors is available, there is an emergency procedure under the National Assistance (Amendment) Act 1951 for applying to a single magistrate without giving notice to the person concerned.

5. HOSPITALS AND MANAGERS

Before the 1959 Act, the crucial legal distinction was between one kind of hospital and another. Nowadays, the crucial distinction is between a hospital and somewhere else, because only a patient who is liable to be detained in a hospital can be given treatment against his will. By no means all the facilities and units provided by the health service are part of a hospital. In section 145(1) of the 1983 Act, a "hospital" is defined as:

"(a) any health service hospital within the meaning of the National Health Service Act 1977; and
(b) any accommodation provided by a local authority and used as a hospital by or on behalf of the Secretary of State under that Act."

This definition includes the three special hospitals, which are provided by the Secretary of State for Health under section 4 of the 1977 Act as part of his general duty to provide a comprehensive health service. It also includes a private hospital, provided that this is specially registered under the Registered Homes Act 1984 as a "mental nursing home" which will receive compulsory patients (1983 Act, s. 34(2) and Sched. 1). It does not include prison hospitals, because these are provided by the Home Secretary under prison legislation.

There is no longer any type of patient who must be sent to a particular type of hospital. Hospitals are free to accept or reject any patient they choose. They cannot be obliged to accept anyone even in an emergency. This was a necessary corollary of the desegregation principle introduced by the 1959 Act. A maternity hospital, for example, could not be made to admit a violently psychotic man. Unfortunately, however, hospitals are equally free to refuse patients for whom their facilities may well be suitable. And there are some prospective patients, particularly those who have appeared before the courts, for whom it is extremely difficult to find any facilities at all.

The decision to accept or reject any patient is technically one for the hospital "managers". In section 145(1) of the 1983 Act, "the managers" are defined as:

"(a) in relation to a hospital vested in the Secretary of State for the purposes of his functions under the National Health Service Act 1977, and in relation to any accommodation provided by a local authority and used as a hospital by or on behalf of the Secretary of State under that Act, the Health Authority or Special Health Authority responsible for the administration of the hospital;
(b) in relation to a special hospital, the Secretary of State;
(bb) in relation to a hospital vested in a National Health Service trust, the trust;

(c) in relation to a mental nursing home registered in pursuance of the Registered Homes Act 1984, the person or persons registered in respect of the home".

What then are the facilities available? And what contribution (if any) can the law make towards ensuring that patients are cared for "under conditions of no greater security than is justified by the degree of danger they present to themselves or others" (Reed, 1992, para. 3.3)?

(a) Ordinary NHS hospitals

The open-door policies which began with the 1959 Act had two components. The first was a dramatic drop in the number of hospital beds for in-patients, particularly in mental illness. From a peak of 149,000 beds in 1955 it has now dropped to about one third of that total. For many years the plan has been to run down and eventually close the old mental illness hospitals, the former asylums, perhaps by the end of this century (Department of Health, 1992). But by 1993, 89 of the 130 hospitals open in 1960 were still open. As the Royal Commission on the National Health Service (Merrison, 1979) pointed out, standards in these hospitals have not been helped, either by the expectation that they would eventually be closed, or by the widely-held view (founded on the work of sociologists such as Erving Goffman) that such places are inevitably harmful to their patients. As the Audit Commission (1994, para. 17) confirm, "people receiving community care, however inadequate, hardly ever wish to return to hospital. Psychiatric hospital care seems to be strongly disliked by most of the people who have experienced it ... ".

It was originally envisaged that the old specialised hospitals would be replaced by smaller community hospitals and psychiatric units in district general hospitals. The former were slow to materialise, while the latter dealt mainly with the acute and more easily treatable cases. They would often take only short-stay patients and some would not accept compulsory patients at all. Yet the major mental illnesses such as schizophrenia remain an intractable problem and the numbers of elderly and demented patients have been rising steadily. In the 1980s there was much concern that "the pace of removal of hospital facilities for mental illness has far outrun the provision of services in the community to replace them" (House of Commons Social Services Committee, 1985, para. 30).

There were many obstacles to progress (Audit Commission, 1994). There is a vicious circle where most of the money is still tied up in hospital beds, which cannot be released until suitable alternative facilities are in place, which in turn needs money, thus sending patients back into hospital unnecessarily, and increasing pressure on hospital beds. There is a difficult division of responsibility for community services, principally between the health services and local social services authorities, and a consequent lack of effective leadership. There is the public resistance which is based upon the perception of mentally ill people as dangerous to themselves and others. But mental health has been identified as one of the five key areas in improving *The Health of the Nation* (Department of Health, 1992) and a great deal of effort is now being put into developing the comprehensive range of services which everyone knows is needed. The goal is that specialist psychiatric services should target their efforts on severely mentally ill people, leaving the primary care services to cater for the less severely ill.

There has also been a sharp decline in the number of mental handicap hospital beds. Although there are many hospital residents who suffer from multiple handicaps requiring skilled nursing and medical care, most people with learning disabilities require no more medical attention than anyone else. It is now seen as an accident of history that so many of those in residential care were in institutions inherited by the health service (Merrison, 1979). *Care in the Community* (DHSS, 1981a) estimated that up to 15,000 could be discharged immediately if appropriate services were available elsewhere. The number of resident patients in mental handicap hospitals fell from 60,000 in 1964 to 30,000 in 1989. The fall has continued at the same rate since then (Emerson and Hatton, 1994). Allied to these developments was the growing feeling that compulsory powers are hardly, if ever, appropriate for people with learning disabilities.

This leads us to the second component of the open door. The policy not only tries to return patients to the community, but also to maintain open conditions within the hospital itself. Although there are still around 900 "low security" beds in ordinary NHS hospitals, the old custodial role has been rejected in favour of the more conventional style of hospital treatment or the newer concept of a therapeutic community (Bluglass, 1985). Ordinary hospitals found it more and more difficult to manage the more challenging patients on open wards within usual staffing levels. This led to a considerable rise between the early 1960s and the early 1970s in the numbers of patients transferred from ordinary mental illness hospitals to the maximum security special hospitals (Parker and Tenant, 1979). It also led to an increasing reluctance to admit offender patients, particularly on restriction orders, to ordinary hospitals. The fall was particularly marked in mental handicap hospitals.

Two sections of the 1983 Act are aimed at meeting the difficulties in securing a hospital bed for patients who really need one. First, as there is nowhere which can be forced to accept a patient in an emergency, section 140 obliges every health authority to notify all the local social services authorities in their area of those hospitals where there are arrangements to receive patients in cases of "special urgency". This covers both informal and compulsory admissions but stops far short of a positive obligation to supply a bed.

During the passage of the 1982 amendments, a strong case was made for such an obligation, at least towards those disordered offenders who might otherwise have to be sent to prison. These were backed by numerous examples reported by and to MIND (see Gostin, 1977), where judges had felt forced to send disordered offenders to prison simply because no suitable bed could be found. Although there is case law suggesting that the prisons should not be used to fill the gaps in the hospital and social services, there are still cases where the courts have little option. To meet these demands, section 39 of the 1983 Act allows any court which is thinking of making a hospital order or interim hospital order to seek information from the health authority for the area where the patient lives or last lived, or from any other which it thinks appropriate, about hospitals in their area or elsewhere which might be prepared to take the patient. The authority has a duty to supply whatever information it has or can reasonably obtain but not, of course, to supply a bed.

Recently, Crown Court judges have taken to summoning the Secretary of State for Health to explain why a bed cannot be found, and although she has not yet appeared, the beds have usually done so. Under section 1 of the National Health Service Act 1977, the Secretary of State has a duty to provide a comprehensive health service. Under section 3(1)(a) this includes a duty to supply hospital accommodation to the extent that he considers necessary to meet all reasonable requirements. If a patient whose requirement is quite obviously reasonable has been refused a bed, or kept in a special hospital longer than necessary because a bed in a more suitable local hospital has not been provided, or even been sent to prison because no hospital will have him, has this duty been broken?

This point arose in *Ashingdane v. Department of Health and Social Security and Others*, Court of Appeal, February 18, 1980. A Broadmoor patient was refused a bed in his local hospital because of a ban on restriction order patients operated by the nurses' trade union. He launched actions against the union branch secretaries, the DHSS and the area health authority. He claimed that the Secretary of State was in breach of the duty under the 1977 Act and that it was *ultra vires* (outside the powers) of both the Secretary of State and the health authority to take any account of the union ban in reaching their decisions. The actions against the DHSS and the health authority were stayed, for at that time the 1959 Act gave them virtual immunity from action; this was removed by the 1983 Act but a similar action would be equally unlikely to succeed today.

A duty placed by statute upon a public authority to provide certain services does not give rise to a right of action in a private individual to sue for damages (or some other remedy to enforce it directly) unless the statute expressly or impliedly intends this. In *Cocks v. Thanet District Council* [1983] 2 A.C. 286 the House of Lords held that local authorities' decisions under what was then the Housing (Homeless Persons) Act 1977 could only be challenged by way of an application for judicial review under Order 53 of the Rules of the Supreme Court. Judicial review is a discretionary remedy which operates to quash an invalid decision and oblige the authority to take it again, rather than to force the authority to act in a particular way or to award damages for any resulting loss.

The principles are now well-known. The courts will not interfere with the proper exercise of a discretion which Parliament has conferred on some other body. However, the Minister or other body must not exercise his discretion so as to frustrate the purpose of Parliament in conferring it (*Padfield v. Minister of Agriculture, Fisheries and Food* [1968] A.C. 997). The decision-maker must apply his mind to the question. He must apply the right law to the question. He must take into account the relevant considerations and exclude the irrelevant. Even if he has done all this, his decision may still be quashed if it is a decision which no reasonable body in his position could have taken (*Associated Provincial Picture Houses Ltd v. Wednesbury Corporation* [1948] 1 K.B. 223).

The courts have not been afraid to apply these principles to individual decisions made under the Mental Health Act by hospital doctors (see Chapter 7), mental health review tribunals (see Chapter 8) and the Home Secretary (see Chapter 5), and would no doubt do the same with decisions by health authorities or the Secretary of State for Health. It is, however, one thing to challenge the exact operation of the 1983 Act in an individual case and another thing to challenge the exercise of a broad power, or even duty, to provide services for a general or even a particular class of people. It is very difficult to say that an authority has acted unreasonably in deciding its priorities and levels of resources (see *Wyatt v. Hillingdon London Borough Council* (1978) 76 L.G.R. 727). The allocation of funds for any particular area of social need is a matter for political rather than judicial control. Thus, for example, in *R. v. Secretary of State for Social Services, ex p. Hincks*

(1980) 1 B.M.L.R. 93 (see also *R. v. Central Birmingham Health Authority, ex p. Walker* (1987) 3 B.M.L.R. 32), the Court of Appeal rejected an allegation that the Secretary of State had broken his duty under section 3(1)(c) of the National Health Service Act 1977, made by four patients who had been waiting for orthopaedic operations for up to three years because of a shortage of beds in their area. And in *R. v. Cambridge District Health Authority, ex p. B.* [1995] 1 W.L.R. 898, the Court of Appeal would not interfere with the authority's decision to refuse to fund further treatment for a child suffering from leukaemia; the Master of the Rolls because it was not for courts to make the agonising judgments about how best to allocate a limited budget for the maximum advantage of the maximum number of patients, the President of the Family Division because the decision was not "*Wednesbury* unreasonable".

Nevertheless, there may well be some decisions which would fail that test. And if the hospital managers are prepared to offer a bed and a court is therefore able to make a hospital order, it is possible that staff who obstruct the patient's admission are guilty of contempt of court (see the remarks of Lawton L.J. in *R. v. Harding (Bernard), The Times,* June 16, 1983).

(b) Regional secure units

The solution proposed, both for the problems of ordinary psychiatric hospitals and the log-jam in special hospitals, was secure provision within the NHS. As far back as 1961, the Working Party on the Special Hospitals (Emery, 1961) foresaw the problems which the open-door policy would bring and recommended this. The Butler Committee on Mentally Abnormal Offenders were so horrified by what they found at Broadmoor that they rushed out an interim report (1974) recommending the setting up of secure units in each NHS region as a matter of urgency. The revised Report of the Working Party on Security in NHS Psychiatric Hospitals (Glancy, 1974) did the same. Between 1976 and 1982, the government provided considerable sums to develop secure facilities but progress was slow, not least because some regional health authorities found other more pressing (and popular?) uses for the money. Nevertheless, in 1992 there were some 630 places available in permanent regional medium secure units (the target is 1,200 by 1996); there were also over 300 places at interim or other medium secure units; some of the latter cater for patients with learning disabilities (Reed, 1994a).

Now, according to the Mental Health Act Commission "the most fashionable forensic area is suddenly the Regional Secure Unit" (1989, para. 11.9). However, units are usually highly selective in the patients they take and will not accept those who might have to stay indefinitely. The Commission refers to the psychiatric code of "Do not enter box until exit is clear" which means that patients cannot be transferred from a special hospital to a regional secure unit until the unit can be sure that it will be possible to transfer him down (or even up) the security scale in due course. At the same time, their existence can reduce the tolerance of general psychiatric hospitals for the more difficult patients. They are unlikely to fill the gap in caring for "embarrassing patients": the dangerous or the "unrewarding, dependent, chronic and ungrateful" (Scott, 1975; quoted in Bluglass, 1985). It seems safe to assume that the prisons, other hospitals and the community will have to go on finding places for these, hopefully not in cardboard boxes under Waterloo Bridge.

(c) The special hospitals

Under section 4 of the National Health Service Act 1977, the Secretary of State has a duty to provide special hospitals "for persons subject to detention under the Mental Health Act 1983 who in his opinion require treatment under conditions of special security on account of their dangerous, violent or criminal propensities." There are now three special hospitals, each with its own catchment area: Broadmoor was opened in 1863 in response to pressure from the Lunacy Commissioners and others to make special provision for dangerous criminal lunatics; Rampton and Moss Side were opened respectively in 1910 and 1919 and originally catered for difficult mental defectives, whether or not offenders; Park Lane was opened in 1974 to reduce overcrowding at Broadmoor; Moss Side and Park Lane together became Ashworth Hospital (South and North respectively) in 1990. Virtually all their patients are detained, although a few may remain informally for a short while after their detention ceases. Numbers have been dropping steadily in recent years, and stood at just under 1,600 at the end of 1993.

The special hospitals used to be managed directly by the Department of Health. The Report of the Rampton Review Team (Boynton, 1980) found that this had led to a lack of leadership and purpose, which they thought responsible for many of the shortcomings in the system and in the quality of patients' lives. After a transitional phase in which some functions were delegated to management boards for each hospital, the Special Hospitals Service Authority was set up in 1989 (see Special Hospitals Service Authority (Establishment and Constitution) Order 1989, (S.I. 1989 No. 948), amended (S.I. 1990 No. 1905)). This had the strategic task of "developing policies relating to the provision and management" of special hospitals, and then the duty to provide and maintain them, and the functions of hospital managers under the 1983 Act (Special Hospitals Service Authority (Functions and Membership) Order 1989, (S.I. 1989 No. 949), amended by (S.I. 1989 No. 1611), (S.I. 1990 No. 1331), (S.I. 1991 No. 1025)). So far it has not proved possible to integrate the special hospitals into the NHS generally but they are losing some of their isolation from the mainstream.

Applications for admission are considered by a multi-disciplinary hospital advisory committee at each site. The committee will usually require a report from one of the special hospital's own consultants, as well as the doctor currently responsible for the patient. There is no legal category of patient who must be sent to a special hospital. Equally, since the 1959 Act there has been no category of compulsory patient who cannot be sent there. However, around 90 per cent of admissions now come as a result of criminal proceedings, and over 50 per cent are transferred from prison. Roughly two-thirds of restricted patients are in special hospitals; nearly three-quarters of special hospital patients are now restricted (Home Office, 1995a; Department of Health, 1995a). Around half the unrestricted patients are non-offenders transferred from ordinary NHS hospitals. In the early 1960s there was a steep rise in these admissions, as the special hospitals were asked to take patients whom the ordinary hospitals found too difficult to manage (Parker and Tennant, 1979), but there has since been a steady decline. During the 1970s, strenuous efforts were made to reduce the size of the special hospital population by a more stringent application of the criteria derived from section 4 of the 1977 Act (see above).

There undoubtedly were some inappropriate admissions in the past. The best known example is Nigel Smith (referred to by Scarman L.J. in *R. v. McFarlane* (1975) 60 Cr.App.R. 320 at 324). He was admitted to Broadmoor on a restriction order after committing a relatively minor series of frauds. He had no prior history of violence or mental illness, but he did make the mistake of confessing violent feelings towards his mother during an interview in prison with a Broadmoor psychiatrist. Scarman L.J. remarked that "one wonders how the criteria indicated" in what is now section 4 of the 1977 Act "could have been said to have been met." But because there was no other suitable place for him to go, "inevitably he goes to the sort of hospital which should not be cluttered up with cases of his sort."

Perhaps as many as half of all special hospital patients (and most of the women patients) do not need to be there, although over 80 per cent need at least medium secure conditions (Reed, 1994a). In the case of *B. v. United Kingdom*, applic. no. 6870/75, the European Commission on Human Rights declared admissible a complaint that the patient's detention in a special hospital constituted "inhuman or degrading punishment or treatment," contrary to Article 3 of the European Convention on Human Rights. The complaint was based partly on the conditions in Broadmoor, which had appalled the Butler Committee on Mentally Abnormal Offenders (1974 and 1975) and many others, and partly on the deleterious effects of being confined in a place which was inappropriate both to his offences and his needs. The Commission proceeded to investigate the facts, but decided by eight votes to five that there had been no violation of Article 3. The case may have had some effect in speeding up the improvements in Broadmoor. But a patient might still seek judicial review on the ground that it was unlawful, irrational or unreasonable to detain there a person who did *not* require treatment under conditions of special security on account of dangerous, violent or criminal propensities. There must come a point at which the patient does not require any "special security" and the lack of alternative secure facilities becomes irrelevant. In fact, more patients are transferred to community care or ordinary hospitals than to medium secure units (Reed, 1994a).

The obstacles to transferring patients out of special hospitals remain enormous (Dell, 1980; Dell and Robertson, 1988). Many patients will be unable to cope if they are released directly into the community from the highly structured environment of a special hospital (see Boynton, 1980; Cohen, 1981; Blom-Cooper, 1992 for descriptions). The public outcry should they offend again will be much louder than the concern at their continued imprisonment. Transfer to an NHS hospital may encounter opposition from both the staff and the local community (Gunn, 1979). There are still not enough places in medium secure units. The Mental Health Act Commission (see, *e.g.* 1993) regularly highlights the problem of transfer delays, which it attributes to a combination of lack of alternative facilities, slow decision-making by medical and Home Office authorities and the "tendency of some patients to be unobtrusive" (1989, para. 10.1). While there have been improvements since Boynton reported on the "scandal" of Rampton patients who should not be there, sustained effort is required to ensure that special hospital facilities are reserved for those who really need them.

(d) Mental nursing homes

Another possibility is to enter a private hospital, technically a "mental nursing home". These provide around 2,800 mental illness and learning disability beds, perhaps 300–400 of them with some security (Reed, 1994a). Annual admissions from 1987/88 to 1992/3 hovered between five and six thousand (Department of Health, 1995a). They may admit informal patients and, provided that they are registered to do so, all types of compulsory patient (except, technically, those transferred from prison under sections 46, 47 and 48 of the 1983 Act; the reason for this limitation is no longer obvious; the admission figures suggest that it is ignored). If a private hospital is prepared to offer a bed, for example, to an offender who might otherwise have to go to prison, the health authority has power (under the National Health Service Act 1977) to pay the bill; it also has power to discharge the patient. There were 452 formal admissions to mental nursing homes in 1992/3, 125 of them from the courts, a rise of some 61 per cent since 1987/88.

Mental nursing homes were, at first, those former licensed houses and charitable hospitals which were not taken over by the NHS. The private sector is now playing a growing role in all forms of health care. It has always been heavily involved in the care of the elderly, where it can be difficult to distinguish between an ordinary old people's home and a nursing home. Both must be registered under the Registered Homes Act 1984, but with different authorities and under different procedures.

A mental nursing home is defined in section 22(1) of the Registered Homes Act 1984 as:

"Any premises used, or intended to be used, for the reception of, and the provision of nursing or other medical treatment (including care, habilitation and rehabilitation under medical supervision) for, one or more mentally disordered persons (meaning persons suffering, or appearing to be suffering, from mental disorder), whether exclusively or in common with other persons."

NHS hospitals and any other premises exclusively managed by a government department or provided by a local authority are expressly excluded (s. 22(2), (3)). Joint ventures between the public and voluntary or even private sectors are not.

A mental nursing home must be registered with the health authority under Part II of the 1984 Act whereas a residential care home must be registered with the local social services authority under Part I (see Chapter 9). The distinction between them lies in the fact that the former does but the latter does not provide "nursing or other medical treatment", although that term is widely defined. A mental nursing home is only exempt from registration under Part I if it is used solely as such. The Act therefore contemplates dual registration, even for those homes which at the time are being used solely for the one purpose. The dividing line between a "patient", who is receiving nursing or other medical treatment, and a resident, who is receiving other forms of special care, may be very difficult to draw. Many homes will wish to continue to provide care for those residents, particularly the elderly, who cross the line. Health and local authorities are expected to work together to ensure that the burden of dual regulation is not too great (Circulars HSG(95)41 and LAC(95)12).

The line between a nursing home which caters for the mentally disordered and an ordinary nursing home is also important. The dividing line in law is whether the home caters for people suffering, or appearing to be suffering, from mental disorder. Both must be registered under Part

II of the Act, but a mental nursing home must be registered as such, because inspectors have an additional power to examine patients. Otherwise, the requirements are very similar and the Department of Health advised that homes accommodating elderly mentally confused people need not necessarily register as mental nursing homes. It depends upon the number of such patients and the seriousness of their condition (DHSS Circular HC(81)8, LAC(81)4). So here we have just one problem in distinguishing mental order from mental disorder.

Any person (including a company) carrying on a mental nursing home must be registered with the Secretary of State (s. 23(1)), who has delegated this function to the health authorities. Registration may be refused if the applicant, his staff or his premises are unfit for the purpose or his staff are not suitably qualified. There must be either a doctor or a qualified nurse in charge (who need not but in a small home may be the "person registered') and the authority may insist upon qualifications suitable for the home in question, for example in nursing the mentally ill or mentally handicapped. The authority may also specify the number and qualifications of nurses required (s. 25). It must specify the maximum number of patients and may impose other conditions about the type and age-range of patients who may be accommodated (s. 29). Authorities are expected to publish codes of practice, so that consistent standards can be set (Circular HSG (95)41). If a home is to take compulsory patients it must be registered in a separate part of the register (s. 23(5)) and the authority will be interested in the security arrangements.

The Secretary of State makes regulations about the details of applying for registration, record-keeping, visiting and inspection (s. 27), and about the general conduct of and level of services to be provided in nursing homes of all types (s. 26). Under the Nursing Homes and Mental Nursing Homes Regulations 1984, homes must keep a register of all patients, case records on each patient, and a full record of all staff, and these must be retained for at least a year after the last entry or the patient's departure (Reg. 7). Regulation 12 prescribes a long list of facilities and services which must be provided and in mental nursing homes particular importance will be attached to recreational and occupational facilities, as well as such obvious things as furniture, food and fire precautions. Health authorities must inspect homes at least twice a year (Reg. 11) and have powers of entry, not only to registered homes but also to homes which they reasonably believe are being used as nursing homes (Reg. 10). They may decide whether to visit outside normal working hours and whether or not to give advance warning. The inspector may require records, registers and any other information he needs for the inspection, but not clinical records unless he is a doctor. The inspector of a mental nursing home may visit and interview patients in private, and if he is a doctor he may examine them and their medical records, in order to investigate their complaints or where it is suspected that they are not being properly cared for (s. 35(2)).

Failure to register or to display a registration certificate (s. 23(1) and (6)), breach of the conditions relating to patients (s. 29(4)), contravention of the regulations relating to record-keeping, inspection or the provision of services and facilities (ss. 26, 27 and Reg. 12), and obstructing the visiting of mental nursing homes and their patients (s. 35(5),(6)) are all criminal offences, although the penalties are not severe. There is also an offence of holding out a place as a mental nursing home when it is not registered as such (s. 24(2)).

Registration may be cancelled if the "person registered" is convicted of any of these offences (including the failure to provide all the "adequate" facilities and services listed in the regulations), or if anyone else has been convicted of an offence under the Act in relation to the same home, or if the conditions relating to patients have been broken, or on any ground which would have entitled the authority to refuse registration in the first place (s. 28). In urgent cases where there is a serious risk to the life, health or well-being of patients, this may be done by a single magistrate (s. 30). Otherwise, the authority may do so according to statutory procedures which are designed to ensure a fair consideration of the case (ss. 31, 32 and 33 (3)). These latter procedures also apply to the initial decision to refuse registration or to any later variation of the conditions. There is a right of appeal against all these decisions, including that of a magistrate, to the registered homes tribunal (s. 34), constituted under Part III of the Act. If a home has compulsory patients in it when registration is cancelled or the registered person dies, the registration continues in force for two months to enable alternative arrangements for them to be made (s. 36). In practice, of course, health or social services authorities will have to make alternative arrangements for every patient if registration is cancelled.

Recent guidance stresses that the registration and inspection process should not be too onerous or attempt to impose too high a standard; regulation is different from conracting for services, where higher standards may sometimes be sought (Circular HSG (95)41). But it is always difficult to impose high standards upon the private sector if the controlling authority will be faced with having to provide for any patients or residents who are displaced. These difficulties are compounded when NHS mental health facilities are changing so rapidly. Many compulsory patients in mental nursing homes are funded by health authorities which do not have sufficient provision for difficult and offender patients. The Mental Health Act Commission's functions also cover these patients, but the Commission (1989, para. 11.4) has not found it easy to keep up with the rapid growth, especially in the use of secure facilities. Like special hospitals, those units tend to be remote from the patients' homes, offering restrictive environments, and not always able to meet the individual needs of patients. Clearly, the Mental Health Act Commission will be as important in protecting the interests of such patients in the years to come as was the Board of Control in the past.

2 MENTAL DISORDER AND THE GROUNDS FOR COMPULSION

1. PSYCHIATRY IS A PROBLEM

Defining mental disorder is not a simple matter, either for doctors or for lawyers. A disorder of the "mind" is not the same thing as a disorder of the "brain", although the former may be caused by the latter. The Oxford English dictionary definition of mind includes "the seat of consciousness, thoughts, volitions and feelings". But how are we to know when these functions have become so abnormal as to warrant the term "disorder or disability"? It is often said (in psychiatric textbooks) that with a physical disease or disability, a doctor can presuppose a state of perfect or "normal" bodily health (however unusual that may be in practice) and then point to the ways in which the patient's condition falls short of this. A state of perfect mental health is probably unattainable and certainly cannot be defined. The doctor has instead to presuppose some average standard of mental functioning; and it is not enough that the patient deviates from this, for some deviations are in the better-than-average direction. Even if the patient is below average, the doctor still has to decide how far below is sufficiently abnormal, among the vast range of possible variations, to be labelled a "disorder or disability".

If this be so, it must cast doubt upon the *validity* of many diagnoses of mental disorder, for they could never have the scientific objectivity of a finding of physical disorder. However, the distinction between them in practice is nothing like as clear cut. A very similar relativity is involved in determining whether a failure in bodily functioning is thought bad enough to be called a disorder. The patient's evaluation, and to some extent the doctor's, will be influenced by social and cultural norms. The diagnosis will at first be a hypothesis, which will act as a guide to treatment and may give some indication of the future course of the disorder, but may well have to be modified as more is learnt about its underlying causes, either in the particular case or in general.

Some disorders of the mind are the result of bodily defects (such as syphilis or arterio-sclerosis) and can be approached in much the same way: by alleviating the painful or distressing symptoms while recognising the connection between them and the underlying defect, which may (or more often may not) be capable of remedy. There is a school of psychiatric thought which believes that all mental disorders worthy of the name will eventually be traced to physical or organic causes and can thus be fitted into this conventional disease model. On this view, where the cause is not yet known, psychiatry is simply at the same stage as medicine has been (and still is) with many physical disorders: the stage of minute observation and recognition of distinct clusters of symptoms, categorising them into discrete syndromes, alleviating the pain and distress which they cause to the patient and attempting to predict the future course from similar cases, while at the same time searching for some clue to the underlying defect. Obstetricians do not, for example, refuse to treat the effects of toxaemia of pregnancy simply because they do not yet know what causes it.

The advantage of this model of mental disorder from the legal point of view is that it is *potentially* capable of limiting the scope of psychiatric intervention and competence—it lays no claim to solving all the ills that flesh is heir to. The disadvantage is that it enables physical treatments whose effects are scarcely understood to be employed for disorders which have not yet been shown to have a physical cause. This is all very well if the patient understands the position and agrees. It is not so obvious why the hypothesis of a physical cause should justify the imposition of such treatment against the patient's will. Nor does it explain why the doctors are so sure that a physical cause will some day be found for some disorders but not for others. Even in the case of the most serious illnesses, schizophrenia and the affective (mood) disorders, the hypothesis upon which the whole edifice is built has yet to be conclusively demonstrated.

Then there are other schools of psychiatric thought which, in varying degrees and varying combinations, reject the notions of organic causes, of discrete disease entities, and of the more radical physical treatments. They seek other causes and other solutions. Their various therapies may be aimed at the patient's individual psyche or at its interaction with family or societal pressures. The disadvantage of these psychotherapeutic models from the legal point of view is that they can carry the province of psychiatry far beyond the normal concerns of the medical profession, into the wider ills of the family and society. There is no necessary connection with medicine at all. This could be a serious objection if these models are used to give a spurious scientific objectivity to attempts to explain or to excuse an offender's behaviour. From the patient's point of view, however, the advantage is that their methods of treatment can usually only succeed with his free co-operation.

There is yet a third school of thought, which concentrates, not on the causes of the disorder, but on attacking its behavioural manifestations. This school has developed systems of behaviour modification which rely upon the consistent reinforcement of desired behaviour and the equally consistent discouragement of bad (see Royal College of Psychiatrists *et al.*, 1980; Boynton, 1980). Lawyers may find it particularly curious that offenders are removed from the penal system (which claims very similar objectives) for this purpose, but in theory the treatment is much more intensive and aimed at the particular problems of the patient himself. It can claim to do wonders for just those patients whom many more conventional psychiatrists now admit that they cannot treat, those whose disorders are manifested mainly by their anti-social or inadequate behaviour. Unless it is allied to a clear distinction between the normal and the abnormal, therefore, it is an obvious recipe for enabling offenders to escape their just deserts while confining some relatively harmless non-offenders.

These various models offer ample scope to the anti-psychiatrists within the profession itself, let alone to outsiders. The organically-minded are accused, for example, of failing to enter into the patient's own view of his life and to grasp the underlying rationality of what he says and does (found particularly in the work of Laing); or of perverting the concept of disease or illness to justify the imposition of treatment upon socially inconvenient people, both for their own and society's ends (found particularly in the work of Szasz). Those attacked, on the other hand, tend to accuse the anti-psychiatrists of ignoring the problems of the really ill and concentrating on the much pleasanter (and in America at least more profitable) task of ministering to the neuroses of the middle classes. Clare (1980), for example, points out that the countries in which the practice of psychiatry is most controversial are also those (the USA and the former U.S.S.R.) in which the widest definitions of the most serious illnesses are employed.

He argues that the majority of those in the NHS would claim to do their best to incorporate the good features of every approach into their clinical practice. The so-called "medical model" is not synonymous with the organic theory of mental disease, for it can encompass a sympathetic understanding of the patient's experience, a broad-minded evaluation of the complex of possible causal factors, and a cautious approach to treatment. But its prime claim is to apply the ordinary medical methods to the identification of the disorder, so that, for example, no-one is labelled a schizophrenic without exhibiting the precise symptoms which have been agreed to indicate this particular diagnostic category. Once criteria have been laid down and practitioners properly trained in their use, psychiatric diagnosis can indeed become very *reliable*. In other words, the chances of two or more psychiatrists coming up with the same label for the same patient become as good as, if not better than, those in any other branch of medicine.

Unfortunately, however, this does nothing to answer the question of its *validity*. If we all agree what a table looks like we have a fairly good chance of identifying a particular object as a table and our disagreements will be about not-quite-table-like objects. We will also be better at table-spotting than anyone else because we have had so much training and experience at it. We may even have acquired a certain skill in repairing broken tables. (Psychiatrists will quite properly say all of these things.) None of that proves that our account of what made it a table, still less what made it break, has any validity. Some would argue, for example, that the varying rates of diagnosis of mental illnesses in men and women, or in members of different racial groups, are at least in part a reflection of invalid accounts of the illnesses involved (Showalter, 1987; Littlewood and Lipsedge, 1993; see also Barnes, Bowl and Fisher, 1990). After all, a high degree of reliability in the identification of witches was achieved by the witch-hunters of the seventeenth century by just the same methods as the present-day psychiatrists employ.

In any case, these accounts of the nature and causes of mental affliction provide us with no sort of justification for allowing psychiatrists to confine and treat patients against their will. We do not permit surgeons to remove appendices simply because they are better at identifying when an appendix is diseased and at performing the operation. When neither the disease nor the cure is universally agreed, there is even less justification. This is certainly not to argue that a justification does not exist, merely that it does not lie in the expertise of the psychiatrist alone. But before considering what it might be, we must consider what English law has to say on the subject.

2. THE LEGAL CATEGORIES OF MENTAL DISORDER

The Mental Health Act makes two vital distinctions. First, for admission for assessment (ss. 2 or 4) or removal to a place of safety (ss. 135 or 136), the patient need only be suffering from some "mental disorder". For longer term admission for treatment (s. 3), or reception into guardianship (s. 7), or for a court hospital or guardianship order (s. 37), interim hospital order (s. 38), or transfer during sentence (s. 47), he must have one of the four specific forms of mental disorder: "mental illness", "severe mental impairment", "psychopathic disorder", or "mental impairment". Secondly, admission for treatment, hospital orders (but not interim hospital orders), and transfers during sentence all distinguish between the *major* disorders of mental illness and severe mental impairment, which justify admission even if hospital treatment is unlikely to do the patient any good, and the *minor* disorders of psychopathic disorder or mental impairment, which only justify admission if treatment is likely to make him better, or at least prevent his getting worse. Remands to hospital for treatment (s. 36) and transfers of unsentenced prisoners (s. 48) can only happen where the patient is suffering from a major disorder.

As well as the implications for the liberty of the subject, therefore, the precise meaning of these terms has great practical importance. But added to the intrinsic difficulties of defining them is the fact that the Act does *not* distinguish between the forms of disorder which justify long-term civil commitment and those which permit the therapeutic rather than penal disposal of criminal offenders. Many people might wish to take a narrower view of the grounds for forcibly detaining and treating a non-offender than of the circumstances justifying a court in sending an offender to hospital rather than to prison. The only scope for this, however, lies in the additional criteria for civil commitment (discussed in section 3 later), which replace the discretion of the court or the Home Secretary in criminal cases and are intended to keep civil compulsion to a minimum.

All the compulsory powers of admission to hospital or guardianship require that the patient either *is or is believed to be currently suffering* from mental disorder or the required form of it. For an admission to hospital for assessment (including an emergency admission) (s. 2(2)(a)) or for treatment (s. 3(2)(a)), or reception into guardianship (s. 7(2)(a)), or for a hospital or guardianship order (including a restriction order) (s. 37((2)(a)) or an interim hospital order (s. 38(1)(a)), transfer from prison to hospital (ss. 47(1)(a), 48(1)), or remand to hospital for treatment (s. 36(1)), the patient must actually be suffering from the mental disorder in question. The same is required when any of the long-term powers is renewed (s. 20(4)(a)). For a remand to hospital for reports (s. 35(3)(a)), there must be "reason to suspect" that he is; for an entry warrant (s. 135(1)) he must be "believed" by the approved social worker so to be; and he must so "appear" to a police officer taking him to a place of safety (s. 136(1)).

Some mental disorders are permanent, although they may not always be of the required nature or degree. Others come and go. In some of these, the symptoms may be controlled by medication but are likely to return if medication is discontinued. In *Devon C.C. v. Hawkins* [1967] 2 Q.B. 26, it was held, in relation to a person whose epilepsy was controlled by drugs, that "so long as drugs are necessary to prevent the manifestation of disease, the disease . . . remains". Such a person, then, is still suffering (see Blom-Cooper, Hally and Murphy, 1995). But there is always a difficult balance to be struck between the advantages and disadvantages of keeping patients on long-term medication. If the patient does not have symptoms which currently require medication, then it is difficult to say that he "is suffering" from the disorder, even if his psychiatrist believes that it may well recur in due course. The psychiatrist might regard him as a sick person whose illness is in remission, while the patient might see himself as a well person whose illness may return.

(a) "Mental disorder"

Section 1(2) of the Act defines "mental disorder" as "mental illness, arrested or incomplete development of mind, psychopathic disorder and any other disorder or disability of mind." Quite clearly, therefore, it is more than a handy collective noun to embrace all the four specific forms of disorder mentioned in some sections of the Act: "arrested or incomplete development of mind" is wider than "severe mental impairment" and "mental impairment"; and "any other disorder or disability of mind" takes in conditions which are not included in any of the other terms. Section 1(3) does, however, provide that a person cannot be dealt with under the Act as suffering from mental disorder, or from any specific form of it, "by reason only of promiscuity or other immoral conduct, sexual deviancy or dependence on alcohol or drugs."

There are two possible reasons why mental disorder sufficient for the short-term powers is so much wider than the four forms needed for the long-term powers. First, what is now "admission for assessment" used to be "admission for observation", with the clear implication that a short period of observation might be needed before a firm diagnosis could be made. Secondly, removal to a place of safety gives no right to impose treatment without consent, and there used to be considerable doubt about whether admission for observation did so: detention and observation may be thought justified where forcible treatment is not. However, under the 1983 Act patients admitted for 28 days of assessment may be treated in exactly the same way as those admitted for treatment (s. 56(1)). In practice the initial compulsion is usually what matters. Many patients admitted for assessment remain as informal patients (Department of Health, 1995a). But whether they do so through ignorance, inertia, the effects of treatment or a genuine willingness cannot be known. There is also the problem, well-documented in the USA, that once the label "patient" is attached to any person, not only do medical and nursing staff interpret his behaviour in that light, but he too may adopt "patient-like" behaviour in order to conform to their expectations and make life more tolerable.

We must therefore consider what the law means, first, by each of the four specific forms of disorder and then by the two terms which make "mental disorder" into a wider concept.

(b) "Mental illness"

Although the law regards it as a major disorder, "mental illness" is defined nowhere in the Act. The Percy Commission (1957) were much more concerned with the definitions of subnormality and psychopathic disorder and assumed that mental illness would be construed in the same way that "unsoundness of mind" and "lunacy" had been construed in the past. This was almost certainly limited to what were then termed psychotic conditions (and possibly not to all of them). They also assumed that these did not encompass disturbances of personality or behaviour. These were dangerous assumptions, for there is evidence that during the nineteenth century lunacy had been stretched, from its common law origins in dangerous madness, so as to enable families and workhouses to unload their enfeebled elderly or incorrigibly troublesome members onto the asylums (Scull, 1979). Similarly, some modern psychiatrists may assume that mental illness simply refers to whatever disorders are left once the various forms of handicap and psychopathic disorder are subtracted (Rollin, 1969).

31

One solution would be to ask the psychiatrists themselves to distinguish the concept of "illness" from that of "disorder." Thus they might agree that an "illness" entails a "mental change involving an obvious departure from normal health" (for which in due course an organic cause is likely to be found); whereas other conditions are not illnesses but "extreme variations in personality from a hypothetical norm". This approach coincides with the Butler Committee's (1975, para. 1.13) definition of mental illness as a "disorder which has not always existed in the patient but has developed as a condition overlying the sufferer's usual personality".

But this approach would not distinguish between the serious illnesses which used to be termed psychoses (principally schizophrenia, affective (mood) disorders such as manic-depressive or major depressive illness, and the various disorders associated with physical conditions, such as senile dementia or delirium tremens) and the various conditions which used to be termed neuroses (such as anxieties, phobias, obsessions, and depression). The International Classification of Diseases (10th revision, ICD–10, World Health Organisation, 1992) has now abandoned the distinction and groups disorders according to common themes or descriptive likenesses. Some conditions which do not involve the gross symptoms popularly associated with "madness" also result from a "change involving an obvious departure from normal health", can be just as disabling and involve just as little acceptance of the need for treatment. Obvious examples are the eating disorders which have a higher death rate than the traditional illnesses.

The opportunity for the courts to supply a more precise definition of mental illness arose in the case of *W. v. L.* [1974] Q.B. 711. The patient, a young man of 23, had put a cat in a gas oven; had later made a cat inhale ammonia and then cut its throat with a cup; had hanged a puppy in the garage; had strangled a terrier with wire; had threatened his wife with a knife; and last had threatened to push her downstairs as a means of disposing of the baby she was expecting. This was clearly enough to fall within the definition of psychopathy (section (c) later); but at the time, being over the age of 21, he could not be obliged to remain in hospital for longer than 28 days unless he committed a criminal offence or could be termed "mentally ill". The doctors were divided in their opinions, but there was one who described him as suffering from an "episodic epileptoid psychosis".

The Court of Appeal decided that he was both psychopathic and mentally ill. Lawton L.J. provided the only authoritative statement in English law on the meaning of "mental illness":

> "The words are ordinary words of the English language. They have no particular medical significance. They have no particular legal significance ... ordinary words of the English language should be construed in the way that ordinary sensible people would construe them .... I ask myself, what would the ordinary sensible person have said about the patient's condition in this case if he had been informed of his behaviour to the dogs, the cat and his wife? In my judgment such a person would have said 'well, the fellow is obviously mentally ill'."

It is impossible not to think of this as the "man-must-be-mad" test. It simply adds fuel to the fire of those who accuse the mental hygiene laws of being a sophisticated machine for the suppression of unusual, eccentric or inconvenient behaviour (and in this country without due process of law).

It pays scant regard to the painstaking efforts of psychiatrists to distinguish mental health from mental illness by means of carefully described deficiencies, not in behaviour, but in mental functioning. It draws no recognisable distinction between illness and personality disorder. It tells us nothing about why some people who are cruel to animals should be regarded as responsible for their actions and some should not.

As Cavadino (1991a) points out, lay people's understanding of mental illness is notoriously limited or faulty. It would make more sense to focus on the commonly accepted medical meaning of the phrase. This seems to be what both the other judges, Lord Denning and Orr L.J., did in *W. v. L.* [1974] Q.B. 711. But if so, we would lose any link with the concepts of the past, which are either limiting or protective depending on your point of view.

The DHSS Consultative Document on the 1959 Act (1976) canvassed the possibility of a closed definition of mental illness which would require one or more of the following characteristics: (i) more than temporary impairment of intellectual functions shown by a failure of memory, orientation, comprehension and learning capacity; (ii) more than temporary alteration of mood of such degree as to give rise to the patient having a delusional appraisal of his situation, his past or his future, or that of others or to the lack of any appraisal; (iii) delusional beliefs, persecutory, jealous or grandiose; (iv) abnormal perceptions associated with delusional misinterpretation of events; (v) thinking so disordered as to prevent the patient making a reasonable appraisal of his situation or having reasonable communication with others.

This was identical to the definition of "severe mental illness" suggested by the Butler Committee for the purposes of a verdict of "not guilty by reason of mental disorder", save that "more than temporary" is substituted for "lasting"; following further consultation with psychiatrists, the Butler Committee's definition has also been adopted for that purpose in the Law Commission's draft criminal code (1989). In the event, however, the attempt to provide a definition in the 1983 Act was abandoned, ostensibly because the lack of it was not thought to have caused any difficulties in practice (DHSS *et al.*, 1978). Of its very nature, lack of precise definition will not cause problems to the people who operate the law; but it may very well do so for their patients. If statutory definition would be too inflexible and restrictive, there may be scope for other forms of guidance (Cavadino, 1991a). In the mean-time, it is to be hoped that practitioners will limit their intervention to cases exhibiting mental symptoms which bring them within the precise and recognised categories of mental disease. They might also bear in mind the definition suggested by the Northern Ireland Review Committee on Mental Health Legislation (MacDermott 1981):

> " . . . a state of mind of a permanent or temporary (but not merely transient) nature in which the individual exhibits such disordered thinking, perceiving or emotion as impairs his judgment of his situation to the extent that he requires care, treatment or training in his own interests or in the interests of other persons."

In the Mental Health (Northern Ireland) Order 1986, article 3(1), this is subtly altered to "a state of mind which affects a person's thinking, perceiving, emotion or judgement to the extent that he requires care or medical treatment . . . " At least these focus attention upon *why* it is that some people may be treated differently by the law from others whose actions are inconvenient or damaging either for themselves or for others.

(c) "Psychopathic disorder"

This same problem arises in an even more acute form with the "minor" disorder of psychopathy, defined in section 1(2) of the Act as "a persistent disorder or disability of mind (whether or not including significant impairment of intelligence) which results in abnormally aggressive or seriously irresponsible conduct on the part of the person concerned."

In the nineteenth century, the term "moral insanity" was coined to describe cases which did not exhibit the obvious symptoms, such as delusions or hallucinations, associated with lunacy. It originally meant "madness, consisting in a morbid perversion of the natural feelings, affections, inclinations, temper, habits, moral dispositions, and natural impulses, without any remarkable disorder or defect of the interest or knowing and reasoning faculties . . . ." (Prichard, 1835). This may approximate to the modern concepts of neurosis and personality disorder but has no specific connection with antisocial behaviour. "Moral" in those days meant "emotional" or "psychological" rather than the reverse of "immoral". In Germany, the term "psychopathy" or "constitutional psychopathic inferiority" was used for a whole range of conditions where the patient's personality deviated from some supposed biological norm.

The idea of a specific disorder closely associated with antisocial behaviour seems to have stemmed from the observation that there were people whose persistent and apparently incorrigible misbehaviour began at a very early age. In England, these were termed "moral imbeciles", with the obvious risk of confusion with the originally wider concept of moral insanity and the quite different condition of intellectual imbecility. Because neither were thought to be covered by the concept of "lunacy", the Mental Deficiency Acts of 1913 and 1927 were passed to provide for the confinement of both the intellectually and the morally defective. The two were defined separately in the Acts, but their association led inevitably to doubts about whether the morally defective could be confined if they were not intellectually subnormal.

The Percy Commission (1957) wished to make it clear that disordered personalities of normal intelligence could be dealt with under the new Act. By that time the concept of psychopathy had changed. Efforts to categorise and define specific personalities which might be called pathological had concentrated on predominantly "aggressive" or predominantly "inadequate" characteristics. From this it was a short step to the Percy Commission's conclusion that there was a mental *disorder* called psychopathy, which could be defined largely in terms of the adequacy of the person's social functioning. Hence they suggested a third category of mental disorder, after mental illness and severe mental subnormality, covering "any type of aggressive or inadequate personality which does not render the patient severely subnormal but which is recognised medically as a pathological condition." If it included "marked limitation of intelligence" the term "feebleminded psychopath" was proposed. But because of the obvious libertarian objections, the Commission proposed age limits on the prolonged detention of those who had not offended against the criminal law (see further section 3(b) later).

The Commission were still attacked for suggesting too wide a criterion for compulsory hospitalisation, and for failure to distinguish sufficiently between personality disorder and mental handicap. The resulting statutory definition of psychopathy therefore emphasised the connection with serious antisocial behaviour, and provided for a separate definition of non-severe mental handicap. It is questionable, therefore, how far the concept has come from the old idea of "moral imbecility" (Anderson, 1962). Yet the original meaning had been quite different, and psychiatrists are by no means agreed on the existence of a specific clinical entity corresponding to the statutory definition. The closest approximation in the International Classification of Diseases (ICD–10, F60.2) is "dissocial personality disorder":

> "Personality disorder, usually coming to attention because of a gross disparity between behaviour and the prevailing social norms, and characterised by:
> (a) callous unconcern for the feelings of others;
> (b) gross and persistent attitude of irresponsibility and disregard for social norms, rules and obligations;
> (c) incapacity to maintain enduring relationships, though having no difficulty in establishing them;
> (d) very low tolerance to frustration and a low threshold for discharge of aggression including violence;
> (e) incapacity to experience guilt or profit from experience, particularly punishment;
> (f) marked proneness to blame others, or to offer plausible rationalisations, for the behaviour that has brought the patient into conflict with society."

Not surprisingly, the concept of psychopathy has been particularly criticised in its application to criminal offenders. Why should this particular group of offenders be singled out for special treatment? Are they a particular group at all? How is it possible to distinguish the mentally disordered psychopath from the mentally normal recidivist? Is it not circular to conclude that a person is disordered because he commits crimes and then conclude that his disorder should at least partially excuse those crimes (see particularly Wootton, 1959)?

There may be a tendency to apply more elastic concepts of mental disorder for the purpose of treating rather than imprisoning a criminal offender than would be thought appropriate in compelling a non-offender to accept treatment. Particular examples are alcohol or drug abuse and some forms of sexual deviation (see, *e.g. R. v. Mental Health Act Commission, ex p. X.* (1988) 9 B.M.L.R. 77, p. 146, later; Fennell, 1988). These have commonly been thought to be "all in the mind" and thus treatable by psychiatric methods. Yet to deem them mental disorders suggests that a man may be insane simply because of his inconvenient, damaging or self-destructive behaviour. Because of this, the DHSS (DHSS *et al.*, 1978) suggested that they should be excluded from the definition of mental disorder for the purposes of civil commitment, but that the courts should remain free to impose a hospital order after a criminal offence. In the result, section 1(3) excludes those whose *only* problem is promiscuity, immoral conduct, sexual deviancy, alcohol or drug dependence from *all* the categories of mental disorder, and thus from the ambit of hospital and guardianship orders (although requirements for the treatment of alcohol or drug abuse may now be included in supervision orders) unless there is some other mental disorder as well.

A good example of circularity arose in *R. v. Mental Health Review Tribunal, ex p. Clatworthy* [1985] 3 All E.R. 699, where a hospital order (initially with restrictions) had been made following two offences of indecent assault in 1967. The diagnosis was psychopathy but, as Mann J. pointed out, "the effect of [section 1(3)] is apparently to prevent there being a condition of psychopathic disorder when the abnormally aggressive or seriously irresponsible conduct consequent upon the persistent disorder or disability of mind is conduct which is a manifestation of sexual deviancy." If this be so, on what logical basis are promiscuous, immoral or sexually deviant conduct, alcohol and drug abuse excluded but violence and dishonesty not?

But even supposing that the psychiatrists can point (as they could not in the *Clatworthy* case) to signs of mental pathology which are independent of the tendency to commit crimes, such as the lack of normal feelings or motivations associated with his behaviour, the case for special treatment is still not made out. A psychopath who has been made the subject of a hospital order is apparently no more likely to go on behaving badly in the future than is a similar but "normal" offender who has been sent to prison (Walker and McCabe, 1973). There is at present no convincing evidence of whether or not they can be treated: some may respond to different treatment, in a range of settings, but it cannot yet be determined what will work for whom (Dolan and Coid, 1993; Reed, 1994b). They are often the most troublesome and inconvenient of patients.

The result is that, far from amounting to an excuse, the label "psychopath" is likely to do an offender more harm than good. If a hospital place cannot be found, the court may be tempted to impose a prison sentence at the top end of the range because, by definition, he is more than usually dangerous. The Butler Committee thought that responsibility for psychopaths should lie principally with the prison rather than the hospital services. They suggested that a hospital order should not be made unless there was at least a suspected additional mental or physical illness or disability *and* a prospect of benefit from hospital admission. The DHSS (1976; DHSS *et al.*, 1978) recognised that "psychopath" had become a damaging label involving much stigma, but did not want to remove the possibility of treatment from those who might be helped by it. The statutory definition remains much as it was in the 1959 Act but there is now an additional "treatability" criterion on admission (p. 43, later).

Following the 1983 Act, there was also concern that psychopathic offenders may have to be discharged from hospital if they are not suffering from a disorder warranting treatment there, even though they may offend again if released (see DHSS and Home Office, 1986; Peay, 1988). The very generous interpretation given in the courts, both of "medical treatment" and of "treatability" (see pp. 42, 195, later) may provide some solution. The recent Report of the Department of Health and Home Office Working Group on Psychopathic Disorder (Reed, 1994b) however commends the idea of a "hybrid order" which sets the tariff sentence for the offence but keeps open the option of whether this would be served in prison or under a restriction order.

The Reed Report also proposed that the term "psychopathic disorder" in the Mental Health Act should be replaced by the more generally understood and less stigmatising term "personality disorder," provided that this was not further defined. Such a major extension of the circumstances in which long-term compulsory detention and treatment could be imposed may solve the professional dilemma and offer the chance of humane disposal to a wider range of offenders, but raises serious questions about the justifications for imposing long-term detention and treatment in hospital upon both offenders and non-offenders alike.

(d) "Mental impairment" and "severe mental impairment"

The common law distinguished "idiots" (who have no understanding from birth and are presumed incurable) from "lunatics" (who may have lucid intervals or even be cured). The early lunacy legislation included idiots, but the Idiots Act 1886 was the first to provide separately for the confinement of both idiots and "imbeciles". This left out of account people who were neither mad nor severely handicapped, but suffered from disturbed or inadequate personalities, manifested mainly in the quality of their social functioning. Hence the Report of the Royal Commission on the Care and Control of the Feeble-Minded of 1904 to 1908 (Radnor, 1908) recommended that local authority institutions be provided for them as well as for idiots and imbeciles.

The Mental Deficiency Acts of 1913 and 1927 defined four categories of mental defect, itself defined in 1927 as "a condition of arrested or incomplete development of mind existing before the age of 18 whether arising from inherent causes or induced by disease or injury". The first category were "idiots", who were unable to guard themselves against common physical dangers such as fire, water or traffic. Their mental age when adult was said to be that of a pre-school child. "Imbeciles" could guard against physical dangers but were incapable of managing themselves or their affairs. Their mental age would be about that of a nursery or infant school child. The "feebleminded" were the largest group. Though neither idiot nor imbecile, they were thought to require care, supervision or control for their own protection or that of others. The last group were the "moral defectives" who became the psychopaths of today (see (c) earlier).

The Percy Commission wanted to do away with this outdated terminology and also the strict legal separation between the care of lunatics and defectives. Hence they recommended a uniform set of procedures to cover both mental illness and mental handicap. The main result was to remove psychopathy from its association with mental handicap and it is now usually regarded, if anything, as a psychiatric disorder. The 1959 Act also replaced the three grades of defect with the major disorder of "severe subnormality" and the minor disorder of "subnormality". Both required limitation of intelligence. For severe subnormality, this had to be such that the patient was incapable of leading an independent life or guarding against serious exploitation.

Later developments cast doubt on the validity of the 1959 Act's elegant scheme. The terminology has changed yet again. The World Health Organisation (1980) now distinguishes between a handicap and a disability.

"The term 'disability' summarizes a great number of different functional limitations .... People may be disabled by physical, intellectual or sensory impairment, medical conditions or mental illness .... The term 'handicap' means loss or limitation of opportunities to take part in the life of the community on an equal level with others. It describes the encounter between the person with a disability and the environment ... " (United Nations, 1994, p. 9).

The people with whom we are concerned here have a learning disability.

Before the 1982 amendments, there was a vigorous campaign to take learning disabilities out of the Act altogether. The association with mental illness could suggest that people with learning disabilities are invariably disturbed in their thinking, feeling or behaviour, when this is very far from true. They argued that the need for civil commitment, if it arose at all, stemmed not from the disability as such, but from some additional psychiatric illness or behaviour disorder (which might even be the result of how supposedly normal people had reacted to their disability). Learning disabilities cannot be "cured" in the way that psychiatric disorders can be cured, although a person's level of functioning may be improved by skilled and patient education. If patients are committed to hospital, therefore, they will find it much harder to obtain their release.

This is a particular problem with hospital orders. A mildly disabled person knows only too well that, although hospital may be a pleasanter place than prison, he may have to stay there for a great deal longer. A special hospital is particularly ill-suited to improving his chances of surviving in society. The Rampton Review Team (Boynton, 1980) recommended that severely handicapped patients should not be in Rampton at all. In fact, the courts have often been cheated of their humane intentions by the reluctance of NHS hospitals to accept patients with learning disabilities from them. Only gradually is it being accepted that special facilities should be developed for people who present the "double challenge" of learning disabilities and behavioural problems.

The Butler Committee (1975) did not want to deny the chance of a therapeutic disposal, but recommended that the court should have evidence from a specialist in mental handicap. The DHSS (DHSS *et al.*, 1978) concluded that non-offenders might still have to be compelled in order to protect them from exploitation. MIND (1978) responded that "it is a curious society which, in order to prevent abuse of its vulnerable citizens, suggests confinement for the abused, while allowing freedom for those who exploit." Of course, the same could be said of those who abuse children. The removal of the child, even against his will, is not always worse than leaving him in the detrimental environment. Nor does compulsion inevitably mean confinement in an institution. Guardianship, at least in its 1959 Act form, could provide a measure of protection in the community.

The result was an unsatisfactory compromise. The 1983 Act defines "severe mental impairment" as "a state of arrested or incomplete development of mind which includes severe impairment of intelligence and social functioning and is associated with abnormally aggressive or seriously irresponsible conduct on the part of the person concerned" (s. 1(2)). "Mental impairment" is "a state of arrested or incomplete development of mind (not amounting to severe impairment) which includes significant impairment of intelligence and social functioning and is associated with abnormally aggressive or seriously irresponsible conduct on the part of the person concerned" (s. 1(2)). This means that for all the longer term powers, admission for treatment under section 3, hospital orders and transfers from prison, but also guardianship, the patient's learning disability *must* be associated with "abnormally aggressive or seriously irresponsible conduct". This may not make much difference in criminal cases (arguably *all* offending is seriously irresponsible) but presents difficulties especially with guardianship. On one view, most if not all severely disabled people are also "seriously irresponsible" in the sense that they cannot take responsibility for their own conduct. A broad approach would make guardianship available to protect them. It would, however, defeat the object of the changed definition, which was to exclude from the Act those who did not also exhibit psychopathic behaviour. On any view, it excludes those so profoundly disabled that they cannot engage in "conduct" at all.

The changed definitions are welcome in their insistence that there must be impairment of social functioning as well as of intelligence. It has been said that they are not terms of art and so must be construed as ordinary people would construe them. "Severe mental impairment" is to be judged by comparison with people of normal intelligence and social functioning rather than with mentally handicapped people generally (*R. v. Hall (John)* (1987) 86 Cr.App.R. 159). There is no rule of thumb to distinguish "severe" from "significant" impairment, still less to distinguish the significantly impaired person from the "dull but normal". This was never an easy matter, even in the days when it was thought to be governed by the scientific measurement of intelligence or of "mental age". The Percy Commission thought that all the former idiots and imbeciles and some of the feeble-minded would be in the severely subnormal category. They suggested a mental age of below about seven and a half to nine, or an IQ of 50 to 60, would be a "strong pointer" to severe handicap. They made no suggestion at the upper end. The International Classification of Diseases (World Health Organisation, 1992, F70) puts "mild mental retardation" at an IQ of 50 to 69. Standardised tests for which local cultural norms have been determined should be used. And for a definite diagnosis "there should be a reduced level of intellectual functioning resulting in diminished ability to adapt to daily demands of the normal social environment" (p. 227). Many psychologists would now doubt that the concept of intelligence is capable of governing the matter. A person with an IQ score in the 80s may be handicapped by the inadequacy of his social functioning, while a person with a lower score may be much more capable. It is good that the new definitions bring this out, but they do serve to emphasise how subjective and value-laden the assessment of degrees of impairment can be.

(e) "Arrested or incomplete development of mind"

The campaign on behalf of people with learning disabilities did not succeed in excluding them from the short-term powers of compulsion. "Arrested or incomplete development of mind" remains an ingredient of "mental disorder" which is sufficient for admission for assessment or removal to a place of safety. The Act does not limit it to "severe mental impairment" and "mental impairment". The phrase dates back to the old mental deficiency legislation. It would seem to cover any appreciable failure to meet the normal milestones of mental development, whether this is caused by genetic or constitutional factors, or by environmental shortcomings in childhood, or by damage to or disease of the brain. It could even cover other things than intellectual development. But it would *not* cover the subsequent degeneration of a mind which had been fully developed. The mental infirmities of old age would not be included here, although they may be included as a mental illness, at least if they amount to a psychosis, and they might amount to "any other disorder or disability of mind".

(f) "Any other disorder or disability of mind"

Once again, this residuary category is sufficient for the short term powers and there is no reason to suppose that it is simply a handy collective noun for the four specific disorders. The example given in Parliament during the passage of the 1959 Act was brain damage caused by an injury or physical disease such as encephalitis (although the results of this might often amount to one of the other disorders). As ordinary words of the English language, "any other disorder or disability of mind" seem to mean any mental condition which deviates sufficiently from the supposed norm to be called abnormal and which is sufficiently deleterious (as abnormally high intelligence, for example, usually is not) to be called a disorder.

If so, this is both too wide and too vague to justify even the shortest invasion of liberty, let alone detention for up to 28 days with the risk of forcible psychiatric treatment. The DHSS (1976) argued that to be more specific, but to include all the suitable candidates for compulsion, might in practice *extend* the categories of those at risk. As it is, many psychiatrists probably do not address their minds to the law's distinction between mental illness and mental disorder and only recommend any form of compulsion for people whom they consider to be mentally *ill*. On the other hand, they are unlikely to restrict that concept to what used to be termed psychoses. In practice, "mental disorder" probably means any condition of mind which has been recognised and described by psychiatrists sufficiently often to appear in the standard psychiatric textbooks.

But those textbooks (and the International Classification of Diseases) deal separately with disorders of the mind and diseases or injuries to the brain. Even if the present statutory definition is wide enough to cover them both, the Law Commission (1995) have proposed a new concept of "mental disability" as part of the test of whether a person is capable of taking a particular decision for himself (p. 48, later). This would cover "any disability or disorder of the mind or brain, whether permanent or temporary, which results in an impairment or disturbance of mental functioning" (para. 3.12).

3. THE ADDITIONAL CRITERIA FOR CIVIL COMMITMENT

In 1957, the Percy Commission (para. 317) set out the principles which they believed would justify the use of compulsion in a world where all care and treatment was, if possible, to be provided without it. First and foremost, there had to be a pathological mental disorder for which the patient required hospital or community care. Secondly, this care could not be provided without compulsion because the patient or his family would not accept it. So far, so good: but the Commission went on to suggest two additional requirements which were crucial. Thirdly, if the patient would not accept treatment, there should be "at least a strong likelihood that his unwillingness is due to a lack of appreciation of his own condition deriving from the mental disorder itself." Finally, there should be one of two advantages to be gained: *either* a "good prospect of benefit to the patient from the treatment proposed—an expectation that it will either cure or alleviate his mental disorder or strengthen his ability to regulate his social behaviour in spite of the underlying disorder, or bring him substantial benefit in the form of protection from neglect or exploitation by others:" *or* a "strong need to protect others from anti-social behaviour by the patient."

However, the Commission did not suggest that these principles should be expressed. Instead, they recommended a scheme which distinguished between the various types of disorder in a way which they believed would translate their views into action. Their third principle would be achieved by restricting long-term treatment to the mentally ill or severely subnormal. Their fourth principle would be achieved by the additional criteria in the grounds for commitment. As modified in the 1983 Act, there are now *three* matters of which the recommending doctors must be satisfied, in addition to the diagnosis of mental disorder already discussed. These are summarised below, before the full meaning of each is discussed:

(i) For admission for *assessment*, the patient's disorder must be "of a nature or degree which warrants the detention of the patient in a hospital for assessment (or for assessment followed by medical treatment) for at least a limited period" (s. 2(2)(a)). For admission for *treatment*, the patient's disorder must be "of a nature or degree which makes it appropriate for him to receive treatment in a hospital" (s. 3(2)(a)).

(ii) If the patient is suffering from *psychopathic disorder* or non-severe *mental impairment*, he can only be admitted for *treatment* if medical treatment in a hospital is "likely to alleviate or prevent a deterioration of his condition" (s. 3(2)(b)).

(iii) For admission for *assessment*, it is also required that the patient "ought to be so detained in the interests of his own health or safety or with a view to the protection of other persons" (s. 2(2)(b)). The equivalent in an admission for *treatment* is that "it is necessary for the health or safety of the patient or for the protection of other persons that he should receive such treatment and it cannot be provided unless he is detained under this section" (s. 3(2)(c)).

Because the definitions of the various forms of mental disorder are so wide, it is these three additional requirements that theoretically distinguish the "sectionable" from the "unsectionable" patient. But how effective are they in doing so?

(a) "Of a nature or degree . . . "

This is meant to ensure, at the very least, that the *type* or *severity* of the patient's disorder is currently such that he ought to be in hospital (p. 30, earlier). Compulsory admission should not be used if the patient could be cared for equally well in the community. This criterion does go some way towards insisting that patients are cared for in the "least restrictive environment" possible. In practice, doctors in NHS hospitals will insist that they are not going to admit any patient who does not need to be in hospital, because pressure on their beds is so great.

Thus, this criterion should exclude from compulsory admission an increasing number of patients who ought not to be in hospital at all and are only there because the community does not have appropriate facilities for them. This is particularly true of long-term residents in mental handicap hospitals, where compulsory powers are in any event rarely used. This criterion should also exclude, at least from compulsory admission for treatment, those patients for whom medical treatment *in a hospital* is no longer appropriate.

But what of those who could survive quite well in the community if only there were some way of insisting that they have their regular injections of the long-acting drugs which keep their symptoms under control? Under the 1959 Act, it was theoretically possible to do this by transferring them into guardianship, although in practice it was hardly ever done. Under the 1983 Act, a guardian has no right to force the patient to accept treatment, although he may insist that the patient goes to a clinic where treatment is available, or is visited by a community nurse. The same is true of a patient subject to supervised after-care under the Mental Health (Patients in the Community) Act 1995.

In *R. v. Hallstrom, ex p. W.; R v. Gardiner, ex p. L.* [1986] Q.B. 1090 McCullough J. held that it was only "appropriate" for a patient to receive medical treatment in a hospital if her condition required *in*-patient treatment. It was not, therefore, possible to admit a patient for whom in-patient treatment was not appropriate, with a view to granting immediate leave of absence so that she could be obliged to take her medication outside hospital. There was, as the judge acknowledged, a case for giving doctors the power to impose treatment outside hospital.

> "There is, however, no canon of construction which presumes that Parliament intended that people should, against their will, be subjected to treatment which others, however professionally competent, perceive, however sincerely and however correctly, to be in their best interests. What there is is a canon of construction that Parliament is presumed not to enact legislation which interferes with the liberty of the subject without making it clear that this was its intention."

Fine words, but in section 145(1) medical treatment is defined to include "nursing and care, habilitation and rehabilitation under medical supervision." In *R. v. Mersey Mental Health Review Tribunal, ex p. D., The Times*, April 13, 1987, therefore, it was held appropriate to continue to detain a patient in a special hospital even though there was nothing other than nursing care which could be given to him.

Might this requirement go further than requiring that the patient's condition is bad enough for him to be in hospital? If it must be bad enough to "*warrant his detention*" does this not ask for a *moral* judgment about whether it is bad enough to *force* him to go? Beebe, Ellis and Evans (1973) provide an illustration in the case of Mrs X, who was a socially isolated 65-year-old Viennese refugee Jewess. Her G.P. reported to the mental welfare team that she was again becoming paranoid. The team agreed (with some reservation because of cultural factors). Paranoia is undoubtedly a mental disorder, although it may be either a personality disorder or a psychotic paranoid state. Mrs X would probably have been better off in hospital for her own sake. Nevertheless, the team thought themselves unable to compel her to go, because "she was sufficiently in contact with reality".

Taken seriously, this requirement could come close to the Percy Commission's third principle: that the patient's unwillingness to enter hospital should result from a failure to appreciate his need for treatment, which failure is caused by the mental disorder itself (and not, for example, by ordinary independence of mind, dislike of hospitals, or distrust of doctors). But this is no longer required for an admission for treatment. The changed wording simply insists that the patient's condition is bad enough to "make it appropriate for him to receive medical treatment in a hospital." There is no mention of its being appropriate to *compel* him to go. The law-makers must have assumed that whenever a patient was suffering from one of the four specific forms of disorder which was bad enough to require hospital treatment, it was bound to be bad enough to justify forcing him to go. But is that right?

(b) Treatability

The Percy Commission put "treatability" forward as a condition for the commitment of *all* patients, apart from those whose detention was necessary to protect other people from antisocial behaviour. But the present requirement applies only to the long-term detention of psychopathic or non-severely impaired patients. In civil commitment, it replaces the age limits which were contained in the 1959 Act: such patients could not be compelled to enter hospital for treatment over the age of 21, although once there they could be kept till 25 or even longer if "dangerous". Those age limits were put there to meet a serious libertarian point. These patients are not suffering from those gross distortions of perception, thinking or mood which are involved in a diagnosis of serious mental illness. Nor are their capacities so impaired that they are no more capable of looking after themselves than a small child. They have an apparently pathological inability to avoid seriously antisocial behaviour. The Percy Commission believed that permitting such people to be detained *before* those tendencies had manifested themselves in a criminal offence had exposed a wide range of social misfits to confinement without trial. This had certainly happened to some unmarried mothers, confined for their "moral defect". The Commission believed that it was only permissible to detain such people in hospital after they had committed crimes, or for a short period of observation, or while they were still growing up. But once they were adults, they were entitled to the same presumption of innocence as the rest of us.

In the years that followed, this point was forgotten. The age limit was seen as an arbitrary restriction upon the hospitals' power to provide treatment where they thought it might do good. Some people (*e.g.* the Court of Appeal in *W. v. L.* [1974] Q.B. 711, p. 32, earlier) clearly thought that there ought to be some form of preventive detention available for people who were not mentally ill but whose doctors thought them dangerous. The doctors, on the other hand, did not want to be expected to provide preventive detention, even if the person had committed a crime (*particularly* if the person had committed a crime). They wished it to be emphasised that they could not be expected to receive such patients unless there was some prospect of benefit from treatment. If there was such a prospect, they saw no reason for limiting civil compulsion to the young.

Hence the age limits were abolished in 1983. But both for an admission for treatment and for a hospital order the psychopathy or non-severe impairment must be such that hospital treatment is "likely to alleviate or prevent a deterioration of his condition." This concept of making the patient better, or at least preventing his getting worse, is difficult to apply where the condition is of constitutional origin and cannot be "cured" by conventional psychiatric treatment. Some hospitals offer behaviour modification or milieu therapy (although this may not be easy to distinguish from providing an environment in which the behaviour is unlikely to recur). Others offer psychotherapeutic treatments which require the patient to co-operate, but the fact that he refuses to do so does not make his condition untreatable (*R. v. Cannons Park Mental Health Review Tribunal, ex p. A.* [1994] 2 All E.R. 659, C.A.). In effect, then, the new "treatability" test is designed to protect the hospitals from any responsibility towards patients whom they do not want, but it provides no protection at all for the patient who does not want the hospital (Gunn, 1979).

The 1983 Act did go some way towards meeting the original purpose of the treatability test by applying it to the *renewal* of both an admission for treatment and an ordinary hospital order (though not a restriction order) for patients with all four forms of disorder (s. 20(4); p. 88, later). But in the case of mental illness or severe mental impairment, an alternative is that the patient would be unlikely to be able to care for himself, to obtain the care which he needs or to guard himself against serious exploitation. There are two curious features about this. The first is that the Percy Commission proposed treatability as an *alternative* to the need to protect other people. But in the 1983 Act it is a condition in its own right. That means, for example, that the detention of an ordinary hospital order patient cannot be renewed unless treatability (albeit with the alternative of inability to care for himself) can be shown. On the other hand, treatability has *not* been written into the circumstances in which a mental health review tribunal *must* grant a discharge (s. 72(1)(b); see p. 194, later). Although the tribunal must take it into account in exercising its discretion to discharge (s. 72(2)(a)), it may refuse to discharge a patient who could not have been admitted in the first place and who will have to be released at his next renewal date (see *R. v. Cannons Park Mental Health Review Tribunal, ex p. A.* [1994] 2 All E.R. 659, C.A.).

(c) "In the interests of his own health and safety or for the protection of other persons"

This requirement was the one designed to implement the Percy Commission's fourth and final principle, of "treatability" or protection. In practice, however, psychiatrists commonly believe that it means that the patient must be dangerous to himself or others (see even Clare, 1980). Bean (1980), for example, found that, while a high rating for psychiatric disorder was needed before the patient would be admitted to hospital at all, whether he was admitted informally or compulsorily depended mainly on his "dangerousness" rating. These psychiatrists are to be commended for their caution, although they may be using the term dangerousness in a very loose sense. But in fact, as is now stressed in the Code of Practice (Foreword and para. 2.6), this is *not* what the law requires.

The Act uses the criterion that the patient is likely to "act in a manner dangerous to other persons or to himself" for the quite different purpose of preventing his nearest relative from discharging him (s. 25(1); p. 167, later). Where an Act of Parliament uses two different phrases it is presumed to mean two different things. In this case, it is clear that the criteria for the initial admission to hospital were meant to be broader than those for keeping him there against the wishes of his family.

The difference between the two phrases is quite obvious. A patient is only dangerous *to himself* if he is likely to kill or injure himself, either deliberately or through extreme self-neglect. But a patient may need hospital treatment "in the interests of his own health or safety" whenever this is the best way of providing the appropriate care or treatment or of safeguarding him against the risks, temptations or other stresses to which he might be subjected outside. Once the doctor has reached the conclusion that the patient's disorder is bad enough to make it appropriate for him to receive treatment in a hospital, it follows that his detention will be necessary for his own health, if not his safety, if he is unwilling to go voluntarily.

Of course, there may be some patients whose condition is not bad enough to warrant hospital admission for their own sake but is bad enough to warrant it for the sake of other people. If the law required such patients to be *dangerous*, there would have to be a risk that they would attack and harm someone. But the Act simply requires that it be necessary to "protect other persons". This leaves it to practitioners to decide who those other persons might be and what they are entitled to be protected from. A good illustration (from personal experience) is Mrs Y. She displayed none of the first rank symptoms of schizophrenia (thought control, auditory hallucinations or delusions) but was described by her psychiatrist as "bats". She was a very bad house-keeper, was loud, argumentative and often irrelevant in conversation, and made a thorough nuisance of herself by pestering and arguing with her neighbours. Significantly, her own psychiatrist remarked that it had been a mistake to give her a "good" council house with house- and garden-proud neighbours. Most of the usual drugs had been tried and he did not suggest that keeping her in hospital was likely to do her any good at all.

So how far was he entitled to go in trying to protect other people from her? Does the Act simply intend that they should be protected from physical harm? Or can it at least be extended to protecting families from the enormous physical and mental strain which caring for a disordered relative can impose? Or from the emotional and sometimes financial suffering caused by living with someone who is clearly going out of his mind? Or from the developmental damage suffered by the children of parents who cannot cater adequately for their intellectual and emotional needs? Or from the irritation and nuisance suffered by neighbours of people like Mrs Y? The general consensus would probably stop at around the third point on this scale but the law does not insist that the psychiatrist does. The only confident statement is that the protection of property alone is not enough.

(d) Consenting or incapable patients

The patient may be suffering from mental disorder; it may be serious enough to warrant hospital admission or make hospital treatment appropriate; if he is psychopathic or impaired, he may be "treatable"; and the admission or treatment may be necessary in his own interests or those of others. But should he be compelled, even if all these conditions are fulfilled, if *compulsion* is not necessary, either because he is willing to go or because he is in no state to object?

Of course, there are cases in which the compulsion of an apparently willing, or a non-objecting, incapable, patient is in fact necessary (see Code of Practice, para. 2.7). There may be well-founded fears that he will soon change his mind. Beebe, Ellis and Evans (1973) give the examples of the schizophrenic woman who asked for the security of the hospital but warned that her voices might tell her to leave, or the alcoholic who had frequently left before and was plagued by intrusive thoughts that he should kill his wife and child. The patient may be willing to stay in hospital but unwilling to accept the medical treatment which his doctor thinks necessary. The patient may be incapable of expressing a view either way, but the doctor may be reluctant to rely upon the common law doctrine of necessity (p. 136, later).

45

But what if an informal admission is only inappropriate for administrative reasons? Tales abound of hospitals that will not admit patients out of normal hours, or without a prior interview with the hospital psychiatrist, or during industrial action, without the clear mark of urgency which a compulsory admission provides. And what is the position when the psychiatrist concentrates on discovering symptoms of mental disorder and whether the patient is "dangerous" without exploring his willingness to seek treatment (see, *e.g.* Chief Medical Officer, 1966; Oram, 1972; Roy, 1968; Bean, 1980)?

Section 2 (admission for assessment) requires that the patient's condition warrant his *detention* and that he ought to be so *detained* in the required interests. If the only reason that detention is thought warranted is that the hospital has administrative objections to an informal admission or no-one has bothered to consult the patient, these conditions have not been fulfilled and he should not be sectioned. Section 3 (admission for treatment) does not use those words, but does require that the appropriate hospital treatment "cannot be provided unless he is detained under this section" (s. 3(2)(c)). Those words are meant to limit the use of compulsion to those cases in which the compulsion as well as the treatment is necessary. Unfortunately, they might be stretched to include the administrative cases, although not the cases where no-one has bothered to consult the patient.

Of course, if the patient is willing to enter hospital, he may also be willing to be "sectioned" if this is necessary to secure him the appropriate bed. Section 131(1) (p. 8, earlier) was meant to make it clear that there was nothing to prevent hospitals admitting patients informally if they wished. It was not meant to mean that patients could be railroaded against their will into hospital without bothering to use the compulsory procedures. But does it also mean that the Act's procedures cannot be used if they are not necessary to overcome his objections? The point may be academic, because no wrong would be done to the patient if he were prepared to consent to all the implications of a "section". But those who sectioned him might be guilty of the offence of making a false statement in the admission forms, contrary to section 126(4) (p. 247, later).

4. COMMENTARY

The law in effect allows the professionals to use compulsion whenever *they* need to do so in order to give the patient the hospital treatment which they think he needs. Ought there to be more to it than that? We must start from the assumption that mentally distressed or disabled people are people like anyone else and entitled to the same rights as others and then ask what will entitle us to take away those rights.

The Act suggests two different justifications for civil commitment. The first is the person's own health or safety. The problem here is whether it is ever justifiable to take away a person's freedom solely for his own sake. Mill (1859) argued that self-protection was the only object for which mankind was justified in interfering with another's freedom. A man must be allowed to go to the devil if he wishes, provided that he does not infringe the equal rights of other people in the process. The argument is familiar in the seatbelt and smoking controversies of today. The usual answer is that these particular examples of self-neglect result in a disproportionate claim on the resources of the NHS, to the detriment of other patients or taxpayers.

But in the case under discussion, the result will probably be a smaller rather than a greater claim on public expenditure. Indeed, Sedgwick (1982) has pointed out that some of the implications of anti-psychiatry, although it has been enthusiastically espoused by many on the left, are extremely attractive to those on the right who wish to limit the provision of public facilities for mentally disordered people.

The easy answer is that Mill's argument was never intended to apply to people who are incapable of participating in the system of rights and duties implied by the concept of equal freedom. A child must be brought up and educated to a point where he is capable of participating, whether he or his parents like it or not. We must want for him the very minimum that he would want for himself, whatever else he might want (Freeman, 1980). Can we apply the same idea to mentally disordered people? One difficulty is that childhood can be defined by reference to an objective and easily proved criterion. A second difficulty is that the purpose of the intervention is to enable the child eventually to take his place as a fully responsible member of society.

To take the second difficulty first, some anti-psychiatrists have argued that compulsory psychiatric intervention is of no help to the patient. If mental illness is defined by reference to the psychiatrist's own standards of normality, by definition he takes no account of the standpoint of the very person he is supposed to be helping. The patient's conduct appears irrational or inappropriate because the doctor cannot put himself in the patient's place. For these reasons, he can do little to help. In fact, he can only make matters worse. The label "mentally ill" places the patient too low, and indeed may imprison him in an institution which can only do damage (Goffman, 1961), while the label "psychiatrist" places the doctor so high, that effective communication between them is ruled out (Laing, 1959; Laing and Esterson, 1971). This must be doubly so where the normal relationship of trust between doctor and patient is destroyed by the imposition of compulsory powers.

It is indeed curious that two centuries of laws have been designed on the assumption that psychiatrists can cure their involuntary patients. Yet in the nineteenth century the percentage of cures was extremely low, particularly among pauper patients (Scull, 1979). Even today, numerically the most important problems are the incurable diseases of old age and the major functional psychoses, where the symptoms may be treated but not the cause. However, there are many patients whom the doctors can help and in some cases, particularly depression, they can be tolerably confident that they will be able to produce such an improvement that the patient will be glad that his wishes were overborne. The same can apply to people with learning disabilities. They can benefit from patient and skilled education for participation in society, although this is not usually a task for the medical profession.

But is the fact that the doctor can bring about such an improvement that the patient will thank him in the end enough? Of course it is not. I may be glad when the dentist has taken my teeth out, but he cannot do so by force. There still must be something about the patient which disqualifies him from the right to make that choice. The law has hitherto paid far too little attention to the precise mental qualities which add up to a disqualification. It has assumed that a diagnosis of mental illness or mental disorder is enough and that once such a diagnosis has been made, we can take it for granted that the refusal to accept help is the result of that diagnosis, rather than of ordinary stubbornness, political or religious conviction, or a

47

different approach to the calculation of the odds. But how should we approach the question of capacity to make the choice?

There are several possibilities. We could look at the usual criterion for enjoying ordinary legal rights. This depends upon understanding in broad terms what is involved in making the decision and the effects of making it. Eccentricity, caprice, forgetfulness, the inability to make choices which others regard as sensible or wise or good, these do not disqualify. The minimum requirement is to know what one is about. This is a very useful criterion when it comes to the status of people with learning disabilities, because their disorder consists mainly in a deficiency in just this quality. Once they have reached a certain point, there is no reason to believe that the disability alone will distort their capacity to participate in the system of rights and duties of which we speak.

The same test can also be applied to mental illness. But the patient's consciousness may be unimpaired and his understanding distorted in a rather different way. He knows where he is and what he is about. He can understand what he is told. But the way in which he thinks about things may be quite different from other people. It is not, or should not be, that he has different moral, political or religious views. It is that the kinds of perception and the kinds of thinking which lead him to make decisions based upon what he knows are not the same as other people's (this is reflected in the Butler Committee's attempted definition of serious mental illness on p. 33, earlier).

The Law Commission's (1995) proposed test of whether a person is incapable of taking a particular decision encompasses each of these ideas. It covers, first, someone who is unable because of mental disability (as defined on p. 40, earlier) "to understand or retain the information relevant to the decision, including information about the reasonably foreseeable consequences of deciding one way or another or of failing to make the decision"; but this would not include someone who is able to understand an explanation of that information "in broad terms and simple language". Secondly, however, it covers some-one who, although he can understand the relevant information, is unable because of his mental disability—for example his inner compulsions or susceptibility to outside pressures—to make a "true choice" based upon it. Expressly, a person is not to be regarded as incapable for this purpose merely because he makes a decision which would not be made by a person of "ordinary prudence". The Law Commission's proposals are meant for decisions about personal welfare, physical health care and financial matters, but not for those which are dealt with under the Mental Health Act. But is there any reason in principle or practice why they should not apply just as much to the decision to enter hospital for psychiatric treatment or to accept, say, E.C.T. as they do to treatment for physical disorders (see *Re C (Refusal of Medical Treatment)* [1994] 1 FLR 31, p. 139, later)?

But suppose that we have found that the patient lacks capacity on some test or other. Many would argue that this is a minimum requirement for compulsion for the sake of his own health, even if we know that we can do him some good. Equally, however, even if we know that we cannot do him any good, he still lacks capacity. Is there any reason why we should not treat him like a perpetual child? The justification for helping the child to reach maturity is not there, but neither is the qualification for participation in legal rights and duties. We would obviously still owe him the duties of humanity, to provide him with the necessities which might promote the development of his physical, mental and emotional health as best we can.

There is no reason at all to do this in a particularly restrictive environment, out of touch with everyday life. We ought never to give up hope that one day he might improve or progress and this can best be promoted by as much contact with ordinary life as is possible. But it need not involve recognising the right to equal freedom until he becomes qualified to exercise it. We must still beware setting that threshold too high.

These arguments apply to the compulsion of mental patients wherever it is to take place. They do not lead to their being locked up in secure institutions, unless these are more likely to make them better or are in fact more humanitarian than the alternatives. They would only allow patients to be kept in surroundings which are as conducive as possible to their successful rehabilitation. They would certainly bring with them a concomitant right to appropriate treatment and care.

What about the other possible justification for compulsion? The Act refers to the protection of other persons. For people who reject the arguments above this is the only possible reason for intervention. But what are other people entitled to be protected against? They are certainly entitled to some protection against conduct which the law defines as criminal. There is a need for society to admit that in some cases it can protect itself against these, even though it cannot demonstrate the offender's blameworthiness in the usual way (Kittrie, 1971). But how far beyond the confines of the criminal law is the civil law entitled to go? At present, it goes far beyond being "dangerous" and indeed there are other things against which people may legitimately claim protection. But we ought to know what they are.

The other question is whether the machinery of civil commitment either can or should be used for this purpose. It has, as we shall see, enormous advantages over the criminal process, not only for the authorities but also for the person concerned. But the risks involved are also manifest. If in effect we are creating a special sort of crime called "antisocial mental disorder", should we not admit it?

However, we should also bear in mind Carson's (1989a) stricture that "Legalistic approaches are not well known for being successful in ensuring that more resources are obtained for patients or that higher standards are consistently enforced but other approaches are not either." Even if psychiatry is a problem, law is a problem too. The law is a tool of intervention as well as a protection against it. Legal interventions deserve just as much scrutiny as do medical. Both the legal and the medical models can serve to restrict, not only the use of compulsion, but also the provision of appropriate resources or beneficial outcomes for all disabled or disordered people. Hence the developing idea (see Carson and Wexler, 1994) that medicine and law should work together to determine what their therapeutic goals are and how best these might be achieved.

3 THE ROLE OF SOCIAL WORKERS, FAMILIES AND DOCTORS

Each of the three procedures for compelling a non-offender to go into hospital consists of an application made to the hospital managers, either by the patient's nearest relative or by an approved social worker (ASW), supported by the recommendations of one or two doctors. There are two curious features about this. The first is that the doctor never has the final word. He cannot force either the relative or the social worker to act. The second is that the final decision can either be made by a detached professional or by a lay person who is closely involved with the patient. The reasons for this lie in the different procedures laid down for private and pauper patients in the old lunacy legislation.

1. PATIENTS AND PAUPERS

The common law allowed anyone to restrain a dangerous lunatic. Any relative, friend or neighbour who was prepared to foot the bill could arrange for him to be confined in a private madhouse or public hospital, without going to the trouble and expense of invoking the Crown's ancient jurisdiction over the person and property of those found lunatic by inquisition. Libertarian lawyers such as Lord Mansfield (see *Coate's Case* (1772) Lofft 73) were clearly troubled by this and the first Act for regulating Madhouses (1774) made it unlawful for them to take patients without the written and sealed order of a physician, surgeon or apothecary. In 1828, the Act to regulate the Care and Treatment of Insane Persons in England extended this idea to the public subscription hospitals (but not yet to Bethlem) and laid down a procedure which was remarkably like that of today. An order was made by the person who would see that the bill was paid, and supported by two medical certificates (except for a short-term emergency confinement, where one was enough). This pattern continued, with refinements, until 1890. Then for the first time, it was laid down that the initial petition should, if possible, be made by the husband or wife or a relative of the patient and, except in an emergency, the order of a judicial authority was required. At first the doctors had been seen as a protection against unscrupulous families and madhouse keepers. By the end of the nineteenth century, the patient was thought to need protection against unscrupulous doctors as well.

For pauper or vagrant lunatics, however, the position was quite different. The earliest Acts expressly dealing with the confinement of lunatics were the Vagrancy Acts of 1713 and 1744, which were designed to prevent a variety of social misfits wandering about and becoming a charge on parishes other than their places of origin. Two justices were allowed to confine "persons who by lunacy or otherwise are furiously mad or so disordered in their senses that they may be dangerous to be permitted to go abroad" even if they were not chargeable to the parish as paupers. Those who were might in any event be disposed of as the parish officials thought fit. Increasingly, this meant confinement, usually in the poorhouse or workhouse, although some were sent to charitable hospitals and more and more to the private madhouses. There, the condition of pauper lunatics was so terrible that the first aim of the reform movement was to set up county asylums where they might be better cared for (see Chapter 1). The next step was to devise procedures which would oblige the poor law officials to identify suitable candidates and send them there. These generally involved the parish overseers, and later the relieving officers, in bringing pauper or vagrant lunatics before the justices, who could then direct them into an asylum. The early nineteenth century reports and statutes chronicle the battle between the reformers' ambition to secure proper care and treatment (as they saw it) in an asylum or hospital and the more economically-minded poor law authorities. As early as 1811, however, the justices had to call for medical assistance before issuing a warrant to take the patient to an asylum. The patient's family had nothing to do with it, unless they were prepared to assume financial responsibility, in which case they were allowed to discharge him if he was not actually dangerous. The Lunacy Act 1890 brought together all the procedures for both paying and non-paying patients, but the differences between them remained until the National Health Service Act 1946.

The procedures under the Mental Deficiency Act 1913 allowed parents to commit their young or severely handicapped children without any judicial order, provided that there were two medical certificates. More commonly, defectives were committed by judicial order on the petition of a relative, friend or relieving officer, again with two medical certificates. It was this Act which introduced the idea that one of the doctors should be specially approved for the purpose. But it also allowed a policeman or relieving officer to take an abandoned, neglected or ill-treated defective to a place of safety without any medical certificate at all.

With the dismantling of the old poor law administration following the Local Government Act 1929, the relieving officer became the local authority public assistance officer, but he continued to be "duly authorised" under both the lunacy and mental deficiency legislation to operate the admission procedures for non-paying patients. Under the Mental Treatment Act 1930, "pauper lunatics" became "rate-aided persons of unsound mind" but it also became possible to admit them direct to certain hospitals for a short period without any medical certificate at all.

That Act began to make cautious moves in the direction of community care, authorising local authorities to establish psychiatric outpatient clinics and to arrange after-care. Already, with the setting up of the first training course for psychiatric social workers at the London School of Economics in 1929, there was an idea that social workers might have a professional role to play in the care of the mentally disordered. With the establishment of the NHS in 1948, the responsibilities of local health authorities to provide services for the care and after-care of many types of patient were expanded. The particular function of arranging the compulsory admission of mental patients was given to them, shorn of its connection with the relief of financial need, which was transferred to central government. Many of the former public assistance officers stayed as mental welfare officers, duly authorised as before. But the authorities' other duties meant that they were now recruiting an entirely different type of worker to undertake social case work as part of their care and after-care functions. Their training, skills and outlook were radically different from those of the former public assistance officers. In some places their roles were not fully integrated until after the 1959 Act.

That Act did away with the need for judicial involvement in compulsory admission (unless it was necessary to gain entry to private property by force). The Percy Commission (1957, para. 390) thought the magistrate more of a rubber stamp than a genuine safeguard. The best protection was "that the working of the new procedures should be in the hands of people who have the sort of knowledge and experience needed to form a sound judgment on the questions at issue." The Commission had no doubt that these people were doctors. Stronger safeguards would be provided by requiring more than one medical opinion, by insisting that one of the doctors was specially qualified to give it, and by removing the power to detain patients without medical advice.

The report gives little attention to why, in that case, it was necessary for the relative or mental welfare officer to be involved at all, although there is discussion of the methods of overcoming the relative's objections. It was assumed that the age old practice of an application by a relative or local official should continue. Much emphasis was given to improving services for patients in the community. But it does not seem to have occurred to the Commission that trained and experienced social workers might not be content to see themselves as errand boys for the family or the doctors. Nevertheless, although "no responsible relative or mental welfare officer would lightly disregard or dissent from [the doctors'] advice," (para. 404) the report conceded that in the last resort both must be free to do so. Social workers have increasingly asserted both their professional independence and the importance of the judgments which they are qualified to make. This has called into question the role of the relative, whose only qualification is proximity to the patient. Not only may this "distort detached perception", but he "may himself be an integral part of the patient's mental disorder" (Gostin, 1975).

2. SOCIAL WORKERS AND RELATIVES

(a) The approved social worker: definition and role

Under the 1959 Act, local authorities were free to appoint any or all of their social workers as mental welfare officers as they thought fit. Practice varied. Some appointed all their field-workers. Some appointed only those with a special interest in the work, who might include former untrained duly authorised officers as well as trained psychiatric or hospital social workers. One problem was that, after the creation of the new all-purpose departments under the Local Authority Social Services Act 1970, specialist training courses gave way to all-purpose generic training and field-workers might no longer be able to concentrate on clients with whom they had special skills or experience. A further problem was the ambiguity of the social worker's role under the 1959 Act. Was he simply a substitute for the absent or reluctant relative? Or a junior member of the clinical team devoted to providing for the patient's needs as the doctors saw them? Or a truly independent professional with skills which were just as relevant to the decision as those of the doctors?

The 1983 Act tried to shift the emphasis towards a fully independent professional role. The functions which were previously entrusted to mental welfare officers (MWOs) are now carried out by approved social workers (ASWs). An ASW is an officer of a local social services authority appointed by his authority for this purpose (1983 Act, s. 145(1)). Authorities must appoint sufficient social workers for the task (s. 114(1)), but these must be people whom the authority can approve "as having appropriate competence in dealing with persons who are suffering from mental disorder" (s. 114(2)). In doing so they must have regard to the matters directed by the Secretary of State (s. 114(3)). In effect, these require a Certificate of

Qualification in Social Work (CQSW) or equivalent; appropriate experience; and an appropriate level of professional competence (DHSS Circular, LAC (86)15; see CCETSW, 1993). Procedures should be determined locally but approval should not be for more than five years at a time. Numbers approved should also depend on local conditions, but ASWs should be engaged in a wide range of mental health work rather than confined to statutory duties.

Behind these bland instructions lay quite a battle, reflecting the same ambiguities about the social worker's role as there had been before. The original training scheme was criticised, not only for restricting the numbers who might enter the examinations, but also for concentrating too heavily on legal and psychiatric knowledge, rather than on the social factors and social work strategies involved, both in assessment and in finding alternatives to hospital admission and detention (Barnes, Bowl and Fisher, 1990; Prior, 1992). While specialisation and experience may strengthen the social worker's independence, in a way which may be difficult to achieve if "doing a section" is a rare event, this must be balanced against the risk of becoming too closely identified with the medical viewpoint.

As will become apparent, the ASW's role in relation to the family, the doctors, the patient himself, and the services which are to be provided, contains some major contradictions (Prior, 1992). The tasks given him by the legislation fall into three broad categories. First are his powers to gain access to mentally disordered people living in the community who may need his help. These are discussed in Chapter 4. The second and most important category consists of his role in the process of arranging compulsory admission to hospital. This is discussed in detail in this chapter. He has a similar but much less frequently invoked role in arranging reception into guardianship in the community, and in that case he is also to be involved in carrying out the responsibilities of a guardian on behalf of his authority or in supervising the work of a private guardian. This is discussed in Chapter 9. Thirdly, an ASW is amongst those who are entitled to recapture absconding or escaping compulsory patients. This is discussed in Chapter 7.

But once a social worker has been involved in compelling a patient to go into hospital, he has very little part to play in what happens thereafter. The ASW has no legal voice in the treatment of the patient while in hospital or in whether the patient is ready to be discharged. Unlike the nearest relative, he has no power to discharge the patient. This is one reason why social workers find their role in compulsory admission so much more troubling than their role in taking children into local authority care. An ASW may be asked to supply a social inquiry report for the hospital (see below) or for a mental health review tribunal (see Chapter 8) or to arrange the after-care for which his authority is responsible when the time comes for the patient to be discharged (see Chapters 7 and 9), but these tasks may also be given to non-approved social workers. His formal role in the arrangement of after-care under supervision, which is similar but not identical to his role in arranging reception into guardianship, is discussed in Chapter 7.

(b) The nearest relative: definition and role

The patient's nearest relative is normally determined by taking whoever comes first on the list of relatives (s. 26(1) and (3)). If there is more than one in the same category, the elder is preferred regardless of sex (s. 26(3)).

But any relative who is caring for the patient or with whom the patient ordinarily resides (or, if now an in-patient, last lived with or was cared for by) is promoted to the top of the list (s. 26(4)). This is particularly likely to affect people looking after their elderly relatives, who might otherwise yield to an older or closer relative. It does not, however, promote those relatives who give most devoted care while the patient is in hospital unless they also did so before he went in. It could also lead to difficult conflicts between those with whom the patient lives and those who claim to be caring for him.

People whose parents were not married to one another are regarded as related only to their mother's side of the family and not to their father unless he "has" parental responsibility for them (s. 26(2)); he cannot have this once the children are grown up, however close their relationship was or now is. This is out of line with the general rule (in the Family Law Reform Act 1987, s. 1(1)) that relationships are to be traced without regard to whether or not a person's parents were married to one another.

Anyone who does not "ordinarily reside" in the United Kingdom, Channel Islands or Isle of Man must be ignored if the patient does reside here (s. 26(5)(a)). A person under the age of 18 must be ignored unless he is the patient's spouse (or recognised cohabitant, see under spouse below) or parent (but who would "section" a tiny child?) (s. 26(5)(c)). Curiously, a relative who is himself a mental patient (informal or compulsory) is not automatically ignored, although he may be replaced by a county court (see section 2(d) later). The list of relatives is as follows:

Spouse. A husband or wife comes first even if aged under 18, but must be ignored if they are permanently separated, either by agreement or under the order of a court, or if one of them has deserted the other (s. 26(5)(b)). These are not exactly easy questions for a social worker or hospital to determine, especially at short notice. Desertion means the intentional withdrawal from cohabitation, without the other's consent or a good excuse. To be separated by agreement or court order used to require an agreement or order which formally relieved the parties of their common law duty to live together. Such agreements are very rare, as are decrees of judicial separation, which are now the only court orders short of divorce technically having that effect. But in reality orders excluding or keeping a spouse from the matrimonial home or (at least if they are living apart) prohibiting one spouse from harassing, molesting or otherwise interfering with the other produce the same result. Common sense would now extend the phrase to all agreements to live apart, formal or informal, and all court orders regulating the spouses' lives apart, even if they simply deal with financial provision or the upbringing of children. The phrase would not cover spouses who have been living in different places for some time (usually involuntarily) but still regard themselves as a couple and intend to resume cohabitation when they are able to do so.

If the patient is not married, or if his spouse must be disregarded because of permanent separation (under s. 26(5)(b)), then a person who has been living with the patient "as the patient's husband or wife" (which is thought to refer only to hetero-sexual cohabitants as same sex marriages are not allowed) for at least six months and is still doing so (or was until the patient went into hospital) must be treated as a spouse (s. 26(6)). Perhaps wisely, a cohabitant does not become nearest relative simply because the patient's spouse is not ordinarily resident in the United Kingdom (so must be disregarded under s. 26(5)(a)). Such a situation is by no means far-fetched in these days of international migration; any adult relative resident here would then become nearest relative in preference to the cohabitant; this result may be sensible, but it certainly adds to the difficulty of the social worker trying to make such sensitive judgments on the ground.

Son or daughter. This includes adopted children, but not stepchildren or an unmarried father's children (see s. 26(2) above). If there are several, the eldest is preferred regardless of sex (s. 26(3)), subject now to the preference given to the "caring" relative.

Father or mother. The 1983 Act places father and mother on an equal footing, so the elder or carer will take priority (s. 26(3)), but unmarried fathers do not count unless they have parental responsibility (see s. 26(2) above). Children under 18 are hardly ever subject to compulsory powers but the nearest relative is usually the older parent. However, a guardian appointed by a court or a deceased parent, a person with whom a child is to live under a residence order (s. 28), or a local authority having parental responsibility under a care order, is nearest relative (except where the child is married: s. 27).

Brother or sister. Grandparent. Grandchild. Uncle or aunt. Nephew or niece. Within these categories, the principles applicable to sons or daughters also apply. The eldest in any category usually comes first, regardless of sex, relatives of the whole blood are preferred to those of the half-blood, and children of unmarried parents are treated as if they were the marital children of their mothers, but unrelated to fathers who do not have parental responsibility for them (s. 26(2) and (3)), and the caring relative is promoted (s. 26(4)).

Non-related caretakers. The list now ends with any person who is not a relative within any of the above categories, but with whom the patient ordinarily resides (or did so before he was last admitted to hospital) and has done so continuously for at least five years (s. 26(7)). Such people come last in the list but may gain promotion because of the rule in section 26(4). They can never be treated as the nearest relative of a married patient unless the spouse can be ignored because of permanent separation or desertion.

Wards of court. If the child is a ward of court, no application for compulsory admission to hospital can be made without the court's leave and the functions of nearest relative can only be exercised by or with leave of the court (s. 33(1),(2)); reception or transfer into Mental Health Act guardianship is not allowed at all (s. 33(3)), presumably because the child is already in the guardianship of the court; supervised after-care is subject to any direction of the court (s. 33(4)).

Authorising another to act. The legal nearest relative can always authorise someone else to perform his functions (under regulation 14 of the Mental Health (Hospital, Guardianship and Consent to Treatment) Regulations 1983), provided that that person is not excluded under section 26(5). The authority must be in writing and given to the person authorised, with notice to the hospital managers if the patient is already detained in hospital, to the local social services authority if the patient is in the authority's guardianship, and to both the local social services authority and the guardian if the patient is in private guardianship. Authorisation can be revoked at any time in the same way. This is obviously a sensible provision for the nearest relative who has little contact with the patient. But there is no requirement to register the authorisation with the local authority before any question of compulsion arises. A social worker may perhaps only discover that it has been given when he contacts the nearest relative, which rather defeats the object of the exercise.

Appointment by a county court. If there is no nearest relative or the nearest relative is in some way unsuitable, the county court has power to appoint someone to perform the task. This is more frequently used as a method of overriding the wishes of the patient's family and will be discussed in section 2(d) below.

The nearest relative has a role parallel to that of an ASW in arranging the patient's compulsory admission to hospital or reception into guardianship but unlike the ASW he has a right to object to admission for treatment or to guardianship; this is discussed in section (c) below and Chapter 9. Unlike the ASW, he also has power to discharge a civil patient from detention or guardianship, although discharge from hospital may be prevented if the patient would be likely to act dangerously were he to be released. He has no right to object to after-care under supervision, but must be consulted and informed unless the patient has requested otherwise. These are discussed in Chapter 7. Whenever he cannot himself discharge the patient, except when he has been prevented from discharging a patient admitted for assessment, he may apply to a mental health review tribunal. This is discussed in Chapter 8.

(c) Arranging compulsory admission: the relative and the social worker

Under section 11(1) of the 1983 Act, applications for compulsory admission to hospital either for assessment or for treatment may be made either by an ASW or by the patient's nearest relative. Even if the professional opinion of the ASW is that the application should not be made, he cannot prevent the relative from making it (perhaps, in the case of an emergency application, on the recommendation of the family doctor or of a locum with no previous knowledge of the family at all). In practice, of course, the ASW carries the necessary forms and knows about the admission policies of the local hospitals. He may therefore be tempted to deny the relative access to these. This would be most improper, for the Act gives the relative the right to apply whatever the social worker may think.

However, wherever a patient is compulsorily admitted on the application of his nearest relative (except on an emergency application), section 14 requires the managers to notify the local social services authority, for the place where the patient lives, as soon as practicable. The authority must then arrange as soon as practicable for a social worker to interview the patient and provide the hospital with a report on his social circumstances. This need not be done by an ASW, but it will be all the more helpful if it is. The hospital doctors need as much information as possible about the context in which the incident or behaviour which triggered the admission took place, and also about other methods of handling the problem, and this is what an ASW should be trained to assess. It was obviously intended that this duty should apply to all compulsory admissions except those which only last for 72 hours. Unfortunately, the section does not make it entirely clear whether it applies when an emergency admission is converted into an ordinary admission for assessment. Ideally, the hospital should have an objective social assessment as soon as possible after any admission in which it was not available beforehand (or if available was ignored).

On the other hand, the nearest relative cannot prevent the ASW from making an application for admission for assessment. But either before or within a reasonable time after making such an application, section 11(3) requires the ASW to do what he can to inform the person (if any) who appears to be the patient's nearest relative, not only of the admission but also of the relative's right to discharge the patient. As an admission for assessment only lasts for 28 days, or 72 hours if in an emergency, "within a reasonable time" must mean as soon as possible. But when telling the relative of his power to discharge, it would be wise also to tell him that the patient's doctor may prevent this if the patient "would be likely to act in a manner dangerous to other persons or to himself" (s. 25(1)).

However, if an ASW is proposing to make an application for the patient's long-term admission for treatment (or, for that matter, reception into guardianship), he *must* consult the person (if any) who appears to be the nearest relative. The only exceptions are where this is not reasonably practicable or would involve unreasonable delay (s. 11(4)). In theory, this should hardly ever be so, because an admission for assessment gives ample time to trace and consult the relative. The Code of Practice (para. 2.13) advises that practicability refers to the availability of the nearest relative and not to how appropriate it is to inform or consult him. In practice, admission for assessment is often used as a short-term admission for treatment, after which it is hoped that no further compulsion will be necessary. The Code therefore requires the ASW wherever possible to ascertain the nearest relative's views of the patient's needs and his own and to tell the relative why he is considering an application and what it will mean.

Whether or not he has been consulted, the nearest relative has the right to prevent an admission for treatment (or a reception into guardianship). He must notify his objection, either to the ASW who propose to make the application, or to the local social services authority (s. 11(4)). The Act does not insist that the ASW obtain the relative's positive consent, but he must record in the application whether he has consulted the relative and, if so, that the relative does not object (see Mental Health (Hospital, Guardianship and Consent to Treatment) Regulations 1983, Form 9). An application which states that the wrong person has been consulted as nearest relative is not "duly completed", (*R. v. South Western Hospital Managers, ex p. M.* [1993] Q.B. 683). If the relative does object, the ASW cannot make the application (s. 11(4)) and if he does so the patient's detention will be unlawful (*Re S.-C. (Mental Patient: Habeas Corpus), The Times,* December 4, 1995; see pp. 83 and 174, later). He may, however, apply to a county court for the relative to be replaced, on the ground that the objection is unreasonable (see section 2(d) later).

More commonly, however, the patient's relatives are anxious for him to be admitted, but would like the ASW to take the responsibility. This is natural enough. He is familiar with the procedures and relatives are often anxious that the patient should not feel betrayed or let down, or even know that his family no longer feel able to cope with him. Some social workers believe that it is good practice to encourage the nearest relative to face facts and to take responsibility for an admission which the family wants. The more common view, adopted in the Code of Practice (para. 2.30), is that the social worker should shoulder the burden and a 24-hour ASW service should be provided to ensure this (para. 2.32). His professional training should enable him to withstand and overcome any antagonism from the patient. If this is impossible, it is far more important for the patient's own future health and well-being that the patient should retain a good relationship (if he has one) with his family than with the social worker.

ASWs can come under a great deal of pressure to act, not only from families but also from G.P.s and others. What is their legal position? The 1983 Act insists that they do at least consider the case. If the nearest relative of a patient living in the area of a local social services authority "requires" this, the authority *must* direct an ASW as soon as practicable to consider the patient's case with a view to making an application (s. 13(4)). There is no discretion to refuse, however unreasonable the demand. This caused a great deal of worry initially, but apparently formal requests are very rare (Barnes, Bowl and Fisher, 1990). The Code of Practice (para. 2.33) requires local authorities to issue guidance to their ASWs on what amounts to a "request", and whether one can be accepted through a G.P. or other professional, and to have explicit policies on how to respond to repeated requests where the patient's condition has not significantly changed. But the duty only applies to a "patient", who is defined (in section 145(1)) as a "person suffering or appearing to be suffering from mental disorder." The social worker may decide not to make an application, but if so, he must give the relative a written explanation.

Section 13(1) does impose a positive duty upon an ASW to make an application, but only if three conditions are fulfilled. First, the patient must be physically present in the area covered by the social worker's local authority (this means their whole county or metropolitan district, not simply the area covered by an "area team"). Section 13(3) makes it clear that an ASW also has power to act outside his own local authority. This is most desirable if the patient is his own client, but there is no legal duty to do so. Secondly, the ASW must be "satisfied" that the application ought to be made. He has no duty to act in any case which he does not himself judge to merit it, whatever the family or the doctors may say. Thirdly, if he is satisfied that the application should be made, he has the duty to make it himself if he "is of the opinion, having regard to any wishes expressed by relatives of the patient or any other relevant circumstances, that it is necessary or proper for the application to be made *by him*" (s. 13(1); emphasis supplied). This is a clear hint that he should be ready to do the job himself if this is what the family wants.

Before an ASW makes any application for admission to hospital, he *must* "interview the patient in a suitable manner and satisfy himself that detention in a hospital is in all the circumstances of the case the most appropriate way of providing the care and medical treatment of which the patient stands in need" (s. 13(2)). This can present difficulties, both legal and practical.

What is meant by an "interview"? We tend to think of a two-way oral exchange, such as happens on television or radio or when we apply for a job. If the ASW on the spot cannot communicate with a patient who speaks a different language or is deaf and dumb he should try to find an ASW who can do so, or a professional interpreter, preferably one who understands psychiatric interviewing. He should avoid using the patient's relative if he can (Code of Practice, para. 2.11). Communication difficulties can add to the problems of making an accurate assessment of people from certain ethnic minorities, for example some Asian women. But what if the patient cannot communicate at all or (perhaps understandably) refuses to do so? The Oxford English Dictionary contains old definitions which involve only a personal meeting, or getting a "view, glance or glimpse." Could that be enough to be "suitable" in such cases? The problem with this suggestion is that the Act also requires that any applicant, whether relative or social worker, has "personally seen" the patient, either within the 14 days which end on the date of the application (s. 11(5)) or, in an emergency application, within the past 24 hours (s. 4(5)). An interview suggests something more, although possibly only an attempt by the social worker to communicate in the best way possible with the particular patient before him. The Code of Practice advises that patients should not be interviewed through a closed door unless there is a serious risk to other people (access should be obtained by warrant under section 135 instead). Interviews should be put off if the patient is suffering the effects of sedation, drugs or alcohol, unless action is urgent because of his disturbed behaviour. If none of this helps, the assessment "will have to be based on whatever information the ASW can obtain from all reliable sources" (para. 2.11). The patient should see the ASW alone, unless the patient would like someone else to be there or the ASW has reason to fear physical harm (para. 2.12). The division between medical and social work components of the task will be explored later (see section 5). In law, the social worker may disagree with both the family and the doctors. In practice, he should be sure of his ground before doing so.

In the debates leading up to the 1982 amendments, many suggested that the powers of the nearest relative should be removed. An independent social assessment was certainly needed in addition to the medical opinions, but the relative could not supply it. He had no professional knowledge, either of mental disorder or of the facilities available for treatment. He was too closely involved with the patient to judge the situation dispassionately and might easily assume that the only response to a crisis was immediate admission to hospital. Yet it was for exactly the same reasons that the DHSS (DHSS *et al.*, 1978) argued that the relative should retain his powers. "Some relatives may prefer to feel that they are in control of the situation, and they will be in the best position to judge when they are unable to cope any longer with the patient." Despite this, the DHSS also hoped that the strengthened role and expertise of the social worker would in fact lead to their making even more of the applications than they already did. In fact, it appears that only a tiny minority of applications are made by a nearest relative, as social workers receive very few requests for reports under section 14 (Barnes, Bowl and Fisher, 1990).

(d) Replacement of the nearest relative by a county court

A county court may appoint an acting nearest relative, under section 29 of the 1983 Act, as a way either of supplying a relative for a patient who has none, or more commonly of overriding the wishes of the relative he has. Proceedings tend just to make double figures each year. Application to the court may be made by any relative, any other person with whom the patient is living or was living just before going into hospital, or an approved social worker (s. 29(2)). There are four possible grounds (s. 29(3)):

(a) that the patient has no nearest relative or that it is not reasonably practicable (perhaps because of the patient's mental condition) to discover whether he has one or who it is; or

(b) that the nearest relative is incapable of acting because of mental disorder or other illness; or

(c) that the nearest relative unreasonably objects to the making of an application for admission for treatment or for reception into guardianship; or

(d) that the nearest relative has exercised, or is likely to exercise, the power to discharge the patient without due regard to the patient's welfare or the interests of the public.

The situation in ground (c) is the only one in which the health or social services are likely to be seriously troubled. But when is a relative being unreasonable?

In *W. v. L.* [1974] Q.B. 711 (see also p. 32, earlier) the patient, who was both psychopathic and mentally ill, had threatened his wife and the baby she was expecting. His admission for observation was about to run out and the baby had been born. His wife objected to an admission for treatment. She was confident that she could keep him under control with the drugs prescribed. No doubt she did not wish to break up the family and jeopardise her husband's employment just at the birth of their first child. The Court of Appeal decided that the test was not what the relative subjectively considered reasonable, but what an objectively reasonable relative would do in the particular circumstances of the case. In this case, a reasonable person would regard it as too great a risk, particularly to the baby, to have the husband home until he had been cured. The wife was therefore replaced as nearest relative so that the application could be made.

But will it ever be reasonable for the relative to disagree with the professional opinions? In *B. (A.) v. B. (L) (Mental Health Patient)* [1980] 1 W.L.R. 116, the law report does not explain why both the doctors and the social worker considered an application necessary. Two doctors had recommended it, but as their examinations had been more than seven days apart, their recommendations were not technically sufficient to found an application. The mother objected and the county court judge thought her objection unreasonable. On appeal, the mother complained that she had not seen the medical opinions and that she could not be unreasonable if these were not sufficient. The Court of Appeal held that it was enough that her solicitor had seen the reports and that the applicant did not have to "get his tackle in order" before going to the county court. That may be done after the court has ruled on whether the objection is unreasonable.

The second point is fair enough, for the evidence on which the social worker takes the case to court will probably be out of date before he comes to make the application. Unfortunately, the judgment in this case is couched in such a way as to suggest that the mother *must* have been unreasonable, simply because the two doctors had recommended admission. This cannot be right. First, the Act's scheme relies upon the independent concurrence of the applicant and doctors as an effective protection for the patient. It was never intended that the decision should be left solely to the doctors. As the Act gives the relative a veto unless the court decides otherwise, it clearly contemplates that the court should evaluate the reasonableness of the relative's attitude in the light of all the available evidence, and not simply rubber-stamp the original doctors' views. Secondly, in *W. v. L.* the court had likened the process to that of dispensing with a parent's agreement to an adoption order on the ground that the agreement is unreasonably withheld. In adoption cases, the court is not allowed simply to substitute its own judgment for that of the parent. It must decide whether the parent's decision falls within the range of possible decisions which a reasonable parent might make. Sometimes, there are two reasonable views open to such a person, and the court must not then interfere simply because it would have chosen the other one (*Re W. (An Infant)* [1971] A.C. 682) (this was the test applied by Croydon County Court in *N. v. S.*, January 1, 1983, quoted in Gostin, 1986, para. 8.07).

There is one reported example of a county court judge declining to find the nearest relative unreasonable. In *S. v. G.* [1981] J.S.W.L. 174, the judge took as his starting point the merits of the doctors' case for detention, stating that "it is vitally important that matters about which doctors have to be satisfied should be clearly proved." The doctors disagreed about the precise diagnosis, but they had no doubt that the patient was mentally ill. Equally, however, his detention was no longer necessary in the interests of his own health or safety. The question was whether it was necessary for the protection of other persons. The judge concluded from the evidence that it was not. Hence the father's objection could not be unreasonable. The judge did not have to consider whether there might be two reasonable views.

This case is only an illustration of the approach which the county court judge may take, for it cannot bind others. But it would seem logical for him to consider whether there is a case for the admission for treatment (or guardianship—even if the local social services authority might not accept it; see Re B., November 29, 1985, quoted in Gostin, 1986, para. 8.07) before deciding whether the relative's attitude to it is reasonable. In S. v. G. above, the father had obtained an adjournment in order to seek evidence from two other psychiatrists and they had reached a different conclusion from the recommending doctors. If the judge had heard the case when it was first listed, he would have granted the application. But the situation may change very rapidly and a short delay before the hearing may well strengthen the relative's case.

In the meantime, section 29(4) provides that if the patient is detained for assessment and an application for the replacement of the nearest relative on ground (c) and (d) is made before the 28 days run out, the patient may still be detained for assessment (which includes treatment) until the application has been finally disposed of. This includes the time limited for appealing from the county court to the Court of Appeal and the time taken for any such appeal to be heard or withdrawn. If the nearest relative is replaced, the patient may be detained for a further seven days to enable the formalities of an admission for treatment to be completed. All of this can take a long time, during which the patient has no right to apply to a mental health review tribunal; he might have been better off if his relative had agreed to the admission after all.

The court may appoint either the applicant or any other able and willing person to act as nearest relative, but if the applicant is an ASW the court must appoint his local authority rather than him (s. 29(1)). If a local authority is given the powers of a nearest relative, it must arrange for the patient to be visited in hospital and do whatever else would be expected of the patient's parents (s. 116). This obviously involves far more than the legal functions of a nearest relative. The displaced nearest relative can apply for the patient's case to be reviewed by a mental health review tribunal once in every 12 month period after the order (s. 66(1)(h) and (2)(g)). However, if he was displaced on ground (c) or (d), he cannot apply to the county court for the order to be discharged (see s. 30(1)(b)). The order will automatically lapse when the patient ceases to be liable to be detained (or subject to guardianship) or if no application is made for his detention or guardianship within three months of the order (s. 30(4)).

If the order was made on ground (a) or (b), the court itself may specify a maximum duration (s. 29(5)) and the displaced relative can apply for it to be discharged (s. 30(1)(b)). If the person displaced has ceased to be the nearest relative under section 26, for example because the patient has married, the new nearest relative may apply for the order to be discharged (s. 30(1)(b)). The person appointed as acting nearest relative may always apply for discharge (s. 30(1)(a)) or for its variation to appoint someone else instead (s. 30(2)). So may any relative if the person appointed dies

(s. 30(3)). An ASW may apply for the variation of the order, but not for its discharge (s. 30(2)). Thus a person displaced for unreasonableness cannot regain his position unless the patient is discharged or his replacement agrees.

Nevertheless, the commitment procedures assume that the patient is an irrational being whose liberty may properly be removed by extra-judicial process. His nearest relative, on the other hand, is assumed to be a rational individual, whose voice in the patient's future may only be removed after due process of law. In some families, it must be difficult to decide who should be labelled "patient" and who "relative," but the consequences of that initial allocation are crucial for all concerned.

3. PARENTS, CHILDREN AND LOCAL AUTHORITIES

Mental Health Act compulsion is hardly ever used for patients under the age of 16. It is even more difficult to make reliable diagnoses of mental disorders in children than it is with adults. There are also other means of overcoming any opposition, either from the child or from his family, to whatever care or treatment is thought most appropriate to his needs.

If the child is under 17, the local authority may apply for a care or supervision order. They must first prove (a) that the child is suffering or likely to suffer significant harm (including harm to his mental health or development); and (b) that the harm or likely harm is attributable to the care or likely care given to the child not being what it would be reasonable to expect a parent to give to him (or to his being beyond control) (Children Act 1989, s. 31(2); they must then show that the order will not only be consistent with the paramount consideration of the child's welfare but also be better for the child than any other order the court might make or making no order at all (1989 Act, s. 1(1),(3),(5)).

A care order confers parental responsibility upon the local authority, although this can only last until the child reaches 18 (1989 Act s. 91(12)). The authority become the child's nearest relative (1983 Act, s. 27); but they also have a wide discretion to decide where the child is to be placed (1989 Act, s. 23); this includes the same power as a parent to arrange for the child's informal admission to hospital (*R. v. Kirklees Metropolitan D.C., ex p. C. (A Minor)* [1993] 2 FLR 187, C.A.; see further p. 65, later). Where a local authority have parental responsibility for a child patient, they must arrange for him to be visited in hospital and do whatever else would be expected of his parents (1983 Act, s. 116).

A supervision order does not confer parental responsibility on the authority but may contain requirements for psychiatric examination and/ or treatment (1989 Act, ss. 31(1), 35, Sched. 3, paras. 4, 5). The requirements are almost identical to those in probation or supervision orders made in criminal proceedings (p. 115, later). More commonly, these examinations are directed as part of the investigations pending the full hearing of a care application (1989 Act, ss. 44(6)(b), 38(6)). It is also possible to order a full assessment of a child reasonably believed to be suffering or likely to suffer significant harm before any other proceedings are begun (1989 Act, s. 43). However, a child who has sufficient understanding to make an informed decision may refuse to consent to such a requirement in a supervision order (1989 Act, Sched. 3, paras. 4(4)(a), 5(5)(a)) or to submit to an examination directed by the court (1989 Act, ss. 44(7), 38(6), 43(8)).

An alternative to care proceedings is to invoke the inherent (non-statutory) jurisdiction of the High Court to protect the welfare of all children, usually by making the child a ward of court. The procedure has been used to challenge particular decisions of parents whose general care of the child cannot be criticised. Thus the court can prohibit a treatment proposal supported both by the parents and by the doctors. This happened, for example, when Heilbron J. decided that the sterilisation of an 11-year-old girl with Sotos' syndrome was not in the child's best interests (*Re D. (A Minor) (Wardship: Sterilisation)* [1976] Fam. 185). On the other hand, the court may allow treatment which the parents oppose. This happened, for example, when the Court of Appeal sanctioned an operation to save the life of a Down's syndrome baby after the parents had decided that it would be kinder to allow her to die (*Re B. (A Minor) (Wardship: Medical Treatment)* [1981] 1 W.L.R. 1421).

Under the Children Act 1989, however, disputes about any particular aspect of parental responsibility can be resolved by a "specific issue order" (s. 8(1)), so that the inherent jurisdiction should rarely be necessary for this type of case (see *Re H.G. (Specific Issue Order: Sterilisation)* [1993] 1 F.L.R. 589; *Re R.(A Minor)(Blood Transfusion)* [1993] 2 F.L.R. 757; *c.f. Re O. (A Minor)(Medical Treatment)* [1993] 2 F.L.R. 148). Most non-parents, including local authorities, need leave to apply for a specific issue order; before granting leave the court must consider the type of order to be applied for, the applicant's connection with the child, any risk that the application itself would cause harmful disruption to the child, and if the child is being looked after by a local authority, the plans of the authority and the wishes of the parents. It is likely, therefore, that the educational psychologist who made the child a ward of court in *Re D.*, above, would be given leave under these criteria (see s. 10(1), (2), (9)). A specific issue order cannot be made if a child is in care under a care order (1989 Act, s. 9(1)), so the local authority may then have to seek leave to invoke the inherent jurisdiction to resolve the issue (1989 Act, s. 100(3); as happened in *Re W. (A Minor)(Medical Treatment: Court's Jurisdiction)* [1993] Fam. 64, below). But local authorities can no longer use the jurisdiction to obtain care or supervision orders, or an aspect of parental responsibility (1989 Act, s. 100(2)) or an order which they could obtain in any other way (1989 Act, s. 100(5)), such as a specific issue order where the child is not in care (see *Re R. (A Minor)(Blood Transfusion)* [1993] 2 F.L.R. 757, a point which seems to have been missed in *Re S. (A Minor)(Medical Treatment)* [1993] 1 F.L.R. 376 and *Re O. (A Minor) (Medical Treatment)* [1993] 2 F.L.R. 148).

Under the inherent jurisdiction, the court may override the objections even of a child who would otherwise be able to decide for himself (*Re W. (A Minor) (Medical Treatment: Court's Jurisdiction)* [1993] Fam. 64, C.A., which concerned a 16-year-old girl with anorexia nervosa; *Re R. (A Minor) (Wardship: Consent to Medical Treatment)* [1992] Fam. p. 11, C.A., which concerned a 15-year-old girl with fluctuating psychotic behaviour and suicidal tendencies; in *South Glamorgan County Council v. W. and B* [1993] 1 F.L.R. 574, it was held that this could even override the child's statutory rights of refusal in the 1989 Act, but this must be controversial).

The court could only override a child's wishes under a specific issue order if this was "an aspect of parental responsibility" (1989 Act, s. 8(1)). The power of a parent to consent to treatment on behalf of his child is another reason why Mental Health Act compulsion is rarely necessary. But the extent of that power is controversial. Certainly, if a 16 or 17-year-old is capable of expressing his own wishes and wishes to go into hospital, his parents cannot prevent him (1983 Act, s. 131(2)). Further, his consent to any surgical, medical or dental treatment which would otherwise be a trespass to his person is as effective as it would be if he were of full age (Family Law Reform Act 1969, s. 8(1)). The common law requires only a broad understanding of what is proposed in order for any consent to be effective (see Chapter 6). Below that age, the House of Lords decided in *Gillick v. West Norfolk and Wisbech Area Health Authority* [1986] A.C. 112 that a child might have capacity to decide for him or herself (although they differed on the precise test of capacity).

Logically, if a child has the capacity to consent he also has the capacity to object. But Lord Donaldson M.R. has twice said (in *Re R.*, above, where the other two judges did not support him; and in *Re W.*, above, where one judge did but the other did not) that not only the court, but also anyone with parental authority, may give an alternative consent which can override the child's objections. There is also at least one High Court case stating that a local authority do not need to apply to the court for an order authorising treatment if the child is in care (*Re K., W. and H. (Minors) (Consent to Treatment)* [1993] 1 F.L.R. 854). Nevertheless, it is doubtful whether the children involved in any of these cases had the capacity to take their own decisions. It is an unattractive thought that a parent, or even a local authority, may authorise the forcible treatment of a competent adolescent without any of the safeguards attached either to court proceedings or to admission under the Mental Health Act.

If a child of any age is not capable of making the decision or expresses no view, then his parents can undoubtedly consent on his behalf, subject, of course, to the overriding powers of the courts to decide what is best (and to the understanding that some decisions, for example in relation to sterilisation, should always be referred to the court; see Chapter 6).

Not surprisingly, the Code of Practice describes the legal framework as "complex" (others might use a different epithet) (para. 30.3); but it accepts that parents and local authorities as well as courts can override a child's refusal, although that refusal is an important consideration in making clinical judgments (para. 30.7.d). In practice, however, it advises that young people should be kept as fully informed as possible about their care and treatment; their views and wishes must be taken into account; unless statute specifically overrides, they should generally be regarded as having the right to make their own decisions (and in particular treatment decisions) where they have sufficient "understanding and intelligence"; and any intervention should be the least restrictive possible and result in the least possible segregation from family, friends, community or school; all children in hospital should receive appropriate education (para. 30.2).

With the best will in the world, parents of handicapped or mentally disturbed children will find it hard to put their children's interests first all the time. Equally, the children's welfare may be damaged even further if they are forced into confrontation. Hence Gostin (1975) argued that parents should not be able to "volunteer" their children for admission to mental hospitals without some additional check, such as an automatic review by a mental health review tribunal.

In *Parham v. J.L. and J.R.* 444 U.S. 584 (1979), the United States Supreme Court accepted that these children did have liberty interests which required protection. But the majority considered that the independent judgment of the hospital's medical superintendent was sufficient, not only where the child was in the care of his parents but also where he was a ward of the state. The minority accepted that a prior hearing might do more harm than good to relationships within the natural family but argued for a subsequent review. Where the child was a ward of the state, however, there were no such relationships to be damaged. Nor could it be assumed that the authorities would share the natural inclination of parents to put their children's interests first. Thus the minority considered that children in care should not be admitted to mental hospitals without a prior judicial hearing.

In this country there are restrictions on the circumstances in which children being looked after by a local authority (whether compulsorily under a court order or by arrangement with their parents) or accommodated by health authorities, NHS trusts, local education authorities, or in residential care homes, nursing homes or mental nursing homes (see Children (Secure Accommodation) Regulations 1991, reg. 7) may be kept in "accommodation provided for the purpose of restricting liberty." This includes locked wards in mental hospitals, regional secure units, and other secure facilities (*R. v. Northampton Juvenile Court, ex p. London Borough of Hammersmith and Fulham* [1985] F.L.R. 192). Children cannot be kept in such places unless they are likely either (a) to abscond from other accommodation and to suffer significant harm if they do, or (b) to injure themselves or others if kept anywhere else (1989 Act, s. 25(1); different criteria apply to children remanded to local authority care in criminal proceedings). No child can be kept in secure accommodation for more than 72 hours in any 28 days without the authority of a court (1991 Regulations, reg. 10(1)); the court can authorise up to three months more (reg. 11) and then further periods of up to six months at a time (reg. 12). The child must be given an opportunity of legal representation (1989 Act, s. 25(6)) and a guardian *ad litem* will be appointed for him unless the court thinks this unnecessary. Admission to secure accommodation, including a youth treatment centre, does not automatically bring with it the power to impose treatment without consent. This is governed by the general principles outlined above.

These rules do not apply to children who are detained under the Mental Health Act 1983 (1991 Regulations, reg. 5(1)). They may be treated against their will, but the safeguards may be preferable, for they include access to the Mental Health Act Commission, mental health review tribunals, and second opinions for the more controversial treatments (see Chapters 6 and 8). There would, indeed, be something to be said for regarding all children in psychiatric hospitals or secure facilities as detained patients for these purposes. There is more concern about the mentally ill or behaviourally disturbed children in such facilities than about the now very small numbers of mentally handicapped children in long-stay mental hospitals. In order to ensure that these are not forgotten, however, sections 85 and 86 of the Children Act 1989 require notification to the local social services authority if any child is, or is intended to be, accommodated by a health or local education authority, or in a residential, nursing or mental nursing home, for more than three months. The authority must then consider whether his welfare is adequately safeguarded and promoted and what services it might provide for him.

4. THE DOCTORS

(a) Their qualifications

Applications for admission to hospital under section 2 (for assessment) or section 3 (for treatment), or for reception into guardianship under section

7, must be supported by the recommendations of two doctors (ss. 2(3), 3(3) and 7(3)). An application for admission for assessment in an emergency under section 4 requires the support of only one (s. 4(3)). An application for after-care under supervision is made by the patient's responsible medical officer (RMO) supported by an ASW and another doctor (ss. 25A(5), 25B(6)). A warrant under section 135(1) to gain entry to private premises and remove the patient to a place of safety can only be executed if a doctor is present (s. 135(4)), although the patient can be taken to hospital without any formal recommendation. Medical evidence is also required for an order to remove a person to a hospital or other place under section 47 of the National Assistance Act 1948 (discussed in Chapter 4), although in this case it is the normal procedure which requires one doctor and the emergency version which requires two. The only compulsory civil procedure in which the support, or at least the presence, of a doctor is not required is the police power to remove a person from a public place to a place of safety under section 136 (discussed in Chapter 5).

Whenever the Mental Health Act requires the recommendations of two doctors, one of them must be on the list of those approved by the Secretary of State under section 12(2) "as having special experience in the diagnosis or treatment of mental disorder." Approval is delegated to Regional Health Authorities, who should set up regional advisory panels, to whom they may delegate the function. They should ensure that there are enough approved doctors spread across the region, with "out of hours" availability and at least two on the staff of any unit taking detained patients. "Special experience" is a necessary but not always sufficient qualification for approval (*R. v. Trent Regional Health Authority, ex p. Somaratne, The Times*, December 10, 1993) and the Department of Health guidance (Circular No. HC(90)21, extended to March 31, 1996) lays down no hard and fast definition of "special experience". Like the Percy Commission (1957), the Department does not expect approval to be limited to qualified psychiatrists, let alone consultants; applications from others, such as G.P.s and prison medical officers, are to be positively encouraged; but it does now expect three years' post-registration clinical experience, including six months in a psychiatric training post which involves dealing with detained patients. Criteria may have to be adjusted, up or down, in the light of local demand and supply. Approval is usually for a period of five years at a time.

It may come as a surprise that all approved doctors are not at least qualified psychiatrists. The problem is that these are still in short supply. The Royal College of Psychiatrists only came into being in 1971 and has made great efforts to bring post-graduate training into line with that of other specialisms. Membership of the College (or the equivalent, including the former Diploma of Psychological Medicine) obviously constitutes "special experience" but the Departmental guidance stops short of requiring it. Nor does it require current practice in psychiatry, although it stresses the need for "up-to-date knowledge, skills and attitude". Learning disabilities are very different from psychiatric illnesses, and it would obviously be sensible if doctors whose only special experience is with the one should not make recommendations about the other. However this cannot be made a condition of approval. The Department's guidance simply observes that in practice doctors would "probably not wish" to act in cases in a category with which they are not normally concerned. Even approval does not guarantee that the doctor will be familiar with the legal requirements: indeed, an ASW may well be more knowledgeable than the doctor. But there are still too few approved doctors to go round.

In all applications, one of the doctors must, if practicable, have "previous acquaintance" with the patient (s. 12(2)). If it has not been possible to use such a doctor, the applicant must explain why (Mental Health (Hospital, Guardianship and Consent to Treatment) Regulations 1983, Forms, 1, 2, 5, 6, 8, 9, 17 and 18). This is thought particularly important in an emergency application, where the solitary doctor need not be an approved specialist, although previous acquaintance is still only required if practicable (s. 4(3)). Sometimes an approved doctor will know the patient beforehand, for example because of previous treatment in hospital or a domiciliary visit. But it was originally expected that the patient's general practitioner would supply the second recommendation, having the background knowledge to set the psychiatric symptoms in context. The Code of Practice expects this even if the consultant does know the patient and if it is not possible the second doctor should also be approved (para. 2.25). Whether the G.P. is any safeguard for the patient must be doubted. He usually has little knowledge of psychiatry or experience of mental disorder. He is under much more pressure than the hospital psychiatrist to consider the welfare of his other patients in the family or neighbourhood. Psychiatrists often claim that they spend more time resisting the pressure to admit patients than forcing them in (see, for example, Bean, 1980). But once the specialist has decided to admit the patient, the G.P. is unlikely to disagree. Whatever his experience, qualifications or private views, the structure of relationships between specialists and G.P.s is not such as to encourage him to do so.

Even so, there will still be emergency admissions where the patient has the protection neither of a specialist nor of a doctor who knows him. Many psychiatric emergencies arise in inner cities with floating populations, at times when one doctor is deputising for another, or where there is no psychiatric emergency team to make domiciliary visits at all hours. But these admissions may not always be lawful (see the report of the Divisional Court's decision in *R. v. D'Souza* [1992] Crim. L.R. 119, a House of Lords case discussed on p. 80, later). It could well be "practicable" for the proposed applicant to chase up a doctor who does know the patient, even though that doctor is not on duty or does not usually make domiciliary visits. Administrative arrangements are not the sole criterion for what is practicable in the eyes of the law.

In practice, of course, it is often extremely difficult to obtain a hospital bed unless a doctor from that hospital has already seen the patient. The law, however, does not insist that one of the doctors must be on the hospital staff. Indeed, it starts from the presumption that both of them should be independent of it. This is because of the spectre of collusion which dominated the procedures for paying patients in the past. Thus no recommending doctor may be, or be related to, a person who receives or has an interest in the receipt of any payments made on account of the maintenance of the patient (s. 12(5)(d)). This would include having a financial interest in an admitting private mental nursing home. More importantly, the doctor may not be on the staff of the admitting hospital or nursing home, or be related to a doctor who is (s. 12(5)(e)), although relationship to any other member of the hospital staff does not matter. Otherwise, it is not unlawful for a doctor to recommend the admission of a patient whom he intends to treat as a private patient, but the Code of Practice points out that it is "undesirable" for him to do so (para. 4.3).

Despite this, it was always intended that the great majority of compulsory patients would be admitted on the recommendation of their hospital doctor. Thus, provided that the patient is to be admitted to an NHS hospital as a non-paying patient, one of the recommending doctors (or the sole doctor in an emergency) may be a member of its staff (s. 12(3)); both doctors may be so, provided that three conditions are fulfilled: (a) getting an outside doctor would cause a delay involving serious risk to the patient's health or safety; (b) one of them works at that hospital for less than half the time that he is contracted to work for the NHS; and (c) if one of them is a consultant, the other does not work (either there or elsewhere) in a grade in which he is under that consultant's direction (s. 12(4)). For the purpose of all these rules, however, a G.P. who works part time in a hospital is not regarded as a member of the hospital staff (s. 12(6)).

It is difficult to know what the rules can hope to achieve. They prevent a doctor recommending the admission of someone who is to be his private patient at a hospital where he is on staff or has a financial interest and they prevent a consultant getting together with his registrar or house officer or even another full time consultant at that hospital. But if the aim was to provide two genuinely informed opinions, these might have been more satisfactory than the consultant and G.P. If, on the other hand, the aim was to reassure the patient, he is unlikely to appreciate the niceties. In any event, the rules do not prevent action which he may find equally suspicious. There is, for example, nothing to stop a consultant at the admitting psychiatric hospital from joining with his house officer at the general hospital from which the patient is to be transferred.

There are other rules aimed at securing the doctors' independence. They cannot be partners (s. 12(5)(b)), nor can one be employed as an assistant by the other (s. 12(5)(c)), and they must not be related to one another, or to a partner or assistant of the other (s. 12(5)). A recommending doctor cannot be the applicant (s. 12(5)(a)), the applicant's partner (s. 12(5)(b)), or employed as an assistant by the applicant (s. 12(5)(c)), nor can he be related to any of these people (s. 12(5)). Finally, no recommending doctor can be related to the patient himself (s. 12(5)). "Related" means being the husband, wife, father, father-in-law, mother, mother-in-law, son, son-in-law, daughter, daughter-in-law, brother, brother-in-law, sister or sister-in-law of the person concerned.

No doubt these rules do an excellent job in ensuring that a psychiatrist does not conspire with his assistant to place his wife in a mental nursing home which he runs, but they also invalidate the recommendation of a doctor who happens to be the brother-in-law of some totally disinterested doctor on the hospital staff.

(b) The medical recommendations

Each doctor must have "personally examined" the patient (s. 12(1)). The Act does not define an examination, which presents much the same difficulty as the social worker's interview. An interview might include holding a conversation through a locked door, but an examination implies that the doctor must at least see the patient. If access cannot be negotiated, a warrant must be obtained, or the police called to see whether they have any lawful power of entry (Code of Practice, para. 2.20). On the other hand, it is difficult to hold an interview with someone who cannot or will not speak, but it may be possible to examine him. Nevertheless, if patient and doctor cannot understand one another, a professional interpreter who understands psychiatric terminology and if possible the patient's cultural background should be used if practicable; the Code emphasises the need to avoid any possible pre-conceptions based on the patient's sex, social and cultural background or ethnic origin (para. 2.19).

If there are two doctors, their examination may be joint. But if they examine separately, not more than five days may elapse between the days on which their examinations took place (s. 12(1)). They should always discuss the case with one another (Code, para. 2.21). Preferably, both should discuss it with the applicant and one must do so (para. 2.22).

The Act does not specify that the recommendation must be signed at the same time as the medical examination. But it is important to state both dates accurately on the forms, for two reasons. First, the recommendations must be *signed* on or before the date of the application itself (s. 12(1)). Clearly, one should not make an application and then go looking for evidence to support it. Secondly, the application only remains valid for 14 days beginning with the date of the last medical *examination*, or in an emergency admission, for 24 hours beginning with the time when the examination actually took place or the application if earlier (s. 6(1)). If the patient does not arrive at hospital within these time-limits, it is unlawful either to take him or to detain him there. The only exception to this timetable is where a second medical recommendation is provided after an emergency admission to convert it into an ordinary admission for assessment (s. 4(4)). This can obviously happen after the application has been signed, but in all other respects it must comply with the Act's requirements.

Medical recommendations may be single or joint but must be in the forms prescribed by the Mental Health (Hospital, Guardianship and Consent to Treatment) Regulations 1983. Joint forms should only be used for joint examinations (Code, para. 2.23). Recommendations on forms required for one section cannot be used for another, which may be important to the social worker choosing between ordinary and emergency admissions for assessment. For admission for assessment, the Act only requires the doctors to confirm that the statutory grounds are made out (s. 2(3)). The forms do not expressly require them to give any diagnosis or reasons for their opinions about this, but they must explain why informal admission is not suitable (see forms 3 and 4). In an emergency application, the Act similarly does not require reasons (s. 4(3)), but the prescribed form requires the doctor to state how long a delay would be caused by waiting for another doctor, why this might result in harm, and whether that harm would be caused to the patient, to those now caring for him, or to other people. He must also state when he first learned that the patient's condition was causing such anxiety that it might warrant an immediate admission to hospital that day, the day before, within the last week, or more than a week ago (form 7). In an admission for treatment, or reception into guardianship, the Act itself requires the doctors to give grounds for their opinions on the patient's state of health and (where applicable) treatability (ss. 3(3) and 7(3)). The forms therefore insist on a clinical description (forms 10, 11, 19 and 20). They must also explain why hospital detention is necessary, indicating whether other methods of care or treatment (such as out-patient treatment or local authority social services) are available and if so why they are not appropriate, and why informal admission is not appropriate. Guardianship recommendations must explain why the patient cannot appropriately be cared for without powers of guardianship.

(c) The responsible medical officer

Once the patient is in hospital, many important legal functions are carried out by the RMO, who may well have been one of the recommending doctors. These are discussed in Chapters 6 and 7. The RMO is defined in the Act as the doctor in charge of the patient's treatment (s. 34(1)). This must mean the psychiatrist who is formally and professionally responsible for the patient in the hospital. There is no formal requirement that he be approved under section 12(2). If a patient is subject to after-care under supervision, however, the Health Authority must ensure that an approved doctor is in charge of his medical treatment (s. 117(2A)(a)). He is the patient's "community responsible medical officer" (CMRO) (s. 34(1)) whose role is explained in Chapter 7. The same person can be the patient's RMO, CMRO and even supervisor (s. 34(1A)).

5. DOCTORS AND SOCIAL WORKERS: ASSESSING THE PATIENT

The ASW and the doctors can themselves override any objections of the nearest relative to an admission for assessment. They will usually be able to persuade a county court judge to override his objections to an admission for treatment or a reception into guardianship. But what can a doctor do if there is no ASW willing to apply? Many doctors have an invincible belief that they have a common law duty to treat their patients and they also have a very natural professional desire to do so. The common law does indeed impose upon them a duty to take reasonable care of their patients. But apart from a limited doctrine of necessity (discussed in Chapter 6), this does not entitle a doctor to impose treatments which his patient does not want, still less to interfere in the life of a person who has not even agreed to become his patient. The Mental Health Act procedures allow medical intervention in circumstances far wider than those which the common law would allow. Those procedures accept that any individual social worker may refuse to act on the medical recommendations. The doctor may then advise the nearest relative of his right to apply, but he should never do this in order to avoid involving an ASW in the assessment (Code, paras. 2.30, 2.31).

It is one thing to say that the ASW has the right to act independently and quite another thing to put it into practice. The doctors are likely to see him, at best, as a junior member of a professional team which is devoted to securing the best possible care and treatment for the patient. At worst, they will see him as little more than a messenger to supply the forms, arrange transport to hospital, and smooth over any difficulties with the patient and his family (see Bean, 1980). A social worker is bound to share something of the medical approach. He is professionally concerned with the assessment of need and the provision of care. Any professional person is likely to believe that his expert knowledge and experience make him better equipped to solve a problem than are the lay people whose problem it is. The law in fact gives social workers much more power to impose solutions upon their clients than it gives to doctors.

However, although the old poor law or duly authorised officer probably had few qualms about taking a patient to hospital against his will, the modern social worker is likely to find this much more difficult. It is not only that "to be able to impose a course of action by physical force if necessary upon another human being is such a violation of the rights of personality that in normal conditions the social worker's integrity no less than the patient's would suffer emotional damage" (Le Mesurier, 1949). Any sensitive person might feel the same, but traditional social work training was based on casework principles, which had much in common with those of psychoanalysis. The implied condemnation of the patient's character and behaviour is the opposite of a non-authoritarian or "non-judgmental" attitude towards him and compulsion scarcely allows him any "self-determination". It can also seem a confession of the failure of the social worker's or a colleague's casework techniques and one which could jeopardise the building of a successful relationship with the client in future. The social worker is also committing the client to a situation which is quite outside his control, yet with modern community care policies the patient may be out of hospital and needing his support in a relatively short time. Casework principles no longer figure so prominently in social work training, but any modern course is bound to include sociology, in which the views of the "anti-psychiatrists" (diverse though these are) may be aired. Students may also learn of research which suggests that the roots of a compulsory admission lie far below the comparatively late appearance of the psychiatrist upon the scene, in the "complex struggles and negotiations in families and other social groups about behavioural norms." Research also suggests that "the issue of compulsion arises mainly when the 'patient' refuses to accept the definitions of 'illness' and 'health' insisted upon by his significant others" (Jordan, 1981; see Bott, 1971; Lawson, 1966). They will be aware of class, gender and ethnic biases in the recognition and treatment of mental disorder (e.g. Littlewood and Lipsedge, 1993; Showalter, 1987) and most of them will have come into the profession with a commitment to redressing the more glaring inequalities in society.

Nevertheless, the role inevitably places the ASW in a position of authority over his client. If he believes that all mental illness is a myth invented by psychiatrists as part of the structure of social control over the disenfranchised classes, the job is not for him. Part of his task is to reconcile his assessment of the patient's needs with his respect for the patient's rights and integrity. In this he is no different from the doctors, many of whom are now just as sensitive to these issues as any social worker. The other part of the social worker's task is to reconcile the different pressures from the patient, his family, the doctors and his own assessment of the situation. This in the end comes down to identifying a proper sphere of professional competence within which the social worker may disagree with the doctors, for of his right to disagree with both patient and family there can be no doubt.

The law is not very helpful. It reserves the social worker's right to refuse the medical advice. But the forms expect the doctors to certify that the grounds for admission exist and to explain why informal admission or other solutions are not appropriate. The applicant has only to confirm the procedural details and explain why (if this be so) he could not find a doctor who knew the patient beforehand. Section 13(2) does expect him to interview the patient and satisfy himself that detention in hospital is the most appropriate way of providing the care and medical treatment which the patient needs. But it stops short of requiring the social worker to satisfy himself about what that care and treatment is or why it is needed. Yet it is essential for practitioners to confront the issue of what is properly a medical problem and what is properly a social problem or a mixture of the two. Places where this has been done by co-operation between the health and social services seem most successful in finding alternatives to compulsory admission (Barnes, Bowl and Fisher, 1990).

The Code of Practice (para. 2.6), requires everyone concerned in the assessment to consider, not only the statutory criteria, but also: the patient's wishes and view of his own needs; his social and family circumstances; the risk of making assumptions based upon his sex, social and cultural background or ethnic origin; the possibility of misunderstandings which may be caused by other medical/health conditions including deafness; the nature of his illness or behaviour disorder; what may be known about him by relatives, friends and other professionals (but assessing how reliable this is); other forms of care or treatment, including whether the patient would accept informal or out-patient treatment; the needs of the patient's family or others with whom he lives; the need for others to be protected from the patient; the impact that compulsion would have on his life after discharge; the burden on those close to the patient of a decision *not* to admit compulsorily; and the appropriateness of guardianship. Only then should the applicant, in consultation with the other professionals, judge whether the statutory grounds are satisfied and decide accordingly (unless it is too urgent to consider all these factors). This sounds like putting the horse before the cart. In fact, each of the three main components in the grounds can contain both a medical and a social element.

The first is a diagnosis of mental disorder or a specific form of it. The doctors involved may be most reluctant to concede the social worker any voice in this question and the latter must obviously tread delicately. But it is necessary to set the patient's behaviour into its social, familial and cultural context in order to make a proper assessment of its meaning. ASWs ought to be able to recognise behavioural symptoms of mental disorder and mental impairment, and to appreciate the impact of the cultural and ethnic background of clients. The Code, however, expects the doctor to decide whether the patient is suffering from mental disorder and assess its seriousness and the need for further assessment and/or treatment in hospital (para. 2.18).

The next component is that the disorder is bad enough to warrant (or make appropriate) the patient's detention in hospital. This assessment must be affected by the fact that enforced medical treatment can only be provided in hospital. Much will therefore depend upon whether medical treatment is needed and the social worker will rarely be in a position to challenge the doctor's opinion about certain types of treatment. He may, however, be able to suggest and arrange for other types of care to be given and in different settings. As yet, however, it appears that social work assessment is more successful in reducing the use of compulsory admission than in identifying alternative sources of care and treatment in the community (Barnes, Bowl and Fisher, 1990).

The final component is that detention is necessary in the interests of the patient's own health or safety or for the protection of others. The social worker may not be able to disagree with the opinion that certain treatments are necessary for the patient's own health, but he should be able to ascertain whether it is necessary to use compulsory admission in order to secure them. Sometimes it may be possible to do so in less restrictive conditions. Sometimes it may be possible to explore whether the patient is prepared to accept treatment voluntarily. If he is, compulsion should only be considered if his current mental state, together with reliable evidence of past experience, indicates a strong likelihood that he will change his mind before he gets to hospital with a resulting risk to himself or others (Code, para. 2.7).

Bean's research (1980) suggests that this issue is not always adequately covered by the doctors, who concentrate upon finding symptoms of mental illness and assessing "dangerousness". In practice, he found, it is the dangerousness rating which determines whether an admission is informal or compulsory. The social worker obviously has a part to play in assessing this. There may be specific features of a particular illness about which the psychiatrist will be more knowledgeable, but in general "psychiatrists have not shown themselves to be particularly skilled at predicting dangerousness. Nor have they been too astute in distinguishing the potential suicide from the pretender" (Clare, 1980). According to Clare, the reason for the popular belief that they have some special skill lies in the equally erroneous belief that most psychiatric patients are actually or potentially violent. They are not. But there is now increasing evidence of an association between acute psychotic conditions and violence to self or others and a developing expertise in risk assessment (see Crichton, 1995). Few psychiatrists have gone as far as Clare in attempting to dispel this faith in their omnicompetence, but there is a great deal of American research casting doubt upon it (see, for example, Steadman, 1979). It is equally doubtful whether social scientists have any sufficiently precise knowledge of the causes of dangerous behaviour to enable them to make valid predictions (compare Prins, 1975, with Webb, 1976). But if these are possible at all, they must be based upon the interaction between the patient and his social circumstances (see, for example, Hepworth, 1982).

In considering the "protection of other persons", the Code (para. 2.8) states that it is essential to assess both the nature and the likelihood of risk and what level of risk others are entitled to be protected from, taking into account: reliable evidence of risk to others; any relevant details of the patient's mental history and past behaviour; the degree of risk and its nature (too high a risk of physical harm or of "serious, persistent psychological harm" indicate a need for compulsion); and the willingness and ability of those with whom the patient lives to cope with that risk.

The Code is all about inter-disciplinary co-operation. The ASW should involve any community psychiatric nurse or home care staff concerned with the patient (para. 2.16). Everyone must try to consult everyone else about the patient's needs and the alternative ways of supplying them. If they have done this and set out their views clearly to one another, "there is nothing wrong with disagreement" (para. 2.28). If there is an unresolved dispute, they must not abandon the patient and his family, but look for an alternative plan (para. 2.29). The decision not to apply should be as well thought-out, and explained to the family and other professionals, as is the decision to apply (paras. 2.3, 2.26, 2.27).

However, as Barnes, Bowl and Fisher (1990, p. 150) argue, for the ASWs

> "assessment to be truly independent it should not be based on borrowings from psychiatry, but derive from the skills of social workers in understanding how social pressures can affect individual behaviour, and how the relationship between the individual and the social world can be changed by practical assistance, therapeutic relationships, and temporary or more permanent removal from the source of stress."

If so, what can be the justification for the continued legal role of the patient's nearest relative? The point of lay involvement is to counter-balance the over-mighty power of the professionals who know what's best for us. The relatives are the last people to supply the detached and confident judgment required to do this.

4 THE MACHINERY OF CIVIL COMMITMENT

The grounds upon which applications for compulsory admission to hospital under the Mental Health Act may be made, the role of social workers, doctors and relatives in making them, and the short-term power to detain an existing hospital in-patient for the purpose, have already been covered in earlier chapters, but there are many procedural details still to be mentioned. These include the process of getting the patient to hospital, the duration and possible renewal of his detention there, and the monitoring of the admission documents. The alternative procedure for admitting some people, particularly the elderly, under the National Assistance Act 1948 is also covered. But before all this, we must first consider how the doctors and the social workers can gain access to the patient in a crisis.

1. GAINING ACCESS

The three "sections" in Part II of the 1983 Act will not always give the authorities adequate power to deal with a psychiatric crisis. There is no power to apprehend or detain a person until an application has been "duly completed" (see s. 6(1)). This cannot be done unless the applicant has personally seen the patient (s. 11(5)) and a social worker applicant must also interview the patient (s. 13(2)). Any application must be "founded on" the requisite medical recommendations (ss. 2(3), 3(3), and 4(3)). To give these the doctors must have personally examined the patient (s. 12(1)). The difficulty is illustrated by the case of *Townley v. Rushworth* (1963) 62 L.G.R. 95.

The defendant's wife had signed an application form for his emergency admission but the doctor had not yet made the medical recommendation. When the doctor went to the house with another relative and two police officers, the defendant told them to leave. The doctor replied that the defendant must go to hospital whether he wanted to or not and began to prepare an injection. One of the officers restrained the defendant from leaving the room. Seeing a scuffle, the other officer came up and the defendant punched him on the nose. The doctor then injected the defendant and summoned an ambulance. Only after that did the doctor sign the medical recommendation. Subsequently, the defendant was convicted of assault occasioning actual bodily harm to the police officer. His appeal to the Divisional Court, however, was allowed. As the application form had not been duly completed by the addition of the medical recommendation, the four people in the house had no power to restrain the defendant, and indeed were trespassers. As they were trespassers, the defendant was entitled to use reasonable force to resist them. So, "unless it is to be said that a householder is to sit down and submit, not only to his liberty being infringed in his own house, but also to assault by injection, and to his liberty being removed in hospital, I cannot say that to hit out with the fist is an unreasonable use of force" (Lord Parker of Waddington C.J., at p. 98).

Lanham (1974) has argued that the decision is wrong and that the Act itself authorised the doctor to do what he did. He suggests that because the

77

recommendation can be signed after the application form (provided that both are on the same day) a signed application is enough to authorise the doctor to enter the premises and make his examination. This cannot be right. An application does not authorise anything until it is duly completed and the provisions quoted above indicate that this cannot happen until the recommendation has been made. Indeed, the court itself went too far, because Lord Parker assumed that all would have been well if the doctor had signed the recommendation beforehand. This he was not entitled to do unless he had examined the defendant very recently. In any event, under section 6(1) a duly completed application merely authorises the taking and conveying to hospital of the patient. There is no reference to entering premises, which is provided for elsewhere by the procedure for getting a magistrate's warrant if entry is refused (see (c) below). Practitioners should not assume that completing the forms, even if it can lawfully be done without seeing the patient immediately, is sufficient to justify entry to private premises, with or without force.

(a) Common law powers of detention

On the other hand, the court in *Townley v. Rushworth* (1963) 62 L.G.R. 95 did not consider whether the common law might have provided lawful justification for what was done. Although Carson (1982a) has argued otherwise, the common law undoubtedly permitted that a "private person may without an express warrant confine a person disordered in his mind who seems disposed to do mischief to himself or any other person" (Bacon's Abridgement, cited in Clerk and Lindsell, 1989, para. 17.47). In *Black v. Forsey* 1988 S.L.T. 572, the House of Lords held that such a power was part of the common law of Scotland. It was this, rather than any statutory authority, which justified the admission of non-pauper patients to madhouses and hospitals in the early days. It could easily be taken too far—hence Lord Mansfield's strictures in *R. v. Coate* (1772) Lofft 73 that keepers of madhouses should be taught "that the circumstances of the case alone could support their action", that "everything must appear strictly, with all diligence and due advice, to be done for the best" and that "all unnecessary severity, all confinement other than for the best purpose of the unhappy person's recovery" would be subject to censure; but he had no doubt that such a power existed. When the Act for regulating Madhouses was passed in 1774, it was designed to provide additional procedural protection, but left the common law grounds for confinement untouched (see s. 31). Lord Campbell C.J. applied the same approach to the Lunacy Act of 1845, which gave statutory protection to people acting under the certificates and orders which it prescribed, but not to the people actually making the orders. Thus in *Fletcher v. Fletcher* (1859) 1 El. & El. 420, he found for a plaintiff against an uncle, who had committed the nephew in the reasonable belief that the nephew was insane but who did not allege that there was actual insanity at the time: "By the common law of England no person can be imprisoned as a lunatic unless he is actually insane at the time." There are several cases dealing with the effect of failure to comply with the Act's procedures and taking contradictory views. But both Lord Denman C.J. in *Shuttleworth's Case* (1846) 9 Q.B. 651 and Coleridge J. in *R. v. Pinder, Re Greenwood* (1855) 24 L.J.Q.B. 148 stated that the common law would permit them to refuse to release an insane person who was dangerous either to the public or to himself. And in *Scott v. Wakem* (1862) 3 F. & F. 147, Bramwell B. directed the jury that if the defendant (who was a surgeon) "had made out that the plaintiff was, at the time of the original restraint, a dangerous lunatic, in such a state that it was likely that he might do mischief to any one, the defendant would be justified in putting a restraint upon him, not merely at the moment of the original danger, but until there was reasonable ground to believe that the danger was over" (indeed he went further than this, and suggested that if the plaintiff's wife had called the defendant in to cure her husband of delirium tremens, or if the plaintiff himself had afterwards approved of what was done, the defendant would have been justified, providing that he did no more than was necessary and proper in the circumstances). Finally, in *Symm v. Fraser* (1863) 3 F. & F. 859, Coleridge C.J. directed the jury that the defendant doctors might have succeeded in a plea of justification (they had in fact pleaded that they were not responsible for what was done by attendants whom they had sent after being called in by the plaintiff herself), because what they had done had resulted in the preservation of her life and health, and the prevention of serious mischief to herself or others, while she was suffering from delirium tremens.

Subsequent legislation has at least made it clear that those who operate the statutory procedures correctly have lawful justification for what they do. It even provides some protection for those who operate them incorrectly (s. 139(1); p. 249, later). The 1983 Act does not expressly abrogate the common law power.

However, the House of Lords decided in *Black v. Forsey* 1988 S.L.T. 572 that the Mental Health (Scotland) Act 1984 contains a comprehensive code which impliedly removes any common law powers of the hospital authorities. Private individuals, however, may still restrain a person who is actually insane and who seems disposed to do mischief to himself or others. A reasonable belief in insanity is not enough. And as the common law tended to contrast the dangerous lunatic with the harmless eccentric it may be that a reasonable belief in dangerousness is also not enough. In *Sinclair v. Broughton* (1882) 47 L.T. 170, the Judicial Committee of the Privy Council stated that there was no law permitting a magistrate or police officer (in India) to confine a person "in consequence of a bona fide belief that a person is dangerous by reason of actual lunacy;. . . a fortiori, this cannot be done in the case of a bona fide belief of danger from impending lunacy." But these remarks could be understood in several ways. In any event, it is clear that the powers are limited to doing what is necessary and proper for as long as the danger lasts.

It is not at all clear whether the common law gives a right of entry to private premises. Lanham (1974) has argued that "where a person has a power to arrest the insane and dangerous he can also enter the latter's premises to make the arrest." He bases this on the analogy of the common law power to break into premises to prevent a felony and arrest the offender or to follow a felon into his house in order to arrest him. But a power of arrest does not invariably carry with it the right to enter premises by force and there is no case acknowledging this right in relation to the insane. Indeed, in *Anderdon v. Burrows* (1830) 4 C. & P. 210, Lord Tenterden C.J. implied the contrary. In any event, all the common law rules allowing police officers to enter premises without a warrant, apart from those to deal with or prevent a breach of the peace, were abolished in section 17(5) and (6) of the Police and Criminal Evidence Act 1984 (PACE). This does not, however, exclude the possibility that others have such a power.

Of course, there may be some other occupier of the premises who is entitled to grant entry. If the defendant in *Townley v. Rushworth* (1963) 62 L.G.R. 95 had owned his house jointly with his wife, she could at least have prevented their being trespassers, although there might still have been an assault before the forms were signed. Indeed, it ought to be the case that a wife's rights to occupy the matrimonial home also give her the right to license visitors whether her husband likes it or not (and this was held to be so, at least in the case of domestic violence against her, in *R. v. Thornley* (1980) 72 Cr.App.R. 302). Similarly, a patient living in a flat or bed-sitter may not always have exclusive rights of occupation, so that the landlord may be entitled to authorise entry.

A police officer has power under section 17 of PACE to enter premises without a warrant for five purposes; three cover the execution of an arrest warrant granted in criminal proceedings or arrest without warrant for certain offences, including any which could be punished with five or more years' imprisonment (s. 17(1)(a),(b),(c)). An officer can also enter to "recapture a person who is unlawfully at large whom he is pursuing" (s. 17(1)(d)). In *D'Souza v. D.P.P.* [1992] 1 W.L.R. 1073, the House of Lords held that a compulsory patient who is absent without leave from hospital is "unlawfully at large" but the entry has to be almost contemporaneous with the chase; so the police were not "in the execution of their duty" when they simply called at the patient's home and forced entry after being refused access. The final purpose is "of saving life or limb or to prevent serious damage to property" (s. 17(1)(e)). This could cover a person who has gone berserk or is about to commit suicide. The police also have a common law power of entry where a serious breach of the peace is being committed, but the essence of a breach of the peace is putting other people in fear for themselves and the disturbed behaviour of a patient alone in a locked room can scarcely do this.

Hence the Mental Health Act Code of Practice advises (para. 2.20) that if direct access cannot be obtained and delay to negotiate access is not desirable, then a warrant under section 135 (see (c) and (d) later) must be obtained or the police called to see whether they have any relevant power of entry.

(b) Entry under section 115

Section 115 empowers an approved social worker (ASW) to enter and inspect any premises which are not a hospital and in which a "mentally disordered patient" is living, if he has reasonable cause to believe that the patient is not under proper care. The premises must be in the area of the local social services authority which appoints him, and he must, if asked to do so, produce some duly authenticated document (for which no statutory form is laid down) showing that he is such a social worker. Section 145(1) defines a "patient" as a person who is suffering or appears to be suffering from mental disorder: but the addition of the words "mentally disordered" in section 115 could limit this power to those who are in fact disordered.

The power is undoubtedly useful, but it is aimed at discovering and protecting patients who for some reason may not be receiving proper care, and not at producing a situation in which the patient may lawfully be "sectioned". Thus, it relates only to an ASW, although once there he may be able to persuade the occupier to allow entry to a doctor as well. Secondly, it is only exercisable "at all reasonable times" and it is debatable whether this includes the middle of the night, even if a serious psychiatric emergency threatens, although in that case it probably does. Finally, while it might grant a defence to a social worker who entered without permission or stayed when asked to leave, it certainly does not permit him to gain entry by force. If he is acting within his powers, however, it is an offence for anyone to obstruct him without reasonable cause (s. 129).

As part of their comprehensive scheme for the protection of vulnerable people (p. 217, later), the Law Commission (1995) have proposed replacing this power with a wider one to enter and inspect premises and interview the person in private.

(c) Warrants under section 135(1)

Under section 135(1), an ASW may lay an information on oath before a magistrate, at any time or any place. It must appear to the magistrate "that there is reasonable cause to suspect that a person believed to be suffering from mental disorder—(a) has been, or is being, ill-treated, neglected or kept otherwise than under proper control, in any place within the jurisdiction of the justice, or (b) being unable to care for himself, is living alone in any such place." The magistrate may then issue a warrant, which need not name the patient (s. 135(5)) but must specify the premises to which it relates. It is addressed to any police officer (who need not be named) and not to the ASW, but in executing it the police officer must take with him an ASW (not necessarily the informant) and a doctor (s. 134(4)). The warrant authorises the police officer to enter, by force if need be, the specified premises, and, if thought fit (it is not clear by whom), to remove the person to a place of safety, with a view to making an application for compulsory admission or guardianship or other arrangements for his treatment or care (s. 135(1)).

A "place of safety" is defined for this purpose as "residential accommodation provided by a local social services authority under Part III of the National Assistance Act 1948 . . . " (see Chapter 9), a hospital or mental nursing home (see Chapter 1), a police station, a residential home for mentally disordered persons (see Chapter 9), or "any other suitable place the occupier of which is willing temporarily to receive the patient" (s. 135(6)). The DHSS advised that a police station should only be used for a short time while an ASW makes appropriate arrangements (DHSS, 1987, para. 291).

A patient who is removed to a place of safety under this section may be detained there for up to 72 hours (s. 135(3)). There is therefore no need to "section" the patient once entry has been gained to the premises, even if he is reluctant to come to hospital. Neither this section nor an emergency admission under section 4 gives any statutory power to treat the patient without his consent, and there is much to be said for delaying the stigmatising process of "sectioning" until the situation has cooled down somewhat. Only a handful of people are admitted to hospital under section 135(1) (Department of Health, 1995a), although an unknown number of other warrants may result in "sections", informal admission, removal to another place, or no action being taken at all.

This provision is the obvious answer to the problem of gaining entry. Social workers should certainly not attempt forcible entry by themselves, and, as we have seen, the police power to do so without a warrant is limited. But getting a warrant is bound to cause some delay, which could be dangerous if the patient is suicidal or destructive. Even then, Carson

(1982a) has pointed out that the grounds are not apt to cover every case in which a compulsory admission might be appropriate. A seriously ill, depressed or suicidal person may be quite able to care for himself and may not be ill-treated or neglected by anyone else. Nor is he necessarily "being kept otherwise than under proper control".

Once again, as part of their comprehensive scheme for the protection of vulnerable people (p. 217, later), the Law Commission (1995) have recommended replacing this power with a simpler power to obtain entry by warrant, which might if necessary be coupled with or followed by an order for assessment or for temporary removal to protective accommodation.

(d) Warrants under section 135(2)

Section 135(2) deals with the problem of entry once a patient has become liable to compulsion under the Act (or under the Mental Health (Scotland) Act 1984). Information may be laid before a magistrate by any constable or other person who is authorised under the Act to take a patient to any place, or to take into custody or retake a patient who is liable to be so taken or retaken. It must appear to the magistrate: (a) that there is reasonable cause to believe that the patient is to be found on premises within the magistrate's jurisdiction, and (b) that admission to the premises has been refused or a refusal is apprehended. Once again, the warrant authorises any police officer to enter the premises, by force if need be, and remove the patient. The police officer may be accompanied by a doctor and by any person authorised to take or retake the patient, but it is not essential (s. 135(4)). Now that the House of Lords have decided (in *D'Souza v. D.P.P.* [1992] 1 W.L.R. 1073; p. 80, earlier) that the power of entry under section 17(1)(d) of PACE is limited to actual pursuit of absconders, there may be more need to seek such warrants.

2. ORDINARY AND EMERGENCY ADMISSION FOR ASSESSMENT

(a) Ordinary admission under section 2

An ordinary application for admission for assessment must be made on Form 1 (prescribed by the Mental Health (Hospital Guardianship and Consent to Treatment) Regulations 1983, reg. 4(1) and Sched. 1), by the patient's nearest relative or someone authorised by him or by a county court to act, in which case the authorisation must be attached, or on Form 2 by an ASW (s. 11(1)). The applicant must have personally seen the patient within the 14 days ending on the date of the application (s. 11(5)). Form 2 requires the ASW to state whether or not he has yet told the nearest relative about the application and the relative's power of discharge, but he has no legal obligation to consult the relative beforehand (compare the Code's guidance discussed in Chapter 3). The application must be "founded on" two medical recommendations each in Form 4, or a joint medical recommendation in Form 3, complying with the requirements of section 12. The application is made to the managers of the particular hospital and must be personally delivered to their authorised officer (reg. 3(2)).

An application "duly completed in accordance with the provisions of this Part of this Act" is sufficient authority for the applicant, or any person authorised by the applicant, to take the patient and convey him to hospital at any time within the defined period (s. 6(1); see overleaf). The forms no longer state that they are accompanied by the medical recommendations, but it is hard to see how an application can be founded on something that has not yet been done. The documents give no authority to take the patient anywhere other than the named hospital. This has caused problems where physical treatment (for example for an attempted suicide) is urgently needed, but it is known that the general hospital will not admit compulsory patients. Should the application be made to that hospital, so that the patient can be taken there for life-saving treatment in casualty, and then a fresh application made so that he can be taken to the psychiatric hospital which will admit him? Or should the application be made to the psychiatric hospital, with the intention of taking a detour to the general hospital en route? The former is more in keeping with the letter of the law, but the problem is one which the administrators should not allow to arise.

Getting the patient to hospital is the applicant's task. An applicant ASW should choose "the most humane and least threatening" means of transport "consistent with ensuring that no harm comes to the patient or others" (Code, para. 11.4). Often, an ambulance will be best (para. 11.6) and this comes within the health authority's duty to provide ambulance services (DHSS, 1987, para. 36). A car should only be used if the patient will not be a danger (Code, para. 11.7). The police should be asked to help if he is violent or dangerous (para. 11.8). If the applicant authorises others to take the patient, it is advisable to do so in writing. No more force may be used than is reasonably necessary to effect the purpose (*e.g.* see *Allen v. Metropolitan Police Commissioner* [1980] Crim. L.R. 441) but the applicant should not be held responsible for the excesses of delegates whom it was reasonable to call in and who should have known better.

If the patient escapes, either before he can be apprehended or on the way to hospital, he may be recaptured by the person who had his custody immediately before the escape, or by any police officer, or by any ASW (s. 138(1)(a) and s. 137(1)). But this only applies during the period of 14 days beginning with the date of the second medical examination. If the patient does not arrive at the hospital within that period, there is no power to take him there, or to admit him if he gets there (s. 6(1) and (2)). If the proposed patient learns of the application before he is taken, he might be well advised just to go away for a fortnight. Provided that he does arrive in time, however, the "duly completed" application is sufficient authority for the managers to detain him there in accordance with the Act (s. 6(2)).

The hospital is also protected by section 6(3), which provides that any application "which appears to be duly made and founded on the necessary medical recommendations may be acted on without further proof of the signature or qualification of the person by whom the application or any such medical recommendation is made or given or of any matter of fact or opinion stated in it". However, these provisions cannot turn an unlawful detention into a lawful one: if the proper requirements have not in fact been fulfilled, the application is not "duly completed" for the purpose of section 6(1) and (2) (see *R. v. South Western Hospital Managers, ex p. M.* [1993] Q.B. 683); and section 6(3) does not mean that the detention can continue simply because the documents *look* correct (see *Re S.-C. (Mental Patient: Habeas Corpus), The Times*, December 4, 1995, Court of Appeal, p. 174, later).

It is lawful to take a patient to the named hospital, even though that hospital has not already agreed to admit him. But unless the hospital does agree, the patient will have to be released immediately on arrival. It is therefore advisable to have arranged the bed in advance. The doctor should arrange the bed (Code, para. 2.18.d), but the ASW should telephone to confirm time of arrival, should ensure that the documents arrive at the same time, and get there himself as soon as possible to oversee the admission process (Code, paras. 11.9–11.11). If the patient is admitted, the managers must make a record of this in Form 14 (reg. 4(3)) and of the receipt of the medical recommendations in Form 15 (reg. 4(4)).

Once admitted to hospital, the patient may be detained there for up to 28 days, beginning with the day on which he was admitted (s. 2(4)). But he may be discharged before then, either by the RMO, or by the hospital managers, or (in certain cases) by his nearest relative (see Chapter 7) or by a mental health review tribunal (see Chapter 8). If he wishes to apply to a tribunal, he must do so within 14 days. Once the 28 days have elapsed, the patient may remain in hospital informally (s. 131(1)) but he cannot be further detained unless other compulsory powers are taken *before* the admission for assessment runs out (s. 2(4)). There is no power to renew an admission for assessment and it is clear from section 5(1) and (6) that an admission for assessment cannot be replaced with a second admission for assessment or with a "holding power" under section 5(2) or (4). Thus, unless the patient becomes subject to a court order or Home Secretary's direction, any further detention must be by an application for admission for treatment, the grounds for which are more restricted. The only situation in which the admission for assessment can itself extend beyond 28 days is where before that date an application has been made to a county court for the replacement of the nearest relative. If an admission for assessment runs out before anything else is done, there is no power to detain the patient either under the Act (*R. v. Wilson and another, ex p. Williamson, The Independent,* April 19, 1995) or at common law (*Black v. Forsey* 1988 S.L.T. 572).

The Act does not specify what period must elapse between separate admissions for assessment. A series of these, interspersed with periods in the community or as an informal patient, might effectively avoid the more stringent criteria of admission for long-term detention and treatment. Worse still, in *R. v. South Western Hospital Managers, ex p. M.* [1993] Q.B. 683, it was held that a patient could lawfully be admitted under section 3 when the doctors had made their recommendations only the day after a tribunal had ordered her discharge from admission under section 2. The tribunal had found that her illness (an affective disorder) was not such as to warrant her detention in hospital for assessment and had accepted her assurance that she would comply with her lithium treatment. Refusing habeas corpus, the judge said that the applicant and doctors were not bound by the tribunal's decision on the facts; but if he was wrong about that, the circumstances had changed because there was now good reason to believe that she would not comply with her treatment. (In some cases, such a decision might be so unreasonable as to justify judicial review, but another judge had already decided otherwise in this case; judicial review and habeas corpus are discussed in Chapter 7). In practice, however, only a relatively small proportion (around 15 per cent) of section 2 admissions move on to section 3; the great majority become informal (Department of Health, 1995a).

(b) The choice between sections 2 and 3

Once in hospital under section 2, the treatment which can be given to the patient is the same as that which may be given to long-term compulsory patients. For this reason, it has been argued that admission for assessment should have been abolished. It allows a serious intervention in the patient's life, but the grounds are more appropriate to a short period of observation alone. It is usually throught best to treat as little as possible during a period of observation and assessment. According to the Code, section 2 "pointers" are: unclear diagnosis and prognosis; need for an in-patient assessment to formulate a treatment plan; need to judge whether the patient will accept treatment voluntarily; need to judge the likely effectiveness of a treatment which can only be carried out under Part IV of the Act (see Chapter 6); need for further assessment of a patient previously admitted compulsorily who has since changed; and where the patient has not previously been admitted, whether compulsorily or informally (para. 5.2). Section 3 "pointers" are: a previous admission, a disorder already known to the team and a recent assessment by that team; a patient unwilling to remain as needed when a section 2 expires; or who is judged to need treatment beyond the 28 days, in which case the section 3 should not wait until the 28 days are nearly up (para. 5.3). Decisions should *not* be influenced by a desire to avoid consulting the nearest relative; or the fact that the proposed treatment will last less than 28 days; or the fact that a patient detained under section 2 will have quicker access to a tribunal than one detained under section 3 (para. 5.4). It is hard to tell whether the Code believes the last to be a good or a bad thing. This advice may explain why the relative use of section 3 is rising.

(c) Emergency admission under section 4

This is simply a short cut version of an ordinary admission for assessment. By itself, it lasts for no more than 72 hours, and gives no power to impose treatment. But it may easily be converted into an ordinary 28-day admission, with power to treat, once the patient is in hospital.

The application must be made on Form 5 or 6 and the applicant must have seen the patient within the previous 24 hours (ss. 11 (5) and 4(4)). Only one medical recommendation is required, on Form 7, and the doctor need not be an approved specialist, but he must "if practicable" know the patient beforehand (s. 4(3)). If he does not, the applicant must explain why it was not practicable to use one who did. It may be "practicable" to use the patient's own doctor if he can easily be traced but does not wish to come out because he is not "on call". Both applicant and doctor must state that in their opinion it is of urgent necessity for the patient to be admitted and detained under section 2 *and* that compliance with the Act's requirements for that section would involve "undesirable" delay. This can only refer to the need to obtain two recommendations, one from an approved specialist. Thus it is clear that section 4 should only be used where the need for admission is so urgent that a second or approved doctor cannot be found in time. The doctor must explain why. It would therefore be inappropriate to use an emergency application following detention of an in-patient under section 5 (p. 10, earlier; Mental Health Act Commission, 1987 and 1989). It is also wrong to use section 4 simply because it would be more convenient for the second doctor to examine the patient in hospital (Code, para. 6.4).

The procedure for removing the patient and admitting him to hospital is the same as for an ordinary section 2 admission. But the patient must arrive at the hospital within the period of 24 hours beginning at the time of the medical examination or at the time of the application, whichever is the earlier (s. 6(1)(b) and (2)). The application may be signed before the recommendation, provided that they are signed on the same day (s. 12(1)).

An emergency application ceases to have effect once 72 hours have elapsed from the time of the patient's admission to hospital, *unless* a second medical recommendation is given and received by the managers within that time, and the two medical recommendations together comply with all the usual requirements of section 12 (apart, of course, from the requirement that both must be signed on or before the date of the application) (s. 4(4)). Once that recommendation is given and received, therefore, the admission is *automatically* converted into an ordinary section 2 admission. The authority to detain is extended to 28 days, but beginning on the day on which the patient was originally admitted under section 4; and the patient may then be treated in the same way as an ordinary section 2 patient. There is no need to bring in the nearest relative or an ASW to make a fresh application. Indeed, as the patient has already been admitted for assessment, the effect of section 5(1) and (6) is that this cannot be done without allowing the emergency admission to lapse for some time. There is nothing to prevent the patient applying to a tribunal the moment he is admitted under section 4. If the second medical recommendation is not forthcoming, of course, the application will be otiose. But if the recommendation is given, valuable time may be saved.

(d) The choice between sections 2 and 4

Emergency admission is the most controversial of the three "sections". From having been the most commonly used it has now become the least popular of all the three sections. If compulsion is reserved for those cases where it is genuinely essential, it is not surprising that this often happens in an emergency. The Code says that an "emergency arises where those involved cannot cope with the mental state or behaviour of the patient" (para. 6.3), which sounds more like the reason for any admission. But it goes on to say that there must be evidence of: a significant risk of mental or physical harm to the patient or others; and/or a danger of serious harm to property; and/or a need for physical restraint of the patient.

There are considerable regional variations, not only in the use of any form of compulsion, but also in the relative use of the various sections. Although there are special pressures in some inner cities, it is unlikely that the incidence either of "sectionable" mental disorder or of genuine emergencies varies between regions to anything like the same extent. In Camden in 1966 (Roy, 1966) virtually all "night calls" which required compulsion were handled under the emergency procedure; but by 1969 to 1971 (Beebe, Ellis and Evans, 1973) a policy of using approved psychiatrists whenever possible on emergency calls had been introduced; there was then a much higher proportion of ordinary short-term admissions. Recent research similarly indicates that it is local attitudes, policies and practices which explain variations in the use of hospital admission and compulsion, rather than the differing needs of the client population (Barnes, Bowl and Fisher, 1990).

The main criticism of emergency admission is that the patient may be deprived of the protection of a psychiatric opinion before his admission to hospital. The risk is that partisan or inexperienced relatives, social workers and G.P.s will react to a crisis with an over-hasty admission, after which the damage is done. The best solution might be an emergency admission on the recommendation of an approved psychiatrist, for this could give the minimum intervention with the maximum protection. But an emergency admission can easily be converted into one giving the full power to treat. Further, while the evidence suggests that psychiatrists *may* be an effective safeguard against inappropriate *admission*, it does not suggest that they are such an effective safeguard against inappropriate *compulsion* (Bean, 1980; Barnes, Bowl and Fisher, 1990).

Clearly, therefore, no one should choose an emergency admission unless there is a genuine and urgent need to admit the patient before the right two doctors can be found, and without realising that the consequences for the patient may be just the same as in an ordinary admission for assessment. If an ASW feels obliged to make an emergency application but is not satisfied with the reasons for the non-availability of the second doctor, he must get a senior to take it up with the health authority (Code of Practice, para. 6.6).

Both the numbers and the proportion of emergency admissions have been dropping steadily in recent years (from 29 per cent of formal admissions of non-offenders in 1984, to 13 per cent in 1989/90, and less than 7 per cent in 1992/93). Those of ordinary admissions for assessment mostly have been rising (from 54.5 per cent, to 66 per cent, but most recently down to 60 per cent). But the greatest proportional increase has been in the use of section 3 (Department of Health, 1995a).

3. ADMISSIONS FOR TREATMENT UNDER SECTION 3

There have always been fewer admissions for treatment than for observation or assessment, but the proportion of section 3 admissions has been rising, from 14 per cent in 1984 to 20.7 per cent in 1989/90 and 33.3 per cent in 1992/3 (Department of Health, 1995a). Once again there are regional variations in the rate per 1,000 population. The greatest proportion of resident patients at any one time will, of course, be detained under the longer term powers.

(a) Application and admission

The application may be made either by the patient's nearest relative, or someone authorised by that relative or a county court to act as such, on Form 8, or by an ASW on Form 9. The relative must usually be consulted and may either object or signify his lack of objection. This and the means of overriding the relative's objections are discussed in Chapter 3. The applicant must have seen the patient within the 14 days ending on the date of the application (s. 11(5)) and a social worker applicant must have interviewed the patient (s. 13(2)). Two medical recommendations complying with section 12 are necessary and Forms 10 or 11 require them to be far more explicit than for an admission for assessment. The procedure for taking the patient to hospital, recapturing him if he absconds before getting there, and admitting him to the hospital is the same as in an ordinary admission for assessment (section 2(a) earlier). He must therefore arrive at the hospital within the period of 14 days, beginning on the date of the second medical examination (s. 6(1)(a)).

(b) Duration and renewal

The rules governing what may happen to the patient in hospital are the same as those for an ordinary admission for assessment (see Chapter 6). The differences between them lie in the grounds for admission and in the potential duration of the patient's detention. Once admitted to hospital for treatment, the patient may initially be detained for six months beginning with the day on which he was admitted (s. 20(1)) but he may be discharged before then, either by the RMO, or by the hospital managers, or (in certain cases) by his nearest relative (see Chapter 7), or by a mental health review tribunal (see Chapter 8). He may apply to a tribunal at any one time during those first six months. He may remain in hospital informally after the authority for his detention has lapsed or he has been "discharged" from detention (s. 131(1)).

Once the patient has been detained for six months, the authority for his detention can be renewed for a further period of six months and thereafter for periods of one year at a time (s. 20(2)). The RMO must examine the patient within the period of two months ending on the day on which the authority to detain would expire. If the RMO considers that the requisite conditions are fulfilled, he must make a report to the managers on Form 30 (s. 20(3) and reg. 10(1)). But before making the report, he must consult one or more people who have been professionally concerned with the patient's medical treatment. These may be other doctors, nurses, psychologists or other therapists (s. 20(5)).

The criteria for renewing the patient's detention are set out in section 20(4). In all cases, the RMO must believe that it is necessary for the patient's own health or safety or for the protection of other persons that he should receive medical treatment in a hospital and that this cannot be provided unless he continues to be detained (s. 20(4)(c)). The RMO cannot think this if it is not appropriate for the patient to receive in-patient treatment in hospital or if he is not currently detained (as opposed to liable to be detained) because he is on leave (*R. v. Hallstrom, ex p. W.; R. v. Gardiner, ex p. L.* [1986] Q.B. 1090). Where the RMO is of the opinion that the patient is suffering from mental illness or severe mental impairment of a nature or degree which makes it appropriate for him to receive such treatment in a hospital, the RMO must also believe *either* that such treatment is likely to alleviate or prevent a deterioration of his condition *or* that the patient, if discharged, is unlikely to be able to care for himself, to obtain the care that he needs or to guard himself against serious exploitation (s. 20(4)(a) and (b)). Where the RMO is of the opinion that the patient is suffering from psychopathic disorder or mental impairment of the appropriate nature or degree, the RMO must also believe that medical treatment in a hospital is likely to alleviate or prevent a deterioration of his condition (s. 20(4)(a) and (b)). Thus the same conditions which were necessary at the initial admission must also be fulfilled at its renewal, but the "treatability" test (see p. 43, earlier) is now also applied to the "major" disorders, unless the patient would be unable to fend for himself if discharged.

If the report is made to the managers, the authority for the patient's detention is renewed automatically for the appropriate period from the expiration of the current period (s. 20(2) and (8)), *unless* the managers decide to discharge the patient despite the RMO's advice (s. 20(3)). The object of the report is to enable the managers to consider the patient's case and they should not simply rubber stamp the RMO's recommendation. If the detention is renewed, the patient must be informed and a new right to apply to a mental health review tribunal arises.

(c) Reclassification

At renewal, the RMO may decide that the patient is suffering from a different legal category of mental disorder from that which was originally specified. If the additional criteria appropriate to the new form of disorder are also satisfied and the detention is renewed, the application will be amended accordingly (s. 20(9)). There is also a procedure for reclassifying the form of the patient's disorder at other times (s. 16). Again, the RMO makes a report to the hospital managers, this time on Form 22 (prescribed under reg. 6), after consultation with one or more other professionals involved with the patient's medical treatment (s. 16(3)). The effect of a reclassification "downwards", from mental illness or severe mental impairment to psychopathic disorder or mental impairment, is that the RMO must also report whether further medical treatment in hospital is likely to alleviate or prevent a deterioration of the patient's condition. If the patient is not "treatable", his detention is automatically ended (s. 16(2)). A reclassification "upwards" has little practical effect. The major disorders are subject to a less stringent "treatability" test at renewal, but the RMO will have to reconsider the whole case then anyway and could always change his mind about the form of the patient's disorder once more. Nevertheless, the patient and his nearest relative must be informed of *any* reclassification under this section (s. 16(4)) and each has a right to apply to a mental health review tribunal. It will therefore be much simpler to leave the question of reclassification until renewal. Otherwise, a great deal of extra work may be caused by something which will have no practical effect except for a very few psychopathic or mildly impaired patients, whom the RMO might just as well have discharged instead.

4. TRANSFER FROM GUARDIANSHIP

Under section 19(1)(b), a patient under guardianship may be transferred to hospital. The transfer is effected by the responsible local social services authority on Form 27, but only after a procedure which is virtually identical to an ordinary admission for treatment (reg. 8(3)). An ASW must make the application on the usual form, and the usual rules about consulting the nearest relative and the duties of the social worker apply. The application must be founded on medical recommendations in Forms 28 or 29, which are virtually identical to those for an admission for treatment. The application must be accepted by the hospital and the local authority must be satisfied that a bed will be available within 14 days beginning with the day on which the transfer is signed. The authority must also have taken such steps as are practicable to inform the nearest relative of the proposed transfer. Once the transfer has been authorised, the patient may be taken to hospital by an officer of the local authority or by anyone authorised by them, but must arrive there within the 14 days beginning with the date of the second medical examination (reg. 9(1)(b)). The hospital must then record the admission on the usual form.

This suggests that the patient will then be regarded as an ordinary admission for treatment on that date. He certainly has the usual right to apply to a tribunal within six months. But section 19(2)(d) provides that Part II of the Act is to apply to him as if the original guardianship application were an application for admission for treatment and he had been admitted to hospital at the time when he was originally received into guardianship. Strictly speaking, the renewal dates should be calculated from the reception rather than from the admission. In practice, no one in the hospital will know when that was.

5. PATIENTS DETAINED BEFORE THE 1983 ACT

There are now only a handful of patients (mostly in special hospitals) who have been detained there since before the 1959 Act came into force. Some were transferred from the penal system and are now treated as though they were subject to a transfer direction, with restrictions, under section 46, or 47 or 48 with 49, as appropriate (1983 Act, Sched. 5, para. 37; see also paras. 38 and 39). Some of these "mental defectives" might remain subject to civil compulsion after their court orders ceased, and are like ordinary hospital order patients today, in that their nearest relatives have no power to discharge them (para. 34(4)). In other respects, however, both they and the patients originally admitted under the civil powers in the Lunacy and Mental Deficiency Acts are to be treated as if they had been admitted for treatment under Part II of the 1983 Act (para. 34(1)). The only difference between them and patients admitted since the 1959 Act is that the authority for their detention may still be renewed for periods of two years at a time (paras. 34(2) and 33(1), (2) and (4)). However, the procedure for renewal is the same, and this includes the new criteria laid down in section 20(4) (para. 34(3)). Those originally admitted for treatment for "minor" disorders under the 1959 Act lost the benefit of the repealed age limit of 25, and could be detained until their detention next came up for renewal, when it was governed by the new criteria.

6. SCRUTINY AND RECTIFICATION OF DOCUMENTS

The 1959 Act removed the central check on the validity of admission documents which had been exercised by the Board of Control, and the job is now done by the hospital management (reg. 4(2)). This should be formally delegated to a few officials who have an adequate knowledge of the Act (Code, para. 12.1). There are a few circumstances in which minor mistakes in applications or medical recommendations can be rectified, under section 15(1), or a fresh medical recommendation substituted for one which is insufficient, under section 15(2) or (3). These do not apply to orders made by a court, which may on occasions be just as defective.

Section 15(1) permits any application or recommendation "which is found to be in any respect incorrect or defective" to be amended by the person who signed it, provided that the hospital managers consent. This may be done within 14 days of the patient's admission (although of course an emergency admission can never last longer than 72 hours unless it is converted into an ordinary admission for assessment).

"Incorrect" probably means "inaccurate" in the sense of mis-stating names, dates, places or other details which had they been correctly stated would have justified the admission. It does not mean that a document which accurately reflects the facts can be rectified if those facts do not fall within the legal requirements. For example, a frequent fault is that the medical recommendations are undated or dated later than the application (see s. 12(1)). If in fact they were signed on or before the date of the application, the mistake can be rectified. But if they were signed later, then the application is invalid and the detention illegal.

"Defective" probably means "incomplete" in the sense that all the information required in the forms has not been given. It cannot mean that forms which are complete and accurate statements of the facts can be falsified in order to provide legal justification for detention where none exists. Thus a form may be amended if a vital date or qualification is omitted: but not if the date which is accurately stated contravenes the Act's time limits (DHSS, 1987, para. 58) or if the person signing the document is not qualified to do so (para. 52) or if it wrongly states that the nearest relative has been consulted (*R. v. South Western Hospital Managers, ex p. M.* [1993] Q.B. 683). According to Bingham M.R. in *Re S.-C. (Mental Patient: Habeas Corpus, The Times*, December 4, 1995 (see also pp. 58, 83, 174), there is "nothing in that section which enables a fundamentally defective application to be retrospectively validated". Further, an unsigned form cannot be regarded as an application or recommendation at all (DHSS, 1987, para. 52).

In one respect, however, section 15 does permit the remedying of a genuine deficiency which might otherwise invalidate the admission. If one of the two medical recommendations required for an ordinary admission for assessment or for admission for treatment is "insufficient to warrant the detention of the patient", the matter can be cured by obtaining a fresh recommendation which is sufficient. The hospital managers should notify the applicant (not the person who signed the document as under section 15(1)) and if a fresh medical recommendation is received within 14 days of the patient's admission, the application is treated as if it had been valid from the outset (s. 15(2)).

This procedure may be used where one (but only one) of the recommendations does not disclose adequate grounds for the admission. This is unlikely in an admission for assessment, where all the doctor has to do is put his signature to a printed form containing all the necessary statements, although he does now have to explain why informal admission is not appropriate. It is more likely in an admission for treatment, where he has to give a clinical description of the patient's mental condition and elaborate on other possible methods of care as well as the suitability of informal admission. If he fails to convince the scrutinising officer (the Code, in para. 12.4.b, advises that a medical scrutiny must be arranged), then the recommendation may be "insufficient" but could be remedied by a fresh one, provided of course that the facts warranted it. The new recommendation could be provided by the same or a different doctor.

The same procedure can be used where the two recommendations are good in themselves but taken together do not fulfil the Act's procedural requirements (s. 15(3)). The obvious example is where neither doctor is an approved specialist, but the section may also apply where the dates of their examinations were too far apart (see s. 12(2) and (1)). A fresh recommendation may cure this, and it need not comply with the requirements about the interval between the examinations or about signing the recommendation on or before the date of the application (s. 15(2)(a)). But together the new recommendation and the old must comply with every other requirement in the Act (s. 15(2)(b)).

One discrepancy which can never be cured in this way is where the doctors do not agree on at least one of the four forms of mental disorder in an admission for treatment (s. 15(4)). Nor can the procedure apply where it is the recommendation in itself, rather than in its relationship with the other one, which is bad: for example, where one of the doctors is not qualified at all, or where he is disqualified from making the recommendation because of his relationship with one of the other people involved. It could certainly not be used to render lawful the detention of a patient who had arrived at hospital more than 14 days after the date of the second medical examination, for it is not then the recommendation which is insufficient. Thus the mistakes which can be put right under section 15 are very limited.

7. THE NATIONAL ASSISTANCE ACT PROCEDURES

Patients may also be compulsorily admitted to hospital or other types of residential care under section 47 of the National Assistance Act 1948 and its emergency version in the National Assistance (Amendment) Act 1951. It is not known how many orders are made each year. But it does seem clear that they almost always relate to elderly or aged people who are living alone and are no longer looking after either themselves or their homes as well as the people around them would wish. Grey (1979) traces the origin back to the Webbs' Minority Report of the Poor Law Commission of 1909, which referred to the need "for some power of compulsory removal of infirm old men or women who refuse to accept an order for admission to the workhouse, and who linger on, alone and uncared for, in the most shocking conditions of filth and insanitation." But they saw this, not as an aspect of poor relief, but of public health. And it was in that guise that forerunners of the present provision appeared in local Acts for Bradford and London (and perhaps other places) during the 1920s. There is obviously a delicate borderline between the physical and the mental infirmities of old age, and there are many cases in which the National Assistance Act and Mental Health Act procedures are alternatives. The relative merits and demerits are, however, by no means easy to assess.

(a) The grounds

The grounds for proceeding under the 1948 Act have three components: (i) that the person is suffering from grave chronic disease *or*, being aged, infirm or physically incapacitated, is living in insanitary conditions; *and* (ii) that the person is unable to devote to himself, and is not receiving from other persons, proper care and attention; *and* (iii) that his removal from home is necessary, either in his own interests or for preventing injury to the health of, or serious nuisance to, other persons (s. 47(1) and (2)).

It is important to remember that the person must either be suffering from "grave chronic disease" or living in "insanitary" conditions. Harvey (1979) gives as a typical example of the use of the power an old lady called Agnes. She was apparently quite fit, but caused concern to neighbours and her doctor by her occasional reluctance to turn off the gas. Yet she had a home help and was apparently very critical of the quality of the help's work. Where was the evidence, either of grave chronic disease or of her living in insanitary conditions? At its widest, insanitary may mean "injurious to health", but it is normally associated with the spread of infection or lack of proper sanitation.

It is also necessary that the person be unable to look after himself *and* not be receiving proper care from other people. This raises even more explicitly than the Mental Health Act the question of whether the person could cope at home if only the right sort of community services were available: "the definition of need is a function not only of the person's disability but of the level of services available in the community" (Grey, 1979). Although the Act refers only to what is, or is not, being provided, it would be as well to consider also what *could* be provided before taking such a drastic step.

It is also now known (see Norman, 1980) that removing elderly people from their own homes, particularly when they are reluctant to accept this, is likely to lead to a swifter deterioration than leaving them at home would have done. It may therefore be difficult to say that removal is necessary in their own interests, and conditions would have to be very bad indeed before they constituted a risk to the health of other people, or even a serious nuisance to them. A nuisance in law is something which causes either physical damage to the neighbours' property or a substantial interference with its use and enjoyment. None of this, therefore, suggests that section 47 is simply a way of overcoming the reluctance of an old lady who might be safer or more comfortable in an old people's home.

(b) The full procedure

The full procedure under the 1948 Act is initiated by the community physician, who is employed by the health service and not the local authority. He certifies in writing to the district local authority that the grounds exist. But in the non-unitary authorities the district local authority is not the local social services authority which is responsible for arranging residential accommodation and providing social services to people in their own homes. Thus, although the local authority makes the application to the local magistrates' court, the social workers who may have been helping the old person will not necessarily be involved.

Seven clear days' notice of the hearing must be given to the person concerned "or to some person in charge of him" (s. 47(4)(a)). This last is a curious idea, as by definition the proposed patient is not being properly looked after by those around him, so that it seems most unjust to deprive him of his right to notice by giving it to them instead. Seven clear days' notice must also be given to the "person managing" the place to which it is proposed to remove the patient, unless that person is heard in court (s. 47(3)). The "manager" of a hospital is a person with whom we are familiar under the Mental Health Act (p. 17, earlier) but who is the person managing a local authority old people's home? The officer in charge may be extremely reluctant to receive a resident in defiance of the normal principle that these are voluntary residences with none of the author-itarian connotations of the workhouses of the past. But his local authority employers, in whose name the home is managed, may on occasions think differently. It would seem that the authority, rather than the individual, is the "person managing" for this purpose. But even though they must be given a hearing, the section does not expressly state that they must agree to accept the resident.

The court must hear oral evidence of the allegations in the certificate. If they are then satisfied of these, and that it is "expedient" to do so, they may order the removal of the patient to a "suitable hospital or other place" (s. 47(3)). The actual "removal" is the task of an officer of the applicant local authority, who must be specified in the order, but who may call upon the ambulance service to provide transport (s. 47(2) and (10)). The court fixes the duration of the order, up to a maximum of three months (s. 47(4)). But the court may extend this for further periods of up to three months, provided once again that the patient or some person in charge of him (who could presumably be the officer in charge of the home) is given seven clear days' notice (s. 47(4) and (7)). On the other hand, once six weeks have gone by since the original order or any extension, the patient (or someone acting on his behalf) may apply to the court for the order to be revoked (s. 47(6)). This time, seven clear days' notice must be given to the community physician (s. 47(7)). In practice, however, the chances of rehabilitating an old person who has been removed from home in this way are extremely slim. He will probably remain where he is whether or not the order continues in force. There is no other right of appeal, save on a point of law to the High Court.

The magistrates' court may vary the place at which the person is to be kept, provided once again that the manager is either heard or given notice (s. 47(5)). If the person is kept in hospital, the accommodation is free. If he is in a local authority home, the usual procedure for levying charges from him applies. If he is somewhere else, the local authority must pay, but can seek to recover from the person by those same procedures (s. 47(8) and (9); see Chapter 9). This is controversial enough where people volunteer, however reluctantly, for residential care; where they are forced to accept it, it must feel like adding injury to insult.

(c) The emergency procedure

However controversial and deficient the full section 47 procedure may be, it does at least provide one form of judicial hearing, usually with notice to the person whose life is to be disrupted. There is, however, an emergency version in the National Assistance (Amendment) Act 1951, which is probably more frequently used. The district community physician and a second doctor (usually, but not necessarily the G.P.) must both certify that in their opinion the person fulfils conditions (i) and (ii) for the full procedure and that it is necessary to remove him in his own interests and without delay (s. 1(1)). This then permits several modifications to the basic procedure.

First, the application may be made by the district community physician himself, provided that the local authority has given him general authorisation to do so (s. 1(3)). Secondly, it may be to a single justice, rather than to a full magistrates' court (s. 1(3)). The requirement of seven clear days' notice to the person concerned is waived (s. 1(1)), and the order can be made *ex parte* (s. 1(3)), that is without any notice at all. The requirement of notice to the manager of the hospital or home is also waived, provided that it is shown that he has agreed to have the person (s. 1(2)). The magistrate must still have oral evidence of the grounds. Any order made under the emergency procedure can only last for up to three weeks (s. 1(4)) and the right to apply for revocation after six weeks is therefore inapplicable. An application to the full court, with the appropriate notice, is necessary to obtain an extension. But an extension may very well not be necessary once the initial break with home has been achieved.

(d) What does an order allow?

The Acts are by no means clear about what may be done with the person once he has been removed. Section 47(1) of the 1948 Act declares that the purpose of the provisions is to secure "the necessary care and attention" for the people concerned; and section 47(3) provides that the court may order their removal to the hospital or home, and their "detention and maintenance therein". It seems that the 1951 Act was expressly passed because a doctor had been unable to persuade a person with a broken leg to go to hospital for treatment. Yet the Acts say nothing about imposing medical treatment, as opposed to care, attention and maintenance, without the patient's consent. In this they are very like the Mental Health Act 1959, which seems to have assumed that getting the patient to hospital was the only problem: what happened once he was there could safely be left to the clinical judgment of the doctors. Nowadays, however, we are very much less inclined to read such powers into statutes which do not expressly contain them (see Jacob, 1976), and it would be most unwise to go beyond the limits of what is permitted by these Acts and by the common law.

The greatest objection to these procedures is that they do not distinguish between people who have the capacity to decide for themselves, but choose to lead a life which others would find uncomfortable, and people who are unable to choose for themselves. The Law Commission (1995) have proposed the replacement of these powers, along with those in sections 115 and 135(1) of the 1983 Act, with a comprehensive scheme for the protection of vulnerable people living in the community which seeks to do this (p. 217, later).

8. COMMENTARY

Which would you rather be? Admitted to a hospital or old people's home under the National Assistance Act or "sectioned" under the Mental Health Act? The National Assistance Act conforms much more closely to the model of due process, because it involves an arbitration by an independent outsider. In practice, however, the person most nearly affected is not usually given notice of the proceedings, and no arbitration takes place. The Percy Commission thought that the intervention of a judicial authority in such circumstances was little more than a rubber stamp and they were probably right. It would be different if the person concerned were given notice, the right to representation, and a full-dress hearing before his liberty was infringed. But apart from the procedure for finding lunatics by inquisition, that has never been on offer to mental patients, even during the so-called triumph of legalism under the Lunacy Act 1890. The biggest objection to the present commitment procedures is that a person's rights are so crucially affected by the initial decision that he is a "patient". This defines whether he or his nearest relative is to be regarded as a rational human being. This defines whether he can be taken to hospital, detained, and given treatment without anything at all in the nature of due process ever having taken place. And the label "patient", as we all know, is extremely sticky.

On the other hand, the procedure does have enormous attractions. It is quick. It is private. It was naive of the Percy Commission to believe that it would do away with the stigma of certification, for there is certainly a stigma in being "sectioned". But it could be less than that involved in any of the earlier procedures, if only because the consequences are now so much less drastic. It is meant to protect both the patient's liberty and his needs better than a trial would do, by involving just those people who might be expected to assess them both properly. It does assume that all the participants will be able to act independently of one another. But in fact the only entirely free agent is likely to be the hospital consultant, who controls access to his own beds. Other doctors will find it hard to disagree with him. Relatives and social workers may find it easier to do so, but their dual responsibility places each in a difficult position. The social worker's duty to interview is an important step in involving the patient in his fate at the outset. But where everyone is concerned to balance the competing values of the patient's liberty and his needs, one or the other can be knocked off balance. Bean (1980) suggests that if other doctors and social workers are permitted to disagree with the consultant, "unstable interaction" is caused, to the detriment of the patient. But there must be some point to the legal formalities. They cannot just be pieces of paper that have to be filled in properly, as a timetable that must be kept, but not as a mechanism for substantial consideration of whether the case for compulsory intervention exists.

Even if in fact everyone involved bends over backwards to avoid railroading the patient into hospital, there are good reasons for the European Convention on Human Rights to insist on a speedy judicial review of the merits of the patient's detention (Art. 5(4)) and for mental health review tribunals to be given the job. The patient admitted for assessment still has to apply for it, and it may take place almost at the end of his detention; but it should have a retrospective effect on how everyone sees his case and a prospective effect on how others are seen in the future. There is much to be said for the English way of doing things. In practice, whatever the procedures, they will only be invoked where the professionals feel a need for them. If they can deliver the care and treatment they think the patient needs, without invoking the Mental Health Act or any other legislation, they will most assuredly do so. The patient who is vulnerable to this sort of attention can be as much in need of the law's protection as the most obviously sectionable psychotic.

5 MENTALLY DISORDERED OFFENDERS

The fact that a person who is alleged to have committed a criminal offence may be mentally disordered can affect the normal processes of the law at several points. He may never be reported to the police, if the people aggrieved do not consider him morally responsible for what he has done. The authorities may decide not to prosecute, for they have almost complete discretion and a variety of alternatives. If a prosecution is launched, he may be remanded or transferred to hospital before being dealt with, or be found unfit to stand trial. At the trial, mental disorder may occasionally provide a defence to the charge or allow the court to choose a therapeutic rather than a penal disposal. Even if a prison sentence is chosen, the Home Secretary may later transfer him to hospital.

The official policy is to divert as many mentally disordered offenders as possible away from prosecution or penal disposal and towards the health and social services (Home Office Circular No. 66/90). In a perfect world, according to the Final Report of the review into services for these patients (Reed, 1992), they should be cared for with a proper regard of the quality of care and the needs of individuals, as far as possible in the community rather than in institutions, under conditions of no greater security than is justified by the degree of danger, so as to maximise rehabilitation and the chances of sustaining an independent life, and as close as possible to their own homes and families. In practice, reality "often falls a long way short of what is desirable" (Reed, 1992, para. 3.1). But progress, even in implementing the proposals of the Butler Report on Mentally Abnormal Offenders (1975), has been slow. Neither the law, nor the policy, is likely to keep mentally disordered offenders out of prison unless there are enough suitable alternative services for them (Fennell, 1991a).

1. POLICE POWERS

(a) Detention under section 136

A police officer may remove to a place of safety any person whom he finds in a "place to which the public have access" and who appears to be suffering from mental disorder and in immediate need of care or control, provided that the officer thinks the removal is necessary in the interests of the person concerned or for the protection of other persons (s. 136(1)). The officer need not suspect that a criminal offence has been committed, let alone an arrestable offence. No magistrates warrant, written application or medical evidence is required, as it normally would be if the person were on private premises. A "place to which the public have access" covers more than public highways and open spaces where all are free to come and go as they please. It includes places like railway platforms and football grounds and car parks, to which members of the public are admitted on payment, or shops and public houses, which are only open at certain times of the day. These are not included at other times, but while they are open the concept may cover parts of the premises to which general access is denied. Even if some members of the public are not allowed in, a place may qualify if others are admitted *qua* public, for example to a hospital accident and emergency department. A place would not qualify if people are only admitted as lawful visitors to private premises, for example, when passing through a garden to get to the front door. Whether lifts, landings and staircases serving a block of flats qualify will depend upon whether and how access is controlled. A communal balcony was assumed to be public in *Carter v. Metropolitan Police Commissioner* [1975] 1 W.L.R. 507 (overleaf) and open walkways linking dwellings on a housing estate were so found in *Knox v. Anderton* (1983) 76 Cr.App.R. 156.

The definition of a place of safety is the same as that in section 135 (s. 135(6); see p. 81, overleaf), which includes both a hospital and a police station. Once at the place of safety, the person may be detained for up to 72 hours "for the purpose of enabling him to be examined by a registered medical practitioner and to be interviewed by an approved social worker and of making any necessary arrangements for his treatment or care" (s. 136(2)). The section gives no power to impose medical treatment without consent (s. 56(1)(b)). It is not an emergency admission. Once the person has been seen and any necessary arrangements made, the authority for his detention lapses (Code of Practice, para. 10.8).

The Code stresses the need for health, social services and police to have a clear local policy (para. 10.1), in order to ensure quick and competent assessment by a doctor *and* an ASW (para. 10.2), to define the responsibility of the police and other professionals involved (para. 10.3) and to monitor its use with a view to reducing it (para. 10.4). Although a hospital is generally thought preferable to a police station as a place of safety, the Mental Health Act Commission (1993, para. 10.7) prefers a mental health facility outside hospital: assessment on a psychiatric ward is not appropriate for someone who may not need admission at all, an accident and emergency department may have no suitable room, and some hospitals find it difficult to handle disturbed behaviour. Distance can also be a problem (Bean et al., 1991). The Code merely advises that preferred places of safety should be identified by local agreement, bearing in mind the effect of the setting on the assessment of the patient (para. 10.5).

Section 136 is technically a power of arrest for the purpose of the Police and Criminal Evidence Act 1984 (PACE). The person arrested is entitled to have someone else informed (PACE, s. 56); and if held in a police station, to have access to legal advice (PACE, s. 58); the Code says this should be facilitated in other places if requested (para. 10.9). The PACE Code of Practice on Detention, Treatment and Questioning (see section 2 later) applies. On the other hand, if a person is detained in hospital, there is a right to information under section 132 (see Chapter 6), and it would be good practice to do the same in a police station (Code, para. 10.11). Whenever possible the doctor should be "approved" (and few police surgeons are). Whatever the doctor's view the patient should still be seen by an ASW (paras. 10.12 to 10.15).

Hospital admission statistics (Department of Health, 1995a) suggest that use of this section is declining and in any event rare outside London. However, cases where the person is taken to a police station or elsewhere are not centrally recorded. Even if he is later admitted to hospital, this may well be under a different section or as an informal patient. The practice in any area will depend upon the willingness of local hospitals to accept referrals direct from the police, the availability of doctors and ASWs to go to police stations if asked, the policies of the particular police force and the attitudes of individual police officers. Even in London, research suggests that police involvement is far greater than indicated in the section 136 admission figures (Rogers and Faulkner, 1987).

Given its broad terms and the lack of any medical opinion before the person is detained, the power is clearly open to abuse. Whether it is in fact abused is more debatable. Both Rollin (1969) and Walker and McCabe (1973) found that the police used it instead of arresting an obvious offender who seemed equally obviously disordered. As Walker and McCabe point out, "Almost any behaviour of a markedly abnormal kind in a public place can be made the basis for some sort of charge." Most of the patients had been in hospital before. The police seemed reluctant to put a person in hospital without medical advice unless he was known to have been there already or his behaviour was so obviously bizarre that the "man must be mad" test (p. 32, earlier) would apply. But if, as Bean *et al.* (1991) found, the police use it to keep their options open when they discover an offender who appears to be mentally disordered, it is hard to understand why the Government refused to implement the Percy Commission's original recommendation that there should always be grounds for arresting the person instead.

The DHSS (DHSS *et al.*, 1978), however, thought that the power was most often used "where a person's abnormal behaviour is causing nuisance or offence." In *Carter v. Metropolitan Police Commissioner* [1975] 1 W.L.R. 507, the one reported case, a woman with no history of mental disorder was taken to hospital by the police following a dispute with her neighbours. Her version was that at the time she was standing calmly in the doorway of her own flat. The police version was that she had telephoned them to say that there was trouble but that she had "not started screaming yet" and was found on the communal landing, shouting abuse and with excrement on her hands. The court found the police version more credible and refused her leave to sue (under what is now section 139; see p. 249). It is obviously controversial that the law should permit the police to handle this sort of problem by making an instant diagnosis and arranging detention in a hospital or elsewhere without any medical or social work advice. Moreover, the *Carter* case concerned an inter-racial dispute and it seems clear that Afro-Caribbeans are over-represented in police referrals, not only in comparison to the general population but also to other methods of psychiatric admission (Rogers and Faulkner, 1987; Barnes, Bowl and Fisher, 1990; Bean et al, 1991).

Doubts about the reliability of police diagnosis are not on the whole borne out by research. Patients referred by the police have been found to show high rates of chronic mental illness, or to be at least as disturbed as those admitted under sections 2 or 4, but to be even more socially isolated and out of touch with the community services (Fahy, 1989; Bean et al, 1991; Mokhtar and Hogbin, 1993). From this perspective the police provide a valuable extra source of referral of people who desperately need it and may even be under-using their powers (Mokhtar and Hogbin, 1993).

There may still be cause for concern about the legality or propriety of much that is done (Rogers and Faulkner, 1987; Bean et al, 1991). For example, most arrests were in public but some were on private premises; the police did not realise that it was an arrest for PACE purposes; social workers were rarely involved in assessing patients taken to hospital or to accident and emergency units, whereas they were called to patients in police stations; often no form was completed so that the patient's status was ambiguous; hospitals generally required section 136 documentation even though an informal admission might have been appropriate; the section appeared to be used more as a means of admission and detention than for the purpose of assessment; and most of those admitted to hospital were given medication. Some of these findings were confirmed by Barnes, Bowl and Fisher (1990) who suggest that section 136 may be used by hospitals for de facto admission for assessment without involving a social worker. Interestingly, there is evidence that families of mentally ill people value the service provided by the police more highly than that of professionals, especially social workers (National Schizophrenia Fellowship, 1990).

(b) Diversion, interrogation and prosecution

Apart from section 136, there are several other options open to the police when they encounter a possible offender who may be mentally disordered. If he is known to be an absconding compulsory patient, they may simply detain and return him to hospital under sections 18 or 138; if he is on leave of absence, they may contact the hospital to recall him, so that section 18 will apply (see Chapter 7). If he is not already a compulsory patient, they may be able to persuade him to co-operate while they set in motion the processes for an ordinary informal or compulsory admission. They might even rely upon the common law power to arrest the insane (see Chapter 4). Alternatively, they may make use of their powers of arrest for the offence suspected, or in the prevention of crime or a breach of the peace, and consider diversionary options later.

Theoretically, they must tell him at the time under which of these powers they purport to detain him. In practice, they may refrain from putting a label on the detention until the decision between arrest and diversion has been made (Bean et al., 1991). Part of the process of deciding will be to interview the suspect. However, special procedures are now laid down in the Code of Practice for the Detention, Treatment and Questioning of Persons by Police Officers, issued under PACE (Home Office, 1995b). These apply where an officer suspects (or is told in good faith) that a person may be mentally disordered or handicapped or unable to understand the significance of questions put to him or his answers (see Code C and Annex E).

If such a person is detained, an "appropriate adult" must be informed and asked to come to the police station. An appropriate adult is a relative, guardian or other person responsible for his care or custody; or someone (other than a police officer or employee) who has experience of dealing with mentally disordered or handicapped people; or failing these, some other (similarly independent) responsible adult. A trained or experienced person may be more appropriate than an unqualified relative, but the person's own wishes should if practicable be respected. The adult should be there when the detained person is "read his rights" (*i.e.* to tell someone of his detention, to consult a lawyer and to consult the Codes), so if this has been done before he arrives it must be done again. He can request access to legal advice on the detained person's behalf. The object is not to delay this but to ensure that the detained person understands.

Interrogation of a suspected offender may take place (within limits) before or after arrest or detention. It is recognised that although mentally disordered or handicapped people "are often capable of providing reliable evidence, they may, without knowing or wishing to do so, be particularly prone in certain circumstances to provide information which is unreliable, misleading or self-incriminating" (Code C, Annex E, para. E3). Care and, if possible, corroboration of any admissions, are therefore required. It is all too easy for a police officer to extract admissions from a vulnerable or pliant person and then thankfully regard the case as closed without checking the story further. The best known example is Colin Lattimore, who was convicted almost entirely on his own admission of taking part in the killing of Maxwell Confait, although this had taken place at a time when he could not possibly have been there. The risk of unreliable admissions may be increased, now that (under the Criminal Justice and Public Order Act 1994, ss. 34–36) a suspect must be warned that his failure to explain clues, or his presence at the scene of the crime, or to put forward an explanation which he later uses in his defence, may be held against him in court.

Hence, if a mentally disordered or handicapped person has been cautioned before the appropriate adult arrives, this must be repeated when he does. A mentally disordered or handicapped person must not be interviewed or asked to provide a statement without an appropriate adult present, unless a superintendent or above considers that the delay would lead to interference with or harm either to evidence or to other people, or would alert other suspects who have not yet been arrested, or would hinder the recovery of property. Once the risk is averted, the questioning must stop. The adult must be told that he is not there just to observe, but to advise the person being interviewed and to see fair play, and to facilitate communication with him. All this is, of course, in addition to the normal rules and directions about questioning.

A breach of the Code does not necessarily make a statement inadmissible in evidence. But a confession must be excluded unless the prosecution can prove that it was not obtained "(a) by oppression of the person who made it; or (b) in consequence of anything said or done which was likely, in the circumstances existing at the time, to render unreliable" any confession which might be made by him as a result (PACE, s. 76(2)). Breaches of the Code may combine with other circumstances to amount to oppression, which "excites hopes (such as the hope of release) or fears, or so affects the mind of the subject that his will crumbles and he speaks when otherwise he would have remained silent" (*per* Lord MacDermott, adopted in *R. v. Prager* (1971) 56 Cr.App.R. 151). For example, in *R. v. Westlake* [1979] Crim. L.R. 652, the accused had a mental age of 11 or 12 and was kept in custody for 24 hours before his interrogation. He was then questioned repeatedly over the next five days. No attempt was made to have his father present, although this was practicable. There were frequent breaches of the rules and directions and the judge found the form of questioning itself oppressive.

Even if there is no inducement or oppression, the judge still has a discretion to exclude prosecution evidence if in all the circumstances, including those in which the evidence was obtained, admitting it "would have such an adverse effect on the fairness of the proceedings that the court ought not to admit it" (1984 Act, s. 78(1)). Section 82(3) of the Act also preserves the court's common law discretion to exclude evidence which is more prejudicial than probative (*R. v. Sang* [1980] A.C. 402).

Even if the evidence is admitted, section 77 of the 1984 Act requires the judge, in a case which relies wholly or mainly on the confession of a mentally handicapped person made without the presence of an independent person, to warn the jury "that there is a special need for caution" before convicting him in reliance on it. However, in *R. v. Moss, Daily Telegraph* (1990) 91 Cr.App.R. 371, this warning was not enough to make safe a conviction of a man who was just above mental handicap level, which relied solely on confessions made after he had been in custody for nine days, interviewed nine times, and without a solicitor present. The courts, at least, are becoming increasingly alive to the dangers.

The initial decision between prosecution and some form of diversion out of the criminal justice system lies with the police. Earlier studies (principally Rollin, 1969; Walker and McCabe, 1973) suggested that the two most important factors were the nature of the offence and the police knowledge of the offender's history. The police were more likely to prosecute for crimes against property, which are probably thought more blameworthy, involving a higher degree of thought and planning, than are the public order offences which were common amongst the unprosecuted group and often involved outstandingly abnormal behaviour. The unprosecuted offenders were more likely to be seriously ill (or soon discovered to be so) and also less likely to have a serious criminal record. There was also evidence that chance played a large part in these decisions. Whitehead and Ahmad (1970) were concerned that so many of their hospital order patients appeared to have committed minor public order offences directly related to their disorder (such as shouting at their "voices"). Walker and McCabe (1973), on the other hand, discovered several unprosecuted offenders whose crimes were very serious.

Beebe, Ellis and Evans (1973) illustrated how some offenders could manipulate the system: a man picked up as drunk and disorderly announced suicidal intentions, and was pronounced "mental" by the police surgeon. The psychiatric team called to the police station took a different view, as he seemed to have definite plans for the next day and merely wanted them to save him from the magistrate. Because of this disagreement, he probably escaped official action altogether. This illustrates the dilemma facing a social worker or doctor called to the police station. Now that diversion is the official policy, the police could so easily say "section him or we prosecute". The team may be tempted to comply in order to save the patient from a worse fate. But prosecution is by no means invariably a worse fate than being "sectioned" and patients should only be compelled to enter hospital if the circumstances genuinely warrant it.

Once the initial decision to prosecute has been taken, the case will be handed over to the Crown Prosecution Service (CPS), which will review the case in the light of the Code for Crown Prosecutors issued by the Director of Public Prosecutions (Prosecution of Offenders Act 1985, ss. 3 and 10). Under the present Code (Crown Prosecution Service, 1994), there are two stages in the decision (para. 4.1). There must first be enough evidence to provide a realistic prospect of conviction (para. 5.1). Only then will the prosecutor decide whether a prosecution is needed in the public interest. The more serious the offence, the more likely it is to be needed (para. 6.4). But among the factors making it less likely is that "the defendant is elderly or is, or was at the time of the offence, suffering from significant mental or physical ill health, unless the offence is serious or there is a real possibility that it may be repeated. The CPS, where necessary, will apply the Home Office guidelines on how to deal with mentally disordered offenders. The CPS must balance the desirability of diverting a defendant who is suffering from significant mental or physical ill-health with the need to safeguard the general public" (para. 6.5.f; referring to Home Office Circular No. 66/90).

Presumably, the crucial factor here is whether there should be the option either of a custodial penalty or of a restriction order, for other forms of diversion can be achieved without going to court. Otherwise, some might consider that prosecution is unlikely to serve any "useful public purpose" (Butler Committee, 1975). It may, however, serve other useful purposes. Even the most disturbed patient may feel a sense of grave injustice at prolonged detention in hospital without trial. Many professionals now believe that people with learning disabilities should be prosecuted and held responsible where responsibility exists (see Carson, 1989b). This is an essential element in recognition as a human being. It is also important to establish the truth about an incident, especially in an institution. There is a popular conception, apparently encouraged in some quarters, that mentally disordered or disabled people are more likely than others to commit crimes. Mostly they are not. There is evidence that active psychotic symptoms are associated with an increased risk of violence, but the accurate assessment of risk is acknowledged to be a difficult and inexact science (Hodgins, 1993; Crichton, 1995). While diversion out of the criminal justice system is of real benefit to some, we should not forget the advantages of a proper investigation of the evidence and of the alternative disposals. Nor should psychiatrists be asked to make judgments which are more appropriate to the forensic process (Carson, 1992).

2. PROCEDURE BEFORE TRIAL

(a) Obtaining the medical evidence

If the case goes to court, medical evidence must be obtained before any specifically psychiatric diversion or disposal. The written or oral evidence of two doctors is required before a finding that the accused is unfit to plead or not guilty by reason of insanity (Criminal Procedure (Insanity) Act 1964, s. 4(6); Criminal Procedure (Insanity and Unfitness to Plead) Act 1991, s. 1(1)), and for an ordinary hospital order, a restriction order or an interim hospital order (1983 Act, ss. 37(2)(a), 41(2), 38(1)(a) respectively), for a remand to hospital for treatment (s. 36(1)) or committal to hospital with a view to a restriction order (s. 43(1)(a)), and for a guardianship order (s. 37(2)(a)). Only one doctor is required for remand to hospital for reports (s. 35(3)(a)) or for a probation or supervision order with a condition of psychiatric treatment.

One of the two doctors, or the single doctor where only one is required, must be on the "approved" list (s. 54(1); p. 67, earlier). But none of the other rules about medical recommendations apply. The medical examinations could have taken place some time before the court's order. There is nothing to stop the doctors being related to one another, or to the patient, or, more importantly, being employed at the same institution. The DHSS (DHSS *et al.*, 1978) thought that they should not both come from the same prison or hospital (whether or not it was the admitting hospital). The Code of Practice points out that it is desirable for any doctor who has previously treated the patient to prepare a report, and for the reporting doctor to have "appropriate beds at his disposal" (para. 3.7).

No court can send a defendant to hospital unless it has evidence that a bed in that hospital will be available within a stated time. That evidence must be given either by the doctor who would be in charge of the patient there or by some other representative of the hospital managers (ss. 35(4), 36(3), 37(4), 38(4) and 44(1)). As that doctor is likely to be on the approved list, it will often be more convenient for him to supply the necessary evidence of the defendant's mental condition as well. If the court is contemplating a restriction order, it is particularly desirable to have evidence from the hospital as to whether the patient is suitable and the hospital is willing to admit him on those terms (*R. v. Blackwood* (1973) 59 Cr.App.R. 170). The Butler Committee recommended that the admitting hospital should have to agree to the restrictions as well as the admission, but in *R. v. Royse* [1981] Crim. L.R. 426 it was pointed out that protection of the public was a question for the court rather than the doctors and so it has remained.

One of the two doctors must give oral evidence if the court is to make a restriction order (s. 41(2)). Otherwise, the evidence required for Mental Health Act orders may be given in writing, although the court may always insist on the doctor's attendance if it wishes. Written evidence from a doctor or representative of the hospital managers may be admitted without formal proof of the signature or qualifications (s. 54(2)). If the report is not presented on behalf of the defendant, it must be disclosed to his legal representative. If he has none, the substance must be disclosed to him personally, or to his parent if he is a juvenile. The defence is entitled to insist that the doctor gives oral evidence, so that he may be cross-examined, and to call evidence to rebut what he says (s. 52(3)), except where the evidence relates solely to the availability of a bed.

Reports may be obtained either by the prosecution, or by the defence, or at the request of the court. The defence need not accept the prison doctor's verdict that the accused is "fit for disposal as the court thinks fit" and can shop around for more favourable reports (although they may have difficulty in persuading the legal aid authorities to pay for these unless they can show a good reason). This is one explanation for the frustration which can arise when the court is faced with clear evidence that the defendant's mental condition warrants an order but no evidence that a suitable hospital is willing to have him. However, lawyers should also be prepared to subject "favourable" reports to critical scrutiny and be on their guard against the assumption that a hospital order is always a soft option or what the client wants. Once the possibility is raised, a Crown Court judge may well consider adding a restriction order (see Gostin, 1977). Furthermore, the risks to the public can override the duty of confidentiality, so that a psychiatrist instructed on behalf of the defence may make his report available to the court, which may act upon it whether the defendant likes it or not (*R. v. Crozier* (1990) 12 Cr.App.R. (S.) 206).

It is often argued (*e.g.*, by Kenny, 1983) that expert evidence is not suitable for adversarial combat and should be called to assist the court rather than by the parties. This assumes that the court's expert is right and anyone else is wrong, which in a field like psychiatry is manifestly absurd. Judges themselves seem to veer from an exaggerated contempt to an equally exaggerated respect (*e.g.* King, 1981). The Butler Committee rejected proposals for a panel of psychiatrists to advise the courts. Rightly, they did not wish to deny the accused the opportunity of calling his own evidence if he wished. They comforted themselves that the unedifying "battle of the experts" had diminished, since the abolition of the death penalty and the shift of most decisions to the disposal stage.

The Butler Committee were more concerned that many defendants who might benefit from psychiatric treatment could slip through the net. A busy magistrates' court, dealing with an unrepresented defendant on a minor charge, is unlikely to think of getting medical reports unless he shows obvious signs of disorder (Donovan and O'Brien, 1981). The police, prison authorities and even a legal representative may not know of any psychiatric history, unless there is a previous psychiatric disposal which shows up on the criminal record. There is plenty of evidence (*e.g.* Boehringer and

McCabe, 1973) that such people appear in the courts time and again without the opportunity for treatment being taken. Magistrates, however, seem to be more impressed by the defendant's demeanour in court than by his previous history or the nature of the offence, when making their decisions to call for reports. This problem is being addressed by positive diversion schemes in some courts, some with psychiatrists on the spot to make preliminary assessments (Blumenthal and Wessely, 1992; *e.g.* James and Hamilton, 1991).

The Court of Appeal has advised that there should be a psychiatrist's report in cases of arson (*R. v. Calladine, The Times*, December 3, 1975). Prisons tend to obtain at least the medical officer's view on people remanded on charges of murder or serious sex offences. Where a person charged with murder is granted bail, the court must now make it a condition that he is examined by two doctors, one of them approved, unless satisfactory reports have already been obtained (Bail Act 1976, s. 3(6A)).

The Butler Committee were also concerned about the conditions under which a report is prepared. If an accused is remanded in custody, it may be easy to obtain a report, but prison is scarcely the most favourable environment in which to make a psychiatric assessment. If the accused is remanded on bail, the court may make whatever condition appears necessary to ensure that he makes himself available, so that a report may be made to assist the court in dealing with him for the offence (Bail Act 1976, s. 3(6)(d)). This can include a condition of residence in hospital, but unless the accused is separately "sectioned" he is an informal patient whom the hospital cannot detain. All courts have a specific power to remand offenders for reports after conviction. Magistrates may do so (for three weeks at a time in custody and four on bail) without convicting, if they are satisfied that the defendant did the act or made the omission charged (Magistrates' Courts Act 1980, s. 30). The usual presumption in favour of bail applies to all these remands (Bail Act 1976, s. 4(4)).

As recommended by the Butler Committee, section 35 of the 1983 Act provides for remands to hospital for reports. This applies to anyone awaiting trial or sentence in the Crown Court for any offence punishable with imprisonment (including those charged with, but not yet convicted of, murder). Magistrates may only remand after convicting the accused of a prisonable offence, or finding that he did the act or made the omission charged, or with his consent (s. 35(2)). These remands can only be made where bail would be impracticable, so prison would almost always be the alternative. Nevertheless, it was thought that a normal offender might resent being sent to hospital, so the court must have written or oral evidence from one approved doctor that there is reason to suspect that the accused is suffering from mental illness, psychopathic disorder, severe mental impairment or mental impairment (s. 35(3)). There must be the usual evidence that a bed will be available within seven days, beginning with the date of the remand (s. 35(4)).

The accused may be kept in a "place of safety" before he is taken to hospital. For this and other orders under Part III of the Act, a place of safety is a police station, prison or remand centre, or another hospital which is willing to have him for the time being (s. 55(1)). Once in hospital, he must be detained (s. 35(9)) and if he escapes he may be arrested without warrant and must then be brought back to court (s. 35(10)). The Act expressly allows him to obtain his own medical report at his own expense, so that he can ask for the remand to be ended (s. 35(8)). A remand under this section cannot last for more than 28 days at a time

(s. 35(7)), but the accused may be remanded again and again if the doctor states that this is necessary (s. 35(5)). He need not be brought back to court for the purpose, provided that he has a legal representative who is given an opportunity of being heard (s. 35(6)). But the total period cannot be longer than 12 weeks in all and the court can always end it earlier (s. 35(7)).

These remands are an excellent idea in theory. There may be many more than the official figures suggest (Gunn and Joseph, 1993) but they are still in hundreds rather than thousands. The psychiatric services would be swamped if everyone remanded in custody for reports were remanded to hospital instead (Fennell, 1991a). Those who do go to hospital cannot be treated without their consent (1983 Act, s. 56(1)(b)) unless they are "sectioned" under civil powers as well. Views differ about the propriety of doing this, but there is nothing to prevent it. The Code (para. 17.3) advises that the case should be referred back to court, with a view to a remand for treatment, but if there is going to be a delay, consideration should be given to whether the patient meets the criteria for detention under section 3. It might be simpler to have a combined power to remand for assessment and treatment instead.

(b) Hospital care while awaiting trial

If a person awaiting trial or sentence is remanded in custody, the Home Secretary may direct his transfer to hospital under section 48. This applies to civil prisoners, people detained under the Immigration Act 1971, people remanded in custody by a magistrates' court, and any other person who is detained in a prison or remand centre but not serving a custodial sentence (s. 48(2)). In practice, the last means people awaiting trial or sentence in the Crown Court. The Home Secretary must have reports from at least two doctors, one approved, that the prisoner is suffering from *mental illness or severe mental impairment,* of a nature or degree which makes it appropriate for him to be detained in hospital for medical treatment, and that he is *in urgent need* of this treatment (s. 48(1)). The doctors must agree on one form of disorder, even if one of them thinks he is both mentally ill and severely impaired (s. 47(4)).

The Reed Committee (1992, 1994b) proposed that transfer should be available to test the "treatability" of prisoners with psychopathic disorder and that the urgency criterion should be relaxed. They also proposed pilot schemes for "hospital assessment centres" to which people could be transferred before or after conviction.

All transfers have the same effect as a hospital order (s. 47(3)). The patient may be treated; but he may also apply to a mental health review tribunal, even during his first six months in hospital (see Chapter 8). The transfer of a civil or Immigration Act prisoner can never last longer than his detention would have done (s. 53(1)) and the Home Secretary may choose whether to transfer him as an ordinary hospital order or as a restriction order patient (s. 49(1)). If restricted, he may be transferred back to prison, if the Home Secretary is notified by the responsible medical officer (RMO), any other doctor, or a mental health review tribunal, that he no longer needs treatment for mental disorder or that no effective treatment can be given in that hospital (s. 53(2)). The transfer of remand prisoners must take effect as a restriction order (s. 49(1) and (2)), but the precise consequences depend upon the court in which he is waiting to appear.

If the patient is waiting to appear in a magistrates' court, the transfer lasts as long as the remand, unless the court remands him again (which it may do in his absence if he has appeared before the court within the last six months) or commits him for trial in the Crown Court (which again it may do in his absence if the RMO reports that he is unfit to take part). But the magistrates themselves may end the transfer, even if the remand has not expired or the patient has been committed to the Crown Court, if the RMO reports to them that the patient no longer needs treatment for mental disorder, or that no effective treatment can be given in that hospital (s. 52). If and when the magistrates finally deal with a transferred patient, they may be able to make a hospital order, sometimes without in fact convicting him, but they cannot do so in his absence (p. 118, later).

If the patient is waiting to appear in the Crown Court (or elsewhere), the transfer lasts until the court disposes of the case. But the Home Secretary has power to transfer him back to prison, if notified by the RMO, any other doctor or a mental health review tribunal that he no longer needs treatment or that no effective treatment can be given (s. 51(3)). The court itself may end the transfer if notified to the same effect by the RMO, but it may choose to release him on bail rather than transfer him back to custody (s. 51(3)).

However, if the patient is still in hospital when he comes up for trial or sentence, the court may make a hospital order in his absence and without convicting him, provided that three conditions are fulfilled. First, it must be impracticable or inappropriate to bring him before the court. Secondly, there must be written or oral evidence from at least two doctors, one approved, that he is suffering from mental illness or severe mental impairment of a nature or degree which makes it appropriate for him to be detained in hospital for medical treatment. Lastly, the court must think that this is proper, after considering the depositions and any other documents sent to court (s. 51(5) and (6)). The order may be with or without restrictions.

The effect of all this is that both a magistrates' court and the Crown Court may make a hospital order over a transferred remand prisoner without ever trying him. The Crown Court does not even have to be satisfied that he did the act or made the omission charged. This amounts to indefinite detention without trial. Indeed, the transfer alone may have this result, for the court may be persuaded to go on remanding the patient, or to refrain from listing his case, until he recovers enough to be tried (see Gostin, 1977). This is particularly unsatisfactory, now that the law has been changed for defendants found unfit to plead (see section (c) later). Legal advisers should do their best to get the case to court, so that decisions on guilt or innocence and the most appropriate disposal can be made.

A magistrates' court has power to commit direct to hospital an offender who is committed to the Crown Court specifically with a view to a restriction order being made (s. 43). The magistrates must already have convicted the offender and received the evidence necessary for a hospital order. They must also have evidence from the doctor who would be in charge, or some other representative of the hospital managers, that a bed is available, but in this case there is no 28 day time limit (s. 44). Once again, the committal has the same effect as a restriction order, which is scarcely an inducement to bring the case quickly before the Crown Court.

The Butler Committee were concerned that other disordered people might be languishing in prison without proper treatment while waiting for their cases to be heard. Under section 36 of the 1983 Act, the Crown Court has power to remand direct to hospital for treatment people who are awaiting trial or sentence for any offence punishable with imprisonment, except for murder. This is illogical: once a person is convicted of murder, the court has no choice, but a person awaiting trial may never be convicted, and in the meantime might be receiving the treatment he needs. The evidence of mental condition is the same as that required for a transfer from prison, except that treatment must be "appropriate" rather than urgently needed. There must be the usual evidence from the hospital that a bed will be available within seven days. As the object is to secure treatment for the patient's disorder, the usual provisions about medical treatment of detained patients apply (see Chapter 6). Apart from that, however, the effects of the order, its duration and renewal, are the same as in a remand to hospital for reports (see section (a) earlier).

As three months is by no means a long time to be waiting to appear in the Crown Court, these patients may well have to be returned to prison, unless the Home Secretary can be persuaded to make a transfer direction. It is ironic that a transfer ordered by the Crown Court should be so much less drastic in its effects than one which is directed by the Home Secretary. It scarcely indicates a consistent view about whether it is worse to languish in prison without treatment or to languish in hospital without trial. But transfer from prison may well be quicker and can operate as a substitute for trial in some cases. Its use is certainly increasing (Home Office, 1995a).

(c) Fitness to plead

Occasionally a person appearing before the Crown Court may be so disabled that he is unfit to stand trial. This has nothing to do with his state of mind at the time of the alleged offence. The question is whether he has "sufficient intellect" to be able to plead to the indictment and understand the proceedings sufficiently to be able to challenge jurors, take in the evidence, and make a proper defence (*R. v. Pritchard* (1836) 7 C. & P. 303). Someone suffering from amnesia about the relevant events, but who can understand the trial, is fit to be tried (*R. v. Podola* [1960] 1 Q.B. 325). An illiterate deaf-mute, or someone who is incapable of communicating with the court or his legal advisers, may not be (*R. v. Sharp* (1957) 41 Cr.App.R. 196). But the fact that the accused is highly abnormal and cannot act in his own best interests does not necessarily mean that he cannot understand the trial (*R. v. Robertson* (1968) 62 Cr.App.R. 690). The exclusion of amnesia is controversial; if genuine, it can obviously make it impossible for the accused to defend himself and is quite different from mere forgetfulness (Walker, 1981). Another difficulty with the present law is its all or nothing attitude. The accused may be able to understand a trial on a simple charge, but not on a more complicated matter. More controversial still is the emphasis on cognitive ability rather than mental state (Grubin, 1993). This means that there is no necessary connection between these criteria and those required for detention in hospital. It may also mean that it is thought either cruel to the defendant or an affront to the dignity of the court to make him stand trial.

Before the Criminal Procedure (Insanity and Unfitness to Plead) Act 1991, the inevitable result of a finding of disability (as it is technically called) was indefinite detention as a restriction order patient, with the prospect of eventually returning for trial when fit enough to do so. Not surprisingly, very few people claimed to be unfit.

The question is usually raised on arraignment before the trial begins.

Normally it must be decided as soon as it arises (Criminal Procedure (Insanity) Act 1964, s. 4(4)). However, the judge may postpone this until any time before the opening of the defence case, if having regard to the nature of the supposed disability, it is expedient and in the interests of the accused to do so (1964 Act, s. 4(2)); and if in the meantime the jury acquit him on all counts, it will never be decided at all (1964 Act, s. 4(3)). Although the Butler Committee proposed that a judge might decide the issue, it must still be tried by a jury. This will be a different jury from the one which hears the evidence in the case unless the question is decided during the trial, in which case the judge can choose whether or not a separate jury should determine it (1964 Act, s. 4(4)).

If the accused is found fit, then the trial will proceed in the normal way. If he is found unfit, then a jury must still decide whether or not they are satisfied that he did the act or made the omission charged; and if they are not he must be acquitted in the normal way (1964 Act, s. 4A). This requirement to hold as good a trial of the facts as is possible in the circumstances was one of the changes introduced by the 1991 Act, to meet the criticism that the accused might have a perfectly good defence to the charge. Grubin (1991) found that the evidence linking the accused to the offence "seemed good" in more than 80 per cent of cases but the same could probably be said of most prosecutions.

Perhaps more importantly, the 1991 Act also gave the court a choice between five different disposals. Except in a murder case, it can choose whichever is the most suitable:

(i) an order for admission to a hospital specified by the Secretary of State, with a restriction order of unlimited or specified duration (1964 Act, s. 5(2)(a) and 1991 Act, Sched. 1, para. 2(1)(b)); an unlimited restriction order is the only option available for murder charges (1964 Act, s. 5(3) and 1991 Act, Sched. 1, para. 2(2));

(ii) an order for admission to a hospital specified by the Secretary of State as if under an ordinary hospital order (1964 Act, s. 5(2)(a) and 1991 Act, Sched. 1, para. 2(1)(a)); the effect is just the same, except that there are two months rather than 28 days to get the patient to hospital (Sched. 1, para. 1(4); c.f. 1983 Act, s. 40(1), p. 120–121, later);

(iii) a guardianship order under the 1983 Act (1964 Act, s. 5(2)(b)(i)), provided that the court has the evidence required by section 37(1) of the 1983 Act for such an order (p. 128, later) (1991 Act, s. 5(2));

(iv) a supervision and treatment order under Schedule 2 to the 1991 Act (1964 Act, s. 5(2)(b)(ii)), provided that the court has evidence equivalent to that required for a psychiatric condition in a probation order (p. 115, later) (1991 Act, Sched. 2, para. 2(1)(b)); the patient is placed under the supervision of a social worker or a probation officer for a specified period of up to two years and must submit for all or some of that time to treatment by or under the direction of a registered medical practitioner (paras. 1(1), 4(1)); the treatment options are the same as those in a probation order (p. 116, later) (para. 4(2)); and the other details, for example about variation and discharge, are also similar; the main difference is that the patient's consent to the order is not required; and finally;

(v) if this would be the most suitable in all the circumstances of the case, an absolute discharge (1964 Act, s. 5(2)(b)(iii) and 1991 Act, s. 5(4)).

If the patient is sent to hospital with restrictions and these have not been lifted (under section 42(1) of the 1983 Act; p. 124, later), the Home Secretary can send the accused back for trial, either straight from hospital to the court or via a prison or remand centre, if he is satisfied after consultation with the RMO that the patient can properly be tried (1991 Act, Sched. 1, para. 4(1),(2)). Otherwise, the court's order is the end of the matter.

These changes certainly increase the attractions for the accused of raising the issue of fitness. If he has a defence to the charge, he now stands a much better chance of being acquitted altogether (a quarter of those found unfit from 1976 to 1988 were returned for trial of whom 6 per cent were acquitted; see Grubin, 1991). Even if he is found to have done the deed, the options available to the court are all therapeutic rather than punitive. However, because of the limitations of the other disposals, the court is probably still likely to be attracted by a restriction order if the offence charged is at all serious. The defendant may appeal (to the Court of Appeal) against a finding of disability or that he did the deed or made the omission charged, but apparently not against the disposal chosen. On the other hand, if admitted to hospital or guardianship, he can apply to a mental health review tribunal (see Chapter 8); if the grounds for admitting him under the 1983 Act do not exist he will have to be discharged.

Findings of disability are not available in magistrates' courts, but they have a different way of achieving a similar result (White, 1991). They have power to make a hospital order (without restrictions) over a mentally ill or severely impaired defendant without convicting him, provided that they are satisfied that he did the act or made the omission charged (1983 Act, s. 37(3). In *R. v. Lincoln (Kesteven) Magistrates' Court, ex p. O'Connor,* [1983] 1 W.L.R. 335, the accused was so severely handicapped that he was unable to understand what it meant to consent to summary trial on a charge which would usually give him the option of jury trial. The Divisional Court held that the magistrates could have made a hospital order without trying him, although it was stressed that the circumstances in which this would be appropriate were very rare and would usually require the consent of his lawyers. In *R. v. Ramsgate Justices, ex p. Kasmarek* (1984) 80 Cr.App.R. 366, the Court went further and held that magistrates could make a hospital order under section 37(3) even though the defendant had elected trial by jury. The offence must not, however, be one which can only be tried in the Crown Court (*R. v. Chippenham Magistrates' Court, ex p. Thompson, The Times,* December 6, 1995). It is still difficult to understand how the magistrates can be satisfied that he did the deed without holding some sort of trial.

It will also be interesting to see how Crown Court juries cope with having to decide the facts when the accused is unfit to stand trial. In practice there were probably many trials of unfit defendants in the past so the problem may not be so new after all.

3. MENTAL DISORDER AS A DEFENCE

(a) Insanity

The Criminal Procedure (Insanity and Unfitness to Plead) Act 1991 may also have a profound effect upon the willingness of defendants to plead that because of their mental disorder they were not responsible for actions which offended against the criminal law. Until that Act, any defendant who was found "not guilty by reason of insanity" (the "special verdict" laid down by the Trial of Lunatics Act 1883, s. 2(1)) had, like one found unfit to plead, to be detained indefinitely as a restriction order patient in a hospital specified by the Home Secretary. Hence the defence was unlikely to raise the matter unless the consequence of an ordinary conviction was likely to be worse. Even in a murder case, where the sentence has to be life imprisonment, the defence of diminished responsibility (see section (c) later) provided a wider and more flexible alternative. This perception, that a special verdict had a draconian effect to be avoided if possible, was not necessarily borne out in practice. Mackay (1990) showed that although rare, the defence was raised in cases other than murder; that more defendants were sent to NHS than to special hospitals; and that most of those sent to NHS hospitals were discharged within a relatively short time. Even so, most of the case law is not about the difference between guilt and insanity, but about the difference between innocence and insanity: if the judge ruled that the defence amounted to one of insanity, it might be rapidly withdrawn and a plea of guilty substituted.

But after the 1991 Act there is now the same range of disposals on a "special verdict" as on a finding of disability (see p. 109, earlier). This should make the defence of "insanity" more attractive and it will be interesting to see whether this has an effect upon its interpretation in the courts. The present rules were laid down by the judges in response to questions from the House of Lords in M'Naghten's Case (1843) 10 Cl. & Fin. 200. The accused must prove on the balance of probabilities (or to counter his claim of diminished responsibility or automatism the prosecution may prove, but beyond reasonable doubt) that at the time of his act he was "labouring under such defect of reason from disease of the mind as not to know the nature and quality of the act he was doing, or, if he did know it, that he did not know it was wrong."

This provides two different defences. An example of the first is assaulting someone with an axe believing him to be a block of wood. The disorder has negated the existence of the guilty mind, the element of intention or recklessness which depending upon the offence charged, which would normally be required for a conviction. An example of the second is killing someone in the belief that one is God and thus entitled to do it. To that extent, a person with a diseased mind is relieved from the presumption that we all know and understand the law and its relationship to our actions. Neither limb of the defence will excuse a man who knows what he is doing and knows it to be against the law, even though he is acting on the orders of his "voices", or under the delusion that his victim is persecuting him, or in the belief that he has a divine mission to exterminate prostitutes. Still less does it excuse a man whose perception, knowing and reasoning faculties are unaffected, but whose capacity to resist his impulses or conform his behaviour to the law is substantially impaired by his disorder. Attempts to refine the defence in the United States (e.g., Morris, 1978) tend to concentrate on whether these sorts of case should be included.

Most of the English case law, however, is concerned with the distinction between the man who does not know what he is doing because of "disease of the mind" and the man who is not in control of his bodily functions for some other reason (such as a fit of sneezing or sleep-walking) and is entitled to an ordinary acquittal because of "non-insane automatism". What does the law mean by a "disease of the mind"? It is not limited to mental illnesses in the psychiatric sense, which was certainly what the judges were dealing with in M'Naghten's Case, but can include physical and neurological conditions which impair mental functioning, either tempo-rarily or permanently. The judges approach this question in the light of what they now acknowledge to be the purpose of the special verdict, which is not to excuse the defendant but to protect society against the recurrence of dangerous conduct.

In *R. v. Kemp* [1957] 1 Q.B. 399, Devlin J. defined "mind" in its ordinary sense of the mental faculties of reason, memory and understanding. Insanity could therefore include a malfunctioning of these faculties brought on by arterio-sclerosis. This definition was adopted by Lord Diplock in the unanimous but controversial House of Lords decision in *R. v. Sullivan* [1984] A.C. 156 (following *Bratty v. Att.-Gen. for Northern Ireland* [1963] A.C. 383), which concerned the unconscious violence of an epileptic in the post-ictal stage of grand mal. The defence argued that the M'Naghten rules did not apply at all to unconscious movements, as opposed to those carried out in a deluded state of consciousness. But the House held that "not to know the nature and quality of the act" did include not knowing what he was doing at all. The defence also argued that the loss of consciousness was not caused by mental disease, for this could not include a loss of faculties which lasted for such a short time. But their lordships decided that:

> "if the effect of a disease was to impair those faculties so severely as to have either of the consequences referred to in the latter part of the rules, it mattered not whether the impairment was organic, as in epilepsy, or functional, or whether the impairment was permanent or was transient and intermittent, provided that it subsisted at the time of the commission of the act."

However, they did not rule out the possibility of non-insane automatism if a temporary impairment resulted from some external factor, such as a blow on the head or the therapeutic administration of drugs. Such a transitory malfunctioning was held not to be disease of the mind in *R. v. Quick* [1973] Q.B. 910, which concerned *hypo*glycaemia brought on by a combination of insulin, alcohol and lack of food. However, a diabetic who knows that this might make him aggressive or uncontrolled could be sufficiently reckless to justify a conviction for a crime which does not require any specific intent (*R. v. Bailey* [1983] 1 W.L.R. 760). Further, it was held in *R. v. Hennessey* [1989] 1 W.L.R. 287 that malfunctioning brought on by *hyper*glycaemia caused by a diabetic *not* taking his insulin was a disease of the mind. The test is, therefore, not the nature of the underlying disability, but whether it is the disability or some external factor which has caused the loss of control. Sleep-walking is caused by an internal factor which can amount to a disease of the mind, especially if it results in violence and may recur (*R. v. Burgess* (1991) 93 Cr.App.R. 41).

The so-called hysterical dissociated states also cause difficulty, not least to those judges who find it hard to believe that the accused was indeed unconscious of what he was doing. If a man, for example, is driving purposefully and therefore partially in control, "hysterical fugue" is no defence to a charge of doing so recklessly (see *R. v. Isitt* (1977) 67 Cr.App.R. 44; see also *Att.-Gen.s Reference (No. 2 of 1992)*, *The Times*, May 31, 1992). However, the list of "external factors" is not closed. One judge in the Crown Court, for example, has ruled that post traumatic stress disorder, resulting from rape, was not a disease of the mind, so that if it led to complete rather than partial loss of control, the defence of non-insane automatism could be raised (*R. v. T.* [1990] Crim. L.R. 256).

Transitory malfunctionings which are unrelated to any underlying disability should still lead to an acquittal. So should failure to use one's mental faculties, for example when walking out of a shop without paying in a fit of absence of mind, even if this is exacerbated by depression (*R. v.*

Clarke [1972] 1 All E.R. 209). But what if someone suggests that the element of dishonesty, required in many offences against property, is not present, for example because as a result of post traumatic stress disorder he did not realise that he should not have been claiming means-tested benefits while working? Despite *R. v. T.*, this would appear to fall squarely within the second limb of the rules.

The Butler Committee proposed a special verdict of "not guilty on evidence of mental disorder" to cover two situations. The first was where evidence of any type of disorder is put forward to negative the existence of the state of mind required for the particular offence. This would be roughly equivalent to the first limb of the rules but would bring in, they thought, all cases of non-insane automatism. The Committee also favoured a specific exception for transitory states produced by the use or non-use of drugs or alcohol, or by physical injury.

This is very like the present law on automatism, except that the courts do not except non-use of drugs (*Hennessey*) but might except some other external factors (*R. v. T.*). However, it is much wider than the present law in that it would bring within the special verdict people like Mrs Clarke, who did not intend to steal because of a mild mental condition, which might affect any one but still falls within the wide definition of mental disorder in the Act. The Law Commission (1989) expressed surprise at this and in their draft criminal code have limited the special verdict to "severe mental illness" (see p. 33, earlier), pathological automatism which is liable to recur, and arrested or incomplete development of mind (but with misgivings about the last, because it could bring in so many mentally handicapped people who should at present be completely acquitted).

The Butler Committee's second proposal was that the defence should be available whenever the accused was suffering from "severe mental illness" or severe mental handicap (not limited to mental impairment under the 1983 Act). There would be no need to prove any causal connection between the disorder and the offence, for lack of any real blameworthiness could be assumed. This reflects the humane concern of doctors and others who do not like to see the poor in mind even put on trial, let alone punished. Nor do they like to be asked to speculate about precisely what the accused was thinking as he wielded the axe.

This may be practical but it is also unprincipled. In incorporating the substance of the Butler Committee's recommendations into its draft criminal code, the Law Commission (1989) therefore provided that the prosecution might negative this defence by proving the lack of any causal connection between the severe disorder and the commission of the crime. But as yet the Government has shown no inclination to implement any of these recommendations.

(b) Infanticide

This offence was created in 1938 to mitigate the then mandatory death sentence for murder (although these women were generally reprieved). It applies where a woman kills her child of under 12 months when her mind is "disturbed by reason of not having fully recovered from the effect of giving birth to the child or by reason of the effect of lactation consequent on the birth" (Infanticide Act 1938). The court can then impose any penalty it thinks fit and imprisonment is now quite rare. The offence may be ripe for abolition, now that much the same ground is covered by the defence of diminished responsibility, which can also refer to the killing of a child over 12 months or of a different child. The Criminal Law Revision Committee (1980a) wished to retain it, because psychiatrists had suggested several examples which would be infanticide but not diminished responsibility. These all related to the stresses caused by having to cope with a new baby in poverty-stricken or other socially deprived environments, or by not being able to cope with these pressures or to relate properly to the new baby. Clearly, the offence was being used in circumstances far wider than those originally intended. The committee proposed amending it to cover stresses caused by "circumstances consequent on the birth", as well as the effects of the birth itself. But should these amount to an excuse at all? If they should, why should they not apply to fathers? Or to other people who are driven to killing by the intolerable pressures of their surroundings although unprovoked by their victims?

(c) Diminished responsibility

The defence of diminished responsibility was also introduced to mitigate the mandatory sentences of death or life imprisonment for murder. It results in a conviction for manslaughter, for which the sentence is quite at large. It is now accepted that the judge may agree to the plea without a trial where the medical evidence is not challenged (*R. v. Cox* (1968) 52 Cr.App.R. 130; see also *R. v. Vinagre* (1979) 69 Cr.App.R. 104). In 1976 and 1977, for example, the defence was only challenged by the prosecution or the judge in 29 out of the 194 cases in which it was raised, and failed in 18 of these, giving an overall failure rate of less than 10 per cent (Dell, 1982). The accused must be "suffering from such abnormality of mind (whether arising from a condition of arrested or retarded development of mind or any inherent cause or induced by disease or injury) as substantially impaired his mental responsibility for his acts or omissions in doing or being a party to the killing" (Homicide Act 1957, s. 2).

"Abnormality of mind" has been widely construed as a "state of mind so different from that of ordinary human beings that a reasonable man would term it abnormal" (*R. v. Byrne* [1960] 2 Q.B. 396). This is similar to, but even wider than, the "man must be mad" test for mental illness, because it can cover personality disorders including psychopathy, and transient abnormalities of the sort which may result in mercy killings or battered babies. But it is stretching the words "arising from a condition of arrested or retarded development of mind or any inherent cause or induced by disease or injury" to apply them to the latter and there is ample evidence that doctors do this. They, and the Criminal Law Revision Committee (1980a), would prefer to replace the medical criterion with "mental disorder" as defined in the Mental Health Act.

The second element, substantial impairment of responsibility, is a moral question on which doctors have no particular expertise, although they are often asked to express an opinion. Logically, it should have some connection with the legal definition of responsibility for the offence. The problem is then very similar to that in insanity. If someone knows what he is doing, knows it to be wrong, and could have prevented himself if he chose, how can we say that he was not responsible? And how is it possible to have degrees of such responsibility? What the defence is really getting at is degrees of moral turpitude, which is a rather different matter. The Butler Committee's suggestion was that the disorder should be "such as to be an extenuating circumstance which ought to reduce the offence." The Criminal Law Revision Committee, however, thought this too lax and suggested "a substantial enough reason to reduce this offence to manslaughter" (see also Law Commission, 1989). This at least points the jury towards the real issue.

Many, including the Butler Committee (see also Walker, 1981; Dell, 1982) would prefer to solve the whole problem by abolishing both the mandatory life sentence for murder and diminished responsibility, leaving sentencing in all these cases to the discretion of the judge. This would not absolve the judiciary from the need to distinguish those offenders who were scarcely morally reprehensible at all, from those with some degree of blameworthiness, and those so wicked or dangerous that a life sentence is merited. However, abolition at the mandatory life sentence does not necessarily mean that diminished responsibility should go. Juries might shrink from convicting at all if this less stigmatising verdict were not available; and judges prefer to have the benefit of the jury's view in a disputed case. The House of Lords Select Committee on Murder and Life Imprisonment (1989) favoured abolition of the mandatory penalty for murder but also retention of both diminished responsibility and infanticide.

4. SENTENCING

While the law has so far stuck to a very strict view on criminal responsibility, it has now been provided with a wide range of non-penal methods of disposal after conviction. There are five specifically psychiatric orders, and also the possibility that an offender who is sent to prison may later be transferred to hospital. We must also consider what the court might do if a therapeutic disposal is neither available nor appropriate. It cannot defer sentence on condition that the offender attends a psychiatric hospital (*R. v. Skelton* [1983] Crim. L.R. 686).

(a) Psychiatric probation or supervision orders

Probation orders require an offender aged 16 or over to be under the supervision of a probation officer for a specified period of between six months and three years. They may be made in any court for any offence apart, in practice, from murder, but there is no power to order probation without convicting (Powers of Criminal Courts Act 1973, s. 2). Supervision orders are the equivalent for offenders under the age of 18 (Children and Young Persons Act 1969, ss. 7(7)(b)). There is no minimum duration for a supervision order (1969 Act, s. 17) and the supervisor may (and if the child is under 13 and no probation officer is working with the family must) be a local authority social worker rather than a probation officer (s. 13).

The variety of conditions which may be inserted in probation and supervision orders has been steadily growing, but requirements for psychiatric treatment have a longer history than most. Probation was first introduced in 1907 and with the growth of psychiatric out-patient clinics and voluntary hospital treatment in the 1930s, some enterprising magistrates began to use it as an unofficial means of persuading disordered offenders to seek treatment. The position was regularised in 1948, when express power to insert such conditions was granted. Similar conditions can also be imposed in supervision orders made in family proceedings under the Children Act 1989 (p. 63, earlier).

The court must have evidence from one approved doctor (p. 67, earlier) that the offender's mental condition is such as requires and may be susceptible to treatment but is not such as to warrant the making of a hospital order under the Mental Health Act 1983 (1973 Act, s. 3(3) and Sched. 1A, para. 5(1); 1969 Act, s. 12B(1); 1989 Act, Sched. 3, para. 5(1)). Strictly, then, the court cannot choose between the two as the medical requirements are mutually exclusive. If satisfied that arrangements for the treatment have been made, the court can then insert one of three conditions: in-patient treatment in a hospital (but not a special hospital) or mental nursing home, out day-patient treatment at a specified institution or place, or treatment by or under the direction of a named doctor (1973 Act, Sched. 1A, para. 5(2)–(4); 1969 Act, s. 12B(1),(2)(a); 1989 Act, Sched. 3, para. 5(2),(5)(b)). Further than this, the court is not allowed to be precise: the doctor himself may direct analysis or other forms of therapy by another professional under medical supervision. The condition may be imposed for the whole or only part of the period of the order, but a psychiatric condition in a supervision order cannot continue after the patient reaches 18 (1969 Act, s. 12B(2); supervision orders in family cases end automatically when the child reaches 18, 1989 Act, s. 91(13)). A condition can be inserted in an existing order, but only within the first three months, which may be too soon for the supervisor to discover the need (Criminal Justice Act 1991, Sched. 2, para. 13(2)(a)(ii); 1969 Act, s. 15(2)(b); there is no such restriction in the 1989 Act).

The court must explain all the requirements of a probation order and obtain the offender's consent (1973 Act, s. 2(3)). This does not apply to supervision as such, but the consent of a person of 14 or over must be obtained for a psychiatric condition (1969 Act, ss. 12B(2)(b) and 16(7); the 1989 Act requires the consent of a child of "sufficient understanding to make an informed decision", Sched. 3, para. 5(5)). The doctor in charge of a person on probation may himself make arrangements for part of the patient's treatment to be in a different place from the one specified in the order, provided that the patient agrees. This can include arranging in-patient treatment at a place which could not have been specified in the original order. It is unlikely that this means that doctor and patient can agree on in-patient treatment even though the court required only out-patient attendance. It is also unlikely that they can agree on treatment in a special hospital (which ought to be reserved for detained patients), but they might choose a place which was not a hospital or mental nursing home. These changes do not have to be reported to the court, but the doctor must tell the supervisor, and the treatment is then automatically deemed part of the order (1973 Act, Sched. 1A, para. 5(6)–(8); there is no equivalent for supervision orders).

The doctor can also report to the supervisor if for any reason he is no longer willing to be responsible for the patient; or if he thinks that the treatment should continue beyond the period specified, or that the patient needs a different one of the three kinds of treatment, or that he is not susceptible to or no longer requires treatment. The supervisor must then apply to the court for the condition to be varied or cancelled accordingly. The Act does not insist that the court does so, but usually it will have little choice (1991 Act, Sched. 2, para. 14; 1969 Act, s. 15(9),(10); 1989 Act, Sched. 3, para. 5(6),(7)).

So what is to happen if, having given his consent in court (which many might do to avoid a worse fate), the patient later changes his mind and refuses to co-operate with his doctor? Variation or cancellation negates the court's object; and even if the requirement is for in-patient treatment, the admission is normally informal, so that the hospital can neither detain him nor treat him against his will. The doctor can only report to the supervisor, who may take proceedings for breach. In a probation order, the possible sanctions are a fine, a community service order, an attendance centre order if the offender is under 21, or to sentence him afresh for the original offence (1991 Act, Sched. 2, paras. 3(1), 4(1). But it is expressly laid down that a person on probation cannot be dealt with for breach of the order when all he has done is to refuse to undergo any surgical, electrical or other treatment, if the court decides that the refusal is reasonable in all the circumstances (1991 Act, Sched. 2, para. 5(2)). While there are sanctions for failing to comply with some requirements in supervision orders under the 1969 Act, there are none for failing to comply with a requirement for psychiatric treatment. There are no sanctions against a child who fails to comply with a supervision order under the 1989 Act.

Not surprisingly, therefore, opinions differ as to the efficacy of these orders. Therapeutically, it may be preferable to a hospital order because there is less and less need for even the most seriously disordered to be detained in hospital and the order allows a flexible combination of medical care and supervision. On the other hand, evasion is relatively easy, and there have been failures of communication between the medical and supervising authorities. The supervisor is expressly precluded from actively supervising a person on probation while he is an in-patient in hospital (1973 Act, Sched. 1A, para. 5(5)), and the hospital is not always quick to inform him of discharge or non-cooperation. It would help if a clear indication of exactly what was expected of patient, doctor and supervisor is given at the outset (Lewis, 1980). These orders have been the most common form of psychiatric disposal, but their use has been declining.

This could be, at least partly, because it is now also possible to insert in a probation order a requirement for an offender to have treatment for his alcohol or drug dependency (1973 Act, s. 3(3) and Sched. 1A, para. 6). The court must be satisfied of the offender's dependency on drugs or alcohol, that this caused or contributed to the offence in question, and that it requires and may be susceptible to treatment. The treatment required will be under the direction of a suitably qualified person, not necessarily a doctor, but all the other provisions are either (in the 1973 Act, Sched. 1A, para. 6) exactly equivalent to or (in the 1991 Act, Sched. 2) the same as those for psychiatric treatment.

(b) Hospital orders

The 1959 Act gave the courts power to send a wide range of mentally disordered offenders to hospital. Similar powers had existed before then only in relation to "mental defectives", although these included what are now called psychopaths. In theory the choice became a simple one: either the offender was "bad" and should receive the penalty appropriate to the gravity of his offence and his previous record, or he was "mad" and should be committed to the medical authorities for as long as was necessary to cure him. Unless extra restrictions were needed to protect the public, the policy was to make the position of those for whom the courts had chosen a therapeutic rather than a penal disposal as similar as possible to those admitted for treatment under civil powers.

A hospital order can be made for any offence for which the trial court could have sentenced the offender to imprisonment or some other form of custody, apart from murder which has a fixed penalty (1983 Act, s. 37(1)). The Crown Court must actually convict the offender, unless he has already been transferred from prison to hospital before trial or committed to hospital by the magistrates with a view to a restriction order being made. Magistrates, however, may impose a hospital order on a mentally ill or severely impaired defendant without recording a conviction, provided that they are satisfied that he did the act or made the omission charged (s. 37(3)). The offence must be triable summarily (even if the accused has the option of trial by jury) but it appears that they need not always hold a trial in the strict sense (see cases cited at p. 110, earlier).

The medical criteria. Two doctors, one of them approved, must state that the offender is suffering from mental illness, psychopathic disorder, severe mental impairment or mental impairment. The disorder must be "of a nature or degree which makes it appropriate for him to be detained in a hospital for medical treatment." In the case of psychopathic disorder and mild mental impairment, this treatment must be likely to alleviate or prevent a deterioration of his condition (s. 37(2)(a)(i)). The doctors must agree on one of the four forms of disorder, although they may differ about whether he also suffers from any other. The court must specify its conclusion on this (s. 37(7)).

The definitions of the various forms of disorder have already been discussed in Chapter 2, but several points are particularly important here. The residuary category of "any other disorder or disability of mind" is not enough for a hospital order, and neither is the broader concept of mental handicap. The patient must either be mentally ill or he must exhibit abnormally aggressive or seriously irresponsible conduct. The latter may either be the result of a persistent disorder or disability of mind (psychopathy) or allied to severe or significant impairment of intelligence and social functioning (s. 1(2)).

Because the broader categories are excluded, doctors may well have been tempted to apply a wider concept of mental illness. There is certainly evidence of this in Walker and McCabe's study (1973), particularly in relation to sex offenders and drug addicts. The 1983 Act now excludes people whose only problem is promiscuity or other immoral conduct, sexual deviation or dependence on alcohol or drugs (s. 1(3)). If a doctor wishes to recommend a hospital order for such people, he will have to give evidence of some specific psychiatric illness or psychopathic disorder.

It is difficult to judge the effect of the narrower definition of mental handicap. Perhaps most crimes are "seriously irresponsible" even if they are not "abnormally aggressive". But it is just these inadequate and inconvenient offenders who reveal the greatest gap between the expectations of the courts and the policies of the health service. The courts do not like sending handicapped people to prison, and are proving increasingly reluctant to do so (see section (f) below). There is very little secure provision for them outside the special hospitals. Ordinary NHS hospitals do not like having them. This is only partly because they might be difficult to manage. The place for able-bodied people with learning disabilities is in the community, rather than in a hospital, where they can rarely be cured by conventional psychiatric treatment and may have to stay for a very long time before anyone can be satisfied that they are unlikely to offend again.

The "treatability" test reflects the medical view. It reduces still further the scope for sending the less severely disabled offenders to hospital. But it was mainly introduced because the Butler Committee were persuaded that the responsibility for dealing with dangerous psychopaths should be squarely placed on the prison rather than the hospital services. "Much good work" takes place in prison, especially at Grendon Underwood.

Having once been quite anxious to claim that they could alter aberrant personalities, the medical profession now admit that there is often little they can do. The jury is still out on whether hospital treatment can indeed make psychopaths better or at least prevent their getting worse (Reed, 1994b).

In practice, however, it is the requirement that a bed in a named hospital be available within 28 days of the order (s. 37(4)) which means that the doctors can pick and choose. The decision to offer a bed is that of the hospital managers, acting on the advice of the clinical team under the leadership of the RMO. Consultant psychiatrists these days recognise that other professions, particularly the nursing staff who will have day-to-day contact with the patient, must have a voice in deciding who can be accepted on to their wards. But in effect the decision is theirs. The difficulties in finding a suitable bed, and the courts' powers to put pressure upon the authorities to do so, have already been mentioned (see p. 19, earlier).

The judicial criteria. Once it has the required medical evidence, the court must decide whether the order is the most suitable way of disposing of the case, having regard to all the circumstances including the nature of the offence, the character and antecedents of the offender, and to the other available methods of dealing with him (s. 37(2)(b)). The court cannot impose a fine, custodial sentence, probation, supervision or parental recognisances order as well as a hospital order, although it can make other additional orders, for example for compensation (s. 37(8)).

In principle, the court should decide whether punishment or treatment is appropriate and make its choice accordingly. In *R. v. Gunnell* (1966) 50 Cr.App.R. 242, it was held that an offender who deserved punishment could be sent to prison, even though he qualified for a hospital order and a suitable bed was available. Once it has been decided that treatment is appropriate, the court can go on to consider whether a restriction order should be added to the basic hospital order. In practice, however, these neat distinctions are not so easy to apply, partly because an offender can be both "mad" and "bad" (Rollin, 1969), and partly because of the scarcity of hospital beds which the courts regard as suitable.

The court is entitled to take into account the need to protect the public (*R. v. Higginbotham* [1961] 1 W.L.R. 1277). In *R. v. Gardiner* [1967] 1 W.L.R. 464, the Court of Appeal drew attention to the deficiencies of an ordinary hospital order in this respect. The hospital may discharge the patient at any time and is quite likely to do so within a year. It may make little attempt to recapture him if he absconds (although it is no longer so easy to obtain one's discharge simply by remaining at large; see Chapter 7). His detention cannot be renewed beyond the initial six months unless the medical criteria still exist. These include a treatability test which applies even to mentally ill and severely impaired patients, although in a more limited way (see Chapter 4). There are only limited powers to recall him to hospital or to insist upon after-care (although both have become easier; see Chapter 7). Even a restriction order no longer solves all of these problems. In any event, it deals only with the patient's legal status. Unless a bed is found in a special hospital or secure unit (for which a restriction order is not essential) the practical problem of security will remain. Hence the deciding factor for the court is often, not whether a bed is available, but whether a bed which the court thinks sufficiently secure is available (see *R. v. Morris* [1961] 2 Q.B. 237; *R. v. Cox* (1967) 52 Cr.App.R. 130; *R. v. McFarlane* (1975) 60 Cr.App.R. 320; *R. v. Harding (Bernard), The Times,* June 15, 1983).

On the other hand, if such a bed can be found, the courts seem only too happy to accede to the medical recommendations. They have been as vociferous as any in pressing for more NHS secure accommodation. In *R. v. Harding (Bernard), The Times,* June 15, 1983, Lawton L.J. remarked that it was a form of cruelty to keep a mentally sick person in prison. Of course, a hospital order may be equally severe in some cases. Some offenders are likely to remain in hospital for longer than they would have stayed in prison, and in these days of increasing alternatives to custody some might have avoided prison altogether. The utilitarian answer (Walker and McCabe, 1973) is that, however it may seem to the patient, it is not unjust to make the commission of an offence the "occasion" for sending to hospital a patient who ought to be there and who could just as easily have been "sectioned" under civil powers. This is a little too neat. The patient might never have been considered a suitable case for compulsory hospitalisation had it not been for the offence. The offence will undoubtedly colour the views of both the hospital and any tribunal about whether or not he should be discharged (see Peay, 1989).

The law itself is a little inconsistent about the justice of imposing a hospital order. The offence must be punishable with imprisonment. But the courts do not seem to take the triviality of the offence into account and the Court of Appeal has refused to regard a hospital order, even an unlimited restriction order, as "more severe" than a prison sentence (*R. v. Bennett* [1968] 1 W.L.R. 988; *R. v. Sodhi* [1978] Crim. L.R. 565). This means that it can be substituted for a custodial sentence on appeal.

The Butler Committee were similarly ambivalent. In general, they approved heartily of the hospital order system, which accords well with their mixture of therapeutic positivism and concern for the protection of the public. But they did recommend that mentally handicapped people should not be sent to hospital without the evidence of a specialist in mental handicap, because they were concerned about the possible injustice. They also proposed that a hospital order should not be substituted on appeal without the offender's consent. Gostin (1977), on the other hand, suggested that a hospital order should never be made without consent. This is not as radical as it seems. Hospitals much prefer their patients to be receptive to the idea of treatment and consent is already needed to the rather more common probation order with a condition of psychiatric treatment.

The notion that an offender should not be allowed to choose his punishment, while it may have merit, ought not to be applied to orders which are not supposed to be punishments at all. The question is, rather, whether a person whom we are prepared to call an offender should be entitled to the benefit of the normal principle of proportionality in sentencing, unless both he and the court are prepared to waive it.

The legal effect. Ordinary hospital orders are almost indistinguishable from admissions for treatment under civil powers. All the rules relating to the duration and renewal of detention, reclassification, leave of absence, absconding, and discharge by the authorities are the same (1983 Act, s. 40(4) and Sched. 1, Pt. 1). There are only two important differences. First, the patient's nearest relative cannot discharge him, but can instead apply for the case to be reviewed by a tribunal within the same periods that the patient himself can apply (s. 69(1)(a)). Secondly, the offender does not have the right of a civil patient admitted for treatment to apply to a tribunal within the first six months of his admission. This was removed from ordinary hospital order patients when restriction order patients were given

120

rights of application (as a result of the decision of the European Court of Human Rights in *X. v. United Kingdom* (1981) 4 E.H.R.R. 181). Understandably, the Government did not see why restriction order patients should be allowed to go to a tribunal within six months of a court's decision that they were a serious risk to the public. But the right to a review is one of those "set forth in the Convention" and under Article 14 these must be enjoyed by all "without discrimination on any ground such as sex, race, colour, language, religion, political or other opinion, national or social origin, association with a national minority, property, birth or other status." It was feared that restricted patients might complain of discrimination if ordinary hospital order patients could apply when they could not. Hence a right which had existed since the 1959 Act, had never been known to cause difficulties, but might benefit a few patients (of whom Michael Fagan, the Queen's intruder, was one) was taken away.

The hospital order is authority for a police officer, approved social worker (ASW) or any other person directed to do so by the court, to take the patient to the named hospital within 28 days, and for the hospital to detain him (s. 40(1)). Once he is admitted, any previous compulsory admission or hospital order ceases to have effect, unless the new order is quashed on appeal (s. 40(5)). The court may direct that he is kept in a place of safety, usually the prison where he was held on remand, in the meantime (s. 37(4); for the definition, p. 105, earlier). If the Home Secretary finds that, because of an emergency or some other special circumstances, it is not possible to admit him to the named hospital, he may arrange admission to another one (s. 37(5)).

(c) Interim hospital orders

The stark choice between treating an offender as mad or bad was thought, by the Butler Committee and others, to present another difficulty. Unlike a probation order, a hospital order gives no means of returning to court for a more suitable disposal if it turns out that a mistake has been made. It may not matter if an offender is discharged from hospital in a very short time because his illness has been cured or brought under control. It does matter if there has been a mistaken diagnosis (perhaps brought about by his own deception), or if there is no suitable treatment, or if he has refused to co-operate with any sort of treatment. The power to remand to hospital for reports or for treatment may help to avoid these mistakes, but the 1983 Act also allows the courts to have a "second bite at the cherry" through the medium of interim hospital orders under section 38. The court must have convicted the defendant of an offence which would qualify for a full hospital order. There must be evidence from two doctors, one of them approved, and at least one of them employed at the hospital which is named in the order (s. 38(3)). They must state that the offender is suffering from mental illness, psychopathic disorder, severe mental impairment or mental impairment. There is no room here for a tentative diagnosis, as there is in a remand for reports. There must also be "reason to suppose that the mental disorder from which the offender is suffering is such that it may be appropriate for a hospital order to be made in his case" (s. 38(1)). There must be the usual evidence from the proposed RMO or the hospital managers that a bed will be available within 28 days (s. 38(4)). The court's power to require information about possible beds from the regional health authority applies to interim as well as to full hospital orders

(s. 39). The court then has a complete discretion to try an interim order before finally deciding how to deal with the offender.

If an interim order is made, the patient can be kept in a place of safety before he is taken to hospital by a police officer, ASW or other person directed to do so by the court. The hospital must then detain him in accordance with the order (s. 40(3)). The usual provisions about the medical treatment of detained patients apply (s. 56(1)). Otherwise, however, the order is not like an ordinary hospital order. Neither the patient nor his nearest relative may apply to a mental health review tribunal. No one has any right to discharge the patient or even to grant him leave of absence. If he absconds, a police officer may arrest him without warrant and must then bring him as soon as practicable back to the court which made the order (s. 38(7)). The order lasts in the first instance for whatever period the court specifies, up to a maximum of 12 weeks. The court may renew it for further periods of 28 days at a time, up to a maximum of six months in all, if the RMO reports that this is warranted (s. 38(5)). The patient does not have to be there at renewal, provided that he has a legal representative who is given an opportunity of being heard (s. 38(6)). The court may even replace the interim order with a full hospital order without the patient being there, but with the same proviso (s. 38(2)). But if the RMO reports against renewing the interim order or making a full order, or if the court wishes to do something different, he must be brought back to court for the decision about what to do instead.

Once an interim order is at an end, the court has a completely free choice among the disposals available for the offence in question. If the evidence is there, it may make a full hospital order. This means that the patient will have to spend another six months in hospital before his case can be reviewed by a tribunal. On the other hand, the court could choose to impose a penalty. This may be all very well if the offender turns out not to have been mentally disordered after all or to be unsuitable for medical treatment. Even then, it seems undesirable to impose a further custodial sentence if only a short period in custody would have been appropriate. It would be quite wrong to impose an alternative penalty if the hospital order turns out to have been such a wise choice that the offender has already been cured. The court may be tempted to make a probation order with a condition of some form of psychiatric after-care in such a case. But it should not be forgotten that the court could not have done this had it made a full hospital order in the first place.

(d) Restriction orders

Restriction orders are the most controversial form of psychiatric disposal. They were originally an attempt to combine the advantages of a hospital order with the advantages of indefinite preventive detention coupled with a power of recall after release. The decision of the European Court of Human Rights in *X. v. United Kingdom* (1981) 4 E.H.R.R. 181, forced a reconsideration of this.

The court's powers. A restriction order can only be made in the Crown Court (s. 41(1)). If magistrates have convicted an offender aged 14 or more, and have the evidence required for a hospital order, they may commit him to the Crown Court with a view to a restriction order being made (s. 43(1)). If a bed is available, this can be direct to hospital (s. 44). If the Crown Court disagrees with the magistrates, it may only impose an order or penalty which they could have imposed, unless the magistrates have also committed him with a view to a greater penalty than they can give. The Crown Court can remand to hospital for reports or treatment, or make an interim order, as if it had itself convicted the offender (s. 43(2), (4) and (3)).

The court must always have the evidence required for an ordinary hospital order and one of the doctors must attend to give evidence in person (s. 41(2)). This does not have to be the doctor who would be in charge of the patient, although the court must have the usual evidence that a bed will be available. It is obviously important to have the hospital's views about whether restrictions are appropriate, but in the end the matter is one for the judge (*R. v. Blackwood* (1974) 59 Cr.App.R. 246; *R. v. Royse* [1981] Crim. L.R. 426).

The court must consider the restriction order necessary "for the protection of the public from serious harm", having regard to the nature of the offence, the antecedents of the offender, and the risk of his committing further offences if set at large (s. 41(1)). The 1959 Act did not refer to the need to protect the public from serious harm and the Butler Committee believed that orders were being made in cases where their severity was not appropriate. Gostin (1977) could certainly supply examples. Amongst the most obvious was Nigel Smith (see *R. v. McFarlane* (1975) 60 Cr.App.R. 320, p. 23, earlier). He was a "petty fraudster" with no history of violence or even mental illness, who found himself not only in Broadmoor, but also under a restriction order of unlimited duration. Once a court has imposed restrictions, the burden on the offender to justify his release becomes very considerable. It is difficult to say what effect the tightened criteria have had. Hospital orders of either kind are not common and there may be many reasons for the fluctuations in the numbers and proportion of restriction orders. There are also discrepancies between the Department of Health (1995a) and Home Office (1995a) figures. According to the former, there were 347 admissions under restriction orders and 625 under ordinary hospital orders in England in 1992/3, but the Home Office seem to have been aware of rather fewer. However, once there, restriction order patients stay longer and so form a much higher proportion of resident hospital order patients, especially in special hospitals.

In *R. v. Courtney* [1988] Crim. L.R. 730, the Court of Appeal quashed a restriction order upon a man of good character, who had killed his wife while undergoing treatment for depression, because there was no medical evidence that he was a danger to the public at large. In *R. v. Birch* (1989) 90 Cr.App.R. 78, however, it was pointed out that the question was *not* the seriousness of the risk of re-offending but the seriousness of the harm which the public would suffer if he did so. A high probability of repeating minor offences was *not* enough. However, if there was a risk of serious harm, there was no requirement of proportionality: the index offence need not itself be serious (see *R. v. Kean* (1987) 9 Cr.App.R.(S.) 455). Nevertheless, the 1983 Act had not affected the decision in *R. v. Gardiner* [1967] 1 W.L.R. 464: there the Court of Appeal had said that there should be compelling reasons for not imposing restrictions in crimes of violence or the more serious sex offences, particularly if the offender has a similar record or a history of mental disorder involving violent behaviour. *Birch* itself concerned a wife who had shot and killed her husband, and a low risk of repeating such a serious offence could justify a restriction order; but in that case there was no material on which to conclude that the order was necessary. As in *Courtney*, it was quashed, leaving the defendant subject to an ordinary hospital order.

Effects. Restrictions may be imposed for a definite period or without limit of time (s. 41(1)). Unlike prison sentences, the purpose is not to reflect the gravity of the offence in their length but to ensure that the patient is not discharged until he is ready. As there is usually no means of knowing when this will be, the Court of Appeal stated in *R. v. Gardiner* [1967] 1 W.L.R. 464 that unlimited orders should be made unless the doctors could confidently predict recovery within a limited period. The Butler Committee considered that the power to prescribe a time limit was illogical and should be abolished. This has not been done, but the *Gardiner* approach was approved in *R. v. Birch* (1989) 90 Cr.App.R. 78 (see also *R. v. Haynes* [1982] Crim. L.R. 245; *R. v. Nwohia, The Times*, May 18, 1995).

The Home Secretary can lift the restrictions at any time, if he is satisfied that they are no longer necessary to protect the public from serious harm (s. 42(1)). If the patient is still in hospital when the restrictions end, either because the court specified a limited duration or the Home Secretary has lifted them, he is treated as if he had been admitted under an ordinary hospital order on the day the restriction order ended (ss. 41(5) and 42(1)), but he will be able to apply to a tribunal during the first six months. If, however, the patient has been conditionally discharged from hospital before the restrictions end, he will achieve an automatic absolute discharge on that date (s. 42(5)).

While the restrictions last, they are still severe (see further in Chapter 7). The patient cannot be discharged, transferred to another hospital, or even given leave of absence, without the Home Secretary's consent (s. 41(3)(c)). Either the Home Secretary or the RMO may recall him from leave, and the former is not bound by the usual time limit (s. 41(3)(d)). Absconders can be recaptured at any time and so can never obtain their "discharge by operation of law" (s. 41(3)(d)). The Home Secretary has an independent power to discharge the patient, which is more commonly used because the discharge may be absolute or conditional (s. 42(2)). A conditionally discharged patient is subject to compulsory after-care (although not medical treatment) and may be recalled to hospital at any time (s. 42(3)).

The other crucial difference between an ordinary hospital order and a restriction order is that the latter continues indefinitely. For as long as the restrictions last and the patient has not been absolutely discharged, there is no need for his detention to be renewed periodically under section 20 (s. 41(3)(a)). This means that no one is under any statutory obligation to consider whether the criteria for detaining him still apply. It also used to mean that the Home Secretary did not feel under obligation to agree to a discharge simply because there were no longer any medical grounds for keeping the patient in hospital. He might require to be satisfied, not only that the patient was sane, but also that he was safe. Gostin (1977) collected many examples where the Home Secretary refused or delayed a discharge, even though the RMO or a tribunal had reported that the patient no longer suffered from a mental disorder which warranted his detention in hospital for treatment.

Because it appeared that a restricted patient might be detained for much longer than was justified by his mental condition, Gostin (1977) argued that the restriction order was not a therapeutic disposal, but a penalty equivalent to a sentence of life imprisonment. It should therefore be governed, if not by the usual principle of proportionality, then at least by the maximum term of imprisonment applicable to the offence. The point was reinforced by those offenders transferred from prison to hospital. No matter what their condition, their restrictions must cease when their imprisonment would have ceased (see (e) below). Gostin's suggestion, however, was directly contrary to the approach of the Butler Committee. They were more troubled that dangerous offenders had to be released from prison at the end of their sentences and recommended the extension of the principle of indeterminate detention to them.

In the event, the decision of the European Court of Human Rights in *X. v. United Kingdom* (1981) 4 E.H.R.R. 181, put a different complexion on the matter. Having been convicted of a serious attack upon a workmate, X spent two-and-a-half years in Broadmoor before his conditional discharge in 1971. After three apparently blameless years in the community, he was recalled in April 1974. It later turned out that this was because of the alarming things which his wife said to his supervisor when announcing her intention of leaving him. Habeas corpus proceedings were unsuccessful and under the 1959 Act, his right to seek reference to a tribunal did not arise until six months after his recall. Even then the tribunal could only advise the Home Secretary, who took no action until it tallied with the advice of the RMO.

The main plank of his complaint of breaches of the European Convention on Human Rights, and the one on which he succeeded, was the lack of any judicial review of the merits of his recall and detention. This has now been remedied by giving restricted patients rights of application to and review by mental health review tribunals, although the tribunals' powers are more limited than with ordinary hospital order and civil patients (see Chapter 8). But the patient also complained that his second period of detention in Broadmoor was in breach of Article 5(1) of the Convention, which states *inter alia* that: "No person shall be deprived of his liberty save in the following cases ... (a) the lawful detention of a person after conviction by a competent court; ... (e) the lawful detention ... of persons of unsound mind ... ". In the earlier *Winterwerp Case* (1979) 2 E.H.R.R. 387, the court had laid down three minimum conditions for the lawful detention of persons of unsound mind. Except in an emergency, the person must be reliably shown to be of unsound mind, that is, a true mental disorder must be established on the basis of objective medical expertise; the mental disorder must be of a kind or degree warranting compulsory confinement; and the validity of the continued confinement will depend upon the persistence of such a disorder. The Government argued that because X's detention had been ordered after conviction by a competent court, it was justified under Article 5(1)(a) and these requirements did not apply. The European Commission on Human Rights argued that, because the court had chosen a therapeutic disposal, the detention could only be justified under Article 5(1)(e) and therefore the *Winterwerp* requirements must apply. Somewhat puzzlingly, the European Court considered that the detention before his conditional discharge fell within both (a) and (e); they were less sure whether the detention after his recall did so; but they found this unnecessary to decide, because in any event the requirements of (e) would have to be satisfied. On the facts, however, they found no reason to disagree with the Broadmoor doctor's judgment that these did exist when X was recalled to hospital.

The message of this is plain. If the patient is no longer suffering from mental disorder of a nature or degree which makes his detention in hospital appropriate, he should no longer be detained there, no matter how dangerous he may be. The Act provides that the RMO must examine the patient and report to the Home Secretary at such intervals as the latter may require, but not exceeding a year (s. 41(6)). There is still no formal renewal procedure and no express requirement for the Home Secretary to agree to the discharge of a patient who no longer meets the criteria. Nevertheless, in principle he should clearly do so.

In practice, he is more worried that, in particular, people sent to special hospitals as psychopaths may have to be discharged by a tribunal, if not by him, if their present condition makes hospital treatment inappropriate, no matter how serious the offence or how dangerous he may consider them to be (see DHSS and Home Office, 1986; Peay, 1988). The old style restriction order was a remarkably effective method of protecting the public. It is now more difficult to work out whether that protection is better achieved by a restriction order or by a prison sentence with the possibility of a transfer to hospital.

(e) Transfer from prison

Any prison officer will tell you that many of his prisoners are "only 16 shillings in the pound". In a representative study of the prison population in 1988 to 1989, 37 per cent of sentenced male prisoners received a psychiatric diagnosis, but only 2 per cent with psychosis; 3 per cent were judged to need transfer to prison; not all of these had been identified by the prison medical officers (Gunn, Maden and Swinton, 1991). Even if these prisoners are placed in the hospital wing of a prison where the medical officer has psychiatric experience, they cannot expect to receive the treatment which they would get in hospital. The standard of care is not as high (*Knight v. Home Office* [1990] 3 All E.R. 237). There is no statutory power to impose treatment without their consent (Brazier, 1982). However, the Home Secretary can direct that offenders serving prison sentences be transferred to hospital under section 47 of the 1983 Act. This includes offenders serving other types of custodial sentence, those who do not comply with an order to enter into recognisances to keep the peace or be of good behaviour, and those imprisoned for non-payment of fines (s. 47(5)).

The Home Secretary must have reports from two doctors, one of them approved. The prisoner must be suffering from mental illness, psychopathic disorder, severe mental impairment or mental impairment, and the other conditions are also the same as for an ordinary hospital order. Once again, therefore, if the "16 shillings in the pound" offender is not mentally ill and does not behave in an abnormally aggressive or seriously irresponsible manner, he cannot be transferred. If he is psychopathic or mildly impaired, he cannot be transferred unless hospital treatment is likely either to make him better or at least prevent his getting worse. In addition to the medical criteria, the Home Secretary must consider the transfer "expedient", having regard to the public interest and all the circumstances (s. 47(1)). The patient must arrive at the hospital within 14 days of the direction (s. 47(2)), so the Home Office must have secured a bed for him beforehand. However, there is no limit on the time that can elapse between the medical reports and the direction. Long delays are not at all unknown, with an obvious risk of injustice to a prisoner whose condition may not warrant detention in hospital when transferred (Grounds, 1990).

Prisoners may be transferred either with or without restrictions (s. 49(1)). Restrictions are normally imposed if the sentence has some time to run, but they cease automatically at the end of the sentence (s. 50(2)). This date must be calculated with all the automatic parole which the patient would have had if he had stayed in prison (s. 50(3)), but adding on to the sentence any period during which he was absent without leave from the hospital (s. 50(4)). Prisoners serving life sentences cannot be considered for parole during transfer to hospital (*R. v. Secretary of State for Home Department, ex p. H.* [1995] Q.B. 43, C.A.

The transfer has the same effect as a restriction order (s. 49(2)). The patient can apply to a tribunal within the first six months and then as usual, but if they find that he is fit for discharge, the Home Secretary can choose between allowing this or returning him to prison. The RMO must make regular examinations and reports to the Home Office (s. 49(3)). But if the Home Secretary is advised by the RMO or by any doctor, or by a tribunal, that the offender no longer requires treatment for mental disorder, or that no effective treatment can be given him in that hospital (which is not quite the same thing as saying that he is fit for discharge), the Home Secretary can do one of three things. He can leave the patient in hospital for the time being, unless the patient is fit for absolute discharge. Or he can send the offender back to a penal establishment, there to complete his sentence as if nothing had happened. Or he can release the offender on licence, or discharge him under supervision, if there would have been power to do this from the penal establishment (s. 50(1)). Transferred "lifers" are likely to be released, if at all, on a life licence under section 61 of the Criminal Justice Act 1967, rather than by conditional discharge under the 1983 Act (see *R. v. Secretary of State for the Home Department, ex p. Stroud* [1993] C.O.D. 75). If the patient is still in hospital when the restrictions cease, he remains liable to be detained under an ordinary hospital order (s. 41(5)).

A transfer without restrictions has the same effect as an ordinary hospital order (s. 47(2)). It is normally chosen if the prisoner is coming to the end of his sentence, but it can mean that he will remain legally liable to be detained in hospital beyond the time when he would have been released from prison. He may, however, be discharged at any time and will be able to apply to a tribunal even during his first six months. His longer detention was not thought unjust by the Butler Committee, because he could in any event have been compulsorily admitted under civil powers. On the other hand, Orville Blackwood's perception that his detention was unjust may well have been a contributing factor in the events which led to his death while secluded in Broadmoor (Prins, 1993). After the 1959 Act came into force, there was a trend towards later transfers, and Broadmoor began to keep those patients who were considered unfit for discharge at the end of their sentence. Grounds (1990) argues that these patients should be "sectioned" afresh, if at all, when their sentence expires. A tribunal hearing is not enough protection, as the burden is on the patient to prove his fitness, and he should no longer be saddled with the stigma of a criminal commitment.

The Home Office has made considerable progress in getting these prisoners into hospital, but there are difficulties: "far-reaching changes have made obsolete the old notion of transfer from one institution (a prison) to another (a hospital)" (Home Office and DHSS, 1987, para. 6.22). Special hospitals take only the most dangerous patients. Regional secure units were not designed for a long-term semi-custodial role. Ordinary NHS hospitals are part of a network which includes hostels, centres, group homes and other facilities. It takes a considerable effort of imagination on the part of some to see this as an appropriate setting for

127

people sentenced to imprisonment. With developments at the psychiatric prison at Grendon Underwood, and the possibility of another, more appropriate facilities may be available for some prisoners. This is not, however, within the control of the sentencing court.

(f) Guardianship orders

Guardianship could be a very useful order, but in practice it is hardly ever used. It may be made for the same offences and with the same medical evidence as a hospital order, save that the treatability test does not apply, the patient must have reached 16, and his mental condition must be "of a nature or degree which warrants his reception into guardianship" (s. 37(2)(a)(ii)), rather than such as to make hospital treatment appropriate (see pp. 117–118, earlier). Mental handicap is again limited to impairments which are associated with abnormally aggressive or seriously irresponsible conduct.

The duration and procedure for renewal are basically the same as in an ordinary hospital order; so are the rights of application to a tribunal, save that guardianship order patients can apply during their first six months. The effect, however, is quite different. The patient is placed in the guardianship either of the local social services authority or of some other individual approved by them (s. 40(2)). The order cannot be made unless the proposed guardian agrees (s. 37(2)). The details appear in Chapter 9, but the guardian has three powers over the patient. He may decide where the patient should live, and when and where the patient should go for treatment, occupation, education or training, and he may insist that any named doctor, social worker or other person sees the patient at home (s. 8(1)).

He cannot insist that the patient accepts any medical or other treatment on offer, although if that becomes necessary and the medical recommendations are available, he may transfer the patient to hospital. The patient may be recaptured and returned if he absconds from the place where he is required to live. Otherwise, however, there are no sanctions against a patient who refuses to co-operate (although other people might be guilty of harbouring him or obstructing the authorities). The order is therefore quite different from a probation order with a condition of psychiatric treatment, and of course it involves local authority social services rather than probation officers and doctors.

This is no doubt why it has been so little used. The order requires liaison between the doctors, who will have to give evidence, the social services authority, which will have to take at least some of the responsibility, and the courts, who will not usually have a representative of that authority on hand to consult. The Butler Committee recommended closer co-operation with a view to using guardianship more frequently. Section 39A of the 1983 Act obliges local social services authorities to respond to the courts' requests for information about whether they or anyone approved by them are willing to become guardians and if so how they could be expected to exercise their functions under the Act. It is also hard to see why it is possible to make an interim hospital order but not an interim guardianship order (Mental Health Act Commission, 1993).

(g) Alternatives

Courts may be unable to choose a therapeutic disposal, even if they would like to do so. But before imposing a custodial sentence upon an offender who is or appears to be mentally disordered, they must obtain a report from an approved doctor unless in all the circumstances this is unnecessary; and in any case they must consider, not only any information they have about his mental condition, but also the likely effect of a custodial sentence upon his condition and its treatment (Criminal Justice Act 1991, s. 4). If an offender is suitable for and can be placed in a special hospital, then the court should not sentence him to life imprisonment simply to avoid the risk of release by a mental health review tribunal (*R. v. Howell* (1985) 7 Cr.App.R.(S.) 360), unless the circumstances are "unusual and exceptional" (*R. v. Fleming* (1992) 14 Cr.App.R. (S.) 151).

When he is not suitable for or cannot be found a place in a special hospital, a mentally disturbed offender who commits very serious offences is undoubtedly at greater risk of a sentence of life imprisonment than are other offenders. The criteria are, first, that the offences themselves are serious enough to justify very long sentences; secondly, that there is evidence, usually but not invariably medical evidence, of "unstable character" indicating that the offender is likely to go on committing such offences; and thirdly, that the consequences to others will be "specially injurious" (see *R. v. Hodgson* (1968) 52 Cr.App.R. 113; examples include *R. v. Herpels* (1979) 1 Cr.App.R.(S.) 48; *R. v. Dempster* (1987) 9 Cr.App.R.(S.) 176; *R. v. Birch* (1987) 9 Cr.App.R.(S.) 509; *Att.-Gen.'s Reference (No. 34 of 1992)* (1993) 15 Cr.App.R.(S.) 167). However, in *R. v. Pither* (1979) 1 Cr.App.R.(S.) 209 (see also *R. v. J.* (1992) 14 Cr.App.R.(S.) 500), this was confined to exceptional cases where the offender is subject to a "marked degree of mental instability". Persistent delinquent behaviour is not enough. In *R. v. Spencer* (1979) 1 Cr.App.R.(S.) 75 (see also *R. v. Laycock* (1981) 3 Cr.App.R.(S.) 104), the court emphasised that a life sentence should not be imposed unless the offender was also a serious and consistent danger to the public. The defendant was a former mental patient who set fire to a car while labouring under a misguided sense of grievance, but he had taken pains to avoid endangering life, and the court substituted a sentence of five years.

Mental instability has also been taken into account in justifying sentences at the top end of the "tariff" for violent offenders who for one reason or another cannot be sent to hospital (see, for example, *R. v. Scanlon* (1979) 1 Cr.App.R.(S.) 60; *R. v. Walsh* (1981) 3 Cr.App.R.(S.) 359).

Lower down the scale, there have been cases such as *R. v. Arrowsmith* [1976] Crim. L.R. 636, in which a woman with a long history of disturbed and aggressive behaviour was given three years' imprisonment on breach of probation for a minor offence because the medical and social services could not cope with her any longer. But in *R. v. Clarke* (1975) 61 Cr.App.R. 320, Lawton L.J. observed that:

> "Her Majesty's courts are not dustbins into which the social services can sweep difficult members of the public . . . . If the courts became disposers of those who are socially inconvenient the road ahead would lead to the destruction of liberty. It should be clearly understood that Her Majesty's judges stand on that road barring the way. The courts exist to punish according to law those convicted of offences. Sentences should fit crimes."

A £2.00 fine was substituted for a sentence of 18 months' imprisonment upon a former Rampton patient who was admittedly very difficult to handle but had only been convicted of breaking a flower pot.

In *R. v. Tolley* (1978) 68 Cr.App.R. 323, the Court of Appeal preferred the approach in *Clarke* to that in *Arrowsmith*. They ordered the immediate release of a man who had been diagnosed schizophrenic and sentenced to two years' imprisonment for possessing a small amount of cannabis, even though he was obviously doing very well in the prison hospital. A fixed term of imprisonment should not exceed a length commensurate with the gravity of the offence. The fact that his mental condition made it likely that if set at large he would be a danger to himself or others did not justify using the penal system to supplement the shortcomings of the social services and mental health system.

These cases may be seen as part of a judicial campaign to keep mentally disordered people out of prison. To the extent that they emphasise that the punishment should fit the crime, they have been confirmed, in particular, by section 2(2)(a) of the Criminal Justice Act 1991; section 2(2)(b), however, allows the imposition of a longer sentence than is justified by the seriousness of a violent or sexual offence if this is necessary to protect the public from serious harm.

But they were also part of a campaign to persuade the medical authorities to accept responsibility. A good example is *R. v. Porter (Wendy), The Times*, January 22, 1985, where the Court of Appeal substituted an indefinite restriction order in Moss Side for a sentence of life imprisonment, while commenting forcibly on the lack of suitable intermediate facilities. No matter how many secure units are built, however, they will not solve the problem of people like Dawn Clarke, who was repeatedly discharged from Rampton by a tribunal. There are many people who are not dangerous in any sensible meaning of the term, but who are difficult and a nuisance to all and sundry, and for whom there is precious little that hospitals as such can do. Hospitals are not dustbins any more than prisons are. The alternative of good facilities in the community simply does not exist in many places. The courts, and the rest of us, may have to accept that there are some troublesome people whom we must try to tolerate as best we can.

5. COMMENTARY

The Code of Practice proudly proclaims that "those subject to criminal proceedings have the same right to psychiatric assessment and treatment as any other citizen. The aim should be to ensure that everyone in prison or police custody in need of medical treatment for mental disorder which can only satisfactorily be given in a hospital . . . is admitted to such a hospital" (para. 3.1). But views differ on what people need. No one wants the "embarrassing" patients (p. 21, earlier) and the service is poorest for them (Mental Health Act Commission, 1985, para. 11.9). Serious attempts are being made to improve matters (Reed, 1992), but "diversion" is not the answer to everything.

The law and the criminal justice system are still trying to have the best of all worlds. Within the context of a system which is supposed to do justice, they are trying to cure those who might be cured and to protect society against those who cannot. Once again we can start from the proposition that, just as the defendant has the same rights as everyone else, he also has the same responsibilities. The United Nations Declaration on the Rights of Mentally Retarded Persons (United Nations, 1971) states that "if prosecuted for any offence, he shall have a right to due process of law with full recognition being given to his degree of mental responsibility." This can go either way. If he did not do it, he should not be convicted simply because he is mentally handicapped. If he did do it, he is entitled to the same treatment as others. People who break their duties towards society are normally punished, but their punishment must be in proportion to the offence. Punishments should fit crimes, whether trivial or serious. If then we are going to hold a man responsible, we should accord him the right to minimal proportionality, as the judges seem prepared to do. He may be prepared to accept the loss of that right, in the hope that a therapeutic disposal will do him some good, or at least be more pleasant than the alternative. But if he is responsible enough to participate in ordinary rights and duties, perhaps he should be allowed to make the choice for himself.

But what about the people who are really dangerous? Society may have a right to protect itself against them, whether or not they are responsible, and even if there is nothing the medical profession can do for them. This should be a very limited category. We should make it quite clear what we mean by dangerousness. We should be sure that the event of danger presented is sufficient to justify the level of intervention. And we should be able to separate those who are dangerous from those who are not with a higher degree of reliability than we can at present. Mental disorder as such is not the criterion. There are plenty of sane people who are dangerous and plenty of insane people who are not. If we are going to deprive people of either proportionality or the normal principles of guilt and innocence in order to protect society against serious risk, we should be concentrating on the accurate identification and discovery of that risk and on nothing else.

Then we have the people who are not responsible and who are not dangerous. Some of these should be left alone. A person whose mind is not on the job when he does what would otherwise be a criminal act should prima facie be acquitted altogether. The forgetful shopper is not dishonest. The epileptic is not deliberately violent. He is no more a fit candidate for punishment or other intervention than a blind man who swings his stick. He is in most circumstances an ordinary member of society fully entitled to participate as such. There is, of course, much to be said for holding people liable for at least some of their acts, if they know that carelessness or irresponsibility in taking their prophylactic treatment will produce those acts. If they do not exhibit that carelessness, we have no cause to intervene. They are otherwise fully participant members of society.

Lastly, there are a few who do not qualify as participants in the ordinary system of rights and duties, but who behave in criminal ways. Towards them we should probably behave in the same way as we do when considering their ordinary civil rights (p. 48, earlier). This does not involve locking them up, unless this is absolutely necessary, but catering for their needs as humanely as possible and trying to the best of our ability to fit them into ordinary life.

Strange though it may seem, English law already contains within it the capacity to produce most of these results. But it does so in a haphazard and pragmatic way, which depends more on the discretion of the courts than on any carefully considered principles. The main problem is that it assumes that the solution should be governed by the presence or absence of something the psychiatrists call mental disorder, when that may tell us little about the individual or what they can do for him. The second problem is that it assumes a straight dichotomy between punishment and treatment. There are circumstances when neither is appropriate and nothing should be done. There are circumstances when neither is appropriate but something should be done. We have not (yet?) adopted a "hybrid" order which would allow the authorities to hedge their bets (Reed, 1994b).

6 TREATMENT AND MANAGEMENT

This chapter is concerned with the treatment and management of both informal and compulsory patients in and out of hospital. Far and away the most important change of principle introduced under the 1983 Act was the decision to regulate what may happen to compulsory patients while they are in hospital. Under the 1959 Act, it was assumed that they were incompetent to decide upon their medical treatment. It was also assumed that neither they nor informal patients required any special protection against exploitation or abuse. Nowadays we recognise that some protection is required, not only against exploitation or abuse, but also against unjustified interference with their right to take for themselves those decisions which they are capable of taking. But this is not always easy to reconcile with the professionals' duty to provide proper care and treatment for their patients or with the need to control the violent or challenging behaviour of a few of these.

1. TREATMENT AND CONTROL

The common law normally respects the right of any person to decide what shall be done with his own body. Thus any action which involves the use or the threat of force, however slight, upon his person will amount to a tort (and often also to a crime) unless there is consent or some other legal justification for acting without it. There are, of course, psychological treatments and other activities which involve no such force and usually depend upon the co-operation of the patient. Even here, however, the deliberate infliction of psychological harm is a tort, and some patients may well experience group or individual psychotherapy as coercive and distressing (Code of Practice, para. 19.1). Behaviour modification programmes run an even greater risk of interfering with the patients' basic rights. Other measures commonly employed would undoubtedly be tortious. These include conventional medical treatments, such as injections with drugs, operations, and electro-convulsive therapy (ECT). They also include the various forms of restraint or confinement used, ranging from the bodily restraint of one person by another, through periods of "seclusion" in a locked room, to confinement in a locked ward, or eventually in the maximum security conditions of a special hospital.

Under the old lunacy legislation, there was some regulation of what went on in licensed houses, hospitals and asylums, under the overall supervision of the Board of Control and the law was specific about what should be done when "individual mechanical restraint" was imposed. But the 1959 Act made no provision at all for the care and treatment of hospital patients, whether informal or detained. The official view was that this could safely be left to the clinical judgment of the medical authorities and that detained patients could lawfully be given any recognised form of treatment for their disorder, whether or not they consented (although a more cautious view was later adopted towards patients detained "for observation"). Others (notably Jacob, 1976, and Gostin, 1979; but see also the Butler Report, 1975) pointed out that the Act gave no express power to impose such treatment and that the common law might still apply. These doubts obviously increased the attractions of legislating for express safeguards over the use of the more hazardous or irreversible forms of treatment (see NCCL,1973; Gostin, 1975). The case for these was accepted by the Butler Committee (1975), the DHSS (DHSS *et al.*, 1978), and to some extent by the Royal College of Psychiatrists (1981).

The 1983 Act therefore makes it quite clear that most types of detained patient can be given most forms of medical treatment for their disorder without their consent (s. 63). Some treatments, however, including ECT, can usually only be given either with their consent *or* with an independent medical opinion (s. 58). Others, including psycho-surgery, can usually only be given with their consent *and* a second opinion (s. 57). This last provision also applies to informal patients.

The Act does not remove the common law justifications which apply to all patients, informal or detained, in hospital or in the community. These are principally the patient's own consent, whether express or implied, and the doctrine of necessity, as explained by the House of Lords in the leading case of *Re F. (Mental Patient: Sterilisation)* [1990] 2 A.C. 1.

Theoretically, perhaps, providing a patient with the medical treatment which he either wants or needs may be distinguished from controlling his disruptive or violent behaviour, whether for his own good or that of others. The Code of Practice, for example, draws a clear distinction between "time out", which is part of a prescribed behaviour modification programme, and seclusion, which is for use in an emergency (para. 19.9). The common law does provide justifications for controlling any patient's behaviour, principally through the power to prevent him doing harm to other people or to himself or to property, and a combination of the Act and the common law may justify further measures of confinement or control over detained patients.

In practice, however, it is difficult to draw hard and fast lines between treatment and control, because both are occasioned by the patient's mental disorder and the latter may be designed as much for his benefit as that of others. Therefore, what follows addresses each of the legal justifications for measures which might otherwise be unlawful.

(a) Consent

The patient may give his express consent to the invasion of his normal legal rights. This is only a defence where what has been done is what the patient agreed could be done, and it is advisable to make this clear at the outset. This could be particularly important where the patient agrees to embark upon a behaviour modification programme (see Royal College of Psychiatrists *et al.*, 1980), which may involve deprivation of ordinary legal rights through a token economy or periods of time out.

The law requires that consent be "real". It may therefore be invalid if induced by force or fraud. Clerk and Lindsell (1989, para. 17.08) observe that: "it might perhaps be tentatively suggested that the plaintiff cannot give a real consent unless he has in fact the freedom to choose whether or not he should do so." An informal patient who gives his consent under the threat that he will be sectioned might complain that he has been deprived of his freedom to choose. So might a hospital order patient complain, like the prisoner in *Freeman v. Home Office* (No. 2) [1984] Q.B. 524, that the coercive nature of the institution, and the power of the RMO to decide whether he should be released, prevent his consent being freely given. It was decided in that case that whether or not consent had been given was a question of fact in each case: the patient's will may have been overborne by such circumstances, but their existence does not of itself prove this.

Although common law requires that the patient's consent be "real", it does not require that it be fully "informed" upon all the arguments for or against a particular treatment. In *Chatterton v. Gerson* [1981] Q.B. 432, it was held that " . . . once the patient is informed in broad terms of the nature of the procedure which is intended and gives her consent, that consent is real . . . " and the treatment is therefore not a trespass to her person. If she wishes to complain that she was not adequately informed, she must found her claim in negligence, that is, in the failure of the doctor to take such steps as a reasonable doctor would take in all the circumstances to avoid harming the patient. This approach was approved by the House of Lords in the leading case of *Sidaway v. Board of Governors of the Bethlem Royal Hospital and the Maudsley Hospital* [1985] A.C. 871. In discussing what a reasonable doctor would do, only Lord Scarman thought that the doctrine of informed consent had any place in English law. Lord Bridge, with the majority, considered that the decision on what risks should be disclosed was primarily a matter of clinical judgment. However, if there was a substantial risk of grave adverse consequences, disclosure might be so obviously necessary to the patient's choice that no reasonably prudent doctor would fail to make it. In the particular case, there was no legal duty to disclose a 1–2 per cent risk of ill-effects ranging from mild to catastrophic. This approach coincides with the general approach to questions of medical negligence, laid down in *Bolam v. Friern Hospital Management Committee* [1957] 1 W.L.R. 582. The patient had agreed to ECT and was badly injured when it was given without a muscle relaxant. The judge took the view that it was not negligent to do this if a responsible body of medical opinion would have done the same, even if another body of opinion would not. Further, the evidence suggested that even if the patient had been fully informed of the risk, he would have agreed in any event, so that it was not the doctor's failure to warn him which had caused the injury.

Paradoxically, the view that patients need only be given a "broad terms" explanation in order to give a valid consent could help to preserve the autonomy of some patients, particularly those with mild learning disabilities. Goldstein (1975) has pointed out that the transatlantic concept of "informed consent" places more emphasis on what the patient can understand than on what he wants. It may therefore encourage the authorities to deprive people who cannot fully understand of their right to choose what they want. But if only a "broad terms" explanation is required, the corollary should be that the patient is capable of giving consent if he is capable of understanding it. As Glanville Williams (1983, p. 572) suggests: "The consent of a subnormal patient is easily obtained, but that fact does not rob the consent of its validity." However, as we shall see later (pp. 138–139), when it comes to refusal of treatment, the judiciary have been reluctant to adopt such a "minimal competence" approach.

Even if a valid consent has been given, it may be withdrawn. A patient may agree to a course of drug treatment or ECT but withdraw his consent before it has been completed. He may agree to the hospital's practice of locking the ward door at night, or to a programme of behaviour modification involving periods of time out, but change his mind and ask to be released. In principle, a consent can be revoked at any time: the only possible exceptions (deriving from the false imprisonment cases of *Robinson v. Balmain New Ferry Co.* [1910] A.C. 295 and *Herd v. Weardale Steel, Coal and Coke Co. Ltd.* [1915] A.C. 67) are where the patient has only been let in on contractual terms which restrict his right to do so.

Finally, it should be noted that the Mental Health Act 1983 makes special provision for some treatments (see section (e) later), where not only must the patient's consent be "informed" in a special way, but there must also be an independent assessment both of his consent and of the treatment proposed.

Of course, the fact that the patient has consented to a particular treatment does not mean that the doctor is bound to provide it against his better judgment. Hence an "advance statement" of what the patient *does* want (as opposed to an advance refusal of what he does *not* want, see p. 139, later) cannot be binding in that sense: but it may amount to a valid consent and it is an important indication of the patient's preferences and values which ought to be given serious consideration in deciding what will be in his best interests if he becomes unable to decide for himself (British Medical Association, 1995; Law Commission, 1995).

(b) Necessity

Until the decision of the House of Lords in *Re F. (Mental Patient: Sterilisation)* [1990] 2 A.C.1 there was great uncertainty about what could be done for a patient who was incapable of giving a real consent. A major object of the 1959 Act had been to do away with the need for legal formalities for patients, such as the elderly mentally infirm or those with severe learning disabilities, who did not have to be forced to accept treatment. But it did not clarify what could be done without such formalities and it referred (in what is now section 131(1), p. 8, earlier) only to "treatment for mental disorder". It is possible that many incapable patients went without necessary or desirable treatment for physical disorders as a result. It is equally possible that many were given the treatment their doctors thought best without much thought to the strict legal position.

These doubts eventually surfaced in a series of cases about abortion and sterilisation (*e.g. Re T., T v. T.* [1988] Fam., p. 52), although strictly such operations are no different in principle from any other medical (or indeed dental) treatment. It became apparent that there was now no machinery in law for providing a surrogate decision-maker for an incapable person. Thus, even if the person falls within the criteria for compulsory admission to hospital, the Mental Health Act 1983 only permits treatment "for the mental disorder from which he is suffering" (s. 63; see section (e) below). Under the 1959 Act, an incapable patient might have been placed under guardianship; this gave the guardian all the powers of a father over a child under 14, including the power to authorise medical treatment for a child who cannot do so for himself (see p. 65, earlier). Under the 1983 Act, however, the restricted definition of "mental impairment" (see p. 38, earlier) cast doubt on whether many people with learning disabilities can be placed under guardianship; more important, the guardian no longer has power to authorise medical treatment (p. 220, later). Before the 1959 Act, such treatment might also have been authorised under the prerogative powers of the Crown to protect, not only the property but also the persons, of people found to be idiots or of unsound mind by inquisition. However, the royal warrant by which this power was delegated to the Lord Chancellor and other judges was revoked shortly after the 1959 Act came into force, because it was thought that the 1959 Act covered all the necessary ground. It is, to say the least, debatable whether those powers can now be revived, even supposing this would be the best solution to the problem (see, *e.g.* Hoggett, 1988; Grubb and Pearl, 1989).

In *Re F.*, therefore, the House of Lords accepted that there was no-one authorised by law to consent on behalf of an incapable patient; that there was no jurisdiction in the High Court to supply such consent; and that in some circumstances there was no way of doing so under the Mental Health Act or other legislation. However, where a patient was incapable of giving consent, it was lawful at common law to give him such treatment as was necessary to preserve life or health. The obvious example is an unconscious road accident victim; a less obvious example is a patient who has consented to one operation, during which it is discovered that further treatment is urgently required; in both cases, the doctor can carry on with treatment which it would be unreasonable, as opposed to merely inconvenient, to postpone (see the Canadian cases of *Marshall v. Curry* (1933) 3 D.L.R. 260 and *Murray v. McMurchy* (1949) 2 D.L.R. 442, approved in *Re F*). Where the patient is more permanently incapacitated, it is lawful to give any treatment which is in his best interests. What is in the patient's best interests can be judged by the same test as in *Bolam v. Friern Hospital Management Committee* [1957] 1 W.L.R. 582, that is, whether the treatment proposed would be accepted as proper by a responsible body of medical opinion, even if there is another body of opinion which would not do so.

That is therefore the position for most types of treatment. Indeed, not only is it lawful for the doctor to act in the best interests of his patient, it is also part of his general duty of care towards his patient to do so. However, there are some especially sensitive treatments, of which sterilisation is the most obvious example, where it was strongly advised that a declaration should first be obtained from the High Court that it would indeed be in the patient's best interests. Otherwise, the doctor might later be sued for an unlawful trespass to the patient's person and would be liable if the court found that it was not.

This decision was warmly welcomed by doctors, professionals and other carers, but it left many unanswered questions. What procedures should be referred to the court? The House of Lords were concerned that a woman should not be deprived of her fertility without an objective examination of her individual circumstances. The Official Solicitor has given guidance on the procedure and the evidence required (*Practice Note (Official Solicitor: Sterilisation)* [1993] 3 All E.R. 222). But it has also been decided that declarations need not be sought for so-called "therapeutic" sterilisations, not only those to treat an existing disease or condition of the reproductive organs but also those to control excessive menstruation (*Re G.F. (Mental Patient: Medical Treatment* [1992] 1 F.L.R. 293; *Re E. (A Minor)(Medical Treatment)* [1991] 2 F.L.R. 585), or for abortions (*Re S.G. (Adult Mental Patient: Abortion)* [1991] 2 F.L.R. 329).

Declarations are only available in the High Court, which is not anxious to encourage too many applications, perhaps realising that it may not be the best forum to act as a check upon professional practice unless there is a real dispute to be resolved. In *Re H. (Mental Patient)* (1992) 8 B.M.L.R. 71, the deputy judge refused to grant a declaration that a C.T. scan was in the best interests of a schizophrenic woman with a suspected brain tumour; there was no distinction between diagnostic and therapeutic procedures, but he did not wish to send a signal that such procedures should be delayed pending a costly application to the court.

In *Airedale N.H.S. Trust v. Bland* [1993] A.C. 789, the House of Lords were faced with the opposite question, of the legality of withdrawing artificial nutrition and hydration from a patient in a persistent vegetative state (PVS). No doctor can be obliged to provide medical treatment which he does not consider to be medically indicated (*Re J. (A Minor)(Child in Care: Medical Treatment)* [1993] Fam. 15), although of course he must live up to the usual standard of care in reaching that decision. And someone who has assumed the responsibility of caring for a helpless person is not allowed to neglect his basic needs (*R. v. Stone* [1977] Q.B. 354). Their Lordships decided that it was lawful to withdraw artificial sustenance from a PVS patient but once again each case should come to court so that there could be a full investigation and independent evidence obtained (see the Official Solicitor's *Practice Note* [1994] 2 All E.R. 413). In the reported examples, judges have decided that it was not necessary to continue or resume feeding after a gastrotomy tube had become blocked (*Swindon and Marlborough N.H.S. Trust v. S., The Guardian,* December 10, 1994) or dislodged (*Frenchay Healthcare N.H.S. Trust v. S.* [1994] 1 W.L.R. 601). Although the courts have applied the "best interests" criterion laid down in *Re F* (above) to these cases, it is difficult to disagree with Lord Mustill that the stark truth must be faced that these patients have "no best interests of any kind".

When the procedure proposed is not one which should go to court, *Re F.* raises even more difficult questions. Who decides that the patient is incapable of deciding for himself and upon what test? Case law on this question is limited, because the matter will not come before the courts at all if the patient has agreed with what his doctors propose or his co-operation can readily be secured. It is only when the patient has refused treatment that his health carers or family are likely to apply to the court.

The case law (principally *Re T. (Consent to Medical Treatment) (Adult Patient)* [1993] Fam. 95, below and *Bland*) is now quite clear that the refusal of treatment by a competent patient must be respected, even after he becomes incompetent, provided that it is "clearly established and applicable in the circumstances". The BMA Code of Practice on Advance Statements about Medical Treatment (British Medical Association, 1995) accepts this. It was also held in *Home Secretary v. Robb* [1995] 1 F.L.R. 412 (*c.f. Leigh v. Gladstone* (1909) 26 T.L.R. 139) that the prison authorities could lawfully refrain from force-feeding a prisoner on hunger strike. There are two possible exceptions: first on grounds of public policy, for basic care, such as oral feeding and fundamental hygiene; and second (as decided but not fully explored in *Re S. (Adult: Refusal of Medical Treatment)* [1993] Fam. 123), where a mother is about to give birth, for emergency treatment which is immediately necessary to save not only the life of the mother but also that of her unborn child. However, an advance refusal of treatment for mental disorder can be overridden by the express power (in section 63) to impose treatment without consent.

It is always much easier to accept that a patient is competent to say "yes" to a proposed treatment than that he is competent to say "no", especially in life-threatening situations. In *Re T. (Consent to Medical Treatment)(Adult Patient)* [1993] Fam. 95, the Court of Appeal held that the doctors were justified in giving the patient a blood transfusion after an emergency Caesarian section, despite her express written refusal; at the time she had signed the form, she was unable to make a genuine decision, because of the combined effect of her medical condition and pressure from her mother who was a convinced Jehovah's Witness. Unfortunately, it is not clear which of these two predominated or what precise test of unfitness was being applied.

The only case in which the test of capacity is discussed in any depth is *Re C. (Refusal of Medical Treatment)* [1994] 1 F.L.R. 31. A schizophrenic Broadmoor patient with grandiose delusions about his own medical qualifications and experience refused to undergo a below knee amputation for gangrene although advised that he stood an 85 per cent chance of imminent death. The judge rejected the "minimal competence" test, defined as the capacity to understand in broad terms the nature and effect of the proposed treatment. He found helpful one psychiatrist's analysis of the decision-making process into three stages: first, comprehending and retaining treatment information, secondly believing it, and thirdly, weighing it in the balance to arrive at a choice. The judge decided that the patient did understand the relevant information, that there was no direct link between his refusal and his persecutory delusions, and that he had arrived at a clear choice. As it happened, the patient was right, because conservative treatment had succeeded. This three-stage test is very similar to that recommended by the Law Commission (1995) in their Report on Mental Incapacity (see p. 48, earlier).

The Commission have also proposed that the general principle in *Re F.* should be put on a statutory footing, but with modifications and limitations. The "best interests" criterion would no longer be defined by reference to the *Bolam* test and would require practitioners to consider, among other things, the past and present wishes and feelings of the patient himself. There would be a new procedure for submitting disputes or difficulties for decision and order (as opposed to declaration) by the courts. A few controversial decisions, including non-therapeutic sterilisation and organ or tissue donation, would have to go to court; others, including menstrual management sterilisation, abortion and the treatments governed by section 58 of the Mental Health Act 1983 (see p. 145, later), would require an independent second opinion. A person would be able to provide in advance for what was to happen if he became incapable, either by appointing an attorney to take health care (and other) decisions on his behalf, or by making an advance refusal of treatment which was clearly intended to apply to the treatment and circumstances which have arisen, or by a combination of the two, although in neither case could he be refused "basic care" (direct oral feeding, hygiene and the relief of severe pain). The court would still have power to authorise the withdrawal of artificial feeding from a patient in PVS.

The Commission's proposals do not affect the power to impose treatment for mental disorder under the 1983 Act. But it is worth reflecting upon why a competent patient should not be able to refuse in advance to have particular treatments when he becomes disordered: the rationale for imposing them would then have to be found in the protection of others. The user movement has pioneered the development of "crisis cards" and other measures which aim to give the well patient some voice in what is to happen if he becomes acutely ill again. The BMA Guidance on Advance Statements about Medical Treatment (British Medical Association, 1995, para. 7.5) cautiously advises that "When the patient regains insight, advance statements about preferences between equally viable options for future treatment can be discussed and reflected in subsequent treatment plans".

(c) The prevention of harm

It is undoubtedly possible to restrain any patient from doing harm to himself or to others, whether or not he is liable to be detained under the Act. There are four circumstances in which this may be done, but there is a considerable degree of overlap between them, and all are subject to very similar limitations.

The first is covered by section 3(1) of the Criminal Law Act 1967: "A person may use such force as is reasonable in the circumstances in the prevention of crime, or in effecting or assisting the lawful arrest of offenders or suspected offenders or persons unlawfully at large." This applies only to the prevention of a crime which is actually in progress or about to be committed. It cannot apply where there is no crime because the patient is insane within the M'Naghten rules. The second principle was outlined by Lord Diplock in *Albert v. Lavin* [1982] A.C. 546:

> "every citizen in whose presence a breach of the peace is being, or reasonably appears to be about to be, committed has the right to take reasonable steps to make the person who is breaking or threatening to break the peace refrain from doing so; and those reasonable steps in appropriate cases will include detaining him against his will."

Breach of the peace is not necessarily a crime and it may perhaps be caused by one who is insane. A breach of the peace normally takes place in public, but can occur in private property (see *McConnell v. Chief Constable of Greater Manchester Police* [1990] 1 W.L.R. 364); it happens where "harm is actually done or is likely to be done to a person or in his presence to his property or a person is in fear of being so harmed through an assault, an affray, an unlawful assembly or other disturbance" (*R. v. Howell* [1982] Q.B. 416). Thirdly, a person may use reasonable force in self defence or to defend other persons or property. This will almost invariably also involve the prevention of crime. But the object is not to assist in preserving law and order, rather, to enable individuals to escape being harmed by aggressors, and this includes aggressors who are insane. Finally, as we have already seen in Chapter 4, the common law allows a private person to confine a person disordered in his mind who seems disposed to do mischief to himself or any other person. This is limited to those who are actually insane, although this is probably wider than the concept of insanity within the M'Naghten rules. For our purposes it is wider than the preceding three powers, because it enables staff to prevent a patient from doing harm to himself as well as to others.

All four powers can probably be summed up by the proposition that there is a right to restrain a patient who is doing, or is about to do, physical harm to himself, to another person, or to property. But it is likely that all four are subject to the same requirements of "reasonableness" as are imposed upon the prevention of crime under the 1967 Act (see Harlow, 1974; *R. v. Shannon* (1980) 71 Cr.App.R. 192). "Reasonableness" involves two separate propositions.

The first is that the force used is no more than is in fact necessary to accomplish the object for which it is allowed. Nice calculation is not expected of people responding to an emergency, but neither is gross over-reaction to the danger, or the continuation of force once the need for it is over. None of these powers permit anything in the nature of retaliation, revenge or punishment for what has happened. To seclude a patient, including an informal patient, for a short while to "cool off" is permissible. If this is not practicable for some reason, it may be permissible to administer a short term sedative. A prolonged period of solitary confinement (such as was imposed upon a patient suspected of causing a fire, in the case of *A. v. United Kingdom*, applic. no. 6840/74) is unlikely to be allowed.

A prolonged period of confinement or sedation would not be permitted under these principles, even if it was in fact necessary to prevent the patient doing harm. This is because of the second element in "reasonableness", which is that the reaction must be in proportion to the harm threatened. The police cannot shoot to kill in order to prevent someone from riding in a motor vehicle without wearing a seat belt. Moreover, these common law principles should not be used as a substitute for the procedures laid down in the Mental Health Act, which have replaced the hospitals' common law powers to detain the insane (*Black v. Forsey* 1988 S.L.T. 572, p. 79, earlier). It is important to distinguish between the need to control patients who pose an immediate threat to themselves or those around them and the need to keep some detained patients in a secure environment (Code of Practice, para. 18.1).

But what if staff are mistaken, and no harm is in fact threatened at all? Where the *only* defence relied upon is the detention of the insane, it is clear that the patient must indeed be insane and that even a reasonable mistake is no defence (*Fletcher v. Fletcher* (1859) 1 El. & El. 420). It is not clear whether the patient must actually be dangerous, or whether a reasonable belief in the danger is enough (see Lanham, 1974). The point is academic, for if a nurse succeeded in convincing the court that he genuinely believed the patient to be dangerous, it would be very hard to show that he was wrong. For the other three defences, a reasonable mistake will certainly suffice, and there is much debate about whether even an unreasonable mistake will do (but doubted in *Albert v. Lavin* [1982] A.C. 546). Staff acting in pursuance of the Mental Health Act are in any event protected unless it is shown that they acted in bad faith or without reasonable care (1983 Act, s. 139(1); see p. 249, later) but this will probably not help them in their dealings with informal patients (*R. v. Moonsami Runighian* [1977] Crim. L.R. 361).

These principles would support a practice of working out *in advance*, and by consultation between all the people involved, the appropriate response to each type of incident which may be anticipated on the ward. In this way it should be possible to restrict the intervention to the minimum necessary to prevent the threatened harm, to lay down the maximum response to certain types of incident, and to avoid the risk that any incident, however trivial, is met with a standard and often unnecessary over-reaction.

This is certainly the approach of the Code of Practice, which emphasises that physical restraint (paras. 18.9, 18.11) and seclusion (para. 18.15) should be used as little as possible and as a last resort. Seclusion is "the supervised confinement of a patient alone in a room which may be locked for the protection of others from significant harm"; it is not a treatment technique and should not feature as part of any treatment programme" (para. 18.15). The decision can be made either by a doctor or by a senior nurse, but a doctor should immediately be called (para. 18.17). There should always be someone on hand (para. 18.18) and the patient should be checked at least every 15 minutes (para. 18.19). If seclusion continues it should be reviewed every two hours by two nurses and every four hours by a doctor; an independent review by the responsible medical officer (RMO) and other professionals should take place if it continues for more than eight hours consecutively or more than 12 hours intermittently over a period of 48 hours (para. 18.20). Even the control of behaviour by medication requires careful consideration (para. 18.14).

Even in special hospitals, the declared policy (Special Hospitals Service Authority, 1993) now is "to promote alternative approaches to the care and treatment of disturbed behaviour and to limit the use of seclusion to exceptional circumstances". There is always a risk that practices which start as therapy or control can turn into punishment.

(d) "Detention" and discipline

It was accepted on all sides before the House of Lords in the case of *Pountney v. Griffiths* [1976] A.C. 314 that mental hospitals have powers of control and discipline over all their patients. Some control, over and above that necessary to prevent harm, is implicit in the hospital's power to detain compulsory patients. However, the only clear power which is given in the Act is to detain the patient *in the hospital.* Section 5(4) (the nurse's holding power) refers expressly to the need to prevent the patient from leaving the hospital. Section 6(2) gives the managers power to detain a patient admitted under one of the three sections *in the hospital,* while a hospital order (and a transfer direction) gives the managers authority to detain (s. 40(1) and (2)). Thus there is obviously power to keep the patient within the named hospital. But it is most unlikely that this gives the hospital *carte blanche* to detain the patient in whatever conditions it wishes, subject only to its criminal or civil liability for ill-treatment or neglect. Nowadays no-one would think of keeping a patient in the iron cage devised for the Bethlem patient Norris (illustrated in Scull, 1979), but neither should they think of indefinite solitary confinement. In a hospital or unit which is itself secure, this is an easier concept to apply in practice than it is when most of the patients are free to come and go as they please.

Some control may also be incidental to the purpose of treating the patient to the extent that this is permitted by the Act. In *Pountney v. Griffiths* itself, visiting time was regarded as an aspect of the patient's treatment, and thus the act of inducing him to return to the ward when visiting time was over was incidental to it. In a hospital such as Broadmoor, where the secure and highly disciplined environment is itself regarded as a therapy for the patients, the dividing line between what is permitted in the name of treatment and what can only be justified in the name of detention is particularly difficult to draw. But neither concept could be used to justify any and every regime, however harsh, arbitrary or oppressive.

Finally, some control and discipline may be necessary to enable the institution to function as a hospital at all. Glanville Williams (1983, p. 484) suggests that the authorities of a psychiatric hospital possess common law powers of discipline similar to those enjoyed by the master of a ship, which involve "no more than restraining passengers or crew who are endangering the vessel or those aboard, or who are seriously disrupting life aboard". In the case of informal patients who have withdrawn their consent to abide by the hospital's rules, the proper course is not to impose discipline as such, but either to ask them to leave or (where the criteria exist) to impose compulsory powers. Compulsory patients cannot so readily be asked to leave and so cannot be permitted to cause serious disruption to hospital life. Once again, however, this should be governed by the Criminal Law Act concept of reasonableness (see p. 140, earlier): in other words, that any force used is necessary for the purpose permitted and proportionate to the harm presented. The nurse in *Pountney v. Griffiths* (above) was entitled to take hold of the patient to escort him back to the ward but would not have been entitled to beat the patient unconscious.

The advice given by the Code of Practice on locking patients up is consistent with the principles discussed in this and the previous section. The management, security and safety of patients should be ensured by adequate staffing wherever practicable (para. 18.24). However, doors on open wards can be locked for a while because of a patient's behaviour "to keep the environment safe", but the others should be told that they are free to leave on request (para. 18.25). Locks and other devices may be used to prevent informal patients who are not deliberately trying to leave from wandering out accidentally, but consideration should be given to "sectioning" people who persistently and purposefully try to leave (para. 18.27). Detained patients may have to be kept in locked wards or secure areas in ordinary hospitals, but only after careful assessment and for the minimum amount of time (para. 18.28). Patients should never be deprived of daytime clothing or other aids necessary for their daily living as a means of restricting movement (para. 18.31).

Richardson (1993, 1995) has argued that in practice hospitals already have disciplinary rules and sanctions for patients who break them, but these are imposed informally and not necessarily fairly. Rather than blurring the distinction between treatment and discipline or control, it would be preferable to have a proper policy for responding to seriously disruptive or disturbing behaviour on the part of detained patients in a manner which is both therapeutic and fair.

Complaints have been made that conditions in special hospitals amount to "torture or inhuman or degrading treatment or punishment", contrary to Article 3 of the European Convention on Human Rights. In *B. v. United Kingdom* (1984) 6 E.H.R.R. 204 there was no breach, although the overcrowding in dormitories was deplorable. In *A. v. United Kingdom*, Applic. No. 6840/74, however, the complaint was of five weeks' solitary confinement and a friendly settlement was reached which included new guidelines on the use of seclusion in Broadmoor. Nor can an action for damages be ruled out. In *Furber v. Kratter, The Times*, July 21, 1988, the plaintiff was allowed to proceed with a claim for damages for discomfort, suffering and loss of amenity caused by 16 days' seclusion in Moss Side. In a claim for negligence, damage must be proved, but it was "eminently arguable" that discomfort, suffering and loss of amenity would be enough if negligence were shown. No damage need be proved in a claim for false imprisonment, and it had been thought that the conditions of an originally lawful imprisonment might be so intolerable or prejudicial to health as to render it unlawful. However, in *Hague v. Deputy Governor of Parkhurst Prison, Weldon v. Home Office* [1992] 1 A.C. 58, it was held that a prisoner cannot make such a claim; and a compulsory hospital patient is no different in principle.

(e) Medical treatment under the Act

Section 63 of the 1983 Act provides that the "consent of a patient shall not be required for any medical treatment given to him for the mental disorder from which he is suffering, not being treatment falling within [the special safeguards provided by] section 57 or 58 above, if the treatment is given by or under the direction of the responsible medical officer". By section 56(1) this applies to all detained patients, apart from: those held in a "place of safety" under sections 135, 136 or pending admission to hospital under a hospital order; those detained as hospital in-patients under either of the short-term holding powers in section 5; those admitted for assessment in an emergency under section 4 where the second medical recommendation converting it into a full admission for assessment has not yet been given and received; those remanded to hospital for reports; and restricted patients who have been conditionally discharged from hospital.

This statutory power to impose treatment without consent upon the majority of compulsory patients is subject to several important limitations. The first is that it must be "medical treatment": this is widely defined in section 145(1) to *include* nursing and "care, habilitation and rehabilitation under medical supervision". It is not always easy to distinguish milieu therapy in a maximum or medium secure hospital from a system of detention and discipline for its own sake. But for such a system to qualify as treatment, it must be given by or under the direction of the RMO, and it must be designed as treatment for the specific mental disorder from which the individual patient is suffering. Expecting patients to conform to very high or artificial norms of behaviour, to fit into the system for the system's sake rather than their own, or to be punished for their misdeeds prior to their admission to hospital (all of which were reported by the Rampton review team; see Boynton, 1980) can scarcely qualify as medical treatment even under the widest definition. But a carefully designed programme of behaviour modification, or a therapeutic community, which will meet the needs of the particular group of patients for whom it is designed obviously can qualify.

The second important limitation is that the medical treatment must be given for the *mental* disorder from which the patient is suffering. The Act gives no power to impose treatment for physical disorders which are unrelated to any mental disorder within the meaning of the Act. This is not an easy distinction. Some physical disorders can be either the cause or a symptom of a mental disorder: in that case, treating the cause or the symptom is surely treating the mental disorder. In *R. v. Mental Health Act Commission, ex p. X.* (1988) 9 B.M.L.R. 77, it was said that where the patient was mentally disordered and sexually deviant, the two might be inextricably linked, so that treatment for one could be treatment for the other, even though sexual deviancy cannot by itself amount to a mental disorder under the Act (s. 1(3); but see Fennell, 1988). Artificial feeding is a treatment "for" anorexia nervosa (*Re K.B. (Adult)(Mental Patient: Medical Treatment)* (1994) 9 B.M.L.R. 144; see also *Riverside Mental Health N.H.S. Trust v. Fox* [1994] 1 F.L.R. 614) and for other disorders leading to a compulsion to self harm (*B. v. Croydon Health Authority* [1995] 2 W.L.R. 294, C.A.). However, if a severely handicapped woman becomes pregnant, her pregnancy may have been caused in part by her disorder, but it was accepted in *Re F. (Mental Patient: Sterilisation)* [1990] 2 A.C. 1 that sterilisation was not treatment for the mental disorder of a severely handicapped young woman. Also excluded should be the case where the patient's mental disorder leads him to decline treatment for a quite unrelated physical disorder. If a schizophrenic refuses to have his appendix out because his thought control forbids this, it is permissible under section 63 to treat the schizophrenia but not the appendix. However, the patient would usually lack capacity under the test laid down in *Re C. (Refusal of Medical Treatment)*

[1994] 1 F.L.R. 31 (p. 139, earlier) and so could be treated under the common law.

Section 58 lays down extra safeguards which must be observed where detained patients (within the definition given in section 56(1) above) are to be given either of two types of treatment. The first is ECT (prescribed by the Mental Health (Hospital, Guardianship and Consent to Treatment) Regulations 1983, reg. 16(2)). The second is the administration of medicine by any means at any time during a period of detention, once three months have elapsed since the first time *in that period* when the patient was given medicine *for his mental disorder.* These treatments may only be given in either of two circumstances: (a) where the patient consents, and either the RMO or an independent doctor appointed by the Mental Health Act Commission (see p. 154, later) certifies (on Form 38) not only that he has consented but also that he is capable of understanding the nature, purpose and likely effects of the treatment; *or* (b) where the *independent* doctor certifies (on Form 39) either that the patient is not so capable or that he has not consented but that the treatment should be given having regard to the likelihood of its alleviating or preventing a deterioration of his condition. Before giving the second type of certificate, the independent doctor (the "second opinion appointed doctor" or SOAD) must consult two other people who have been professionally concerned with the patient's medical treatment, one of whom must be a nurse and the other of whom must be neither a nurse nor a doctor.

There were more than 8,800 requests for second opinions in the two years covered by the Commission's 1993 report, compared with less than 7,200 in the previous two year period, 46 per cent of them for ECT. The SOAD and RMO agree upon the treatment plan in well over 90 per cent of cases. This is scarcely surprising as both the Commission and the Code of Practice (para. 16.39) advise that the SOAD's role is to decide whether the proposed treatment is "reasonable in the light of the general consensus of appropriate treatment for such a condition" and not whether it is what he himself would have done in the circumstances (see further Fennell, 1993).

Section 57 lays down even more stringent precautions which must be observed before any surgical operation for destroying brain tissue or destroying the functioning of brain tissue, or for the surgical implantation of hormones for the purpose of reducing male sexual drive (the latter prescribed by the Mental Health (Hospital, Guardianship and Consent to Treatment) Regulations 1983, reg. 16(1) but apparently not including the subcutaneous injection of a depot of Goserelin, a "hormone analogue" which reduces testosterone to castrate levels; see *R. v. Mental Health Act Commission, ex p. X.* (1988) 9 B.M.L.R. 77). These treatments may only be given if both of two conditions are fulfilled: (a) an independent doctor and two other people who are not doctors must certify (on Form 37) that the patient is capable of understanding the nature, purpose and likely effects of the treatment and has consented to it; it was said in *Ex p. X.* that the section only requires the capacity to understand rather than actual understanding, but actual understanding would be required for actual consent and the Commission (1991, para. 6.12) have continued to advise to that effect; *and* (b) that independent doctor (after the same consultation as is required under section 58) must certify (also on Form 37) that the treatment should be given, having regard to the likelihood of its alleviating or preventing a deterioration of the patient's condition. This section applies not only to detained patients (as defined in section 56(1) above) but also to informal patients (s. 56(2)). Thus incapable patients cannot be given these treatments at all. Capable informal and compulsory patients can only be given them with consent, a multi-disciplinary assessment of their capacity to understand the treatment, and an independent assessment of whether it should be done. Some might prefer that psychosurgery be banned altogether (Gostin, 1982); there were 274 referrals during the 10 years covered by the Commission's first five reports, the great majority from only one hospital.

The reasoning behind section 57 is partly that these treatments are so intrusive that they should never be given without the patient's informed consent, but also that there are circumstances in which even informed consent is not enough. Patients who run the risk of a long period of confinement in a maximum security special hospital if they cannot be cured may be ready to agree to anything which holds out the prospect of a cure. A striking illustration occurred in *R. v. Mental Health Act Commission, ex p. X.* (1988) 9 B.M.L.R. 77. An informal outpatient who had a long record of paedophile offences challenged the refusal of a certificate for treatment which had succeeded in reducing his sex drive. The refusal was quashed on the ground that section 57 did not apply to the particular treatment involved (see above). But the court would also have held the refusal unfair, irrational or unreasonable, because the Commissioner had applied too high a test of capacity, had no good reason for holding the patient (an intelligent young man) capable on one visit and incapable on the next, and the medical Commissioner had not applied his mind to the beneficial effects of the treatment proposed before concentrating on the alternatives which might be available or preferable. The court itself was obviously reluctant to deprive an intelligent and consenting patient of treatment which he and his doctor thought was doing him good just because the Commissioner thought that his case might be handled differently (nor will it always be easy for the doctor to consult a nurse and another professional involved in the treatment of an informal outpatient). The real answer may have been that the section did not apply at all because the young man was not a "patient" being treated for "mental disorder" but a sexual deviant being treated for his deviancy (Fennell, 1988).

Various other provisions are related to the safeguards laid down in sections 57 and 58. Section 59 provides that any consent or certificate given under either section 57 or section 58 may relate to a "plan of treatment" under which the patient is to be given one or more of the forms of treatment to which the section applies, and the plan need not have a defined time limit. Section 60 allows a patient who has given consent to a treatment, or to a plan of treatment, under either section 57 or section 58, to withdraw his consent to further treatment. Where treatment is given to a detained patient under section 57, or without consent under section 58, section 61 requires the RMO to provide a report to the Commission about the treatment and the patient's condition when the detention comes up for renewal (s. 61(1)(a)) or, for restricted patients, after the first six months of the order or direction and thereafter when he reports to the Home Secretary (s. 61(2)). The Commission can also require him to report at any other time (s. 61(1)(a)). The Commission can then cancel the certificate (s. 61(3)). In practice, few patients outside special hospitals seem to remain in hospital long enough for this review mechanism to apply. If the patient withdraws consent (s. 60), or the Commission cancels a certificate (s. 61(3)), the whole procedure will have to be gone through again, unless the RMO considers that discontinuance of the treatment would cause serious suffering to the patient (s. 62(2)).

Section 62(1) provides that:

"Sections 57 and 58 above shall not apply to any treatment—(a) which is immediately necessary to save the patient's life; or (b) which (not being irreversible) is immediately necessary to prevent a serious deterioration of his condition; or (c) which (not being irreversible or hazardous) is immediately necessary to alleviate serious suffering by the patient; or (d) which (not being irreversible or hazardous) is immediately necessary and represents the minimum interference necessary to prevent the patient from behaving violently or being a danger to himself or others."

Treatment is "irreversible" if it has unfavourable irreversible physical or psychological consequences and "hazardous" if it entails significant physical hazard (s. 62(3)). This provision can easily be misunderstood. It does *not* amount to a blanket permission to impose treatment upon any patient in those four circumstances. The effect is simply to *exempt* those listed emergency situations from the need to comply with the extra safeguards laid down in sections 57 or 58. The legal justification for using the treatment in question must still be found. For detained patients covered by section 56(1) this is supplied by section 63 (p. 143, earlier), but for informal or other detained patients, consent or the common law doctrine of necessity would have to apply. In practice, section 62(1) is unlikely to apply to any treatment covered by section 57; it may sometimes apply to ECT, but is most likely to cover the use of drugs which might otherwise be caught by the three month rule.

2. HOSPITAL PATIENTS' OTHER RIGHTS

(a) Explanations

Whenever any patient is detained under the Act, the hospital managers must do their best to ensure that he understands his legal position (s. 132(1)). Steps have to be taken "as soon as practicable" after the detention has begun, and again if the section under which the patient is detained changes, for example from a section 2 admission for assessment to a section 3 admission for treatment. The steps required are such "as are practicable to ensure that the patient understands" and they must include giving the required information both orally and in writing (s. 132(3)). If it is impossible to explain matters to the patient when he is admitted, the managers should continue their efforts until it does become possible.

The information required is considerable. The patient must understand under which section he is detained and the effect of that section, and the rights of applying to a mental health review tribunal which are available to him under it (s. 132(1)). The hospital must also explain who has the power to discharge him, including the possible bar on a discharge by his nearest relative and the relative's right to challenge this before a tribunal; the hospital's powers to censor his correspondence; the Act's provisions relating to the treatment of detained patients and the extra safeguards where certain treatments are proposed; and the protective powers of the Mental Health Act Commission and the effect of the Code of Practice (s. 132(2)). Unless the patient asks otherwise, the hospital must also "take such steps as are practicable" to supply his nearest relative (if any) with a copy of this information, either at the same time as it is given to the patient or within a reasonable time afterwards (s. 132(4)).

There is also a statutory duty to inform the patient when his detention for treatment or under an ordinary hospital order is renewed (s. 20(3)), when the form of his disorder is reclassified (s. 16(4)), and when his nearest relative is prevented from discharging him (s. 25(2)). The nearest relative must be informed in each of the last two cases; and, unless the patient or the relative has asked that this should not be done, the hospital "must take such steps as are practicable" to warn the nearest relative of the patient's impending discharge from detention, if possible at least seven days beforehand (s. 133). There is still no statutory duty to tell the patient *at the time* when the authority for his detention simply runs out, even though this may be long after he was originally informed of the position.

There is no duty to supply information to the patient's lawyer or to give reasons for any decision. Yet a major source of complaint before the European Court of Human Rights in *X. v. United Kingdom* (1981) 4 E.H.R.R. 181 was that no explanation had been given of the reasons for the patient's recall to Broadmoor after three years on conditional discharge. This was an alleged breach of Article 5(2) of the European Convention on Human Rights, which requires that "everyone who is arrested shall be informed promptly, in a language which he understands, of the reasons for his arrest and of any charge against him". In the event, the majority of the European Court found it unnecessary to rule on the disputed questions of law and fact under Article 5(2). They found this a lesser problem which was necessarily encompassed by the greater problem of failing to provide a speedy judicial review of the lawfulness of the patient's detention (p. 177, later). At such a review, an explanation would inevitably have been forthcoming. The dissenting member of the court, however, considered that the right to an explanation:

"constitutes a safeguard of personal liberty whose importance in any democratic system founded on the rule of law cannot be underestimated. Quite apart from enabling the person detained to make proper preparations for bringing legal proceedings (under Article 5(4)), it is the embodiment of a kind of legitimate confidence or expectation . . . in the relations between the individual and the public powers."

The Department of Health guidance on recalling restricted patients to hospital (HSG(93)20; LAC(93)9; p. 173, later) accepts that explanations must be given, but with care.

The Code of Practice emphasises that "all patients should be given, throughout their stay in hospital, as much information as possible about their care and treatment" (para. 14.1). The purpose is to ensure that patients understand, not only their legal position, but also why they are in hospital. Although there is no legal obligation to do so, the Code insists that it should be made clear to informal patients that they are free to leave hospital at any time. Presumably this includes reminding compulsory patients when their detention expires. Information should also be given in a "suitable manner". Staff cannot do this unless they are properly trained themselves. The Mental Health Act Commission were "dismayed" (1989, para. 13.2) at the lack of staff understanding, particularly of the hospital managers' power of discharge, and at the Department's delay in translating their leaflets into languages patients could understand.

(b) Visitors and mail

Under the 1983 Act, the scope for censoring patients' mail is much reduced. Nevertheless, the managers of any hospital or mental nursing home, acting through a member of staff as authorised censor (s. 134(7)), may open and inspect any postal packet in order to discover whether it qualifies for censorship (s. 134(4)). In practice, however, this is unlikely to happen outside special hospitals. In any other type of hospital, the only interference allowed is to withhold from the post office any outgoing mail addressed by a detained patient to a person who has asked that communications to him from the patient should be withheld (s. 134(1)(a)). Such a request must be made in writing, either to the hospital managers, or to the RMO or to the Secretary of State.

This also applies to patients in special hospitals. But their mail may also be withheld from the post office if the censor considers that it is likely to cause danger to anyone (including someone on the hospital staff), or to cause distress to anyone (other than someone on the hospital staff) (s. 134(1)(b)). Incoming mail for special hospital patients may be withheld if it is thought necessary to do so in the interests of the safety of the patient or for the protection of other people (s. 134(2)). However, neither of these wider powers applies to mail to or from any of the following: a Minister of the Crown or Member of either House of Parliament, a Master or officer of the Court of Protection or Lord Chancellor's Visitor, any of the public sector ombudsmen (the Parliamentary Commissioner, Health Service Commissioner and Local Government Commissioners), a mental health review tribunal, a health authority, local social services authority, Community Health Council or probation and aftercare committee, the managers of the hospital where the patient is detained, any *legally qualified* person instructed by the patient to act as his legal adviser, and the European Commission or Court of Human Rights (s. 134(3)). However, there is nothing to stop any individual named on this list putting in a request under section 134(1)(a) that mail from a particular patient be withheld.

If the hospital censor does inspect and open a postal packet, but does not withhold anything, he must put a written note of that fact, along with his name and that of the hospital, inside before resealing it (Mental Health (Hospital, Guardianship and Consent to Treatment) Regulations 1983, reg. 17(1)). If he decides to withhold it, or anything in it, he must enclose a note to the same effect and describing any item withheld. He must also record in a special register the fact that it has been withheld, the date when this was done, the grounds for doing so, a description of the items, and his name (s. 134(5) and reg. 17(2)).

If the mail is withheld on either of the wider grounds applicable only to special hospital patients (s. 134(1)(b) or (2)) the managers must give notice of this to the patient within seven days, and also to the person (if known) by whom an incoming packet was sent. This must be in writing (s. 134(6)) and must also give the grounds for withholding the packet and the name of the censor and hospital (reg. 17(3)) and an explanation of the Mental Health Act Commission's powers of review. These should be included in the note enclosed with the packet, in which case they are sufficient notice to the person to whom it is addressed (reg. 17(2) and (3)). The sender will require a separate notice. The Commission must review the hospital's decision, if asked to do so (in any way they think sufficient, not necessarily in writing; reg. 18(1)) either by the patient or by the person by whom incoming mail was sent. The application must be made within six months of getting the notice that the mail was withheld, and should include that notice (s. 121(7); reg. 18(2)). The Commission can direct the production of any documents, information or evidence that they reasonably require (reg. 17(3)), including, of course, the offending letter itself. They have complete discretion to overrule the hospital's decision, for whatever reason they think fit (s. 121(8)).

The European Convention on Human Rights, in Article 8, guarantees everyone "respect for his . . . correspondence." Interference by a public body is only allowed where this is "necessary in a democratic society in the interests of national security, public safety or the economic well-being of the country, for the prevention of disorder or crime, for the protection of health or morals or for the protection of the rights and freedom of others." On the face of it, even after the 1983 Act, the censorship of special hospital patients' mail goes rather further than this (and the European Court in the *Golder Case*, (1975) 1 E.H.R.R. 524, considered the list of exceptions closed). In *Y. v. United Kingdom*, applic. no. 6870/75, a Broadmoor patient did complain that he had been prevented from sending a telegram to his parents about his appeal. But as he was not apparently prevented from sending a letter and in any event delivered his message to his mother when she visited him two days letter, the European Commission decided that there had been no material interference. Each letter has to be considered on its merits. Requests to the Mental Health Act Commission are rare (42 in the first eight years of the Commission's operation) but a good proportion succeed (25 during that period) (Mental Health Act Commission, 1985, 1987, 1989, 1991).

As for visitors, the Code of Practice (para. 26.1) takes the view that all detained patients are entitled to maintain contact with and be visited by whomsoever they wish. Restrictions should only be imposed where contact is discernibly anti-therapeutic for the patient or where the behaviour or propensities of a particular visitor are so disruptive or subversive that exclusion is necessary as a last resort (para. 26.2). Otherwise visiting and other forms of contact should be facilitated and encouraged (paras. 26.3, 26.4).

3. HEALTH SERVICE COMPLAINTS

The old Board of Control combined the roles of overseeing the management and general standards of mental hospitals and protecting the interests of individual patients. In 1959, it was assumed that both could safely be left to the internal machinery of the health service. However, a succession of allegations of neglect and misconduct in mental hospitals (see particularly Robb, 1967, and Morris, 1969), and inquiries such as those into the Ely, Farleigh and Whittingham hospitals, revealed that some special oversight of standards in hospitals catering for the most vulnerable patients was still needed. An independent advisory service, staffed by teams of health service staff on secondment, was set up in 1969 to advise the Secretary of State in relation to the elderly or mentally ill. This began as the Hospital Advisory Service but became the Health Advisory Service in 1976. Also in 1976, a National Development Team was set up to provide information and advice, and to encourage good practice, in the provision of both hospital and community services for people with learning disabilities. Neither of these bodies deals with individual complaints or grievances. The Mental Health Act Commission, established by the 1983 Act (see section 4 later), does deal with both general issues and individual complaints, but (with minor exceptions) only in relation to detained patients.

No doubt there will always be scandals in which the mental health services are seen to have let down either the patients or the public. Recent years have produced a particularly rich crop (usefully summarized by Shepherd, 1995). Perhaps increasingly, the focus is upon the failure to identify and provide appropriate services for some particularly disturbed or dangerous patients. But there is still concern about standards within institutions. The most recent statutory enquiry, established by the Secretary of State under section 125 of the Mental Health Act 1983, concerned allegations of improper care and treatment at Ashworth Hospital and the arrangements for handling patients' complaints (Blom-Cooper, 1992). This recommended that individual complaints should be dealt with by the hospitals' own complaints machinery rather than the Mental Health Act Commission. The Commission (1993, paras. 5.2, 6.1) did not agree, but it did draw unfavourable comparisons between its own resources and powers and those of the Health Service Commissioner.

(a) NHS complaints machinery

Under the Hospital Complaints Procedures Act 1985 health authorities and trusts must make arrangements for investigating and dealing with complaints made by or on behalf of any hospital patient about any aspect of his treatment. Section 1 of the Act obliged the Secretary of State to give them directions for this purpose (see DHSS Circular HC(88)37). A senior officer must be designated to receive formal complaints and to investigate all those that do not involve either clinical judgment, serious untoward incidents, disciplinary proceedings, physical abuse of patients, or possible criminal proceedings. These must be referred to even more senior officers for appropriate action. Guidelines for dealing with complaints about clinical judgment were first issued in 1981 (DHSS Circular HC(81)5) and remain as agreed with the profession at that time. The Code of Practice under the Mental Health Act (para. 23.3) expects staff to bring these procedures to patients' attention and to give "reasonable assistance" to patients who are unable to formulate a complaint for themselves. A complaints officer should log complaints and ensure that patients are told the outcome.

The 1985 Act applies in all hospitals, including special hospitals, but it was not until 1992 that the Special Hospitals Service Authority devised new procedures, with an independent investigative element for complaints of ill-treatment or abuse, which were intended to be accessible and effective (see Blom-Cooper, 1992; Special Hospitals Service Authority, 1994). These were welcomed by the Mental Health Act Commission (1993, para. 5.8) which is "not infrequently" told by patients that they are afraid of the repercussions of complaining.

The Government (Department of Health, 1995b) have decided, in response to the review committee on NHS complaints procedures (Wilson, 1994), to introduce a single procedure for all complaints about NHS services, whether in or out of hospital. This would be quite separate from the procedures for disciplining staff and doctors. There would be two stages: first, the provider would try to resolve the complaint as quickly as possible internally, with a deadline of two days for an initial response and four weeks for a full one; second, unless other action can be taken or everything practicable has already been done, a review panel would be established under an independent lay chairman; panels wholly or partly related to clinical matters would be advised by two independent clinical assessors. Special attention should be paid to the need for vulnerable groups to have support and help in making complaints and advocacy schemes are welcomed (although the Government has so far stopped short of making this a legal requirement). The problem is that mental patients' complaints may be seen as a symptom of their disorder or a result of their disability and therefore not taken as seriously as they should be (Law Society, 1994).

(b) The ombudsmen

Certain types of complaint can be taken to the Health Service Commissioner, or NHS Ombudsman, under sections 106 to 120 of the National Health Service Act 1977, or to the Parliamentary Commissioner, "the" Ombudsman, under the Parliamentary Commissioner Act 1967. The posts are held by the same person.

The NHS Ombudsman deals with complaints by or on behalf of a person who has suffered injustice or hardship caused by the hospital or health authorities, either through maladministration (which means inefficiency), or failure in the services actually provided, or failure to provide a service which it is their duty to provide. Many things are outside his jurisdiction. These include serious incidents or major breakdown in services which are the subject of inquiries set up by the Secretary of State. He cannot deal with matters which could be taken to a mental health review tribunal or to a court, unless he is satisfied that it is unreasonable to expect the complainant to do this. He has, for example, been known to investigate complaints that informal patients have been kept in locked wards and in ignorance of their rights.

There are two other important restrictions which the Government now intends to remove. He cannot at present deal with complaints against family health service practitioners. Nor can he investigate "action taken in connection with the diagnosis of illness or the care or treatment of a patient which in his opinion was taken solely in the exercise of clinical judgment" (Sched. 13, Pt. II). This clearly excludes individual treatment decisions, but the dividing line between administrative and clinical matters is not always easy to draw. In a psychiatric unit, such things as physical surroundings and ward routine, although primarily administrative, may be dictated by the clinical policies of the particular consultant. They may be said to amount to milieu therapy or a token economy or the like. Commissioners have generally not regarded these decisions as taken "solely" in the exercise of clinical judgment and have been prepared to investigate. Removal of the restriction will still be an important step.

The NHS Ombudsman and the Mental Health Act Commission have agreed (Mental Health Act Commission, 1991, para. 5.4) that the Commission should deal first with complaints about the circumstances or consequences of detention, and the Ombudsman with other complaints, but where their jurisdictions overlap the patient should approach the Commission first. The Ombudsman has a full-time staff which specialises in complaints handling, while the Commission may have greater expertise in this particular field. But as the Commission is a special health authority under the 1977 Act, its activities are themselves subject to investigation by the NHS Ombudsman.

"The" Ombudsman deals with complaints of injustice caused by maladministration in government departments, including the decisions taken by the Home Office in relation to restricted patients. He accepted a complaint from Sam Kynaston that it had taken two years for the Home Office to act on the RMO's recommendation for a conditional discharge. However, he concluded that there had been no maladministration because of the extensive consultations required. The Ombudsman is only concerned with administrative short-comings, and not with the merits of decisions taken without maladministration. Nor can he investigate matters which could be taken to a tribunal or a court of law, unless satisfied that it would be unreasonable to expect the complainant to do so.

4. THE MENTAL HEALTH ACT COMMISSION

The 1959 Act left mental patients in England and Wales without any independent body which was specifically committed to safeguarding their welfare and interests. Yet patients in Scotland have the benefit of the Mental Welfare Commission, which has a general duty to "exercise protective functions in respect of persons who may, by reason of mental disorder, be incapable of adequately protecting their persons or their interests" (Mental Health (Scotland) Act 1984, s. 3(1)). This covers patients both in and out of hospital, whether informal or compulsory. It includes a variety of functions, such as visiting patients, investigating their complaints, and even discharging them from compulsion. The Commission have championed many causes on behalf of patients, and anyone reading their publications (see 1972, 1975, 1981) would find it hard to understand why the Scots were thought to need such an informed and caring body while the English and Welsh were not.

The main advocates for a Mental Welfare Commission south of the border were the Royal College of Psychiatrists (1981). They undoubtedly hoped that the medical members might provide an informal means of reviewing questions of clinical judgment, by supplying general guidance and second opinions when asked. This might have avoided the need for the more specific restrictions and controls then being proposed by other bodies, such as the National Association for Mental Health (MIND) and the Butler Committee. These bodies tended to favour a patients' advocacy scheme (MIND) or a system of patients' friends (Butler Committee) rather than a new institution. In the event, we now have a combination of controls over certain treatments and a new institution which, among other things, operates those controls. Patients' advocates were provided for in the Disabled Persons (Services, Consultation and Representation) Act 1986, but the relevant sections seem unlikely to be brought into force. The Mental Health Act Commission has nothing like the scope of the Scottish equivalent, because it is almost exclusively concerned with the interests of detained patients in hospital. However, there is the possibility of extending its protective functions to informal patients in the future.

(a) Constitution

The Commission is set up as a special health authority under section 11 of the National Health Service Act 1977 (1983 Act, s. 121(1)). The chairman and members are appointed by the Secretary of State, for varying periods of up to four years (Mental Health Act Commission Regulations 1983, reg. 3). Members are eligible for reappointment, but they may also be removed at any time and for any reason (regs. 5 and 4). There are no qualifications laid down and no maximum or minimum numbers. It has around 90 members, drawn from medicine, nursing, psychology, social work, the law, and lay people. The combined professional interests heavily outweigh the lay and legal members, and the clinical professions may just be in a majority. The need to tread delicately in balancing lay and professional viewpoints (to say nothing of differences within and between the professions) is probably a greater problem for the Commission than the lack of any formal safeguard of its independence from Government.

The Commission may establish its own committees and they may establish sub-committees (reg. 7(3) and (4)). For its first few years, the Commission operated through three regional panels, staffed by three regional offices, with the full Commission meeting twice a year. It now has a centralised staff structure, with seven visiting teams linked to NHS regions and three special hospital panels to handle visiting and complaints, and a series of Standing Committees on its main topics of interest (Mental Health Act Commission 1989, 1991, 1993). The Secretary of State appoints a central policy committee, which has power to co-opt other members (reg. 7(1)). This committee has the statutory tasks of drawing up proposals for the Code of Practice and drafting the Commission's biennial report (reg. 7(2)) and generally oversees the Commission's activities and controls its finances.

(b) Functions

The Commission has six statutory functions under the 1983 Act and the Mental Health Act Commission (Establishment and Constitution) Order 1983, including the power to review the censorship of patients' mail already discussed (section 2(b) earlier).

Reviewing treatment. The Commission appoints the independent doctors and other people to give certificates for treatment under sections 57 and 58 (see section 1(e) earlier; s. 121(2)(c) and reg. 3(2)(c)). These need not be members of the Commission; the doctors usually are not, whereas the non-medical people who certify consent and capacity under section 57 usually are. Allied to this is the second function of receiving reports from the RMO about all treatment which is carried out on detained patients under section 57, and all treatment which is carried out without consent but with a second opinion under section 58. Generally, these reports arrive when a detained patient comes up for renewal, or when the RMO has to report to the Secretary of State about a restricted patient. But the Commission can require a report at any time. The RMO has no obligation to report on the treatment of informal patients under section 57 unless the Commission asks. The Commission can cancel the certificates authorising these treatments, by notifying the RMO. This will usually, but not invariably, prevent the treatment taking place (s. 121(2)(b) and reg. 3(2)(b)).

Reviewing the Act in operation. The Commission has a general protective function over all detained patients. It must "keep under review the exercise of the powers and the discharge of the duties conferred or imposed by this Act so far as relating to the detention of patients or to patients liable to be detained . . . " (ss. 120(1), 121(2)(b) and reg. 3(2)(c)). This covers the admission and detention process, so that the Commission can scrutinise admission documents and consider whether it is happy with the way in which, for example, medical recommendations are being completed. It may also look at practice in relation to renewal of detention, leave of absence and discharge. Unlike the Scottish Mental Welfare Commission, it has no power to discharge patients. It can certainly consider how patients are detained in the hospital, and has taken a close interest in such issues as seclusion and the management of particularly difficult patients. It can also look at other issues relating to the treatment of detained patients, provided that some power or duty contained in the Act is involved. Priorities over the years have included transfer delays, patients' money and benefits, and black and ethnic minority issues. A broad approach to the terms of reference has enabled the Commission also to look at "de facto" detention, compulsory care and after-care in the community, and the treatment of incapacitated people. Most recently it has been at the forefront of the calls for a review of the 1983 Act (Mental Health Act Commission, 1993).

Visiting. The Commission must arrange to visit and interview in private detained patients in both hospitals and mental nursing homes (s. 120(1)(a)). It is left to the Commission to decide whether it will see all patients automatically and how often to visit. This is governed as much by the level of resources allocated as by the perceived need. Priority is given to the special hospitals, where the aim is to contact each patient at least once a year (MHAC, 1993, para. 5.3). Visitors deal with both individual patients and general points and some visits are "out of hours" or unannounced. It is very difficult for any outsider to get a real sense of what life is like, especially in the maximum security environment of a special hospital.

Investigating complaints. The Commission must arrange to investigate complaints (s. 120(1)(b)). These are of two sorts: (i) complaints about something which happened while the patient was detained in a hospital or mental nursing home and which he considers has not been properly dealt with by the management; these can only come from the patient himself and the Commission may insist that he goes through the hospital procedures first; these are serious limitations, especially for severely disabled and special hospital patients who may be unable or reluctant to make complaints themselves; and (ii) any other complaint about the exercise of the Act's powers and duties in relation to someone who is or has been detained; this does not have the same limitations but the view has been taken that if a complaint falls within (i) it cannot be dealt with under (ii). Further, the Commission need never pursue an investigation which it does not consider "appropriate" and its general arrangements can exclude specified types of case (s. 120(2)).

Associated powers. The Commission's investigatory powers are more limited than those of the Ombudsmen. It may visit and interview and a doctor may examine in private any patient detained in a mental nursing home and visitors may also inspect the records relating to the detention and treatment of any patient who is or has been detained in a mental nursing home (s. 120(4)). Health authorities (including the Special Hospitals Service Authority) and NHS trusts are directed to provide them with similar facilities (see DHSS Circular HC(83)19 and DH Circular HC(91)29, Welsh Office Circulars WHC(83)25 and WHC(92)10). But they cannot insist on people helping them or providing them with documents in the way that the Ombudsmen can. Nor have they any specific sanction. They will obviously inform the parties of the results of any investigation, and if the second type of complaint comes from a Member of Parliament, they must report to him (s. 120(3)). The Commission (1993, para. 16.2) would like to reinforce its powers with an official notification procedure, requiring managers to rectify blatant bad practice, with an ultimate sanction of publicity.

Extending its remit. The Secretary of State does have power, after due consultation, to extend these supervisory and investigatory functions to the "care and treatment, or any aspect of the care and treatment" of informal patients in hospitals and mental nursing homes (s. 124(4) and (5)). Curiously, this is wider than the exact wording of their powers in relation to detained patients, and perhaps an indication of what those powers were meant to mean. No doubt it is more important, and more practicable, to concentrate on detained patients, who are only about 5 per cent of the whole. But they already have the protection afforded by the mechanism of their detention and nearly three-quarters of them are mentally ill. Some of the most vulnerable patients in mental hospitals are the severely handicapped or psycho-geriatric cases. They are rarely "sectioned", because this is not needed to secure their co-operation, but they are totally dependent upon the hospital and its staff for their survival and comfort. The Commission has repeatedly pressed for its jurisdiction to be extended, especially to the *de facto* detained, and more recently to the operation of the Act in relation to all patients, including those under guardianship or supervision in the community (Mental Health Act Commission, 1993, para. 16.2).

The Code of Practice. It is the Commission's task to make proposals to the Secretary of State about what should go into the Code of Practice which is required by section 118 of the 1983 Act (reg. 3(2)(d)). It is his task to draw it up, in consultation with other bodies (s. 118(1),(3)). The code must be laid before Parliament, which can reject it by passing a resolution within 40 days (s. 118(4),(5)). The purpose is to give guidance to doctors, managers and staff of hospitals, and ASWs, on the admission of patients to hospital, guardianship and after-care under supervision under the Act; and to doctors and other professionals on the medical treatment of patients suffering from mental disorder (s. 118(1)(a),(b)). The former could cover guidelines for distinguishing informal and compulsory cases. The latter is not limited to hospital patients but does only cover medical treatment. In particular, the code is expected to identify treatments which give rise to such concern that they "should not be given" without both informed consent and a second opinion, even though this has not been made a legal requirement (s. 118(2)). The Commission prepared a draft Code of Practice in 1985. This was apparently found helpful by some practitioners but did not find favour with the Secretary of State. He arranged for an independent working group to draft the Code which was laid before Parliament in December 1989 and revised in 1993 (the vicissitudes of the code's preparation are discussed by Fennell, 1990, Cavadino, 1993, and Richardson, 1993).

Finally, the Commission publishes a report on its activities every second year, which must be laid before Parliament (s. 121(10)). The reports published so far contain many useful comments on the Act and its operation, speak with pride of the invaluable work of the Commission in reducing the sum total of human misery, but leave one ultimately depressed at the remaining level of that misery and of the resources needed to combat it effectively. Rather ruefully, the Commission (1989, para. 11.9) commented on the "dramatic activity" at Broadmoor, and the other special hospitals, prompted by a Report from the Health Advisory Service and the Social Services Inspectorate (1988). The Commission was not able to achieve improvements at Broadmoor until others stepped in, nor did it detect the seriousness of the problems revealed by the Ashworth inquiry (Blom-Cooper, 1992). And the future problems will increasingly lie, not only in special hospitals and secure units, but in private hospitals and "care in the community" which are a great deal more difficult to police in this way.

7 LEAVING HOSPITAL

"Community care" now refers to two different but interconnected policies. The idea that as many as possible of the people being looked after in mental hospitals should be transferred to less institutional settings goes back at least as far as the Percy Commission of 1957. It entails the provision of specialist medical services for them outside hospital. The idea that social services departments should be responsible for assessing and funding the residential and other community care needs of elderly and disabled or disordered people is much more recent. This chapter deals with the first, and in particular with the ways in which a compulsory patient may leave the hospital where he is currently detained, while Chapter 9 deals with the second.

Most patients will need both health and social services, irrespective of whether or not they have been detained in hospital. Since 1991, the authorities have been required to operate the care programme approach for all mentally ill patients and others so far as it is relevant (Circular HC(90)23; LASSL (90)11; but see North, Ritchie and Ward, 1993; Social Services Inspectorate 1995). This should involve a systematic assessment of the patient's health and social care needs, an agreed care plan, a key-worker to monitor its delivery and to make sure the patient does not get lost, and regular reviews of his progress. The Code states that it is the responsibility of the responsible medical officer (RMO) to ensure that a multi-disciplinary discussion takes place to establish a care plan and organise its delivery (paras. 27.6, 27.7). This should consider the patient's own wishes and needs; the views of any relevant relative, friend or supporter; the need for agreement with the receiving health authority; the possible involvement of other agencies; the details of the care plan, covering day care, accommodation, out-patient treatment, counselling and financial and other support, as far as resources allow; the appointment of a key-worker from either health or social services; and the identification of any unmet need (para. 27.9). A timetable and the allocation of responsibility should be agreed and everything recorded in writing and regularly reviewed (paras. 27.10, 27.11).

On top of this, NHS provider units now have to keep supervision registers, rather like the child protection registers (see Guidelines, HSG(94)5). These should identify people under their care outside hospital who are at significant risk either of suicide, or of serious violence to others, or of severe self neglect, as a result of a severe and enduring mental illness or diagnosed personality disorder. Inclusion on the register should be discussed along with the care programme but the decision rests with the patient's consultant psychiatrist (see also Royal College of Psychiatrists, 1991).

There is a specific statutory duty to co-operate in the provision of after-care for some detained patients. Section 117 of the Mental Health Act 1983 requires both the local Health Authority and the local social services authority to provide after-care services (s. 117(2)) for former compulsory in-patients who are resident in or sent to their area on discharge (s. 117(3)). This applies to any patient detained under an admission for treatment, a hospital order, or a transfer direction who then ceases to be detained and (whether or not immediately afterwards) leaves hospital (s. 117(1)). The after-care services themselves are not defined, apart from two specific duties towards patients subject to after-care under supervision (pp. 170, 171, later). They will be a combination of those provided by the health service under the National Health Service Act 1977 and the community care services provided by local authorities (see Chapter 9).

This is a mandatory duty owed to the individual patient. In *R. v. Ealing District Health Authority, ex p. Fox* [1993] 1 W.L.R. 373 a mental health review tribunal had granted a conditional discharge deferred until the conditions were met but the local psychiatrists were not prepared to act so the health authority refused to provide supervision in the community. In judicial review proceedings this decision was quashed and a declaration granted that they had acted unlawfully in failing to make practical arrangements for the patient's after-care. The judge refused to grant an order of mandamus compelling the authority to do so, because the effect would have been to force a doctor to act against his clinical judgment; but there were other steps they could take to resolve matters. It is, however, unlikely that the courts would allow the patient to sue for damages or an injunction in such cases (see the discussion on p. 209, later).

1. LEAVE OF ABSENCE

The RMO can grant leave of absence to any compulsory patient (s. 17(1)), but if the patient is restricted, the permission of the Home Secretary is also required (s. 41(3)(c)(i); see Sched. 1, Pt. II, para. 3(a)). Leave can be given for a special occasion (such as a wedding), or for a definite period (such as a weekend), or indefinitely. It can be extended without bringing the patient back to hospital (s. 17(2)). But it can also be revoked at any time if the RMO thinks this necessary in the interests of the patient's own health or safety or for the protection of other people. Notice of revocation and recall must be in writing and addressed either to the patient or to the person in charge of him (s. 17(4)). The Home Secretary can himself recall a restricted patient from leave (Sched. 1, Pt. II, para. 3(b)). Leave can be subject to whatever conditions the RMO thinks necessary in the patient's own interests or to protect other people (s. 17(1)). These can include staying in another hospital, living with a particular person, or attending a clinic for treatment. The patient is still liable to detention and can be obliged to accept medical treatment, subject to the usual safeguards; but the Code of Practice (para. 20.8) advises that he should be recalled to hospital if it becomes necessary to administer treatment without his consent. The RMO can also direct that the patient remains in the custody of a member of the hospital staff or of some other person authorised in writing (s. 17(3)). The effect of this is that the patient can be recaptured the moment he escapes, rather than if and when he fails to return to hospital.

Most patients cannot be kept on a string indefinitely by giving them leave. They cannot be recalled once the power to detain has lapsed (s. 17(5)). The case of *R. v. Hallstrom, ex p. W.* [1986] Q.B. 1090 effectively outlawed the practice of using prolonged leave of absence as a means of ensuring that patients who did not need to be in hospital could be obliged to go on taking their medication outside it. The court held, first, that authority to detain a patient could not be renewed while he was on leave, because under section 20(3)(b) the RMO's report must be made to the managers of the hospital where he is "detained", as opposed to "liable to be detained" (which was probably a draftsman's slip). Secondly, the patient could not be recalled from leave simply to renew his detention, if it was not in fact appropriate and necessary for him to be detained in hospital for treatment. The Code (para. 20.6) also says that refusal to take medication should not on its own be a reason for revocation.

This means that unrestricted patients can remain on leave of absence for a maximum of one year (the former limit of six months was abolished by the Mental Health (Patients in the Community) Act 1995). Restricted patients can be recalled by the Home Secretary (though not after 12 months by the RMO) at any time (Sched. 1, Pt. II, para. 3(c)). Patients who are on leave can apply to a tribunal just as if they were still in hospital. Tribunals also have power to recommend that unrestricted patients be given leave, although they cannot order it.

The Butler Committee on Mentally Abnormal Offenders (1975) were enthusiastic about leave of absence as a way of providing compulsory after-care. The Code (para. 20.1) also thinks that leave can be an important part of a treatment plan, but emphasises the need for good planning in advance, involving the patient and the people and services who will be looking after him on leave (paras. 20.1, 20.2, 20.3). The after-care provisions of section 117 (see p. 159, earlier) apply: although the patient is still "liable to be detained" he has ceased actually to be so (Code, para. 20.4.a).

Things can go badly wrong whatever the legal label attached to the patient. In 1979, Ronald Sailes committed a particularly brutal murder while on leave from Broadmoor, where he had spent 15 years as a restricted patient and remained for another year as an unrestricted patient. The subsequent Review of Leave Arrangements for Special Hospital Patients (DHSS, 1981b) identified the need for prior consultation between all the disciplines involved with the patient inside hospital, and with the agencies outside it, and to give the latter the information they needed to do their jobs. The police should be told about present and former restricted patients, and others convicted of serious sexual or violent offences, who are given leave, but not usually otherwise. Reconciling the requirements of patient confidentiality and public safety can present problems throughout the system.

2. TRANSFERS

(a) To other hospitals in England and Wales

A patient detained (under or as if under an application) in an ordinary NHS hospital can be transferred at any time without formality to another hospital, or other accommodation, under the same management (s. 19(3)). Even if the patient is restricted, there is no need for the Home Secretary's consent. A patient detained in a special hospital (unless sent there by a court on remand or an interim hospital order) can be transferred to another special hospital at any time by direction of the Secretary of State (s. 123(1)).

A patient so detained in an ordinary NHS hospital can be transferred into another hospital under different management, with only a little more formality (s. 19(1)(a) and Mental Health (Hospital, Guardianship and Consent to Treatment) Regulations 1983, reg. 7(2)). Form 24 must be signed by the authorised officer of the managers of the first hospital, who must be satisfied that the patient can be admitted to the new hospital within 28 days. The form allows the patient to be taken there within that time, by an officer of the managers of either hospital, or by someone else authorised by the receiving hospital (reg. 9(1)(a)). Restricted patients can be transferred in just the same way as unrestricted, provided that the Home Secretary agrees (s. 43(3)(c)(ii) and Sched. 1, Pt. II, para. 5(a)).

This procedure can also be used to transfer patients into and out of the special hospitals. Any compulsory patient originally admitted to an ordinary hospital can be transferred into a special hospital if he meets the criteria and a bed is available. Once there, it can be difficult to obtain a transfer back into an NHS hospital. Transfer to a less secure environment is usually an important step towards obtaining discharge or even leave of absence. The Secretary of State also has power to direct a transfer out of a special hospital (s. 123(2)), but apparently this is never used (Gostin and Fennell, 1992). The same regulations as to transport apply (reg. 9(2)).

The ordinary procedures also apply to patients detained in mental nursing homes. But if they are maintained there by contract with a health authority, the authority (by an authorised officer) can authorise the transfer (reg. 7(4)).

After a patient has been transferred, the authority to detain him is simply amended as if he had been admitted to the new hospital on the date of his original admission (s. 19(2)(a)).

(b) To other parts of the United Kingdom and islands

Any compulsory patient in England and Wales can be transferred to a hospital in Scotland or Northern Ireland, provided that this is in his interests and the necessary arrangements have been made (ss. 80 and 81). Once again, the only exceptions are patients remanded to hospital by a court or on an interim hospital order. Patients under guardianship here can be transferred to guardianship elsewhere in the same way. The transfer of unrestricted patients is authorised by the Secretary of State for Health and of restricted patients by the Home Secretary. Similarly, the Secretary of State for Scotland can transfer compulsory patients from Scotland (Mental Health (Scotland) Act 1984, s. 77), the Department of Health and Social Services for Northern Ireland can transfer unrestricted patients, and the Secretary of State for Northern Ireland can transfer restricted patients (1983 Act, s. 82). Similar powers exist between England and Wales and the Channel Islands or Isle of Man (1983 Act, ss. 83–85 and local legislation), and between Scotland and Northern Ireland (1984 Act, ss. 80, 81) or the islands (1984 Act, s. 82 and local legislation).

The general effect of a transfer is that the patient is treated as if he had been newly admitted under the equivalent law in the receiving country on the date when he arrives there. This is bound to alter the period for which he is liable to be detained. But a patient admitted for assessment here is treated as a short-term admission in the receiving country and vice versa. Similarly, a restriction order or direction must end whenever it would have ended if he had remained in the original country. A person who was qualified to act as the patient's nearest relative in Scotland or England, but who is not qualified under the law of the receiving country, can continue to act. But a court order replacing the nearest relative is treated as if it had been made by a court in the receiving country, for such purposes as amendment and revocation. A hospital receiving a patient transferred here must record the admission date on Form 32 and must tell the nearest relative as soon as possible (reg. 11). The RMO must decide which of the four forms of mental disorder applies and record this on Form 33. If a patient is transferred out of England and Wales, the old application, order or direction ceases to have effect when he reaches the new place (s. 91(1)).

(c) Abroad

The Home Secretary has power to transfer foreign patients out of the country, although he very rarely uses it. The patient must be neither a British citizen nor a Commonwealth citizen with a right of abode under section 2(1)(b) of the Immigration Act 1971. He must be receiving hospital in-patient treatment for mental illness. And he must be detained, either under a civil admission for treatment or under a hospital order, restriction order or transfer direction (s. 86(1)). Patients detained only for assessment, or remanded to hospital by a court or under an interim hospital order, cannot be transferred under this section. This section also applies to patients detained in Northern Ireland and there is an equivalent in the Mental Health (Scotland) Act 1984 for those detained in Scotland.

It must appear to the Home Secretary that proper arrangements have been made, not only for the transfer, but also for the patient's treatment and care in the country where he is going, and that it is in the patient's own interests for him to go (s. 86(2)). In theory, the patient could be sent to any country outside the United Kingdom or islands, but only his own country is likely to accept him. The Home Secretary authorises the transfer by warrant. He may also direct how the patient is to travel to his destination. This can be under escort or in some other form of custody, but obviously the Home Secretary can only insist on this until arrival in the receiving country.

However, these transfers must now be approved by a mental health review tribunal (s. 86(3)). This was suggested by what is now the Commission for Racial Equality. Obviously, the dangers of misinterpretation are particularly great where there are cultural differences and some independent safeguard is certainly desirable. The DHSS (DHSS *et al.*, 1978) expected that the tribunal would "form an opinion on the adequacy of information as to facilities in the receiving country", but that the Home Secretary would still have to make sure that the arrangements had been made. However, the Home Secretary may have other powers to deport the patient, for example under the Immigration Act 1971 or the Repatriation of Offenders Act 1984, where there is no safeguard for the patient's care. He may use these instead (*R. v. Secretary of State for Home Department, ex p. Alghali* [1986] Imm. A.R. 376), unless the patient is so severely ill that it would be inhumane to do so, when his decision might be susceptible to judicial review (*R. v. Secretary of State for the Home Department, ex p. Talmasani* [1987] Imm. A.R. 32, C.A.).

A patient who is subject to a restriction order when he is transferred abroad will remain so subject, in case he returns to this country before it expires (s. 91(2)).

(d) Into guardianship

Any unrestricted patient can be transferred into the guardianship of the local social services authority or a private individual approved by them (s. 19(1)(a) and reg. 7(3)). The procedure is much simpler than a fresh application for guardianship, but it must be done before the compulsory admission runs out. The transfer is authorised by the hospital managers on part I of Form 25 and confirmed by the authority on part II. It may also be authorised by a health authority which is maintaining the patient in a mental nursing home (reg. (4)). The local authority must specify the date on which the transfer will take place and the consent of any private guardian must be obtained.

Guardianship (discussed in Chapter 9) was meant to be an alternative to hospital for patients who did not need in-patient treatment but did need a structure to their lives in the community. However, it has not been widely used as a form of statutory after-care, perhaps because it is a social rather than a health service function and the guardian's limited powers do not include a power to insist upon treatment. The new power of supervised discharge (see 4(b) later) is likely to prove more popular with hospitals and perhaps even with social services.

3. ABSCONDERS AND ESCAPERS

Theoretically, there is no difference between the escape of a dangerous psychopath from Broadmoor and the failure of a harmless schizophrenic to return from a shopping expedition, although the response in practice will be quite different. It is a crime punishable with up to two years' imprisonment to "induce or knowingly assist" any compulsory patient to absent himself without leave or to escape from legal custody, or knowingly to harbour one who has escaped, or to give him help in order to prevent or hinder his recapture (s. 128), It can also be a conspiracy to commit a common law public nuisance, for example to bring in such things as rope, hacksaw, glass cutters and other tools to help a "homicidal lunatic" escape from Broadmoor (*R. v. Soul* (1980) 70 Cr.App.R. 295). The Act itself makes elaborate provision for the recapture of compulsory patients. If necessary, a warrant to gain entry to premises to recapture the absconder can be obtained under section 135(2) (p. 82, earlier); sometimes there may also be a common law or other power of entry (pp. 79, 80, earlier).

(a) Escaping from legal custody

A person is in legal custody if he is required or authorised by or under the Act to be conveyed to any place, or to be kept in custody, or to be detained in a place of safety (s. 137(1)). This usually applies to people on the move or those who have not yet been admitted to hospital (but not to a hospital patient who is simply absent without leave; *D'Souza v. D.P.P.* [1992] 1 W.L.R. 1073, H.L.). Those who take or detain such people have all the "powers, authorities, protection and privileges" of a constable for the purpose (s. 137(2)). This does not mean that they can do what they like. Even constables can only use such force as is reasonably necessary to achieve their lawful object.

A person who escapes from legal custody can be retaken by the person from whom he escaped, or by any police officer, or by any approved social worker. If he has already been compulsorily admitted to a hospital (and escapes, for example, when being escorted back from leave of absence), he can also be retaken by someone on the staff of, or authorised by, that hospital (s. 138(1)). If he is being taken to or from a hospital under any of the Act's transfer powers or under any of the powers relating to people concerned in criminal proceedings or transferred from prison, or if he is being taken to or detained in a place of safety pending admission to hospital under those latter powers, he can also be retaken by someone on the staff of, or authorised by, the hospital to which he is eventually going as well as from the one from which he may be coming (s. 138(4)). (This does not apply to transfers to and from the islands, or to patients remanded to hospital by a court, or those under interim hospital orders, or civil and Immigration Act detainees being returned to prison).

There are important time limits to some of these powers. A patient who escapes from or on the way to a "place of safety" under sections 135 or 136 can only be retaken within 72 hours of his escape or his arrival at the place of safety, whichever expires earlier (s. 138(3)). A patient escaping on the way to hospital under civil powers of commitment can only be retaken if he can be got to hospital within the 14 days which begin on the date of the second medical examination. If it is only an emergency application, he must arrive within 24 hours of the medical examination or the time when the application was signed, whichever is the earlier (s. 6(1)). A patient who escapes before getting to hospital under criminal powers can be retaken at any time (s. 138(5)). But a patient who has already been admitted to a hospital can be retaken within the same time as one who goes absent without leave (s. 138(2)).

(b) Going absent without leave

A patient is absent without leave if he absconds from a hospital to which he has been compulsorily admitted, or from the place where he is required by his guardian to live, or if he fails to return at the expiry of or recall from leave of absence, or breaks a residence condition in his leave of absence. He may be taken into custody and returned to hospital by any police officer, any ASW, or by anyone on the staff of or authorised by, that hospital (s. 18(1)). If he is living in another hospital as a condition of leave of absence, he can also be retaken by someone on the staff of, or authorised by, that hospital (s. 18(2)). The Code requires hospitals to have a clear policy on absconders, including the circumstances in which the police should be involved (paras. 21.2, 21.4). Calls to the police should be kept to a minimum (DHSS, 1987, para. 289) but they should be told at once whenever a dangerous or restricted patient is absent without leave. Sometimes they should be told even though their help is not needed.

An in-patient detained for six or 72 hours under section 5, or a patient admitted for assessment for 72 hours or 28 days, can never be retaken once that time has gone by (s. 18(5)). Patients admitted for treatment can be recaptured within the six months which began on the first day of absence without leave or the end of the current period of detention, whichever is the longer (s. 18(4)). Detention cannot be renewed while a patient is absent without leave; but if he is absent when or during the week before his detention expires, and is either recaptured or returns voluntarily within the time limit, he remains liable to detention for a further week beginning with the day of his return (s. 21, as substituted by the 1995 Act).

If he is recaptured or returns within 28 days of going absent without leave, the hospital can complete the renewal formalities if required; otherwise the detention will continue as if he had never been away (s. 21A, as inserted by the 1995 Act). But if he has been at large for more than 28 days, then the RMO has to review the case, in consultation with an approved social worker (ASW) and one or more other professionals involved with the patient's treatment, and decide whether the renewal criteria exist (s. 21B(1),(2),(3)); if the RMO does not report that they do within a week of return, the patient is no longer liable to be detained even if he otherwise would have been (s. 21B(4)); if the RMO does so report, the patient's detention is renewed from the (presumably earlier) time it would otherwise have expired (s. 21B(5)); if the detention still had some

165

time to run but the report is within the last two months, it will operate like the usual renewal report (s. 21B(7)). The patient can apply to a mental health review tribunal if his detention is renewed (or his disorder reclassified) under this procedure (s. 66(1)(fa) and (fb)). None of this, of course, applies to restricted patients, whose detention does not have to be renewed and who can be recaptured at any time.

The new provisions replace the old rule that any unrestricted patient could achieve his "discharge by operation of law" simply by remaining absent without leave for 28 days. In the days of tight security in psychiatric hospitals, the patient's ability to survive in the community for so long was considered proof that he was not ill at all. This makes no sense these days, and caused particular concern with hospital order patients, as many as 9 per cent of whom were achieving their discharge in this way (Walker and McCabe, 1973). But despite recommendations of the Butler Committee (1975) the rule survived until the 1995 Act.

(c) Hospital remands and interim hospital orders

Patients remanded to hospital or on interim hospital orders, who abscond from the hospital or on the way to or from it, may be arrested without warrant by any police officer and must then be brought before the court which made the remand or order as soon as possible (ss. 35(10), 36(8) and 38(7)). The court can then end the remand or order and deal with the patient in another way. There is no time limit on these recaptures. Other people can presumably act under the usual procedures, where these apply.

(d) Escaping from England and Wales

A patient who would be subject to recapture under sections 138 or 18 if he were still in England and Wales can be retaken and returned from any other part of the United Kingdom, Channel Islands or Isle of Man. Those who can do this include the national equivalents of an English constable and the Scottish and Northern Irish equivalents of an ASW (s. 88). There are also powers to recapture in England and Wales patients escaping from Northern Ireland (s. 87), the islands (s. 89), or Scotland (Mental Health (Scotland) Act 1984, s. 84). Offender patients who escape to other countries may be extradited if this is provided for by treaty between that country and the United Kingdom.

4. SUBSEQUENT COURT ORDERS

A short period of detention in custody under the sentence or order of a United Kingdom court (including a committal or remand) has no effect upon a pre-existing civil admission for treatment or hospital order. If the patient's detention would normally have expired while he was in custody, it does not do so until the day of his discharge (s. 22(2)). He is then treated as if he had gone absent without leave on that day and can be taken back to hospital within 28 days (s. 22(3), inserted by the 1995 Act). The hospital then has the usual week in which to complete the formalities for renewal (s. 21(1) and (2)). The same would apply if he returned to hospital of his own accord.

But if the patient is detained for more than six months (or for successive periods totalling more than six months) a civil admission or ordinary hospital order automatically ceases to have effect (s. 22(1)). A restriction order, however, carries on regardless, (see, *e.g.*, *R. v. Secretary of State for the Home Department, ex p. K.* [1991] Q.B. 270, p. 173, later). But a fresh hospital or guardianship order cancels any previous hospital admission or guardianship, including a restriction order (s. 40(5)). Section 22 applies, however, if that second order is quashed on appeal.

5. DISCHARGE

(a) By the patient's nearest relative

The nearest relative can discharge a patient admitted for treatment or for assessment under civil powers (s. 23(2)), but not under any type of hospital order (Sched. 1, Pt. I, para. 8(b); Pt. II, para. 7(b)). He must serve his order on the managers and may use Form 34 if he wishes (reg. 15(1)). He is entitled to instruct an independent doctor to visit the patient at any reasonable time, examine him in private and inspect the records relating to his detention and treatment, in order to advise on a possible discharge (s. 24(1), (2)). This could be wise because the nearest relative must always give the hospital at least 72 hours' prior notice of his intention. During this time, the RMO can report to the managers on Form 36 (reg. 15(3)) that the patient, if discharged, "would be likely to act in a manner dangerous to other persons or to himself." This prevents the nearest relative from discharging him, not only at once, but for the next six months (s. 25(1)). If the patient is detained for treatment, the relative must be told. He can then apply to a mental health review tribunal within 28 days. The tribunal will have to allow the discharge if they are satisfied that the patient is not dangerous. If the patient is detained for assessment, there is nothing the relative can do, except wait for it to expire and object to any admission for treatment. A relative can be replaced if he proposes to discharge the patient without due regard for the patient's welfare or the interests of the public (s. 29(3)(d)). This will not be necessary where the RMO can bar discharge, but it may occasionally be useful for patients under guardianship, where the RMO has no such power.

(b) By the hospital, RMO or health authorities

The hospital can discharge any patient admitted for treatment or for assessment at any time (s. 23(2)(a)). This includes an ordinary hospital order patient (Sched. 1), but not one remanded to hospital or under an interim hospital order. A restricted patient can only be discharged with the consent of the Home Secretary (s. 41(3)(c)(iii)). Discharge can be ordered either by the RMO or by the hospital managers.

However difficult it may be for the managers to act contrary to their consultant's advice, and however difficult it is to distinguish their role from that of a mental health review tribunal, their independent power of discharge is seen as an important extra safeguard for patients. The Code advises that they may undertake a review at any time, but must always do so if asked by the patient (unless they have done so recently and there is no evidence of change), or during the renewal process, or if the RMO bars discharge by the nearest relative (para. 22.2). It is up to them how to conduct the review, balancing informality with the gravity of the task (para. 22.5). The power can be exercised by any three or more members of the managing authority or trust, or of a committee to which this function has been delegated (s. 23(4)), but these must not be officers or employees of the authority or trust (s. 23(5)). Hospitals are advised to make known the names of those who can be approached. The RMO has no power to prevent the managers acting, even if he thinks the patient is dangerous.

Patients in mental nursing homes may also be discharged by the registration authority, or by any health authority maintaining them there (s. 23(3)). The inspecting officer of the registration authority may visit a patient at all reasonable times, interview him in private and inspect the documents authorising his detention. A doctor instructed by any of these authorities may do all those things and also examine the patient and his medical records (s. 24(3) and (4)). Technically, a discharge is by order in writing (s. 23(1)), but there is no form laid down in the regulations.

The Act does not expressly state when a patient must or may be set free. There is nothing to prevent a discharge even though the statutory grounds for detention still exist. Equally, there is nothing to insist on discharge the moment that they do not. However, the Code of Practice (para. 1.3) advises that patients should be discharged from compulsion "immediately it is no longer necessary". It certainly follows from the scheme of the Act that a patient ought to be discharged if he no longer suffers from one of the required forms of mental disorder, or if his disorder is not of a nature or degree to make hospital treatment appropriate, or if his detention in hospital is not necessary in the interests of his own health or safety or for the protection of others. The criteria allowing renewal also include a treatability requirement, but the criteria requiring a tribunal to discharge do not (see *R. v. Cannons Park Mental Health Review Tribunal, ex p. A.* [1994] 2 All E.R. 659, C.A.). But even if a tribunal would not be required to discharge the patient, it still has the power to do so, and either the RMO or the managers must also have this power if, on balance it would be appropriate.

They may still wonder where they stand if they release a patient who promptly does harm to himself or others. They will have their usual duty of care towards the patient himself; it is debatable whether their liability to him could include the adverse consequences to him of the damage he does to others (although one health authority was reported in July 1995 to have settled such a claim). But what of their liability to the others? In *Holgate v. Lancashire Mental Hospitals Board* [1937] 4 All E.R. 294, the hospital authorities and doctors were found to have failed in their duty of care towards people whom they could foresee would be injured when they allowed a dangerous patient out on licence without adequate supervision. More recently, in *Partington v. Wandsworth L.B.C., The Independent,* November 8, 1989, the parties agreed that the mother and local authority who shared the care of a 17-year-old mentally disabled girl had a duty to take reasonable care to prevent her injuring others, although it was not broken in that case.

However, such a duty of care can only require them to take steps which the law allows them to take. The power to detain a patient in hospital is governed by the Mental Health Act 1983, which obviously confers a discretion upon the RMO and managers. Civil liability will only lie if the act or omission is outside the limits of the discretion conferred by Parliament (*Anns v. Merton L.B.C.* [1978] A.C. 728; not affected on this point by *Murphy v. Brentwood D.C.* [1991] 1 A.C. 398; see also the analysis by Lord Diplock in *Home Office v. Dorset Yacht Co.* [1970] A.C. 1004, reserving his opinion on whether *Holgate* was correct). Thus the hospital or doctor should only be liable if they have exercised their discretion illegally, irrationally or unreasonably (in the sense defined in *Associated Provincial*

Pictures Houses Ltd. v. Wednesbury Corporation [1948] 1 K.B. 223, p. 20, earlier).

Things can go wrong whatever the patient's legal status (see, *e.g.* Spokes, 1988; Dick, 1991). The NHS Executive has given *Guidance on the discharge of mentally disordered people and their continuing care in the community* (HSG(94)27). Nobody should be discharged from hospital unless, and until, those taking the decision are satisfied that he can live safely in the community and that proper treatment, supervision, support and care are available (para. 2). This obviously involves a proper care programme. But for patients with longer term, more severe disabilities, particularly those known to have a potential for dangerous or risk-taking behaviour, there should be an agreed risk assessment, even though this is known to be "at best an inexact science" (para. 28).

(c) After-care under Supervision

Over the years psychiatrists in particular have pressed for some way of trying to ensure that patients keep up with their medication and do not get lost after leaving hospital, while others have resisted any power to impose forcible treatment outside hospital (see particularly, Royal College of Psychiatrists, 1993; House of Commons Health Committee, 1993; Department of Health, 1993). Amendments made to the 1983 Act by the Mental Health (Patients in the Community) Act 1995 have introduced a form of supervised discharge which is legally very like guardianship but operated by the health rather than the social services.

A "supervision application" (s. 25A(2)) may be made by the RMO (s. 25A(5)) of any patient aged 16 or over who is liable to be detained under a civil admission for treatment or an ordinary hospital order (s. 25A(1); or who is subject to a community care order in Scotland and intends to move to England, see s. 25J)). The grounds are that (a) the patient is suffering from any of the four specific forms of mental disorder; (b) there would be a "substantial risk of serious harm to the health or safety of the patient or the safety of other persons, or of the patient being seriously exploited," if he were not to receive the after-care services to be provided for him under section 117 after he leaves hospital; and (c) his being subject to after-care under supervision is likely to help to secure that he receives those services (s. 25A(4)). The RMO also has to consider the services to be provided and the requirements to be imposed (s. 25B(1)(b),(4)), although these are a matter for the after-care authorities and not for him.

The application must be supported by two written recommendations: one from a doctor who will be concerned with the patient's treatment outside hospital, unless there will be no-one other than the RMO, in which case any other doctor will do, and one from an ASW (s. 25B(6)). The doctor certifies all three elements in the grounds (and must agree with the RMO on at least one of the four forms of mental disorder) and the ASW certifies (b) and (c) (s. 25B(7),(8), s. 25C(2)). They can visit and interview the patient (the doctor in private) and inspect his records (s. 25C(3),(4),(5)) but nowhere is it stated that they *must* do so.

The application is addressed to the Health Authority which will be providing after-care services for the patient under section 117 (p. 159, earlier) but before accepting it the Authority must consult the local social services authority (s. 25A(6),(7)). The application must identify the patient's "community responsible medical officer" (CRMO) and also his "supervisor" (s. 25B(5)(d)) who must also supply statements that they will act (s. 25B(9)(a),(b)). While a patient is subject to after-care under supervision, the Health Authority have a duty to ensure that there is always an approved doctor in charge of his medical treatment and a professional concerned with any of the after-care services to supervise him so that he gets them (s. 117(2A); respectively the CRMO and supervisor, see s. 34(1))). There is nothing to stop one person acting as both hospital and community RMO and supervisor (s. 34(1A)).

The application must be accompanied by details of the after-care services to be provided and of any requirements to be imposed upon the patient (s. 25B(9)(c),(d)). Curiously, it is the "responsible after-care bodies" (*i.e.* either the Health Authority or local social services authority involved), rather than the CMRO or supervisor, which can impose those require-ments, either before or after the patient leaves hospital (s. 25D(1),(2)). The requirements are the same as those which a guardian may impose: to live at a specified place; to attend at specified places and times for medical treatment, occupation, education or training; and to insist upon access being given, wherever the patient is living, to the supervisor, any doctor, any ASW or any other person authorised by the supervisor (s. 25D(3)). Unlike a guardian, however, a supervisor or anyone authorised by him has power to convey the patient wherever he is required to live or attend (s. 25D(4)). People demanding to see, take or convey the patient must produce authorisation if asked (s. 25D(5)).

The application can only be made while the patient is liable to be detained (s. 25A(1)). But the supervision lasts from when he leaves hospital (s. 25G(1)). Presumably by then his detention must have ceased (because otherwise section 117 would not apply) but he might have spent some time as an informal patient before leaving. If he is already on leave, it lasts from when his leave expires (s. 25A(9)). The Act does not lay down any time limits between the dates of the application, its accompanying documents or the patient's departure from hospital. In theory the situation could have changed radically by the time he does. In practice he can apply to a mental health review tribunal.

Supervision lasts for the same periods as admission for treatment or guardianship (s. 25G(1), (2)) and may be renewed in essentially the same way by a report from the CRMO to the responsible after-care bodies (s. 25G(3),(4),(7)). The patient's disorder may also be reclassified (s. 25F). Supervision can be brought to an end at any time by direction of the CRMO (s. 25H(1)). It ends automatically if the patient is compulsorily admitted to hospital for treatment or received into guardianship (s. 25H(5)). It is suspended if he is detained in custody or admitted for assessment (s. 25I(1),(2)); but unless he is in custody for more than six months in all, it is extended (if need be) for 28 days after the detention in custody or hospital ends, so that the renewal formalities can be completed (s. 25I(3),(4)); the renewal is backdated to when it would otherwise have been done (s. 25I(5)).

Consultation is built into each point in the formalities. Before applying, the RMO must consult the patient, at least one other professional involved in his medical treatment in hospital and one involved with the after-care services to be provided, and any non-professional carer; he must consult the nearest relative if practicable, but not, if the patient aks him not to, unless the patient "has a propensity towards dangerous or violent behaviour towards others" and the RMO thinks consultation appropriate (s. 25B(1)(a), (2)(a), (b), (3)); any carer or nearest relative consulted must be named in the application (s. 25B(5)(e)). The CMRO must consult the supervisor and the same list before renewing (s. 25G(5), (6)) or ending (s. 25H(2)–(4)) the supervision. The patient and any carer or nearest relative consulted must be informed when an application is made (s. 25B(10),(11)), accepted (s. 25A(8)), or renewed (s. 25G(8)), or the services or requirements are modified (s. 25E(8)); the patient, carer and nearest relative (with the same proviso as for consultation) must be informed if the supervision ends for any reason (s. 25H(6),(7)); or if the supervisor or CMRO is changed (s. 25E(9)–(11)—but in this case the nearest relative need not be told if the patient has asked otherwise). Information must be given to patients both orally and in writing and to nearest relatives in writing.

As with guardianship, there is no power to force the patient to accept treatment and there are no specific sanctions for failure to co-operate, although he can be recaptured if he absents himself from where he is required to live or escapes while being taken from place to place. But the services and requirements have to be kept under review (s. 25E(1)). If the patient refuses or neglects to receive any of them or to comply with requirements (s. 25E(2)), the responsible after-care bodies must review and if appropriate modify these (s. 25E(3)). They must also consider whether it might be appropriate to end the services or have him admitted to hospital (s. 25E(4)). The patient, any non-professional carer, and (with the usual proviso) the nearest relative must be consulted before the services or requirements are modified (s. 25E(5),(6),(7)).

It is not clear why this new arrangement is thought likely to be any more effective than leave of absence and guardianship in keeping tabs on those patients who need to be encouraged to keep in touch and maintain their medication. The most obvious difference is the extent to which this is operated by the health services and medical profession. Although there is no automatic power of recall to hospital, some have seen this as the thin end of the wedge towards compulsory treatment outside hospital. But at least it has been recognised that imposing requirements upon the patient brings with it an obligation to provide him with at least some services. While the patient remains subject to supervised after-care, the authorities cannot conclude that he no longer needs services under section 117 (s. 117(2)). It would be a shame if compelling him became the best way of ensuring that he was offered them.

(d) By the Home Secretary

The Home Secretary's consent is needed before the hospital or RMO can discharge a restricted patient. But the Home Secretary also has his own powers of release (s. 42(2)). These are more frequently used, because he can choose between an absolute and a conditional discharge. These decisions are taken extremely seriously and a high proportion are considered personally by a Minister.

There has always been felt to be a clear division of responsibility between the hospital and the Home Secretary. The RMO would decide whether, on medical grounds, the patient was fit to leave. The Home Secretary would then decide whether it was safe to let him go. This would only be allowed when it was clear that no undue risk was involved, having regard to all the circumstances, including the patient's response to treatment, the prognosis, and the "safeguards which the arrangements proposed offer against recurrence of anti-social behaviour" (Aarvold Report, 1972). Fear of public opinion, as well as fear for the public themselves, led to a very cautious policy. The system was generally very effective in protecting the public (see Walker and McCabe, 1973). But no system can guarantee complete success unless patients are kept in hospital forever, and there has always been much public concern about those (approximately one a year) who commit murder following their discharge. Graham Young, for example, committed murder and other offences by poisoning shortly after he had been released from Broadmoor, where he had been sent because of very similar offences committed when a boy. The resulting Aarvold Report (1972) recommended further safeguards in a minority of cases which were thought to require "special care in assessment". These are referred to an independent Advisory Board on Restricted Patients, consisting of two lawyers, two psychiatrists, a Chief Probation Officer and a Director of Social Services. They advise on about 50 proposals a year for the discharge or transfer of patients, generally from special hospitals, where the risk is particularly great or the prognosis particularly difficult or there are other special circumstances. The Board has no statutory basis. In *R. v. Secretary of State for the Home Department, ex p. Powell*, December 21, 1978, the Divisional Court decided that it was not amenable to judicial review and need not observe the rules of natural justice. The Board's task is to advise specifically on the risks to the public if the patient should be released.

However, under the European Convention on Human Rights, a patient cannot be detained as a "person of unsound mind" unless he has a true and persisting mental disorder of a kind or degree which warrants his compulsory confinement. If he has not, he can no longer be detained in a hospital, no matter how likely he is to misbehave again if set at large. This point was accepted by Lawton L.J. in *Kynaston v. Secretary of State for Home Affairs* (1981) 73 Cr.App.R. 281. Given the very broad definitions of the mental disorders involved, and of the medical treatment for which detention must be appropriate, this is hardly likely to open the floodgates. The Act itself does not require the Home Secretary to consider whether the criteria for detention still exist. Nevertheless, it seems clear that he should do so, whenever he receives the annual report from the RMO or a specific proposal for discharge from that officer.

Under the 1983 Act, restricted patients may also be discharged by mental health review tribunals (see Chapter 8). Why then does a government department, headed by a politician responsible to Parliament, retain the power of discharge? There are two good reasons. First, a patient may well become fit for discharge some time before his next right to apply to a tribunal comes round. Secondly, the tribunal can only discharge him if the criteria for detention no longer exist, whereas the Home Secretary has a much broader discretion. He could grant a discharge where there was still some mental disorder and it was difficult to determine whether hospital treatment was still appropriate. The Home Secretary may also find it much easier than a tribunal to make the necessary arrangements for a conditional discharge.

A conditional discharge has two consequences. Until the restrictions end or the patient is granted an absolute discharge, he remains liable to be recalled to hospital (s. 42(3)). The Home Secretary issues a warrant and the patient can then be taken into custody and back to hospital as if he had gone absent without leave on the warrant date (s. 42(4)). He can be recalled to a different hospital from the one in which he was originally detained, but not to some other establishment. The Butler Committee (1975) were concerned about conditionally discharged patients whose conduct was worrying, but whose medical condition was not suitable for hospital, but agreed that it would be a grave impairment of liberty to provide for recall to prison on mere suspicion.

No criteria for recall are laid down in the Act. The Home Secretary does not have to obtain medical evidence beforehand. If the case is one where a tribunal would be bound to discharge the patient, because the criteria for detention clearly did not exist, then it might be improper to recall him. But the Home Secretary is entitled to recall a patient when he has some reason to believe that the criteria may exist. Thus in *R. v. Secretary of State for the Home Department, ex p. K.* [1991] 2 Q.B. 270, C.A., the patient, who had a long history of offences against women, was conditionally discharged by a tribunal as no longer suffering from mental disorder. He offended again and was sent to prison. While in prison a tribunal once again found that he was not mentally disordered but declined to grant him an absolute discharge. The Home Secretary decided that he was still a danger to women and issued a warrant for his recall from conditional discharge the moment he was released from prison. This was upheld by the Court of Appeal, although if a new tribunal remained of the same view as the earlier ones, the patient would have to be discharged again once his case was heard. McCullough J. at first instance accepted that it would be improper to recall him after that without some change in the circumstances.

The patient is entitled to an explanation, but the advice is to give this in stages: orally as soon as possible after recall and in any event within 72 hours and in writing within 72 hours; the nearest relative should also receive one within 72 hours. Not surprisingly, recalled patients "may be in an excitable and nervous state" (HSG(93)20; LAC (93)9).

The other object of conditional discharge is to provide some compulsory supervision (see Home Office and DHSS, 1987). This will normally be arranged by the hospital, but the choice of supervisor lies with the Home Office. The Butler Report considered the relative advantages of probation officers and local authority social workers. The latter have access to a wider range of community care facilities and may have more experience of mental disorder. The former have more experience of offenders and may have a "more controlling attitude". Where the need to safeguard the public is particularly important, the reports favour a probation officer, but all stress the need for the greatest possible exchange of information and co-operation with the hospital. The Home Secretary can vary the conditions at any time, whether imposed by a tribunal or by himself (s. 73(4) and (5); the power to vary his own conditions is implicit rather than explicit). In due course, he may grant an absolute discharge. This requires a positive act: simply allowing all the conditions apart from the power of recall to lapse is not enough (*R. v. Secretary of State for the Home Department, ex p. Didlick* [1993] C.O.D. 412, D.C.). The patient may also apply to a tribunal for the conditions to be varied or the restrictions lifted altogether. But unless the tribunal grants an absolute discharge, the Home Secretary will still be in effective control of the conditions and how they operate.

Conditionally discharged patients are excluded from the power to impose treatment without consent (s. 56(1)(c)). Attendance for treatment could be a condition, but refusal to accept it would have to be dealt with on the merits of recall rather than by direct action. In theory, recall should not be used as a sanction for breach if there is no reason to believe that the criteria for detention apply. Nor can a conditional discharge be used as a roundabout way of transferring a patient to another hospital, for discharge must mean release from hospital, or at least from having to stay there

(*Secretary of State for the Home Department v. Mental Health Review Tribunal for Mersey Regional Health Authority* [1986] 1 W.L.R. 1170).

6. HABEAS CORPUS AND JUDICIAL REVIEW

An important constitutional remedy for all who consider themselves illegally detained is the ancient writ of habeas corpus. Application is made to the Divisional Court of the Queen's Bench Division of the High Court, or, if it is not sitting, to any High Court judge, at his home if necessary. This should be done by or with the consent of the prisoner, but if he is incapable, a relative or friend can proceed on his behalf. If the evidence shows a prima facie case of illegal detention, the court will issue the writ. This requires the gaoler to produce the body or show lawful justification for holding him. The court is concerned with whether there is legal power to detain the prisoner. It is a complex question, depending upon the precise terms of the particular power which is being claimed, how far the court can go in investigating the truth of the facts alleged by the gaoler or the merits of his case.

At the lowest level, the hospital's power to detain a mental patient depends upon the existence of orders from a court, warrants or directions from the Home Secretary, or applications, recommendations and renewal reports from those authorised to make them under Part II of the 1983 Act. If no such document existed or if the document itself were bad on its face, then the court would have to order the patient's release.

The next level is where the document is apparently valid but has been completed in breach of the procedures required by the Act. The various provisions differ slightly. Some simply say, for example, that the doctors must examine the patient either together or with no more than five days between the days on which their examinations took place, or that an ASW must interview the patient. Others say that the application shall not be made, for example, if the applicant has not seen the patient within the prescribed time, or the ASW has not consulted the nearest relative.

Some such requirements may be mandatory (so that detention in breach of them is unlawful) whereas others simply be directory (so that it is not necessarily so). But it had always been thought that breach of a mandatory requirement meant that the patient had to be released, and if the hospital did not do so, then the court should do so by habeas corpus.

Unfortunately, at least two decisions suggested that the High Court was not prepared to do this. In *R. v. Governor of Broadmoor, ex p. Argles*, June 28, 1974 (see Gostin, 1986, para. 17.07.1), habeas corpus was refused although it was said that the nearest relative had not been consulted when he could have been. The third edition of this book boldly asserted that this decision was "plainly wrong". But in *R. v. South Western Hospital Managers, ex p. M.* [1993] Q.B. 683 (see pp. 58, 83, earlier), Laws J. also refused habeas corpus where the correct nearest relative had not been consulted; he took the view that section 6(3) of the Act (which allows the hospital managers to act upon apparently valid documents; p. 83, earlier) meant that the detention was not unlawful. However, the Court of Appeal has now held, in *Re S.-C. (Mental Patient: Habeas Corpus)*, *The Times*, December 4, 1995, where the social worker made a section 3 application knowing that the nearest relative actively objected, that habeas corpus is "*an* appropriate, possibly even *the* appropriate remedy" in such cases. Section 6(3) might protect the hospital managers, but it could not turn an unlawful detention into a lawful one. Otherwise, in the view of Bingham M.R., the implications would be "horrifying"—the forms might appear to be in order even if the social worker or the doctors were entirely bogus.

In such cases, as Neill L.J. pointed out, the challenge goes to the validity of the application and to the jurisdiction to detain. This may also happen at the third level, where it is sought to challenge the decision to invoke the Act at all. In *R. v. Board of Control, ex p. Rutty* [1956] 2 Q.B. 109 (see also *R. v. Rampton Institution Board of Control, ex p. Barker* [1957] Crim. L.R. 402; *Re Sage* [1958] Crim. L.R. 258), the applicant was a borderline "feeble-minded" patient who had been compulsorily admitted to an institution on the ground that she had been "found neglected". This was curious, because at the time she was living and working in a hospital under the care of the county council. The court held that there was no evidence that she was "neglected" and ordered her release. As a result, it seems that over 3,000 other patients in mental deficiency institutions had to be released. However, it is clear that if there had been some evidence upon which the authorities could reasonably have concluded that she was neglected the court would not have interfered.

A distinction must be drawn between challenge to an essential fact upon which the validity of the detention depends (see *R. v. Secretary of State for the Home Department, ex p. Khawaja* [1984] A.C. 74), where habeas corpus is appropriate, and challenge to an administrative decision (see *R. v. Secretary of State for the Home Department, ex p. Muboyayi* [1992] Q.B. 244), which can only be made by way of judicial review. The patient in *R. v. South Western Hospital Managers, ex p. M.* [1993] Q.B. 683, who had been admitted under section 3 only three days after a tribunal had decided that she should be discharged from section 2, had already tried and failed to obtain judicial review, presumably on the basis that no reasonable hospital could accept an application in such circumstances. The court can review the decision if it is illegal, irrational or so unreasonable that no reasonable authority could make it (*Associated Provincial Picture Houses Ltd. v. Wednesbury Corporation* [1948] 1 K.B. 223; see also p. 20, earlier). It was used, successfully. to challenge the legality of the patient's section in *R. v. Hallstrom, ex p. W.* [1986] Q.B. 1090, p. 160, earlier) but, unsuccessfully) to challenge the Home Secretary's decision in *R. v. Secretary of State for the Home Department, ex p. K.* [1991] Q.B. 270, C.A., p. 173, earlier).

There are important procedural differences between habeas corpus and judicial review: judicial review applications require leave, affidavit evidence can be filed, and a wide range of remedies is available but all are discretionary. It is also likely to take a great deal longer before the decision is quashed. Judicial review *can* be used to challenge a detention which is so fundamentally flawed that habeas corpus would also be available. Matters will not always be as clear cut as they were in *Re S.-C.* (above). But where a detention is clearly unlawful, there should be no question of leave, delay or discretion. Thankfully, the Court of Appeal has now re-affirmed both the importance of the liberty of the subject and the essential role of habeas corpus in protecting that liberty.

8 MENTAL HEALTH REVIEW TRIBUNALS

Mental health review tribunals were the main safeguard devised by the Percy Commission (1957) when they recommended the abolition of judicial commitment. Since the 1983 Act, almost all compulsory patients have been able to apply for a review, including those admitted for short periods of assessment, or on restriction orders, or transferred from prison. Under Article 5(4) of the European Convention on Human Rights, everyone deprived of his liberty by arrest or detention is entitled to take proceedings "by which the lawfulness of his detention shall be decided speedily by a court and his release ordered if the detention is not lawful." In *X. v. United Kingdom* (1981) 4 E.H.R.R. 181, the European Court of Human Rights decided that all people who were detained because they were "of unsound mind", even those originally admitted from the criminal courts, were entitled to a periodic judicial consideration of the merits of their continued detention. Habeas corpus proceedings were not enough because they could not provide a full assessment of the merits. Where the initial admission is not from a court, Article 5(4) applies straightaway, although the European Court thought that habeas corpus might be a sufficient safeguard for a brief period of detention in an emergency.

Mental health review tribunals must be courts for the purpose of the Convention. They certainly count as courts under domestic law for the purpose of contempt of court (*P. v. Liverpool Daily Post and Echo Newspapers plc and Others* [1991] 2 A.C. 370). The Contempt of Court Act 1981 (s. 19) defines courts to include "any tribunal or body exercising the judicial power of the State". The statutory power to restore liberty to those statutorily deprived of it certainly looks like a "power of the State" and tribunals undoubtedly have a duty to act in accordance with the rules of natural justice, which ought to make them "judicial" even if they are not all staffed by judges.

However, tribunals are not part of the ordinary court structure. In fact, they have many advantages over traditional courts of law. Their membership can be tailored to the particular problem and their more flexible and informal procedures to the peculiarities of the subject-matter. They are not stuck in the adversarial model of British court procedure and can adopt elements of the inquisitorial approach. This is most important in mental health cases, where it is vital that the tribunal should not be too overawed by the hospital evidence, but also that the experience should not have an adverse effect on the patient's health and treatment. The difficulty lies in deciding how far it is possible to go in balancing these considerations against the traditional requirements of natural justice.

1. APPLICATIONS AND REFERENCES

(a) The right to apply

Patients admitted for assessment can apply within the 14 days beginning on the day of their admission (1983 Act, s. 66(1)(a) and (2)(a)). Emergency admissions are not excluded, but there will be no need to proceed if the admission is not converted into a full admission for assessment within the first 72 hours. Patients (of any age) admitted for treatment, transferred from guardianship, received into guardianship, or accepted for after-care under supervision can apply during the first six months (s. 66(1)(b), (c), (e), (ga) and (2)(b), (c), (e)). If a patient is accepted in advance for supervised after-care he can apply before he leaves hospital. Patients placed under guardianship by a court can also apply during the first six months (s. 69(1)(b)(i)), but neither hospital order nor restriction order patients can do so. However, patients found unfit to plead or not guilty by reason of insanity and admitted under section 5(1) of the Criminal Procedure (Insanity) Act 1964 can apply in their first six months, and so can patients transferred from prison by the Home Secretary (with or without restrictions), patients transferred from other parts of the United Kingdom, and patients who become ordinary hospital order patients when their restriction orders come to an end (s. 69(2)).

Ordinary hospital order patients, patients admitted for treatment and patients under guardianship or after-care under supervision can apply once within each period for which their detention, guardianship or supervision is renewed (s. 66(1)(f),(gc) and (2)(f),(fa)). This means once during their second six months and in every year after that. Patients transferred from prison without restrictions are just the same as ordinary hospital order patients. Restricted patients of all types have the right to apply within the equivalent periods (ss. 70 and 79). Conditionally discharged restricted patients, who have not been recalled to hospital, may apply within the second 12 months after their discharge, and in every two year period after that (s. 75(2)). Where a tribunal has ordered conditional discharge subject to specified conditions being met (p. 197, later), the discharge dates from the patient's release from hospital after the tribunal has confirmed that the conditions have been fulfilled, and not from the original order (*R. v. Cannons Park Mental Health Review Tribunal, ex p. Martins, The Times,* June 13, 1995). If they are recalled, they are treated as if a new order or transfer had been made on that date, and so can apply during the second six months and in every year after that. But there is also an automatic review after each recall (see section (b) later).

Any patient whose disorder is reclassified under sections 16 or 25F may apply within 28 days of being informed of this (s. 66(1)(d), (gb) and (2)(d)). He is only likely to want to do this if he has been reclassified upwards, from psychopathic disorder or mental impairment to mental illness or severe mental impairment, because this will deprive him of the wider treatability test at his next renewal. If he has been reclassified downwards, he might want to argue that the treatability test is not fulfilled. But even if he shows this, the tribunal does not have to discharge him (see section 6(a) and (e) later).

The patient's nearest relative can also apply within 28 days of being told that the patient's disorder has been reclassified, but the use of "or" in section 66(1)(i) suggests that they cannot both do so. Whenever the responsible medical officer (RMO) blocks the discharge by the nearest relative of a patient admitted for treatment, on the ground that the patient would be likely to act "in a manner dangerous to other persons or to himself" if released, the relative can apply to a tribunal within 28 days (s. 66(1)(g)) and (2)(d)). The tribunal will then have to discharge the patient if they are satisfied that he is not dangerous. This is a more stringent test than the one which usually applies, so the patient will be better off if his relative can be persuaded to take the initiative in this way. The relative does not have the right to apply to a tribunal if he is prevented from discharging a patient admitted for assessment, no doubt because the admission will have lapsed before a hearing can be arranged.

The nearest relative can apply in the other cases where he cannot discharge the patient, although in these the test is the same as that in an application by the patient himself. After a hospital order or a restriction order, he may apply during the second six months and in every year after that (s. 69(1)(a)). After a guardianship order, he may apply at any time during the first 12 months and in every year after that (s. 69(1)(b)(ii)). Where he has been, or was entitled to be, informed that the patient is subject to after-care under supervision, he can apply within the same periods as the patient can (s. 66(1)(ii)). Lastly, after an order taking away his right to act as a nearest relative, he may apply during the first 12 months and in every year after that (s. 66(1)(h) and (2)(g)).

(b) Automatic reviews

Many patients never apply. Some may not be able to do so, some may not know their rights, and others may not want to or be frightened of upsetting either themselves or the hospital staff. Yet when hospitals began to refer cases (through the DHSS) in order to clear the backlog before the 1983 Act came into force, some found that almost all their compulsory patients could be discharged. The prospect of an independent review can certainly concentrate the mind. It was for this reason that the 1983 Act introduced automatic periodic reviews for all compulsory patients. The object is to review their legal status, rather than their care and treatment or whether they should stay in hospital, although this may also be involved. This may need to be carefully explained to some patients, who might otherwise become agitated or distressed.

The hospital managers must refer to a tribunal any patient admitted for treatment under civil powers (including one transferred from guardianship) who has not exercised his right to apply within his first six months (s. 68(1)). They must do this the moment the six months have expired, unless there is then pending a reference by the Secretary of State for Health (see section (c) later), or an application by the nearest relative, or an application by the patient as a result of his reclassification. They must still make the reference even though the patient has exercised his right to apply on renewal. He could then withdraw that, so that it will not be lost, but patients should probably be advised to wait until the hospital reference has been determined before making their own applications. The hospital managers must refer the case if the patient did apply during the first six months but withdrew the application before it was heard (s. 68(5)). None of this applies to hospital order patients or transferred prisoners. But if a patient admitted under the Criminal Procedure (Insanity) Act 1964 does not apply within the first six months, the Home Secretary must refer his case to a tribunal, and again a withdrawn application is ignored (s. 71(5) and (6)).

The hospital managers must also refer any patient admitted for treatment, including an ordinary hospital order patient, if his detention is renewed and three years have gone by since his case was last considered by a tribunal (for any reason). If the patient is under 16, he must be referred if only one year has gone by since his last review (s. 68(2)). It seems clear from this wording that the managers must refer the case, not when the one or three years have gone by, but when the detention is next renewed. Similarly, the Home Secretary must refer the case of any restricted patient who is still in hospital and whose case has not been considered for the past three years (s. 71(2)). This includes restriction order patients, prisoners transferred with restrictions, and patients admitted under the Criminal Procedure (Insanity) Act 1964 (s. 79(1)). It does not include restricted patients who have been conditionally discharged. Many restricted patients, however, will need little encouragement to make the fullest possible use of their own rights of application.

Finally, if a patient who has been conditionally discharged by the Home Secretary or by a tribunal is recalled to hospital, the Home Secretary must refer his case to a tribunal within one month of the day on which he arrives back (s. 75(1)(a)). This is the answer to the precise problem raised by the case of *X. v. United Kingdom* (1981) 4 E.H.R.R. 181. However, such is the delay in obtaining a hearing that there may still not be the "speedy" review required by the Convention (a delay of five months was unacceptable to the Court in *Van der Leer v. The Netherlands* (1990) E.H.R.R. 567).

(c) Discretionary references

The Secretary of State for Health can refer the case of any patient detained under Part II of the Act, or subject to guardianship or after-care under supervision to a tribunal at any time (s. 67(1)). This must include ordinary hospital order patients, to whom most of the provisions of Part II apply without modification and who are certainly detained under them rather than the court order once the first renewal has taken place. The equivalent provision in the 1959 Act was not thought to apply to restricted patients, whose detention does not have to be renewed at all. However, the Home Secretary has power to refer the case of any restricted patient to a tribunal at any time (s. 71(1)). This includes a restricted patient who has been conditionally discharged from hospital.

A request for a reference may be useful if the patient's own rights have been lost on a technicality (for example because a tribunal cannot defer making a decision about a restricted patient even if it would like to do so). Sometimes the situation may change quickly and the next right to apply may be some time away. The DHSS found its power of reference very helpful in ensuring that large numbers of patients whose cases had not been heard for three years did not all have to be referred the moment the 1983 Act came into force. Apart from these, however, the power has been used very little.

(d) Withdrawal, consolidation and postponement

There is no right to apply to a tribunal apart from those expressly provided in the Act and only one application can be made during each of the specified periods (s. 77(1) and (2)). But any applicant can apply in writing to the tribunal at any time for permission to withdraw his application (Mental Health Review Tribunal Rules 1983, r. 19). If that permission is granted, the application can be ignored and the applicant can try again later (s. 77(1)). References cannot be withdrawn.

If there is more than one application pending in respect of the same patient, the tribunal can consider both of them together (r. 18). This does not apply when an application is pending at the same time as a reference. However, the tribunal might think it appropriate to postpone the application to a future date.

References cannot be postponed, but the tribunal may put off the consideration of an application if an application or reference in respect of the same patient has recently been determined (r. 9). It cannot be put off for longer than six months from that earlier determination or the date when the current period of detention expires, whichever is the earlier. The power does not apply at all if the previous determination was before a break or change in the authority for the patient's detention or guardianship. For this purpose, a break or change happens if (but only if) a patient turns into a patient detained for treatment under civil powers or an ordinary hospital order (whether on admission or transfer from prison or guardianship or the ending of restrictions) or when a patient is received into guardianship. So a previous hearing during an admission for assessment will not prejudice the patient's right to an immediate hearing of his application after he is admitted for treatment. Similarly, a patient who has recently been considered as a restricted patient (where the tribunal's powers are more limited) will be entitled to an immediate hearing of his application as an unrestricted patient. Again, the power to postpone does not apply to an unrestricted patient's application following the renewal of his detention or guardianship for the second six months, unless the earlier application or reference was made more than three months after the initial admission or reception. This means that a patient who applies early in his detention will be entitled to prompt consideration of an application early in his first renewal period. But a patient who puts it off or who does not apply at all and so has to be referred to the tribunal may find that the tribunal postpones his own renewal application. This should be to his benefit. Lastly, there is no power to postpone applications following reclassification, or by a nearest relative who has been barred from discharging the patient himself.

The tribunal cannot postpone consideration in this way unless it is satisfied, after making appropriate inquiries of the applicant and the patient, that it would be in the patient's interests. It must state both its reasons and the period of postponement in writing and send a copy to the applicant, the patient, the responsible authority, the Home Office (for restricted patients) and anyone else who has already been notified of the application. Seven days before the period of postponement ends, the tribunal must start the ball rolling again, unless by that time the application has been withdrawn. If there is by then a new application or reference, the two can be dealt with together.

Clearly then, anyone advising a patient or relative whether to apply should give careful consideration to timing, bearing in mind both the automatic references to which the patient is entitled and the tribunal's powers of postponement.

2. INFORMATION, ADVICE AND REPRESENTATION

It is obviously important that both patients and relatives should be aware of their rights. Hospital managers have a statutory duty to do their best to ensure that the patient understands his. This includes giving him the information both orally and in writing and (unless the patient asks them not to) sending a copy to his nearest relative (s. 132). It has always been Departmental policy to provide leaflets, but in the past patients have often not been properly informed (see Greenland, 1970). Hospitals vary in their attitudes towards tribunals. Some enthusiastic doctors see an application as a helpful step in encouraging the patient to take responsibility for himself. Some even see it as a way of sharing or relieving their own responsibility. Others fear that knowing his rights will unsettle the patient and interfere with treatment. Some may see the tribunal as a threat to their professional judgment, although there is no jurisdiction over questions of treatment. Rather more fear that the hearing will drive a wedge between them and the patient. The 1983 Act resolved the argument in favour of a right to information. The Code of Practice (para. 14.13c.) requires managers to ensure that patients know of the existence and role of tribunals and remain aware of their rights to apply. Although the Act does not require this, the Code expects managers to ensure that the nearest relative is similarly informed.

The Code also requires patients to be given "every opportunity and assistance" to exercise those rights, including facilities for representation. Patients are also entitled to independent medical advice. A doctor instructed by or on behalf of any patient or applicant may visit him at any reasonable time, examine him in private, and inspect any records relating to his detention and treatment in any hospital, in order to advise on whether to make an application or to provide evidence for it (s. 76). The same applies to references by the hospital (s. 68(3)) and the Secretary of State for Health (s. 67(2)) but not by the Home Secretary (see s. 71), although it is inconceivable that access would be denied in such cases. Payment for this advice can now usually be obtained under the "assistance by way of representation" (ABWOR) scheme (see below). Although the object is to provide confidential advice to the patient and he should obviously feel free to unburden himself completely, the doctor can disclose information to the authorities if he fears that "decisions may be made on the basis of inadequate information and with a real risk of danger to the public." A psychiatrist who learned, on examining a paranoid schizophrenic patient who had been convicted of manslaughter by shooting 10 years earlier, that the patient was still interested in guns, was not liable in damages for sending a copy of his report to the Home Office (*W. v. Edgell* [1990] 1 W.L.R. 471).

Patients are entitled to have anyone to represent them at the tribunal, as long as this is not another compulsory patient or even an informal patient at the same hospital. The representative must notify the tribunal of his authorisation and his address. He will then be sent all the documents and notices which would normally go to his client and can take the steps that his client could take. But unless the tribunal directs otherwise, the patient can take someone else along to the hearing, in addition to any representative. If the patient does not want to conduct his own case and has not authorised anyone else to do so, the tribunal can appoint someone to act as his authorised representative (r. 10). This should prove particularly helpful in references concerning severely disabled patients who are unable to do anything for themselves. Most compulsory patients, however, are quite capable of instructing someone to represent them. These rules apply equally to any other "party" to the proceedings (see section 4 later).

The tribunal can pay travelling, subsistence and loss of earnings allowances to anyone who attends as a witness or representative of the applicant (apart from a barrister or solicitor). This also applies to the applicant and to the patient if he is not the applicant, although the patient will rarely have far to come (s. 78(7)). But these expenses do not cover any fee for the representative or for an expert witness, nor any expenditure on preparatory work before coming to the hearing. This is still the position if the patient or applicant is represented by someone other than a practising lawyer.

Originally, there was no legal aid for representation in tribunals, although some lawyers would provide help under the "green form" scheme; this provides, subject to means, legal advice and assistance short of representation. In 1982, following pressure from lawyers and from bodies such as the Council on Tribunals, and with the requirements of the European Convention on Human Rights in mind, mental health review tribunals became the first, and so far the only, tribunal in which ABWOR is available (see Legal Aid Act 1988 and the Legal Advice and Assistance Regulations 1989 (S.I. 1989 No. 340)). There is no longer a means test for ABWOR in a mental health review tribunal (reg. 5A, inserted by 1994 S.I. No. 805); but the solicitor must have the approval of the Legal Aid Board to go beyond advice and assistance into representation. This approval may be refused if it appears unreasonable in all the circumstances that it should be granted (reg. 22(6)). Peay (1989) cites a case where ABWOR was denied to a patient who had spent two years in a special hospital, on the ground that he stood no chance of success. The Code of Practice (para. 14.13c) takes an optimistic view, requiring managers to tell the patient of his right to be represented by a lawyer of his choice, of the Law Society's mental health review tribunal representation panel list, and of other appropriate organisations. A member of staff should see the patient personally and give "every reasonable assistance" in securing representation if the patient wants it.

The Board can set a limit on the costs to be incurred and prior approval must be sought for expert opinions and evidence or for any other unusual or unusually large expenditure (reg. 22(7)). Approval for an independent psychiatrist's report should be almost automatic, except perhaps for patients detained for assessment, when there may not be time to obtain one. For reasons which will appear later (see section 5), the role of the medical member on the tribunal is not an adequate substitute for a doctor instructed on the patient's behalf. Approval for independent social workers' reports may be a little more difficult to get, for the tribunal can always call for more evidence from the social services authority. It can also be difficult to balance the advantages of getting these reports against the disadvantage of having to wait for them. Approval for counsel is possible if the "proper conduct of the proceedings" requires it (reg. 23), but with specialist solicitors available (although not compulsory) this should rarely be so.

Legal representation has become very common, although it is not universal and there are regional variations (Blumenthal and Wessely, 1993). There are disadvantages. Speed is obviously important where a client is deprived of both his liberty and his right to object to most forms of medical intervention. Any delay should be caused by his needs and not those of his representative. Unfortunately, representative-induced delays are common in all types of tribunal. This is partly because of the time needed to prepare cases properly: a lawyer is likely to seek an independent psychiatric report and these have a significant influence on delay (Blumenthal and Wessely, 1993). But there is also a professional "culture of delay" in which the convenience of tribunals and representatives is given higher priority than the clients' interests. In the past, there were also relatively few lawyers with much experience of the legal and practical issues involved or in communicating with mental patients. The great increase in tribunal hearings of all kinds, coupled with the development of the Law Society's specialist mental health panel, has done much to remedy this.

Nevertheless, there are real dangers in importing a courtroom style of advocacy into these hitherto informal hearings, which depend so much upon an understanding of the personalities involved. If not only the patient, but also the hospital and on occasions the Home Office, feel the need to employ an advocate, a major advantage of a tribunal will be lost. It was for these reasons that Bell (1969; 1970) advocated a skilled non-legal representation service for some tribunals. Even now, a non-lawyer may be just as helpful, but there remains the problem of finance. Some tribunals may also regret the spread of representation, feeling that they can themselves provide the patient with all the help he needs. Members have certainly developed considerable skill in communicating with patients. They also have power to seek any further information they need. In practice, however, they have not used this as energetically as they might have done. The great advantage of a representative is that he can seek alternative evidence and solutions and articulate these along with the patient's point of view at the hearing. It is scarcely surprising, therefore, that the use of lawyers in tribunals is associated not only with greater delay but also with greater success (Genn and Genn, 1989).

A further advantage of a representative is that he can be shown all the evidence and documents, even if there are grounds for withholding some from the patient. He can remain throughout the hearing, even though the patient (or anyone else) is excluded. The tribunal rules give an authorised representative both of these rights, but only if he is either a barrister or a solicitor, or a registered medical practitioner, or some other person authorised by the patient or applicant whom the tribunal considers to be suitable because of his experience or professional qualification (rr. 12(3) and 21(4)); the tribunal must be able to trust the representative not to disclose to the patient the information which the tribunal has decided should be withheld from him (see section 4(c) later). Professionally, this is ethical because the rules insist upon it, but any representative must beware of colluding too closely with the tribunal to achieve a result which may be in the client's best interests but contrary to his instructions. It is for the doctors, social workers and other professionals to devote themselves to the patient's best interests. A representative must advise his client where he thinks the client's best interests lie, but in the end he must do as instructed. Soberingly, he might also reflect on Peay's (1989) conclusion that it is difficult to assess how many benefits representation brings.

3. THE TRIBUNAL

There is a tribunal for each of the eight health service regions in England and one for Wales (s. 65). Each panel has three types of member: (a) legal members appointed by the Lord Chancellor, who have such legal experience as he considers suitable; normally these are senior practitioners, but some academics have been appointed; (b) medical members appointed by the Lord Chancellor after consultation with the Department of Health; these are usually consultant psychiatrists, but other doctors with psychiatric experience, including community physicians, may be appointed; and (c) lay members, also appointed by the Lord Chancellor after consultation with the Department of Health, who have "such experience in administration, such knowledge of social services or such other qualifications or experience as the Lord Chancellor considers suitable" (1983 Act, Sched. 2). They are expected to have a basic understanding of the health and social services and preferably some interest in or experience of mental health or learning disability. In practice, therefore, "'lay' might be thought a misnomer in relation to the present tribunal lay members, who include mental health professionals, hospital administrators, social workers and nurses" (Mental Health Review Tribunals, Annual Reports, 1993, para.3.5, 1994, para. 3.4). Members are appointed for three years, but this is renewable.

The regional chairman of the tribunal is a lawyer. Technically, it is his job to nominate the members for a particular hearing or class of hearings (Sched. 2 and r. 8). At any time up to the hearing he may exercise the tribunal's powers on preliminary and incidental matters (under rules 6, 7, 9, 10, 12, 13, 14(1), 15, 17, 19, 20, 26 and 28; see r. 5). These include the power to give whatever directions it thinks fit to secure a "speedy and just determination", subject to the Rules (r. 13). These functions can be delegated to another member appointed to act when the chairman is unable to do so (s. 78(6)). In practice he may give general instructions to the tribunal clerks on some matters.

The clerks are civil servants independent of the hospital authorities and accountable to the regional chairmen. Shortage of clerks has been identified as a major cause of the unacceptable delays which have arisen at times following the 1983 Act (Council on Tribunals,1989; 1990), for they have both to process the paperwork and to attend hearings. The tribunal offices in North and South London, Liverpool, Nottingham and Cardiff are reasonably conveniently situated to serve the special hospitals (where a disproportionate number of hearings take place) but have also to serve some very far flung hospitals. More staff have been recruited, but applications rose by nearly 200 per cent in the first 10 years whereas staff levels only went up by 70 per cent over the same period (Annual Report, 1993).

A further function of the regional chairman is to organise conferences and training for members, a much neglected area in the past. Before 1983, members did not sit frequently outside special hospitals and hardly ever met members from the same region, let alone others. They were generally initiated by sitting in on one or two hearings. This was a recipe for wide divergence in practice, which in turn made it difficult to secure consensus. The 1983 rules, coupled with the increase in hearings and greater emphasis on training and the exchange of views, should have led to greater consistency and predictability of approach. Peay's research (1989) revealed that there were divergences both in process and in outcome for apparently similar patients (a finding which is not unique to these tribunals). Others still feel that the training of, and interchange between, members is inadequate (Blumenthal and Wessely, 1993).

For any one case, a tribunal is made up of at least one member from each of the three groups and the lawyer presides. This is not because he is the most important, but because he should be able to conduct the hearing in a fair and judicial manner and advise on any question of law which may arise. But there are no decisions which, under the rules, are reserved for him. Each member is entitled to an equal voice on questions of law, procedure and substance. In practice, Fennell (1979) found that the lawyer was usually the most powerful member, but the doctor's opinions and character are crucial because of his peculiar role. The lawyer may be particularly powerful in cases concerning restricted patients, because these can only be heard by specially approved members (s. 78(4) and r. 8(3)), who are Circuit Judges or Q.C. Recorders with experience of trying serious criminal cases. Without this, it was feared that neither the sentencing courts nor the general public would believe that enough weight would be given to questions of public safety, and even that special hospital doctors might have to modify their treatment plans to ensure that patients were not discharged prematurely. In practice, many applications by special hospital patients are supported by the RMO, who has been unable to persuade the Home Secretary to act. The judicial approach may have led to tribunals taking a greater interest in the index offence and the patient's previous criminal record. But the system is in any event heavily weighted in favour of caution (see section 6, later) and the judiciary do not seem to have made much contribution towards greater consistency in either procedure or substance (Peay, 1989). A shortage of judge-time may also be another factor increasing delays (Blumenthal and Wessely, 1993).

Tribunal members must of course be independent. They must not be members or officers of the "responsible authority" (r. 8(2); see below) or of the registration authority for a mental nursing home, or of an authority which maintains the patient in a mental nursing home. They must not have a close knowledge of or connection with the patient; but a legal member may preside over more than one hearing about the same patient, and other members could probably do so too, provided that there was no reason to question their independence (*R. v. Oxford Regional Mental Health Review Tribunal, ex p. Mackman, The Times,* June 2, 1986). Finally, a member must not have recently treated the patient in a professional capacity. This may seem obvious but psychiatry is quite a small profession. The RMO and medical member will usually know one another, often quite well. If so, it is particularly important to conduct the hearing in a way which avoids any impression of cosy complicity between the tribunal and the authorities.

4. THE PRELIMINARIES

The parties to the proceedings are the applicant, the patient, the "responsible authority" (*i.e.* the hospital managers or the local social services authority responsible for a patient under guardianship), any other person who is notified under rules 7 or 31 (pp. 189, 187, later), and anyone added as a party by the tribunal (r. 2(1)). For restricted patients, the Home Secretary must be notified and receive copies of all the documents and has various other rights. Failure to comply with these has been held to invalidate the proceedings, so important is it that he should be able to represent the public interest (*R. v. Oxford Regional Mental Health Review Tribunal, ex p. Secretary of State for the Home Department* [1988] A.C. 120).

(a) Assessment cases

These must be heard no more than seven days after the tribunal receives the application. This is essential to ensure that these patients have a real right to challenge their detention, but the priority given to them must have contributed to the unacceptable delays facing long-term patients. As time is short, the preliminaries are also shorter and simpler.

The patient must apply in writing, but he can get someone else (perhaps a social worker or a nurse) to do this for him. There is no prescribed form, although the tribunal or the hospital managers will supply a suitable one if asked. The application must indicate that it is an assessment case, and if possible it should give the patient's name, the hospital address, the name, address and relationship of the nearest relative, and the name and address of anyone authorised by the patient to represent him, but that is all. It is hard to see how the tribunal could proceed at all without the second and third items, but it can ask the hospital to fill in any gaps as best it can. The application must be sent to the offices of the tribunal serving the area

186

where the hospital is (r. 30). It would obviously be sensible to send it by first class post and as soon as possible after the patient is admitted. The hospital should supply the address and any other help the patient needs.

The tribunal must then arrange a hearing and notify the patient, the hospital managers, the nearest relative (if this is practicable), and anyone else it thinks should be heard (r. 31). An obvious candidate would be the approved social worker who sectioned the patient, for the tribunal certainly ought to hear why he did so. If the patient has a representative, notices and other material which would normally go to the patient will be sent to him instead and he may take any step which the patient would otherwise have been able to take in the proceedings (r. 10(4)). When the hospital gets notice of the hearing, or earlier if asked (a telephone call would be sensible), it must supply the tribunal with copies of the admission documents. These are the application for admission to hospital and the medical recommendations supporting it (r. 2(1)). The hospital must also supply as much of the information and reports required in long-term cases as can reasonably be provided in the time available (r. 32).

(b) Long-term cases

In other types of case, the method of applying is the same (r. 3). If possible, the application must give the patient's name, his address (which must include the hospital address, or for a conditionally discharged patient the address of the hospital where he was last detained, or the name and address of the patient's private guardian), the section under which the patient is detained, and the name and address of any representative (or whether he intends to authorise one). A nearest relative applicant must also give his name, address and relationship to the patient. Again, the tribunal can ask the responsible authority or (for restricted patients) the Home Secretary to fill any gaps. Once it gets the application, the tribunal must notify the responsible authority, the patient (if he is not the applicant), and the Home Secretary (if the patient is restricted). This must be done even if the application is postponed and this is where the procedure begins again at the end of the postponement, whatever the point it had reached before (r. 4). The same people must be told of any type of reference, but obviously if it has been made by the responsible authority this will take the form of a request for their statement.

Within three weeks at the latest, the responsible authority must send a "rule 6 statement" to the tribunal, and also to the Home Secretary if the patient is restricted (r. 6(1)). This must contain some basic facts, listed in Part A of Schedule 1 to the Rules. These are the patient's full name and age; the date of his admission to the present hospital (or reception into guardianship); the name of any health authority maintaining him in a mental nursing home; details of the original authority for the detention or guardianship (including the section and Act involved) and of any later renewals or changes; the legal category of disorder from which the patient is recorded as suffering (except for patients detained under the Criminal Procedure (Insanity) Act 1964, to whom these are irrelevant); the name of the RMO and the length of time the patient has been under his care; the name and period of involvement of any other doctor who is or has recently been largely concerned in the patient's treatment; the dates, decisions and reasons of any previous tribunal hearings (but not of recommendations relating to restricted patients under the old law); details of any Court of Protection proceedings and receivership; the name and address of the nearest relative or person acting as such; the name and address of any other person who takes a close interest in the patient; and details of any leave of absence given to the patient during the past two years, its duration and where the patient lived.

The authority must also supply an up-to-date medical report on the patient's medical history and present condition, specially prepared for the tribunal (Part B of Sched. 1). Regrettably, in some hospitals this may be the patient's best chance of a thorough consultation with his RMO, although the report could be prepared by another doctor. The authority must also supply a social circumstances report, as far as this is practicable. This should cover the patient's home and family circumstances, including the attitude of the nearest relative, the opportunities for employment and occupation and the housing facilities which would be available if the patient were discharged, the availability of community support and medical facilities, and the patient's financial circumstances. The social circumstances report is a vital factor in any tribunal decision, especially in unrestricted cases.

Reports from a hospital social worker can be very different from those prepared by a fieldworker from the patient's home area, perhaps some distance away. The hospital social worker should know the patient and regard him as the primary client. The patient's rehabilitation will be his main task and he will go to considerable lengths to investigate what might be available outside hospital. But if he is not employed by the social services authority for the patient's home area, he will not have the same access to its facilities as a local fieldworker would have. The fieldworker may have this access, but unless the patient is already his client, he is much less likely to see the patient's rehabilitation as his priority. He may be more involved with the family. This is where a good representative who is prepared to do a certain amount of investigation can be so helpful.

Finally, the hospital statement should, if practicable, give their views on the suitability of the patient for discharge, and any other observations which they wish to make. If the patient is restricted, the Home Secretary must supply a supplementary statement containing any further information he has. This should arrive no later than three weeks after he received the hospital's statement (r. 6(2)). The Home Secretary is solely responsible for statements on conditionally discharged patients, which must arrive within six weeks (r. 6(3)). These must state the patient's full name and age; the history of his present liability to detention (including details of the offence(s) and dates of the original order or transfer direction and of the discharge); the legal category of mental disorder (again not applicable to cases under the 1964 Act); the name and address and period of care of any doctor responsible for the care and supervision of the patient in the community; and the name and address and period of care of any social worker or probation officer responsible for his care and supervision in the community (Part C, Sched. 1). If practicable an up-to-date medical report (if there is a doctor responsible for the patient), a progress report from any supervisor, and a home circumstances report should be supplied. The Home Secretary may also give his views on the patient's suitability for discharge and any other observations (Part D, Sched. 1).

Once these statements have been received, the tribunal must notify the nearest relative (unless he is the applicant), the private guardian of a patient under guardianship, the registration authority of a private nursing home where the patient is liable to be detained, any health authority which is maintaining him in a private nursing home, the Court of Protection if the patient's affairs are under its control, and any other person whom the tribunal thinks should be given an opportunity of being heard (r. 7). The time and place of the actual hearing used to be fixed at this point but the practice introduced in 1993 of fixing section 3 hearings in NHS hospitals as soon as the application is made has helped to reduce delays (Annual Report, 1994). Fourteen days' notice of this must be given to the applicant, the patient, the responsible authority, the Home Secretary if the patient is restricted, and anyone else who is notified of the proceedings (r. 20). For these last, the two notices can obviously be combined. The 14 days can be reduced by agreement with all concerned. In 1987, targets of eight weeks between application and hearing for unrestricted patients and 12 weeks for restricted patients were set. These have proved so difficult to achieve that even the Council on Tribunals (1994) accepts that they may not be realistic. The main delays are with restricted and special hospital patients both of whom were having to wait on average more than half a year to obtain their hearing (Blumenthal and Wessely, 1993).

(c) Disclosing and withholding information

Under the normal principles of natural justice a person is entitled to know the case against him and no information should be available to the tribunal which is not also available to him. However, mental health review tribunal procedure has always been designed on the assumption that full disclosure may be harmful to the very people whom the proceedings are trying to help. Hence the hospital and Home Secretary can indicate that some or all of their statements, or the information supplied in assessment cases, should be withheld because its disclosure would "adversely affect the health or welfare of the patient or others" (rr. 6(4) and 32(2)). They must give their reasons for thinking this, and in long-term cases the information withheld will be sent to the tribunal in a separate document. The rest of the information will be sent to the patient and applicant automatically (rr. 6(5) and 32(3)).

However, the tribunal's normal duty is to send a copy of every relevant document it receives to the applicant, the patient, the responsible authority and (if the patient is restricted) the Home Secretary (r. 12(1)). If the tribunal receives any documents, including these statements, which have not been copied to the applicant or patient, it *must* consider whether disclosure would adversely affect the health or welfare of the patient or others. If satisfied that it would, it must record in writing its decision not to disclose (r. 12(2)). Otherwise, the document must be revealed. This decision is one which can be made by the regional chairman before the hearing (r. 5). But he may find it difficult to do so without seeing the patient, unless the hospital's reasons are obviously bad.

Withholding information is one of the most controversial aspects of tribunal procedure. Medical attitudes vary. Some doctors believe that it is risky even to tell the patient what they think is wrong with him, whereas others believe that it is wrong not to do so. Some believe that candour can only help their relationship with the patient whereas others believe that it can hinder. The criterion, however, is not whether it will damage the doctor-patient relationship, but whether it will damage the health or welfare of the patient or others. Some information may lower the hospital or its staff in the esteem of the patient or applicant, but that cannot damage the welfare of others unless it is likely to provoke the patient to violence. The biggest problem is posed by the views of the patient's family.

They often wish to give these in confidence, because they do not want the patient to know that they feel unable to cope with him at home. Social workers who interview them for the social circumstances report can promise that there will be no automatic disclosure, but the last word will lie with the tribunal. Blanket requests to withhold whole reports may well be turned down, but if good reasons are given for keeping back specially sensitive information the regional chairman may well uphold them and the tribunal hearing the case is unlikely to disagree (Peay, 1989).

If information is withheld from a patient or applicant, it must nevertheless be disclosed to a representative, provided that he falls within one of the qualified categories whom they can trust (r. 12(3)). This information must not be disclosed to the client (directly or indirectly) or to anyone else without the tribunal's permission, nor can it be used for any other purpose than the present proceedings. This is an important reason for having a representative. A patient may be disturbed by such information but the whole purpose of the proceedings is to decide whether he is indeed as ill as the authorities think he is.

These same rules apply to any further information sought by the tribunal itself. This it may do before or during any hearing (again, the regional chairman may do this beforehand) and direct how and by whom it is to be supplied (r. 15).

5. THE HEARING

There must always be a hearing. Under the old rules, the tribunal could determine cases informally, by collecting information in whatever way it wanted. In practice there was always some sort of hearing (Greenland, 1970) and this is now required.

Before the hearing (often, but not always, on the same day), the medical member of the tribunal must examine the patient and do whatever else he thinks necessary to form an opinion on the patient's mental condition. To do this, he may see the patient in private, look at and copy all his medical records (r. 11). The original purpose was to give the tribunal its own objective medical opinion, so that an independent report on behalf of the patient would rarely be needed. This can still be so, but there are at least two problems. First, a doctor who is to play a part in deciding whether the patient is fit for release obviously approaches his examination in a different way from a doctor whose responsibility is to the patient himself. Rightly or wrongly, the proceedings could easily turn into a sort of case conference (Fennell, 1977), in which the RMO and the tribunal engage in discussion about the best solution, usually in the patient's absence. Some medical members can be most helpful in suggesting ways forward which are quite outside the tribunal's formal powers. This may benefit the patient, but it is not always conducive to the objective examination of the medical issues. A report on the patient's behalf can help the tribunal to highlight these.

The other problem with the medical member's role is one of natural justice. His opinion is regarded as part of the tribunal's deliberations rather than a piece of evidence. Traditionally, it was given in confidence and there was no formal opportunity to learn what it was or to challenge it. Some tribunals asked him to give his report before the hearing; this had the advantage that differences between his views and those of the other doctors would usually emerge and be discussed during the hearing, but the disadvantage that members might approach the case with pre-conceived

190

ideas. Others, therefore, postponed hearing his report until the decision-making stage, when there might be no chance to put any of his points to the others. In *R. v. Mental Health Review Tribunal, ex p. Clatworthy* [1985] 3 All E.R. 699, Mann J. observed that it would be contrary to one of the principles of natural justice (see *Mahon v. Air New Zealand Ltd.* [1984] A.C. 808, at p. 821) for a tribunal to decide on a basis known only to themselves. They should therefore ensure that the parties are aware of any new facts or arguments adduced by their medical member and have an opportunity of dealing with them. Peay's research (1989), however, suggested that judicial members still varied in their views.

The hearing itself almost always takes place at the hospital (unless the patient is under guardianship or conditionally discharged). In the past tribunals were often convened for just one case, except in the special hospitals, but although the numbers of cases have risen dramatically since 1984, so have the numbers of places in which patients are detained. The tribunal must sit in private, unless the patient asks for it to be in public and the tribunal is satisfied that this would not be contrary to his interests. Only he has the right to ask for a public hearing. If the tribunal refuses or reverts to privacy during the hearing, it must record its reasons in writing and explain them to the patient (r. 21(1) and (2)). However, there may not be much difference between a private and a public hearing. When sitting in private, the tribunal may admit anyone it likes, on such terms as it thinks appropriate (r. 21(3)). Whether sitting in private or public, it can exclude anyone from all or part of the proceedings for whatever reason it likes. If it decides to exclude the applicant or the patient or their representatives or a representative of the responsible authority, it must again record its reasons in writing and explain them to the person excluded. It cannot exclude a qualified representative of the applicant or patient (r. 21(4)) or a member of the Council on Tribunals (r. 21(6)).

Again, whether sitting in private or public, information about the proceedings and the names of any persons concerned cannot be made public unless the tribunal so directs (r. 21(5)). This prohibition covers the date of the hearing, the evidence and reports before the tribunal, and the reasons for any decision; but apparently it does *not* cover the name of the applicant, the fact that he has applied and the bare result (*P. v. Liverpool Daily Post and Echo Newspapers plc and Others* [1991] 2 A.C.370). The tribunal is a court, so that publishing information about its proceedings in private is contempt (Administration of Justice Act 1960, s. 12(1)(b)). It can also be contempt to publish prejudicial comments before the hearing, but only if the tribunal is in fact likely to be prejudiced by it. In P.'s case the patient himself was granted an injunction to prevent the newspaper publishing information in breach of rule 21(5). As the rule is designed to protect his privacy, it may seem odd that "the names of any persons concerned" do not include his. It is not easy to achieve a proper balance between an individual's right to privacy and the public's interest in the prospect of certain notorious patients, especially if restricted, being released.

At the beginning of the hearing, the presiding member must explain how the tribunal intends to proceed (r. 22(3)). It is also good practice to introduce the members of the tribunal and the other people present, to explain their functions, and to stress that the tribunal is independent of the hospital and all its works. The tribunal may conduct the hearing in whatever manner it thinks most suitable, bearing in mind the health and interests of the patient. As far as it is appropriate, it must try to avoid formality (r. 22(1)). It is certainly common for tribunals to address patients by their given names and sometimes to allow them to smoke. It is not common for patients to address members of the tribunal by their given names. Informality can be a great benefit in all kinds of tribunal, but particularly here where there are advantages in questioning people directly, rather than listening to advocates doing so. But informality can be unpredictable and can lose sight of the basic principles of a fair and open hearing of both sides of the case.

The applicant, patient, responsible authority and anyone else notified of the proceedings may appear at the hearing and take such part as the tribunal thinks proper. So may anyone else with the tribunal's permission. In particular, the tribunal *must* hear and take evidence from the applicant, the patient, and the responsible authority who may hear each other's evidence, put questions to each other, call witnesses and put questions to any witness or other person appearing before the tribunal (r. 21(4)). This rule is subject to the tribunal's power to exclude even these people for some or all of the time, provided that it records and explains its reasons. Nevertheless, the rule clearly contemplates that the two "sides" will be there for most of the time and have much the same rights as parties to an ordinary dispute. The tribunal has power to subpoena witnesses to appear or produce documents and to hear evidence on oath, but this is hardly ever necessary. It is not bound by the usual rules of evidence, in that it can admit things which would not be admissible in a court of law, but it cannot force someone to disclose things which he could not be forced to disclose in court (r. 14). In practice, medical judgments are often based on hearsay evidence from interested parties and the tribunal should be prepared to submit this to critical examination. Once all the evidence has been given, the applicant and patient must be given another opportunity to address the tribunal (r. 22(5)).

At any time before the proceedings end, however, the tribunal (or one of its members) may interview the patient. It must do so if he asks and it must do so without anyone else present if he asks for this (r. 22(2)). In practice, he will usually give evidence at the hearing and the tribunal can ask the representative of the responsible authority to leave while he does so, but this rule guarantees him a private hearing if wanted. There can be no serious objection to this. The doctor does not have a close personal interest in the outcome, such as would make this unfair to him, but there is a very real risk that the patient will be intimidated by the presence of someone who has so much power over him. Tribunals may therefore find it appropriate to take the initiative and ask the patient whether he would like a private word.

The tribunal may ask the patient to leave while others are giving evidence, but it must explain why. It has been very common practice to hear the family of the patient in his absence, as they are often reluctant to speak freely for fear of upsetting him, however, his case may be prejudiced if they do not. Practice with regard to the patient's doctor and other staff has varied. Some have assumed that doctor and patient will be present throughout, some have assumed that they will be seen separately, and some have seen them both together but then offered each a private word. Up to a point, the tribunal can do any of these, but the expectation is that all stay unless excluded.

However, it is clear that the tribunal must hear from both sides. In the past, some tribunals found it possible to hear a case without ever taking evidence from the RMO or any other person who was responsible for the patient's care in hospital. It is difficult to understand how they could possibly examine the issues properly in such circumstances. They can, of course, call for whom they wish.

The rule does not require them to hear the parties in any particular order. Some tribunals like the hospital to begin, partly because they think that in practice the burden of proof should lie on that side, and partly so that the patient will know the case he has to meet. Others believe that the patient wants his "day in court" and will not understand the proper method of proceeding by examination and cross-examination if he is not allowed to go first. This is less of a problem when he has legal representation. Technically, the burden of proof is on the patient or applicant, and he must be given the last word if he wants it (r. 22(5)). Usually he who speaks last would also speak first.

The tribunal can adjourn the hearing at any time to obtain further information or for any other purpose. It can give directions to ensure that it is heard again promptly. But unless it adjourns to a fixed date, it must give at least 14 days' notice of the resumed hearing (or less if everyone agrees). The applicant, patient or responsible authority is entitled to insist that the hearing be resumed, provided that the tribunal is satisfied that this would be in the patient's interests (r. 16). Tribunals have always had these inquisitorial powers and this has been the predominant model in the past. With legal representation, however, there is far more temptation to leave the investigation to the parties themselves.

6. THE ISSUES

The tribunal is not concerned with whether the admission procedures were properly carried out: the legality of the patient's detention can be challenged by habeas corpus or judicial review (*Ex p. Waldron* [1986] Q.B. 824; see Chapter 7). Nor is it directly concerned with how the patient is being treated in hospital. Its task is to decide whether he should be detained there any longer or remain subject to compulsion in the community. Its powers in relation to an unrestricted patient are different from its powers in relation to a restricted patient and both are different from its role in relation to patients transferred from prison.

(a) Unrestricted patients

The tribunal's criteria are not identical to those for the original admission or the renewal of detention, but the general effect is that it must discharge a patient if satisfied that the grounds for detaining him do not exist. If the patient is detained for assessment, the tribunal must discharge him if it finds (a) that he is not mentally disordered at all, *or* (b) that his disorder is not of a nature or degree to warrant his detention in hospital for assessment (or for assessment followed by medical treatment) for at least a limited period, or (c) that his detention is not justified in the interests of his own health or safety or with a view to the protection of other persons (s. 72(1)(a)). These conditions are in the negative. Strictly speaking, the hospital does not have to prove that the grounds exist and it is up to the patient to prove that they do not. The tribunal need only be satisfied on the balance of probabilities, but we all know how difficult it is to prove a negative. It is particularly difficult to prove that you are either sane or safe once the label "patient" has been officially attached to you. However, some tribunals have been prepared to place the evidential burden of proof on the hospital and they may continue to do so. In assessment cases, it should be possible to scrutinise the evidence upon which that initial judgment was made. The incident or behaviour which led to the detention should be fresh in everyone's minds and the issue will not be unduly clouded by what has since happened in hospital. Misinterpretation of events by family, neighbours, social workers, doctors and other hospital staff is not unknown. The quality of the evidence on which their judgments were made can be assessed. These hearings should give an opportunity to clarify matters before the patient embarks upon his career.

If the patient is detained for treatment, under civil powers or under an ordinary hospital order, he must be discharged if (a) he is not suffering from mental illness, psychopathic disorder, severe mental impairment or mental impairment, *or* (b) his disorder is not of a nature or degree which makes it appropriate for him to be liable to be detained in a hospital for medical treatment, *or* (c) it is not necessary for the health or safety of the patient or for the protection of other persons that he should receive such treatment. If the nearest relative is applying because the RMO has prevented him from discharging the patient, the tribunal must also grant a discharge if it is satisfied that, if released, the patient would not be likely to act in a manner dangerous to other persons or to himself (s. 72(1)(b)). The test of whether someone is *dangerous* is obviously narrower than the test of whether he should be in hospital for his own sake or that of others. The tribunal is only obliged to apply the stricter test if the patient's nearest relative has already tried to discharge him. The relative has no power to do this in hospital order cases, and so the wider test will always apply to them.

However, the tribunal does not have to discharge patients who are "untreatable". This is strange, because (as we saw in Chapter 4) a psychopathic or non-severely impaired patient will have to be discharged by the hospital at his next renewal date unless hospital treatment is likely to make him better or at least prevent his getting worse. An untreatable mentally ill or severely impaired patient will have to be discharged on renewal unless he is unable to fend for himself in the community. It is odd that the tribunal may sanction a detention which the hospital could not, but a valiant attempt by the Divisional Court to import treatability into the appropriateness test was overturned in the Court of Appeal (*R. v. Cannons Park Mental Health Review Tribunal, ex p. A.* [1994] 2 All E.R. 659).

However, the tribunal also has a complete discretion to discharge *any* unrestricted patient, short-term or long-term, even though it is not satisfied that he is entitled to a mandatory discharge. In exercising this discretion in a long-term case, it must have regard to the likelihood of medical treatment alleviating or preventing a deterioration of the patient's condition. If the patient is suffering from mental illness or severe mental impairment, it must also have regard to the likelihood of his being able to care for himself, to obtain the care he needs or to guard himself against serious exploitation, if discharged (s. 72(2)). This is a clear hint that the tribunal ought to discharge a patient if the hospital will not be able to keep him at the next renewal.

In practice, the issue does not usually turn on whether the patient is indeed mentally ill. The lack of statutory definition makes it difficult for the non-medical members to disagree if the medical member and the other doctors are agreed on a diagnosis. Nevertheless, it is open to them to question the definition of mental illness which is being employed, remembering that the Act's original progenitors expected this to be a serious illness akin to what used to be called insanity. It is open to them to scrutinise the evidence upon which diagnosis is based. Several of the reported cases do, however, reveal disagreements about whether a patient originally diagnosed as suffering from psychopathic disorder is still suffering from any disorder within the meaning of the Act (*e.g. R. v. Secretary of State for the Home Department, ex p. K.* [1991] Q.B. 270, C.A.). If the patient is not now suffering from the required form of mental disorder, he must be discharged, no matter how much of a nuisance or even danger he may be to those outside or how much more comfortable and well cared for he would be in hospital. This "well-known lacuna" in the Act (Peay, 1989) is of obvious concern to the Home Office (1986) but is the inevitable consequence of a therapeutic rather than a penal disposal.

The patient must also be discharged, even if he is still disordered, if that disorder is no longer a type or severity to warrant (or make appropriate) his treatment in hospital. The disorder may be such that everyone would much prefer it if he could be kept out of harm's way. But that is not the same as to "make it appropriate that he should be detained in hospital for medical treatment." It can scarcely be appropriate to keep him in hospital for treatment if he is not receiving any treatment there, still less if he is out on leave and not receiving any in the community either. It ought not to be appropriate to keep him there for that purpose if there is no medical treatment appropriate to his case. However, the definition of medical treatment "includes nursing and also includes care, habilitation and rehabilitation under medical supervision" (s. 145(1)), which is extremely wide. Further, as treatability is not required, it can still be appropriate to detain a patient in hospital for treatment even though there is no treatment which can do him any good (see *R. v. Mersey Mental Health Review Tribunal, ex p. D., The Times,* April 13, 1987). The fact that he is unwilling to co-operate with the only treatment which might do him any good does not make that treatment inappropriate (*R. v. Cannons Park Mental Health Review Tribunal, ex p. A.* [1994] 2 All E.R. 659, C.A.). Even so, the tribunal should consider whether it is appropriate for the patient to receive whatever he is receiving in a hospital as opposed to somewhere else. Even if it is "appropriate" he must be discharged if it is not "necessary" for his own health or safety or for the protection of other persons for him to receive it.

Nevertheless, tribunals are often concerned with whether the patient still needs medical treatment in the conventional sense. There will be discussion about his medication. The non-medical members can ask the doctors to justify their opinions and to explain the advantages and disadvantages of the various drugs involved. Even if medication is clearly needed, it is usually possible for the patient to receive long-acting injections in an out-patient clinic or from a community nurse. It may be possible for the patient to go on being treated in hospital, but on an informal rather than compulsory basis. The question then changes to whether the patient will be prepared to co-operate with these plans, because he cannot be forced to do so once he has been discharged, although the new form of supervised after-care (see Chapter 7) may provide a greater incentive for him to do so. Tribunals have been known to grant a patient's discharge after accepting his assurances of cooperation, but with the clear threat that compulsion will be reimposed if he actually tries to assert the rights which his discharge theoretically gives. The practice may be difficult to justify, but it can benefit the patient's morale and make some improvement in his legal status. It is surely preferable to the practice of renewing "sections" in order to impose treatment as an out-patient during leave of absence, which was ruled unlawful in *R. v. Hallstrom, ex p. W.* [1986] Q.B. 1090 but probably still continues (see Peay, 1989).

The other issue which often arises is how the patient is going to cope in the outside world, if he intends to leave the hospital rather than to remain as an informal patient. Strictly speaking, this is irrelevant if his condition is not bad enough to make hospital treatment appropriate. But patients who are still disordered will need some sort of care, although not always under medical supervision. The question of whether hospital treatment is appropriate and necessary will often depend upon the alternative. The tribunal will be keenly interested in where the patient might live, whether he could get a job, how else he might occupy his time, and what support would be available from social services, family and community.

Tribunals may find it easier to hold that hospital treatment is both appropriate and "necessary for the protection of other persons" if the patient was originally detained because of his behaviour towards other people (as, *e.g.* in *R. v. Mersey Mental Health Review Tribunal, ex p. D., The Times*, April 13, 1987). Even here, of course, the patient must be discharged if he is not suffering from an appropriate degree of mental disorder. However, even if he has no gross symptom of mental illness, the tribunal may be able to find that he has a pathological tendency to abnormally aggressive or seriously irresponsible behaviour. This question, along with the question of whether he needs to be detained in the interests of other persons, depends upon his ability to resist the influences which triggered his earlier antisocial conduct. Unfortunately, hospital treatment, particularly in a secure unit, makes this difficult to assess. The tribunal has no control over the social skills training and general rehabilitative effort made in hospital. All it can do is to subject its predictions of future behaviour to critical scrutiny and bear in mind that this is an area in which the inter-relationship of mental condition and social situation is particularly important.

Thus, tribunals are often faced with the problem that the patient cannot be discharged unless the hospital has at least been trying to prepare him for it. The worse the hospital, the worse the patient's chances before the tribunal are likely to be. In unrestricted cases, tribunals have some power to influence the rehabilitative effort. First, they may direct the patient's discharge on a future specified date, rather than straightaway (s. 72(3)). This applies to any discharge under section 72(1), presumably whether it is mandatory or discretionary. Logically, however, the tribunal should not delay a discharge to which the patient is immediately entitled. He might only be entitled to a discharge once the necessary arrangements have been made, and a short delay could be proper to enable this to be done. In discretionary cases, a longer period might be appropriate, perhaps where the doctors predict that the patient will be ready in two or three months' time.

Secondly, if the tribunal does not discharge the patient under section 72(1), it may recommend that he be granted leave of absence, or transferred to another hospital, or into guardianship, with a view to facilitating his discharge on a future date (s. 72(3)(a)); alternatively it may recommend that the RMO consider applying for after-care under supervision (s. 73(3A)(a)). Valuable though these powers may be there is no direct obligation on the medical or social services to comply (although there is a duty to provide after-care under section 117). No doubt they will do their best to do so. The tribunal must set a time limit, at the end of which it will reconsider the case if its recommendations have not borne fruit (s. 72(3)(b), (3A)(b); r. 24(4)). The hearing may be reconvened with 14 days' notice, or less if all agree (r. 25(2)). By that time, the tribunal may feel that a discharge is preferable to keeping the patient in hospital any longer.

There are many other suggestions which tribunals often want to make, particularly about preparation within the hospital for life outside. Some medical members take these up during their discussions with the hospital representatives. There is nothing to stop the tribunal making its views clear, both during the hearing and when it comes to give written reasons for whatever it decides.

(b) Restriction order patients

The tribunal must discharge a restriction order patient if it finds (a) that he is not suffering mental illness, psychopathic disorder, severe mental impairment or mental impairment; *or* (b) that his disorder is not of a nature or degree which makes it appropriate for him to be liable to be detained in a hospital for medical treatment; *or* (c) that it is not necessary for the health or safety of the patient or for the protection of other persons that he should receive such treatment (s. 73(1) and (2)). These are exactly the same as the criteria for the mandatory discharge of unrestricted patients and raise exactly the same issues. But tribunals (and indeed hospitals) may be a little sceptical if a person has recently been sent to hospital as a psychopath after committing a very serious offence and then claims (or is thought) to be no such thing. Similarly, the second criterion is not whether hospital treatment will do him some good, but whether it is appropriate for him to be detained there for medical treatment, defined in the very wide sense to include nursing and care, habilitation and rehabilitation under medical supervision (s. 145(1)). Can it be appropriate to detain a patient for these purposes simply because he has already committed at least one serious offence and may do so again? The gulf between pure preventive detention and some sort of medical care and treatment may be very narrow, but it is nonetheless deep, although the decision in *R. v. Mersey Mental Health Review Tribunal, ex p. D., The Times*, April 13, 1987, came close to bridging it. If detention in hospital for this purpose is not appropriate, the patient must be discharged, no matter how dangerous he may be. However, if it is still appropriate, the tribunal is not concerned with whether it is necessary to protect the public from *serious* harm. Unlike the Home Secretary, it has no power to lift the restrictions while leaving the patient to be detained as an ordinary hospital order patient.

If the tribunal is satisfied that the criteria for mandatory discharge are met, it must then choose between an absolute and a conditional discharge. It must grant an absolute discharge if satisfied that it is not appropriate for the patient to remain liable to recall to hospital for further treatment (s. 73(1)). Otherwise, it must discharge him upon conditions (s. 73(2)). Thus a patient may be conditionally discharged even though he is not then suffering from any mental disorder (*R. v. Merseyside Mental Health Review Tribunal and Another, ex p. K* [1990] 1 All E.R. 694, C.A.). The tribunal can decide what the conditions should be. The Act lays down no limits, but the obvious candidates are residence, supervision and medical treatment. It is not possible to impose a condition of continued residence in a hospital, because this would reimpose detention by another route; discharge for this purpose must mean release from hospital (*Secretary of State for the Home Department v. Mental Health Review Tribunal for the Mersey Regional Health*

197

Authority [1986] 1 W.L.R. 1170), although continued informal residence without any condition should still be allowed. The tribunal might insist that he attends elsewhere or as an outpatient for treatment, although the treatment cannot be forced upon him should he refuse it (s. 56(1)). The tribunal may also decide on what he can or cannot do, in the way of going to public houses or other provoking places. The discharge may be deferred until the necessary arrangements have been made (s. 73(7)). The tribunal can then make another decision without a further hearing (r. 25(1)). But if the case is deferred so long that there has been another reference or application in the meantime, the second one supersedes the first (s. 73(7)). This power to defer a conditional discharge does *not* give the tribunal power to defer deciding the case or to reconsider its decision in the light of later developments (*R. v. Oxford Regional Mental Health Review Tribunal, ex p. Secretary of State for the Home Department* [1988] A.C. 120).

The effect of a tribunal's conditional discharge is just the same as a Home Secretary's. He can recall the patient at any time, in theory immediately after an unwelcome decision by a tribunal; but at first instance in *R. v. Secretary of State for the Home Department, ex p. K.* [1990] 1 W.L.R. 168, McCullough J. accepted that this would be unlawful (because irrational or unreasonable) "unless in the meantime something had happened which justified the belief that a different view might now be taken about one of the factors on which his release had depended." Unless the criteria for detention exist, the patient would have to be released when his case is referred to a tribunal within a month of recall. However, the Home Secretary can also vary the tribunal's conditions (s. 73(4) and (5)). Recall apart, there is no sanction for breach of the conditions. If, for example, an alcoholic is discharged on condition that he does not drink (not usually the wisest thing to do), the mere fact that he has a lapse will not invariably justify a recall.

Patients who have been conditionally discharged by a tribunal or by the Home Secretary may apply to the tribunal for the area where they live. The tribunal can then vary the conditions or even impose new ones. Alternatively, it can lift the restrictions altogether (s. 75(3)). This has the same effect as an absolute discharge. Both mean that the patient is no longer subject to any form of compulsion (s. 73(3)).

If a restriction order patient does not qualify for mandatory discharge, the tribunal has no discretion to release him. Tribunals may find it easier to decide that he no longer needs to be in hospital, because of their power to impose conditions and ensure that he is liable to instant recall. Nevertheless, the lack of discretion is unfortunate and even surprising, given the exalted membership of tribunals in these cases. The patient may be so much better that he does not need to be in a special hospital, even though some transitional care in another hospital may be appropriate before he is discharged into the community. This cannot be imposed as a condition of discharge and the formal power to recommend leave of absence or transfer does not apply to restricted patients (*Grant v. Mental Health Review Tribunal; R. v. Mersey Mental Health Review Tribunal, ex p. O'Hara, The Times*, April 28, 1986) because it can only apply to those who do not qualify for a mandatory discharge under section 72(1). Tribunals used to give detailed advice to the Home Secretary when they had no power to discharge patients themselves. He found this advice was most valuable in building up a picture of the patient's progress. Although it was confidential, it could also help the patient to make that progress through the hospital system. The tribunal can still make its views thoroughly clear when giving its reasons for refusing a discharge. These will be sent to the Home Office, and some parts can be withheld from the patient (r. 24(1) and (2)). Presumably tribunals could also make informal comments if they wished. Certainly, unless tribunals can contribute towards the Home Office understanding of individual patients in this way, an important part of the benefit for the patient will be lost (Wood, 1993). The cases in which the tribunal can be satisfied of the grounds for a mandatory discharge will be relatively few and far between: the combination of the patient's burden of proving a negative, the all-or-nothing power to discharge and the natural caution produced by the patient's own history means that the chances of success are very slim. But that does not mean that the whole proceeding need be without value either to the patient or to those in charge of him.

(c) Prisoners transferred with restrictions

If the patient has been transferred from prison under section 47 or 48, together with a restriction direction under section 49, the task of the tribunal is to decide whether or not he ought to remain in hospital. The task of the Home Secretary is then to decide whether to transfer him back to prison, or in some cases to leave him in hospital, or in others to release him into the community.

After hearing the case, the tribunal must notify the Home Secretary whether the patient would be entitled to an absolute or conditional discharge if he were a restriction order patient. If he is entitled to a conditional discharge, it may recommend that he should stay in hospital if he is not released, rather than be returned to prison (s. 74(1)). If the patient was transferred under section 48 (which relates to remand, civil and Immigration Act prisoners), the Home Secretary must transfer him back to prison, unless he is only entitled to a conditional discharge and the tribunal has recommended that he should be allowed to stay in hospital (s. 74(4)). In other cases, the Home Secretary can decide to allow the discharge. The tribunal will do this in the usual way, if it is notified by the Home Office within 90 days of giving its views (s. 74(3)). If nothing is heard from the Home Office within that time, the hospital must transfer the patient back to prison, unless the tribunal has recommended that he is entitled to a conditional discharge but should be allowed to stay in hospital instead (s. 74(3)).

However, even if the patient is not entitled to either sort of discharge, the tribunal can notify the Home Secretary that he no longer requires treatment in hospital for mental disorder or that no effective treatment can be given for his disorder in the hospital where he is. The Home Secretary may then decide to transfer the patient back to prison; alternatively, if the patient was under sentence, he can exercise any power of releasing on licence or under supervision which would have applied from prison (ss. 50(1), 51(3), and 53(2)). There is no power to do this if the patient was originally remanded by a magistrates' court (c.f. s. 52). But even if there is no effective treatment for these patients, the Home Secretary could decide to leave them in hospital for the time being.

(d) Patients subject to guardianship or after-care under supervision

If the patient is subject to guardianship, whether under a court order or civil powers, the tribunal always has a discretion to discharge him. But it must do so if it finds (a) that he is not then suffering from mental illness, psychopathic disorder, severe mental impairment or mental impairment;

or (b) that it is not necessary in the interests of the welfare of the patient, or for the protection of other persons, that he should remain under such guardianship (s. 72(4)). If the patient is subject to after-care under supervision, or will be when he leaves hospital, the tribunal always has power to order that this should cease, or never begin, and must do if satisfied that the criteria (p. 169, earlier) are not made out (s. 72(4A)). While guardianship is rare, and tribunal applications almost unheard of, supervised after-care is expected to be used more often and to generate more applications (Annual Report, 1994).

(e) Reclassification

If the tribunal does not discharge the patient, it may decide that he is suffering from a different legal category of disorder from that recorded in the application, order or direction (s. 72(5)). This will be amended accordingly, with exactly the same effect as a reclassification by the RMO (p. 88, earlier). For an unrestricted patient, it will determine which "treatability" test is to be applied at his next renewal. For a restricted patient, it will have no effect other than administrative tidiness.

7. THE DECISION AND AFTER

The tribunal may reach a majority decision, and where a tribunal with equal numbers is equally divided, the presiding member has a second or casting vote. It must always record its reasons in writing, and where it is satisfied that the grounds for a mandatory discharge are made out, it must explain its reasons for thinking so (r. 23). Giving reasons for one's decision is not the same as stating the legal ground upon which it was made and several High Court cases have emphasised the need to explain fully why the patient has not succeeded (*Bone v. Mental Health Review Tribunal* [1985] 3 All E.R. 330; *R. v. Mental Health Review Tribunal, ex p. Clatworthy* [1985] 3 All E.R. 699; and *R. v. Mental Health Review Tribunal, ex p. Pickering* [1986] 1 All E.R. 99). In *Pickering*'s case, Forbes J. advised tribunals to address themselves separately to the "diagnostic question" of whether the patient was mentally disordered and the "policy question" of whether his detention continued to be necessary.

The decision, with reasons, must be communicated in writing to the applicant, the patient (if he is not the applicant), the responsible authority, the Home Secretary (if the patient is restricted), and to anyone else whom the tribunal directs. This must be done within seven days in long-term cases, or three days in assessment cases (rr. 24(1) and 33). The decision may also be announced orally by the president at the end of the hearing. Wide variations in practice grew up and so guidelines were agreed among members (Annual Report, 1994, Appendix 12). While accepting the need to remain flexible, these suggest that the decision should be announced orally to the patient immediately after the hearing whenever possible. Even if the patient does not get the reasons at the time, he is entitled to a written explanation in most cases. However, if the tribunal considers that full disclosure would adversely affect his health or interests or those of others, it may communicate its decision to him in whatever way it thinks appropriate, and when giving its decision to the others, may do so on whatever condition it thinks appropriate about disclosing it to the patient. It can never keep anything from his qualified representative, although it may prevent him from telling all to his client (r. 24(2)).

There are two ways of challenging the proceedings in a mental health review tribunal, but neither gives a right of appeal against the merits of the decision as such. The first is to apply to the High Court for judicial review under Order 53 of the Rules of the Supreme Court. This requires the leave of a High Court judge and must usually be done within three months of the tribunal's decision. The object is to quash the decision on the ground that the tribunal had erred on a point of law or procedure. The first would arise if it had exceeded its powers, or made an error of law which appeared on the face of the record, or had reached a decision on the merits which no reasonable tribunal could possibly have reached, taking the relevant considerations into account and excluding the irrelevant. The second would arise if it had broken the statutory rules of procedure or the common law rules of natural justice. These are normally separate and cumulative requirements to see fair play. But something which would usually be a breach of the rules of natural justice may be specifically authorised by the tribunal's rules, provided that these are within the powers granted by the Act. Section 78(1) of the 1983 Act gives the Lord Chancellor a great deal of latitude over such matters as the disclosure of documents and the exclusion of people from the hearing. The rules of natural justice are themselves flexible according to the subject-matter, but the courts might be expected to take a strict view of what is required where the liberty of the subject is in issue, were it not for what the Act itself allows. However, the rules do require the tribunal to record and sometimes explain at almost every point when it departs from what would normally be expected. The High Court can examine whether the stated reason is sufficient, either in the light of the ground permitted in the rules or for the proper exercise of a discretion. If something has gone wrong, the appropriate remedy would be certiorari, to quash the decision and get the tribunal to take it again in a proper manner. But this and all the remedies available on judicial review are themselves within the discretion of the court.

The second possibility is for the tribunal to state a case for the determination by the High Court of any point of law arising before it (s. 78(8); see R.S.C. Ord. 56, rr. 7 to 12). It could do this on its own initiative, but in practice it will be asked to do so by one of the parties. The parties for this purpose are the applicant and any of the bodies initially notified of the application or reference. This would enable, for example, the Home Secretary to take the case of a restricted patient to the High Court if he felt that the tribunal had applied the wrong test (for example, on the knotty question of what makes detention in hospital for medical treatment appropriate). A written request to the tribunal to state a case must be made within 21 days after its decision is communicated. If the tribunal then refuses to state a case, or fails to do so within 21 days, the party concerned then has 14 days in which to apply for an order compelling it to do so. Unlike an application for judicial review, the tribunal and other parties must be notified of such an application. But the High Court would probably be looking for a prima facie case on much the same sort of points. Once the tribunal has stated a case, the applicant or, failing him, any party may apply to the court for it to be determined. If the High Court thinks that the tribunal's decision on the question of law raised by the case was wrong, it can give any direction that the tribunal ought to have given under the Mental Health Act.

The case stated procedure has two advantages over judicial review. The High Court has power to return the "case" to the tribunal for amendment

(R.S.C., Ord. 56, r. 11) and Gunn (1986) argues that this includes the power to require it to amplify the statement of facts found if this is incomplete. The High Court also has power to discharge the patient if the tribunal should have done so. On the other hand, in *Bone v. Mental Health Review Tribunal* [1985] 3 All E.R. 330, Nolan J. considered that judicial review was preferable, because affidavit evidence can be filed, it "allows a broader consideration of the issues; and offers a much more comprehensive range of reliefs." The case stated procedure is said to be "most unusual nowadays" (Annual Report, 1993, Appendix 13) despite the fact that in theory at least it could lead to the patient's immediate release.

8. COMMENTARY

The great criticism levelled at tribunals in the past was that they tended to operate more like a case conference or "patient's welfare assessment panel" (Fennell, 1977) than like a court. This is how they saw themselves (Peay, 1981 and 1982). They were usually dealing with patients who had been in hospital for some time and to whom the various labels were firmly attached. Their procedures were not well suited to examining the evidence upon which earlier judgments had been made. The issue was whether the patient was yet ready for a change and if so how to find the best placement for him. The tribunal was interested in getting some "feel" for his present mental state and assessing his needs along with those of his family and the public.

But the normal model of adjudication, based upon the application of fixed rules to proven facts about the past, cannot be expected to apply to these cases. They are more like child care cases than running-down actions. They will always centre round what sort of a person the patient is and how he can be expected to behave in the future. But the best guide to future behaviour is usually how someone has behaved in the past. It is important that the evidence for this should be properly scrutinised and evaluated. It is also important that the legal criteria are properly applied.

There is more than a whiff of regret in some quarters about the greater length, complexity and legalism of hearings these days. But the involvement of lawyers as advocates for patients should focus minds on the proper legal issues; it should lead to a more careful scrutiny of assumptions about the future made on the basis of past events; and it should usually result in an independent psychiatric report. All of this may take time, especially for the inevitably more difficult and complex cases involving special hospital and restricted patients (Blumenthal and Wessely, 1993). It should not necessarily result in a reduction of the structured informality which is so important, not only in trying to make an assessment of the people concerned, but also in reducing the stresses upon those patients who find it difficult to cope with them and the counter-productive feelings of confrontation which such hearings can produce in both patients and their doctors.

There is not much evidence that it has so far led to greater procedural regularity or consistency in approach. The publication of Annual Reports (1993, 1994) is making the system more open. It also reveals genuine efforts both to improve its efficiency and to engender a common sense of purpose and practice amongst members.

Nevertheless, the legal requirements, particularly for restricted patients, are heavily biased in favour of caution and some might say that this is no bad thing. Tribunals cannot conjure up appropriate facilities out of thin air. They ought at least to provide an effective check upon whether the criteria for detention are made out, but this is not quite what the law requires them to do. At least in assessment cases, where the patient has only recently been detained, the burden of proof ought to be placed on the authorities to justify their action. If they cannot do so, there should be some way of "wiping the slate clean" for the patient. On the other hand, if the action was justified, the hearing may come too soon for the patient and he will not achieve another one until some way into his period of detention for treatment. From this perspective, running together the period of detention for assessment and the first period of detention for treatment has its attractions (Wood, 1993). But such a radical step could only be contemplated in the context of the thorough review of the 1983 Act for which many are now pressing.

9 COMMUNITY CARE

"Community care means providing the right level of intervention and support to enable people to achieve maximum independence and control over their own lives" (Department of Health *et al.*, *Caring for People*, 1989). In mental health, however, this has two sides. First, as we have seen in Chapters 1 and 7, it means closing down the old mental hospitals and discharging as many patients as possible into the community. The process began with the Percy Commission and the 1959 Act, but real momentum gathered after two white papers, *Better Services for the Mentally Handicapped* (DHSS, 1971) and *Better Services for the Mentally Ill* (DHSS, 1975). This normalisation policy has been relatively uncontroversial for people with learning disabilities. Their principal need is for social care, education and occupation, rather than specialist health care, unless they have serious physical disabilities as well. The debate is about what sort of residential settings suit them best (see Emerson and Hatton, 1994). The mentally ill have been more troublesome. The concern is not only about the arrangements made for the care of patients moving out of hospital, but also that abandoning the old asylum role and closing beds has led to an increase in those who are not in touch with the system at all, including the homeless "crazies" on city streets and the disturbed or inadequate petty offenders in prison because there is nowhere else for them to go.

Secondly, however, community care should mean a flexible range of health and social services to meet the needs, and enhance the quality of life, of all kinds of vulnerable people, both as an end in itself and so that they are less likely to have to go into hospital or any kind of institutional care. The need for a positive community care policy became more and more apparent as more and more public money was spent on income support for the rapidly growing numbers of vulnerable old people in private or voluntary nursing and residential homes. The Audit Commission (1986) pointed out that at best this simply switched resources from providing hospital beds to providing other types of institutional care, missing out on more flexible, cost-effective alternatives; at worst, there was no care at all, with an often intolerable burden on people's families and a greater risk of neglect or even abuse. The result was the Griffiths Report, *Community Care: An Agenda for Action* (1988), followed by the White Paper, *Caring for People* (1989), and now the National Health Service and Community Care Act 1990. But it is hard enough to transfer resources from one long-term undertaking to another. It is even harder to manage the change from the simple clarity of professional responsibilities within a hospital to the complex, unclear and unco-ordinated responsibilities of numerous agencies and professionals outside it (Clinical Standards Advisory Group, 1995; Social Services Inspectorate, 1995). This is harder still when the administrative and legal structures governing the provision of health and social services are so different.

The legal issues involved can be illustrated from the provisions of the United Nations *Declaration on the Rights of Mentally Retarded Persons* (1971) (see also the *Declaration on the Rights of Disabled Persons* (1975); and *Standard Rules on the Equalisation of Opportunities for Persons with Disabilities* (1994)). The fundamental aim is to recognise the dignity and worth of all human beings and to promote their integration as far as possible in normal life. To this end, it declares that a mentally handicapped person is entitled to certain services. Thus he "has a right to proper medical care and physical therapy and to such education, training, rehabilitation and guidance as will enable him to develop his ability and maximum potential" (Art. 2). He also has the right to "economic security and a decent standard of living" and to "perform productive work or to engage in any other meaningful occupation to the fullest extent of his capabilities" (Art. 3). Wherever possible, he "should live with his own family or with foster parents and participate in different forms of community life. The family with which he lives should receive assistance. If care in an institution becomes necessary, it should be provided in surroundings and other circumstances as close as possible to those of normal life" (Art. 4). The Declaration also expects that appropriate accommodation, education, training and occupation will be provided for mentally handicapped people who need them.

The Declaration also proclaims that a mentally handicapped person "has, to the maximum degree of feasibility, the same rights as other human beings" (Art. 1). The ordinary rights of other human beings, in English law at least, are based on the right of self-determination. But he also has the right to a "qualified guardian when this is required to protect his personal well-being and interests" (Art. 5) and to "protection from exploitation, abuse and degrading treatment" (Art. 6). Unlike the European Convention on Human Rights, the Declaration does not give individuals a right to petition the United Nations institutions if our laws do not live up to these aspirations. But they provide a standard against which our laws can be judged.

Hence the questions posed for individuals are of two kinds. First is whether they have any real entitlement to the services they need, which in turn depends upon the authorities' responsibilities to provide those services, assess individuals' needs, and listen to representations on their behalf. Second is how far people can be given, not only the help and support, but also the protection from exploitation and abuse which they need, without at the same time taking away the independence and freedom of choice which the whole concept of community care aims to promote. This problem arises whether they are living in hospital, in residential accommodation, with their families or independently. But it is particularly relevant now that so many people with some degree of mental disorder or learning disability are trying to live ordinary lives in an increasingly complex world.

1. ASSESSMENT AND ENTITLEMENT

Legal responsibility for providing community services rests with local social services authorities, local education authorities, and health authorities. Most of the services commonly thought of as "community care" are provided by social services authorities; but the dividing line between health and social care for people with mental disorders or disabilities is not easily drawn and has shifted over the years. When the NHS was set up after the Second World War, it was largely responsible for looking after both the mentally ill and the mentally handicapped. The Percy Commission (1957, para. 592) recommended that "no-one should be excluded from benefiting from any of the general social services simply because his need arises from mental disorder rather than from some other cause." Local authorities' powers to provide services for the elderly, disabled and other groups were therefore extended to them. Nevertheless, the health service has continued to play a major role, both in providing hospital accommodation and in developing a network of services outside hospital. There were attempts to promote joint planning and funding, principally in the Health and Social Services and Social Security Adjudications (HASSASSA) Act 1983, but major changes in the delivery of both health and social services came with the National Health Service and Community Care Act 1990.

The object of Part III of the 1990 Act was to implement the recommendation of the Griffiths Report (1988) that local social services authorities should have the task of "ensuring that the needs of individuals within the specified groups are identified, packages of care devised, and services co-ordinated." Funding for this was to come from the transfer to local authorities of sums equivalent to those being paid out in income support for people living in private and voluntary residential and nursing homes. But it was recognised that extra grants would be needed to improve social services for people suffering from mental illness (Local Authority Social Services Act 1970, s. 7E).

The social services defined as "community care services" for the purpose of the 1990 Act (s. 46(3)) are those provided under four statutory provisions. First, there is Part III of the National Assistance Act 1948. Under section 21(2)(a), residential accommodation can be provided for people who need care and attention because of "age, illness, disability or any other circumstances". Under section 29, a variety of services can be provided for disabled people, defined as people who are blind, deaf or dumb, or who are substantially or permanently handicapped by illness, injury or congenital deformity, and people suffering from any kind of mental disorder. Secondly, under section 45 of the Health Services and Public Health Act 1968, arrangements can be made for promoting the welfare of old people. Thirdly, under section 21 and Schedule 8 to the National Health Service Act 1977, services other than residential accommodation can be provided for the prevention of illness, the care of people suffering from illness, and the after-care of people who have been suffering. "Illness" includes any form of mental disorder within the meaning of the 1983 Act. Health authorities have a parallel responsibility to provide facilities for the prevention, care and after-care of "illness", if these are considered appropriate as part of the health service, under section 3(2)(a) of the 1977 Act. Fourthly, there is the duty under section 117 of the Mental Health Act 1983 to provide after-care services for certain detained patients when they are discharged from hospital; this responsibility is also laid upon the health authorities (p. 159, earlier).

Each local social services authority must prepare and publish a strategic "plan for the provision of community care services in their area", which must then be reviewed and updated from time to time (s. 46). The plan should assess needs in the locality, including the need to rehabilitate long-stay mental patients in the community, and set out strategies for meeting them. These should develop a "mixed economy of care", making use of voluntary, "not for profit" and private providers, whenever this is most cost-effective (Department of Health *et al.*, 1989). Authorities should move away from the role of exclusive service provider and into the role of service arranger and procurer. They are also expected to collaborate with their matching health authorities in deciding who does what.

Secondly, the local authority are responsible for assessing individual need for these services. They *must* carry out an assessment (in accordance with any directions given by the Secretary of State) if it appears to the authority that any person for whom they have power to provide or arrange community care services may be in need of them (s. 47(1)(a)). The health authority and local housing authority should be brought into the assessment when necessary (s. 47(3)). Having made the assessment, the authority must then decide "whether his needs call for the provision by them of any such services" (s. 47(1)(b)). Services can be provided on a temporary basis without an assessment if they are urgently needed (s. 47(6)).

"Community care services" do not include those which can be provided for disabled people, again covering people with mental disorders or disabilities, under the Chronically Sick and Disabled Persons Act 1970 or section 3 of the Disabled Persons (Employment) Act 1958. However, under section 4 of the Disabled Persons (Services, Consultation and Representation) Act 1986 ("Tom Clarke's Act"), authorities already have a duty to consider and decide upon a disabled person's need for such services, if asked to do so either by the client or by a carer: that is, someone who is providing him with "a substantial amount of care on a regular basis" but not employed to do so by a statutory agency. The carer's ability to go on doing this has to be taken into account in the assessment (1986 Act, s. 8(1)). The 1990 Act requires the local authority to conduct this assessment along with the main one, even if they have not been asked to do so (s. 47(2)).

The main object of Tom Clarke's Act, however, was to provide for the appointment of "authorised representatives" for disabled people (s. 1). These would negotiate on their behalf for the provision of services (s. 2) and participate in any statutory or other assessment of their needs (s. 3). They would also be able to request an assessment under section 4. It is strongly felt by many of those concerned with especially elderly and mentally disabled people that their main need is for effective advocates of this sort, coupled with a real entitlement to services, rather than for guardianship or other protective mechanisms which diminish rather than enhance their own legal status (see, for example, Age Concern, 1986). While the Government is keen to encourage the development of the advocacy concept, it has so far stopped short of implementing a legal requirement to supply them.

The third element in the 1990 Act scheme is that, having assessed a person's needs, the local authority should set about meeting them in the best available way. The idea (or ideal) is to devise individualised packages of care which should be monitored and reviewed. The aim would be to enable the client to live at home if at all possible and, if not, to consider whether residential or nursing home care would be appropriate. The authority may either provide services themselves or arrange for them to be provided by other agencies, the voluntary or private sector. If the client needs services provided at public expense, it is possible to make some charge, depending on the type of service and what the client can afford (see pp. 210, 214, later). The rest will be paid for by the local authority. Hence, the 1990 Act scheme has moved away from entitlement to cash benefits to pay for residential care for those who could not afford it themselves, towards discretionary powers to provide a range of services for which those who can afford it are expected to pay.

But what can anyone do if the authority fail either to assess his need or provide him with services once assessed? The Secretary of State has a general power to declare local authorities in default if they fail to comply with any of their social services duties, to direct them to comply, and to enforce that direction by an order for mandamus from the High Court

(Local Authority Social Services Act 1970, s. 7D). This has not prevented individuals from seeking judicial review, alleging that an authority have acted unlawfully, irrationally or unreasonably in making decisions about the general quantity or quality of services they will provide (for example, when seeking unsuccessfully to challenge the decision to cease being a direct provider of old people's homes in *R. v. Wandsworth L.B.C. ex p. Beckwith, The Times*, December 15, 1995, H.L.). But might an individual seek a remedy because he himself has been denied an assessment or a service?

Essentially, this is just the same as being denied a hospital bed (p. 20, earlier). Parliament might have intended that people who suffer harm because a public duty of this sort has been broken can sue for *damages*. But Parliament rarely says so expressly and the courts are extremely reluctant to imply it, especially where there are statutory remedies for the breach of duty (such as the 1970 Act, s. 7D), but even where there are none. The leading case is *Cocks v. Thanet D.C.* [1983] A.C. 286, which concerned the duty to house the homeless; even stronger is *X. (Minors) v. Bedfordshire C.C.*[1995] 2 A.C. 633, which concerned the social services authority's duty to protect children from abuse and the education authority's duties to assess and provide for children with special educational needs.

On the other hand, *judicial review* has proved a fruitful means of challenging the authorities' decision-making processes, particularly in homelessness cases. The court might require an authority to think again if it withheld services because of an error of law or because it acted irrationally or unreasonably in considering the client's case and what to do for him, for example by taking irrelevant considerations into account. Much will depend upon the terms of the particular statutory provision relied upon. Thus there is a clear duty to provide an assessment in certain circumstances under section 47(1)(a), but then a duty to decide whether this calls for services to be provided under section 47(1)(b) (p. 208, earlier). But although authorities must obviously operate these duties fairly and sensibly, resources can be a relevant consideration at several points (Schwehr, 1995).

In *R. v. Gloucestershire C.C., ex p. Mahfood, The Times*, June 21, 1995, it was held that an authority were entitled to take their resources into account when assessing a disabled person's need for services under section 2 of the 1970 Act; the needs of the particular individual would have to be considered in the context of the needs of others and the resources available; but if no reasonable authority could conclude other than that some help was necessary, that must be the answer; and once having decided that it was necessary to make some arrangements there was an absolute duty to make them. We have already seen (p. 160, earlier) how judicial review can be used to support the duty to provide after-care services under section 117 of the 1983 Act (*R. v. Ealing District Health Authority, ex p. Fox* [1993] 1 W.L.R. 373).

In practice, although judicial review may help a few individuals or groups where local authorities go wrong, it is no substitute for proper appeal procedures where the merits as well as the legality of decisions can be challenged. Local authorities are now obliged to establish complaints procedures for "qualifying individuals" (that is, people for whom the authority must or may provide or arrange a service whose need or possible need for such a service has come to the authority's attention) or people acting on their behalf (Local Authority Social Services Act 1970, s. 7B; Local Authority Social Services (Complaints Procedure) Order 1990; Complaints Procedure Directions 1990). This must have three stages—an informal attempt to resolve matters, then an internal consideration by the authority, and then a reference to a panel which must have an independent member who is not a member or employee of the authority or any organisation to which the authority have delegated any of their social services functions. Would a reasonable local authority then fail to remedy a complaint which had been found justified after such a process?

· 2. SERVICES FOR ADULTS

(a) Residential care

Local social services authorities must make arrangements to provide residential accommodation, as part of their general duty under section 21(1)(a) of the 1948 Act, for people who are or have been suffering from mental disorder or to prevent mental disorder if they are ordinarily resident in the authority's area or have no settled residence and are simply there. They may also do so for people who are ordinarily resident elsewhere but come to live in the area after discharge from hospital. They may also make arrangements specifically for people who are alcohol or drug dependent (Department of Health Circular LAC(93)10, Appendix 1).

These arrangements may be in the authority's own homes (but as long as suitable accommodation is available, they do not have to have these; *R. v. Wandsworth L.B.C., ex p. Beckwith, The Times,* December 15, 1995, H.L.), or in homes managed by other authorities (s. 21(4)) or by voluntary organisations or others who provide such accommodation for reward (s. 26(1)). If board and personal care are provided, the home must be registered under Part I of the Registered Homes Act 1984, unless it is exempt (see below) (s. 26(1A)). If nursing care is provided, it must be registered under Part II of the 1984 Act, unless provided by an exempt body (see Chapter 1) (s. 26(1B)). Nursing home care can only be arranged with the consent of the patient's own health authority, apart from temporary arrangements in an emergency (s. 26(1C),(1D)). Other sorts of accommodation can be used, as long as the person running it has not been convicted of any offence under the 1984 Act (s. 26(1E)).

Apart from flexibility of service, the object is to apply the same charging system to all kinds of residential care. Health authorities cannot charge for their services, whereas local authorities are required to charge up to the full cost of their Part III accommodation if residents can afford to pay (1948 Act, s. 22). The amount actually paid is determined by a means test (HASSASSA Act, Part VII). Essentially the same system applies to residential care "bought in" from the voluntary and private sector (1948 Act, s. 26(2),(3),(3A)). If hostel accommodation is provided under section 29 of the 1948 Act (p. 213, later), it also comes within this system (1990 Act, s. 44(7)) rather than the discretionary charges which apply to other types of service. Individuals will be entitled to exactly the same housing benefit and income support whether they are living in residential care or at home. This is paid to the local authority, apart from the sum allowed to the client as a personal allowance. The balance is paid by the authority, from their own resources and those transferred in effect from the social security budget. (However, people already in nursing and residential homes when the Act came into force will continue to be funded by income support; 1948 Act, s. 26A, inserted by the 1990 Act, s. 43).

The contribution of the private and voluntary sectors to residential care of all types has already increased dramatically. The number of places in private old people's homes nearly trebled between 1979 and 1986.

Standards are monitored by registration under Part I of the Registered Homes Act 1984, required of "any establishment which provides or is intended to provide, whether for reward or not, residential accommodation with both board and personal care for persons in need of personal care by reason of old age, disablement, past or present dependence on alcohol or drugs or past or present mental disorder" (s. 1(1)). "Small homes", catering for fewer than four people who need care other than managers, employees and their relatives (s. 1(4A), (4B)), need not register in two circumstances, although more may be added by regulations: these are (a) if they are wholly self-managed, so that the only people needing care for whom they cater are their own managers, employees and their relatives (in which case the effect of the definition is that the limit of four does not apply); or (b) they cater for fewer than four children who are fostered there either by a local authority or voluntary organisation or privately (s. 1(4) and Residential Care Homes Regulations 1984, (S.I. 1984 No. 1345), amended (S.I. 1992 No. 2241), reg. 24). A long list of places covered by different legislation are exempt (s. 1(5)). These are, basically, hospitals, children's homes, schools, colleges and universities, and "any establishment managed or provided by a government department or local authority or by any authority or body constituted by an Act of Parliament or incorporated by Royal Charter." Mental nursing homes are also excluded, if that is their sole purpose, but dual registration is necessary for homes which have some residents and some patients and a modified system of optional dual registration is open to small homes which sometimes have both (s. 4).

Both the manager and the person in control of the home (if different) must be registered with the local social services authority for the area where the home is (ss. 3, 5, 30). The authority must lay down a maximum number of residents and can make other conditions regulating the age, sex or category of people who can be accommodated there. These can be varied or added to from time to time (s. 5(3), (4)). The authority can refuse registration if the applicant or any other person concerned in carrying on the home is not fit to be so; or if the premises are not fit, because of their situation, construction, state of repair, accommodation, staffing or equipment; or if the way in which it is intended to carry on the home is such as not to provide the services or facilities reasonably required (s. 9).

In fact, the Secretary of State makes regulations about the facilities and services to be provided, the numbers and qualifications of staff to be employed and to be on duty, the records to be kept, the notices to be given about residents, events such as deaths, and the absences of staff, the information to be supplied by applicants for registration, and the form of the local authorities' registers (s. 16; see Residential Care Homes Regulations 1984, (S.I. 1984 No. 1345) amended (S.I. 1992 No. 2241) and the Code of Practice, *Home Life*). Homes can be inspected without notice at any time of day or night on behalf of either the Secretary of State or the registration authority (s. 17). Authorities must inspect at least once a year (reg. 18). Homes can be inspected at any time on behalf of either the Secretary of State or the registration authority and the regulations also provide for how often this must be done (para. 20).

Registration can be cancelled if the annual fee is not paid, or if the authority could have refused registration, or if the conditions are not complied with, or if the registered person is convicted of an offence under Part I of the Act or regulations in respect of this or any other home, or anyone is convicted of an offence in respect of this home (s. 10). Under the urgent procedure for cancellation, or for varying the conditions or adding a new one, the registration authority can apply *ex parte* to a single magistrate. He can make the order if it appears to him that there will be a serious risk to the life, health or well-being of the residents. The application must be supported by a written statement of the authority's reasons and the order itself must also be in writing. The authority must then service notice of the order and its terms, together with a copy of the supporting statement, on any registered person as soon as possible (s. 11). Otherwise, the normal procedure for refusing registration, or granting it subject to conditions which have not been agreed, or varying conditions, or cancelling registration, involves serving notices on the people concerned and allowing them to make representations to the authority (ss. 12, 13). There is a right of appeal, against the decisions of the single magistrate or the registration authority, to the registered homes tribunal established under Part III of the Act (s. 15).

Some people feel that these powers allow local authorities to insist on higher standards in private or voluntary homes than they achieve in their own homes. The idea was, therefore, that they should have independent inspection units applying the same standards to all homes, including their own (Department of Health *et al.*, 1989, paras. 5.15–5.24). Recent guidance (Circular LAC(95)12) stresses the same principles of consistency, transparency and user-friendliness as in the regulation of nursing homes (see p. 25, earlier). The Act itself provides for inspection by the Secretary of State (s. 48).

The quality of life for residents in all types of home, public or private, is crucially affected by how far the home is prepared to go in allowing them to live their own lives and take their own decisions. There are two aspects to this. The home's own rules may restrict the residents' rights to choose how and where they spend their time. Homes are legally entitled to offer their accommodation on these terms, take it or leave it, despite the fact that their residents have nowhere else to go. More creditably, homes are only too well aware of their common law duty to take reasonable care of their residents. Rules may be devised in order to avoid a claim for personal injuries brought, for example, by an elderly resident who falls downstairs because there was no one to accompany him. However, homes have nothing to fear if they have taken reasonable precautions, or if a resident has chosen to take a risk of which he is perfectly well aware. The second aspect is that staff may be tempted to take decisions for their residents even though the law gives them no power to do so. People are entitled to make their own choices about such things as medical and dental treatment, and how to spend their own money provided that they are capable of understanding in broad terms what is involved. The mere fact that a person lives in residential care, even for the mentally handicapped or elderly mentally infirm, does not remove his right to self-determination in such matters, any more than should the fact that he lives in hospital.

(b) Other services

Social services authorities also have powers to provide or arrange a wide range of training, occupation and leisure activities, as well as help with daily living and obtaining access to other services, for mentally disordered, disabled or elderly people. These can all be provided directly or by arrangement with the voluntary or private sectors (1948 Act, s. 30; 1968 Act, s. 45(3); Circular LAC(93)10).

Once the Local Education Authority's (LEA) responsibilities are over (see section 3 later) social services should assume responsibility for the occupation and training of mentally disordered people, particularly those with learning disabilities. As part of their duty to make arrangements for non-residential services for the prevention, care and after-care of illness, under paragraph 2 of Schedule 8 to the 1977 Act, they must arrange centres (including training centres and day centres) or other facilities (including domiciliary facilities) for this purpose; they may pay people for work done there (Circular LAC(93)10, Appendix 3). Central government still has power to arrange supported employment for seriously disabled people, under section 15 of the Disabled Persons (Employment) Act 1944 (to be amended by the Disability Discrimination Act 1995; see also p. 237, later). Under section 3 of the Disabled Persons (Employment) Act 1958, however, social services authorities have power (and a duty towards people living in their area) to provide sheltered employment for the disabled; and they may provide hostels for people working there, or suitable work at home, under section 29(4)(c),(d) of the 1948 Act.

Social services authorities must, as part of their duties under section 29, provide facilities for social rehabilitation and adjustment to disability and occupational, social, cultural and recreational facilities. They may pay for work undertaken and provide meals. They may also provide holiday homes, free or subsidised travel, help in finding accommodation to enable people to participate in these facilities, contribute towards the cost of employing a warden on warden assisted housing schemes, and provide warden services for occupiers of private housing (Circular LAC(93)10, Appendix 2).

The last two, as well as help with travelling to and from, and meals and recreation in the home and elsewhere can be provided for old people, under section 45 of the Health Services and Public Health Act, whether or not they are also mentally disordered or disabled (DHSS Circular 19/71). District councils have power to provide meals and recreation for old people under Part II of Schedule 9 to the HASSASSA Act 1983. Social services authorities can provide meals-on-wheels (not otherwise provided for), and night-sitter services, recuperative holidays, social and recreational facilities and services for alcoholics and drug addicts under Paragraph 2 of Schedule 8 to the 1977 Act (Circular LAC(93)10, Appendix 3). They must arrange a home help and laundry service for people who need it because of illness, old age or handicap, under paragraph 3 of Schedule 8 of the 1977 Act.

A great many practical things can, and should, be provided for disabled people under section 2 of the Chronically Sick and Disabled Persons Act 1970. These include home adaptations, televisions, and telephones, as well as holidays and cultural and recreational facilities. Once again, this is a duty towards people who are ordinarily resident in the area and for whom they are "necessary". Keeping a register of disabled people living in the area is a duty under section 29 of the 1948 Act (see LAC(93)10, Appendix 4).

Social services authorities must provide a social work service for disabled people resident in their area, under section 29 of the 1948 Act. They must arrange for enough approved social workers, the exercise of guardianship functions, and "social work and related services to help in the identification, diagnosis, assessment and social treatment of mental disorder and to provide social work support and other domiciliary and care services to people living in their homes and elsewhere" and may arrange them "for the purpose of preventing the impairment of physical or mental health of adults in families where such impairment is likely, and for the purpose of preventing the break-up of such families, or for assisting in their rehabilitation", under paragraph 2 of Schedule 8 to the 1977 Act (Local Authority Circular LAC(93)10).

There is power to make whatever charges the authority think reasonable for their non-residential services, under section 17 of the HASSASSA Act. But they do not have to do so and cannot charge more than it is reasonably practicable for the client to pay. This allows the authority to charge for such things as home help, home care, meals on wheels and day care, but the Government accepts that it would not be appropriate to charge for social work support, occupational therapy, advice and assessment of client needs (Department of Health *et al.*, 1989, para. 3.8.5.).

3. SERVICES FOR CHILDREN

(a) Education

Since 1971, it has been impossible to declare any child ineducable. LEAs are responsible for securing that all children in their area, no matter how severe their learning difficulties or disabilities, receive an appropriate education. LEAs have a duty, which may be shared with the funding authority, to ensure that there are sufficient schools suitable for all the pupils of compulsory school age in their area (Education Act 1944, s. 8(1)). They have power to provide for the education of people up to the age of 19 (s. 8(1A)). This is particularly important for young people with learning disabilities, who are often just beginning to make real progress around the age of 16. LEAs also have the power, but not the duty, to provide schools for children below compulsory school age, which is again particularly valuable for those with disabilities (Education Act 1980, s. 24).

In performing this duty, LEAs must have regard to the need for securing that special educational provision is made for pupils who have special educational needs (1944 Act, s. 8(2)(c)). Generally, these children should be educated in ordinary schools (Education Act 1993, s. 160(1)), but only if this is compatible with giving a particular child the special education he needs, with the efficient education of his school mates, and with the efficient use of resources (1993 Act, s. 160(2)). Otherwise, he will usually be educated in a special school. But if the LEA are satisfied that this would be "inappropriate", they may, after consultation with his parents, arrange for some or all of his education to be provided in another way (1993 Act, s. 163).

The procedures for identifying children with special educational needs, and deciding how best to provide for these, are now laid down in Part III of the Education Act 1993 (see Warnock, 1978; Audit Commission and H.M.I., 1992; Department of Education and Science, *Choice and Diversity. A New Framework for Schools*, 1992). These cover all children below compulsory school age and those up to 19 who are still at school (1993 Act, s. 156(5)). Special educational needs means one of three things: (a) that the child has significantly greater difficulty in learning than the majority of children of his age; this concept of learning difficulty is much wider than the concept of learning disability or mental handicap; or (b) that he has a disability which prevents or hinders him from using the educational facilities generally provided for children of his age in the local schools; or (c) that he is under the age of five and likely to fall within either of these categories, or to do so unless special provision is made for him now (1993 Act, s. 156(2)).

LEAs are obliged to identify all the children for whom they are responsible who have special educational needs and for whom it is necessary to decide what special educational provision is called for (1993 Act, s. 165(1),(2)). They are responsible for all the children in their area who are being educated at public expense (1993 Act, s. 165(3)(a),(b)), or who are at school or aged at least two and under compulsory school age and are drawn to their attention as having, or probably having, special educational needs (1993 Act, s. 165(3)(c),(d)). If the LEA think a determination is or is probably necessary they must carry out an assessment (1993 Act, s. 167). Parents can ask the LEA to assess any child for whom the LEA are responsible (1993 Act, s. 173). The LEA can also assess a child under the age of two if the parents consent (1993 Act, s. 175). Early identification is most important and will usually take place during the developmental assessments provided by the health authority. If a health authority or NHS trust think that a child under five probably has special needs, they must tell the parents about this, and also about any voluntary organisation which may be able to help. After giving the parents an opportunity of discussing things, they must notify the LEA (1993 Act, s. 176).

Parents must be involved in the assessment, but they also have a duty to co-operate with any medical, psychological, educational or other examination required (1993 Act, s. 167 and Sched. 9). If the result of the assessment and any representations made by the parents is that it is necessary for the LEA to determine the special educational provision called for, the LEA must make a "statement" of the child's needs and the provision to be made for them (1993 Act, s. 168 and Sched. 10). The parents can also ask for the reassessment of a "statemented" child who has not been assessed for the last six months (1993 Act, s. 172(2)). The statement itself must always be reviewed if there is a reassessment and within 12 months of its making or last review (s. 172(5)). While a statement exists for a child for whom the LEA is responsible, the LEA *must* provide the education specified in it, unless the parents have made suitable arrangements for themselves (1993 Act, s. 168(5)).

The parents can appeal to the special educational needs tribunal against the LEA's decision not to make an assessment for which they have asked (1993 Act, s. 173(2)); or not to review the assessment of a statemented child (1993 Act, s. 172); the tribunal can then order the LEA to carry out an assessment. The parents may also appeal against the decision not to make a statement for any child who has been assessed (1993 Act, s. 169); the tribunal can then order the LEA to make a statement or ask them to think again. Finally, the parents may appeal against the contents of a statement (1993 Act, s. 170); the tribunal can amend or end the statement.

Parents have a duty to ensure that children of compulsory school age receive efficient full-time education suitable to their age, ability, aptitude and any special educational needs they may have (1944 Act, s. 36). If parents do not send such a child to school or make proper alternative provision, the usual enforcement procedures can be invoked (1993 Act, Part IV). The LEA can make a school attendance order requiring the parent to register the child at the school named in the statement (1993 Act, ss. 192 and 196). Failure to comply is an offence (1993 Act, s. 198), as is failure to send a registered pupil to school without a good excuse (1993 Act, s. 199). Alternatively, the LEA may seek an education supervision order under section 36 of the Children Act 1989, requiring the parents and the child to comply with the supervisor's directions about his education. As a last resort, it may be necessary to bring care proceedings on the basis that the child is suffering significant harm because his educational development is being impaired.

(b) Social services

It has been official policy since 1981 that no child should grow up in a mental handicap hospital and very few now do. The Children Act 1989 brought together the social services designed for handicapped or disabled children and those designed for children whose families were for some other reason unable to look after them properly. It tried to combine the best features of each system, so that all children being looked after by social services have the same protection, but wherever possible services are provided in partnership with the parents.

The authority's general duty is to safeguard and promote the welfare of "children in need" and, if consistent with that, to promote their upbringing by their own families (s. 17(1)). "Children in need" include the disabled, as well as those who are unlikely to attain a reasonable standard of health or development, or whose health or development is likely to be significantly impaired, without social services (s. 17(10)). Each authority must keep a register of disabled children in their area (Sched. 2, para. 2). If assessing needs under other legislation, they may also assess needs under the Children Act itself (para. 3). There is a particular duty to provide services designed to minimise the effect of disability and to give disabled children the opportunity of leading lives which are as normal as possible (para. 6). There must be appropriate provision to make available advice, guidance and counselling, occupational, social, cultural or recreational facilities, home help (including laundry), travel to and from these or similar services, and holidays, to children living with their families (para. 8). There are also duties to provide family centres (para. 9); to promote contact between children living away from home, for example in hospital, and their families (para. 10); to prevent ill-treatment and neglect (para. 4); to seek to avoid legal proceedings of any sort concerning a child and his future (para. 7); to provide appropriate day care for pre-school children and care and supervised activities for older children outside school hours and in holidays (s. 18).

These duties simply require the authority to make appropriate provision for disabled children in its area. Under section 20, however, there is a duty to provide accommodation for any individual child "in need" in the area who requires it because there is no-one with "parental responsibility" for him, or he is lost or abandoned, or "the person who has been caring for him [is] prevented (whether or not permanently, and for whatever reason) from providing him with suitable accommodation and care" (s. 20(1)). This is intended to cover families who need respite or long-term care for their learning disabled or mentally disordered children; but there is also a power to accommodate *any* child (even if his parents are able to do so) if this would safeguard or promote his welfare (s. 20(4)). This service is entirely voluntary and the parents may remove the child at any time (s. 20(8)). The authority must safeguard and promote the welfare of any child being accommodated under this or any social services powers

(s. 22(3)) and consult both the child and his parents before making any decision (s. 22(4)). They may arrange any type of accommodation, including their own or private or voluntary children's homes, or fostering (s. 23(2)); but this should be near his home if practicable (s. 23(7)), and for a disabled child "not unsuitable" to his particular needs (s. 23(8)). Most placements are governed by detailed regulations (*e.g.* on fostering). The authority must promote contact with the child's parents, relatives and friends; they must, usually, tell his parents where he is; similarly the parents must keep the authority informed of their address (Sched. 2, para. 15).

A common system of charging applies to all accommodation provided by the authority. It is discretionary, in that contributions may only be sought if the authority consider it reasonable to do so (Sched. 2, para. 21(2)). There is a ceiling of the authority's normal fostering rate for such a child, irrespective of the actual cost which is likely to be much higher (para. 22(5)(a)). Parental means must be taken into account (paras. 22(5)(b) and 23(3)(b)) and disputes about what should be paid can be taken to court (para. 23). Charging anything at all to the parents of a severely handicapped child may seem like adding insult to injury, particularly as they would not be charged if the child were in hospital; but it seemed equally questionable that the poor and disadvantaged parents whose children had to be looked after by others, sometimes against their will, might be charged for it, while the better off parents of a handicapped child were not.

Social services authorities also have welfare duties towards children spending longer than three months in hospital or other health service accommodation, in private and voluntary residential homes, nursing homes and mental nursing homes, or in LEA accommodation, such as boarding special schools.

4. PROTECTION FROM ABUSE AND EXPLOITATION

There is a well-developed system of powers, duties and procedures to protect children from harm (outlined in Chapter 3). There is also a growing recognition of the problems of elder abuse (McCreadie, 1991; SSI, 1992, 1993) and of sexual and other abuse of adults with learning disabilities (Brown and Craft, 1989; Turk and Brown, 1993; SSI, 1994). But there is not such a well-developed system of law and practice to combat it. As we have seen in Chapter 4, an approved social worker may enter private premises and may apply for warrants to gain entry and remove patients to a place of safety, under sections 115 and 135 of the Mental Health Act 1983; alternatively, any social worker may seek the help of the community physician to invoke the powers under section 47 of the National Assistance Act 1948. Together, these scarcely add up to a clear and comprehensive framework for protecting vulnerable people from abuse and neglect in their own homes, while preserving their right to take their own decisions when they can.

The Law Commission (1995) have tried to remedy this. In their proposals, a person is "vulnerable" if he is aged 16 or over, may be in need of community care services (p. 207, earlier) because of mental disorder or disability, age or illness, and is or may be unable to take care of himself or to protect himself against significant harm or serious exploitation. There would be a new duty to investigate if a vulnerable person was thought to be at risk. The existing provisions would be replaced with new powers to enter premises and see the vulnerable person in private; to obtain a warrant if entry were denied; to obtain an order authorising them to carry out an assessment; and as a last resort to remove the person for a short time to protective accommodation. The assumption is that a vulnerable person who is being harmed or exploited will welcome this intervention. But none of these powers should be exercised if the person objects, unless he is or may be suffering from mental disorder or disability: even then, only a short period of assessment or protection would be justified. Something else would be needed in the longer term.

5. GUARDIANSHIP

Guardianship was originally intended as the community care equivalent of compulsory admission for treatment or an ordinary hospital order. The grounds and procedures are still remarkably similar and in theory patients can readily be transferred from hospital to guardianship and vice versa. In practice, even under the 1959 Act, it was hardly ever used and predominantly for mentally handicapped people rather than the mentally ill. The 1959 Act gave the guardian the powers of a parent over a child under the age of 14. No-one in practice was very clear what this meant. Even then, guardianship was not thought necessary unless the patient seemed reluctant to accept the authority of those who were looking after him.

When the Act was last under review, the Royal College of Psychiatrists, the British Association of Social Workers (BASW), the National Association for Mental Health (MIND) and the Butler Committee on Mentally Abnormal Offenders all thought that more use should be made of guardianship. But they disagreed about whether it should become a community treatment, community care or "essential powers" order. BASW (1977) wanted to develop guardianship along the lines originally intended by the Percy Commission, as a full-scale alternative to hospital care. The Butler Committee (1975) and MIND (Gostin, 1977) were particularly concerned about the compulsory supervision of unrestricted patients after their discharge from hospital, but the Butler Committee thought that leave of absence was preferable. This is controlled by hospital doctors, and includes both the power to impose treatment and a right of recall. The Royal College of Psychiatrists (see 1987) have long wanted some form of community treatment order.

Organisations concerned with the elderly and mentally disabled, on the other hand, were generally opposed to a concept which they thought authoritarian, stigmatising and unnecessary. No one seems to have considered whether it might actually be illegal to exercise control over the life and affairs of a handicapped adult without obtaining some statutory power to do so. In 1978, the DHSS were sympathetic to the argument that compulsion outside hospital should be kept to a minimum. They were clearly suspicious of the ability of social workers to handle it properly and of the lack of any effective sanctions for patients who refused to co-operate. Hence, they opted for limiting guardianship to the "essential powers" thought necessary to secure the patient's co-operation with his community care and for excluding the majority of mentally handicapped people.

Since then, of course, there has been renewed concern about the lack of any health service powers over patients in the community. The new powers of supervised after-care (see Chapter 7) are the result. The procedures and effects are very similar to those for guardianship but they are operated by different people. In the meantime both the Law Commission (1993, 1995) and the Department of Health (1994) have been considering the future of guardianship.

218

(a) The grounds

In both civil and criminal cases, the patient must be at least 16 years old (Mental Health Act 1983, ss. 7(1) and 37(2)(a)(ii)). He must be suffering from mental illness, psychopathic disorder, severe mental impairment or mental impairment, of a nature or degree which warrants his reception into guardianship under the Act (ss. 7(2)(a) and 37(2)(a)). There is no need for the disorder to be "treatable", because the object is not medical treatment as such. But the definition of mental impairment means that guardianship cannot be used to help people with learning disabilities unless their impaired intelligence and social functioning is also associated with abnormally aggressive or seriously irresponsible conduct (s. 1(2); p. 38, earlier). This limits its ability to protect people with multiple handicaps such as Beverley Lewis, a rubella victim who died of neglect while living with her mother, herself a schizophrenic who resisted all attempts to help them. Beverley may have been "seriously irresponsible" in the sense that she was unable to take any responsibility for herself at all, but whether this amounted to "conduct" is doubtful. It was certainly not the draftsman's intention.

The second criterion in a civil case is that "it is necessary in the interests of the welfare of the patient or for the protection of other persons that the patient should be so received" (s. 7(2)(b)). The reference to welfare indicates that guardianship is meant to help the patient and improve his general quality of life. The alternative of protecting other people is unlikely to arise very often, because the guardian's powers are not exactly effective in doing this. For a court order, there is no reference to the patient's welfare or the protection of other people, but the court must consider it the most suitable method of dealing with the case, in all the circumstances (s. 37(2)(b)). As hospitals have become more reluctant to accept offenders with learning disabilities, guardianship might well provide a suitable alternative if only courts and social services authorities could be persuaded to adopt it. But there is no power to make an interim guardianship order to test this out.

Guardianship is now used predominantly for people with mental illness, two thirds of them over 65, who fall into two groups: the elderly mentally infirm, to back up care in their own homes or residential accommodation, and younger people with psychotic illnesses, to ensure support and follow-up in the community (Department of Health, 1994; Cox, 1994). Its use has increased, but only from 41 new cases in 1982/3 to 226 in 1992/3. The reasons are not difficult to imagine (Gunn, 1986; Fisher, 1988; Cox, 1994).

(b) The procedures

Courts can make guardianship orders for the same offences and with the same sort of medical evidence as is required for an ordinary hospital order (p. 128, earlier). In civil cases, the application for reception may be made either by an approved social worker (ASW) (on Form 18) or by the patient's nearest relative (on Form 17) (s. 11(1)). As with an application for admission to hospital for treatment, the ASW must if possible consult the nearest relative and cannot apply if the relative objects (s. 11(4)). But he could then ask the county court to replace the nearest relative on the ground that the objection was unreasonable (s. 29(3)(c); p. 60, earlier). This may not be easy to show, especially if there is doubt about whether the criteria for guardianship apply at all. It is obviously not contemplated that the nearest relative might become guardian himself, so as to provide a limited form of "extended minority" for someone with severe learning disabilities.

The application must be founded on the recommendations of two doctors (s. 7(3)). Forms 19 and 20 require them to give a clinical description of the patient's mental condition and to explain why he cannot appropriately be cared for without powers of guardianship. The implication is that guardianship is to be avoided unless the patient will not accept care without it. The rules about the medical examinations, the doctors' qualifications and relationships with one another and with the other people involved are the same as those for compulsory admission to hospital (see p. 66, earlier). Neither doctor may be, or be related to, the proposed guardian (s. 12(7)). There is nothing to prevent the applicant proposing himself as guardian, but neither the nearest relative nor an ASW is at all likely to do so.

The application is always addressed to the local social services authority and must reach it within 14 days of the second medical examination (s. 8(2)). If the proposed guardian is a private individual, the application must state that he is willing to act, but is ineffective unless accepted on his behalf by the local social services authority for the area where he, not the patient, lives (s. 7(5)). Otherwise, the proposed guardian may be any social services authority, not necessarily the one for the area where the patient lives. But the application has no effect unless it is accepted by the authority proposed as guardian (s. 8(1)). Authorities are unlikely to accept responsibility for patients to whom they owe no legal duty to provide care. Even where they do owe a duty, they may not approve of providing it compulsorily, or welcome the extra responsibility entailed. Similarly, a court cannot make a guardianship order unless satisfied that the proposed guardian is willing to act (s. 37(6)). If he is a private individual, he must be approved by a local social services authority (s. 37(1)). Guardianship is effective the moment the order is made or the application accepted.

(c) The effect

According to the Code of Practice (para. 13.3) guardianship should only be used as part of a comprehensive care plan and is inappropriate if no such power is needed to achieve any part of this (para. 13.4). The guardian has three powers over the patient, to the exclusion of any other person who might have them: (a) to require the patient to reside at a place specified by the guardian or by the local social services authority; (b) to require the patient to attend at places and times similarly specified for the purpose of medical treatment, occupation, education or training; and (c) to require access to the patient to be given, at any place where the patient is residing, to any doctor, ASW or other person similarly specified (ss. 8(2) and 40(2)).

The guardian can therefore insist that the patient attends a clinic for treatment, or receives a visit from a doctor or a nurse. But should the patient refuse the treatment, the Act gives no power to force it on him (see s. 56(1)). And while the guardian can insist upon the patient's seeing certain people, he cannot insist upon the patient's not seeing certain people, however undesirable. This caused difficulty in *Cambridgeshire C.C. v. R.* [1995] 1 F.L.R. 50 (p. 233, later). A young woman with learning disabilities had been in local authority care for many years as a result of serious sexual abuse for which her father had been convicted and imprisoned. When she expressed an interest in contact with her family, they began to put pressure on her to return to live with them and the local authority were anxious to protect her. Guardianship would not have been much help and so they tried to obtain a declaration that they were entitled to restrict such contact. The difficulty lay in identifying any right, whether of the young woman or the local authority, which was being infringed and so the declaration was refused.

Another difficulty is that there is no express power, equivalent to that in section 6(1) and (2) for hospital admissions, to convey the patient to the place where the guardian requires him to live (the Law Commission, 1995, have recommended that there should be; but the Department of Health, 1994, propose to wait and study the impact of supervised after-care, where there is such a power). Hence the Code of Practice (para. 13.9) states that guardianship should not be used solely in order to transfer an unwilling person to residential care. However, a patient who "absents himself without permission" (s. 18(1)(c)) from the place where his guardian requires him to live can be recaptured in the same way as a hospital patient who goes absent without leave (p. 165, earlier). The implication, at least, is that he must have been taken there first. The Code also states that guardianship should not be used to require a patient to live in a hospital save for a short time while another place is found (para. 13.9).

As an imposition of authority, therefore, guardianship is without teeth. There is no sanction (other than recapture) for disobeying any of the guardian's instructions. So the Code of Practice advises that for guardianship to work the patient will have to recognise the guardian's authority and be willing to work with him (para. 13.5.a). If so, one wonders how it can be "necessary" in achieving the plan. Some people, however, may respond to apparent authority however toothless in fact it may be.

The Code does suggest that the guardian should be willing to act as the patient's "advocate" in securing the services needed to carry out the care plan (para. 13.5.b). His more limited legal duties are laid down in the Mental Health (Hospital, Guardianship and Consent to Treatment) Regulations 1983. A private guardian is under the supervision of the responsible local social services authority, for he must comply with its directions when exercising his powers and duties. He must appoint a doctor as the patient's "nominated medical attendant" and notify the name and address to the authority. He must notify his own and the patient's address to the authority straight away, and any permanent change in either address beforehand or within seven days. If he moves into a different local authority area, he must give all these particulars to the new authority and also tell the old one what has happened. He must also furnish the responsible authority with whatever reports or other information about the patient it requires, and tell it as soon as possible if the guardianship comes to an end (reg. 12).

Whoever is the guardian, the responsible local social services authority must arrange for the patient to be visited at regular intervals. This must be at least every three months, and at least one visit annually must be by an approved doctor (reg. 13). The Mental Welfare Commission for Scotland (1970; but see 1992) were enthusiastic about guardianship, perhaps because of the long-standing Scottish tradition of boarding-out handicapped people on remote crofts and farms. They pointed out that statutory duties ensure that someone keeps an eye on patients who may well need support and protection from outside. They may also, unfortunately, increase the reluctance of local authorities to take it on.

If a private guardian dies or resigns (by written notice to the authority) the authority automatically takes over for the time being, but could transfer the patient into the guardianship of another individual (s. 10(1)). The authority, or someone authorised by it, may also exercise the functions of a private guardian while he is incapacitated in some way (s. 10(2)). A private guardian may also be replaced by order of a county court, on the application of an ASW, if he has performed his functions negligently or in a manner contrary to the patient's interests (s. 10(3)).

The patient can be transferred from one guardian to another on the authority of his existing guardian (Form 26), provided that this is confirmed by the incoming responsible social services authority, which must specify a date, and agreed by any proposed new private guardian (reg. 8(2)). The form of the patient's disorder may be reclassified on Form 23, by his nominated medical attendant if he is in private guardianship, or by the responsible medical officer (RMO) if the guardian is a local authority (s. 16(5)). The RMO means the medical officer authorised by the authority to act, either generally or in any particular case or for any particular purpose (s. 34(1)). Reclassification has no legal effect, because there is no distinction between the different forms of disorder for the purposes of guardianship, but it keeps the paperwork in order.

The role of a private guardian is very like that of a foster parent, which reflects its origins in the Scottish boarding-out system. It is inappropriate for care within the patient's own family and is even more rarely used than local authority guardianship: only 16 of the 382 guardians in post in 1993 were not local authorities. The Law Commission (1995) have recommended that private guardianship be abolished.

(d) Duration and termination

Like hospital admission for treatment, guardianship lasts initially for six months, but may be renewed for a further six months and then for a year at a time (s. 20(1)). The RMO or nominated medical attendant must examine the patient within the last two months of the period, and report to the guardian and to the responsible social services authority on Form 31 if the grounds for guardianship still exist. This automatically renews it, unless the authority decides to discharge the patient (s. 20(6), (7) and (8)). The patient can be discharged at any time by the RMO, by the responsible local social services authority, or in civil cases but not in court orders (section 40(4) and Sched. 1, Pt. I) by his nearest relative (who may use Form 35 and must serve the order on the authority) (s. 23(2)(b)). The RMO cannot prevent the nearest relative from discharging the patient, but an application could be made to a county court to replace the relative on the ground that he was proposing to discharge, or had discharged, the patient without due regard to the patient's welfare or the interests of the public. Interestingly, the private guardian or the nominated medical attendant of a patient with a private guardian cannot discharge the patient. The powers of mental health review tribunals to do so are discussed in Chapter 8. Transfer from guardianship to hospital and from hospital to guardianship are discussed in Chapters 4 and 7 respectively.

6. COMMENTARY

English law still cuts a pretty poor figure on both sets of issues outlined at the beginning of this chapter. In theory, the welfare state has accepted the "ideology of entitlement" (Gostin, 1983a). The courts, however, have largely abandoned the enforcement of that ideology to the politicians. They, as we know, have traditionally found it hard to persuade themselves or their constituents of the public good involved in developing community services for the mentally disordered. The public good in keeping them out of sight is so much more obvious. Significantly, the most progress has been made in education. Here the law is much more explicit and is allied to a century-long tradition of universal provision. There is not, and never has been, any such tradition in the social services. In relying on social services to allocate resources for community care packages, the element of universal provision involved in income support for people in nursing and residential homes has been lost. But at least the nettle of providing incentives towards a better range of community services has now been grasped.

At the same time, we are getting better at respecting people's ordinary legal rights and autonomy. There is much more consciousness of the status of residents in homes and of the need to enhance their independence as well as the quality of their care. In theory, the "essential powers" approach to guardianship also has advantages, in providing a framework for both advocacy and protection with the loss of very little legal status for the patient. In practice, however, it is seen as cumbersome, stigmatising, toothless and unnecessary. It is not designed to provide a substitute decision-maker for an adult who is unable to take decisions for himself. Nor is it designed to legitimate the decisions which are made by family and other carers.

With the increasing number of elderly and mentally disabled people living in the community, there have been calls for a new, more flexible institution, along the lines of the limited guardianship systems introduced in several Australian States and Canadian Provinces. These can cover decisions about property as well as personal care, but limit the guardian's powers to what is necessary for the particular patient, and in one case at least these are linked to a clear entitlement to the services which it is decided that he needs. Without such entitlement, many in this country feel that there is no need for increased legal authority over mentally disabled people. However, a lack of authority in law does not mean a lack of authority in practice, and the absence of legal safeguards can easily lead to exploitation or even abuse. Hence the Law Commission's Report on Mental Incapacity (1995) combines recommendations for the protection from abuse of vulnerable adults of all kinds with an entirely new scheme for making decisions, or appointing managers to make decisions, on behalf of those who cannot do so for themselves. The problems caused by the lack of such a system will become even more apparent when we discuss the ordinary legal rights of mentally disordered and disabled people in the next chapter.

10 ORDINARY LEGAL RIGHTS

Many ordinary legal rights can be affected by a person's mental disorder. In most cases, the legal position turns on the individual's capacity to perform the particular function in question. It does not depend upon whether or not he is in hospital, or whether he is an informal or a compulsory patient. Nor does it usually turn on his capacity to perform the function well or wisely, but on whether he can understand in broad terms what he is doing and the effects of doing it. If he cannot do so, others may sometimes have the right to take the decision for him. But this should always depend upon there being a proper legal justification. It should not happen simply because others think that they know best.

The underlying philosophy of the United Nations *Declaration on the Rights of Mentally Retarded Persons* (1971; see p. 205, earlier) is that they should enjoy the same rights as other people, to the maximum degree of feasibility (Art. 1). But if they are unable to exercise those rights in a meaningful way, or it becomes necessary to restrict or deny them, there should be legal safeguards against every form of abuse. "This procedure must be based on the evaluation of the social capability of the mentally retarded person by qualified experts and must be subject to periodic review and to the right of appeal to higher authorities" (Art. 7). The same is required under the United Nations *Declaration on the Rights of Disabled Persons* (1975, Art. 4).

English law does not have a single comprehensive procedure for doing this (Law Society, 1989; Law Commission, 1991, 1995). The old prerogative powers of the Crown might in theory have done so but in practice did not and were abandoned in 1960. Decisions about health care and personal welfare can be taken by others, either under the limited Mental Health Act procedures or under the common law doctrine of necessity, where the High Court may sometimes be called upon to decide what is lawful (p. 135, earlier and p. 233, later for examples). Decisions about a person's property and affairs can be delegated before he loses capacity to an attorney who is given power to act even after the donor becomes unable to act for himself. Alternatively, they may be taken over by the Court of Protection. Of course, there are some rights, including rights of citizenship, and the right to consent to marriage or sexual relations, which can only be exercised by the person concerned.

1. RIGHTS OF CITIZENSHIP

(a) Standing and voting in elections

At common law, "persons of unsound mind" and "idiots" can neither vote nor stand in elections. But these terms probably depend upon the usual test of legal capacity: at the time of voting, can the individual understand in broad terms what he is doing and the effects of doing it? If the person is on the register and turns up to vote, the question is one of fact for the officer presiding at the polling station. People are in practice asked only their name and address and whether they have already voted in the election. If they can answer, they are allowed to vote and the result is unlikely to be challenged.

However, in order to vote, a person must first be registered, and to be registered he must normally be resident in the constituency or ward on the qualifying date. An informal or compulsory patient may still be resident in his home constituency. This depends on such factors as the length of absence, his intention to return, and any legal restraint on his return home. Some compulsory patients may be entitled to register (provided that someone remembers to put them on the form or they remember to check) whereas others may not. But if a compulsory patient cannot be treated as resident at home, he cannot be treated as resident at the hospital where he is detained (Representation of the People Act 1983, s. 7(1)).

Similarly, an informal patient cannot be treated as resident at the hospital, if it is one which is "maintained wholly or mainly for the reception and treatment of persons suffering from any form of mental disorder" (s. 7(2)). Patients in such hospitals used to be entirely disenfranchised, whereas those in general hospitals were not. This was probably a breach of Article 3 of Protocol No. 1 to the European Convention on Human Rights, which binds the contracting countries to "hold free elections at reasonable intervals by secret ballot, under conditions which will ensure the free expression of the opinion of the people in the choice of the legislature." Although certain limited groups may be disqualified, the restrictions should not be arbitrary (*W.X.Y.Z. v. Belgium*, (1975) 2 D.R.E.Comm. H.R. 110). A disqualification which depends upon a person's address, rather than his capacity to vote, is clearly arbitrary. But if residents in the large old mental hospitals were allowed to register there, the results of local, if not national, elections in places where there were large mental hospitals might well have been affected. Hence a different procedure was devised for registering people who are voluntary patients in these hospitals (Representation of the People Act 1983, s. 7(2) to (9); see DHSS Circular No. HC(83)14).

During the 12 months before a qualifying date, the patient may make a declaration, provided that he can do so without assistance (unless this is required because of blindness or some other physical incapacity). This must state that on the date of the declaration, and on the next qualifying date, unless the two are the same, he is or will be a "voluntary mental patient" at a "mental hospital". It must give the address of the hospital, but also the United Kingdom address where the patient would be resident if he were not in hospital, or, if he cannot give such an address, any address (apart from a mental hospital) in the United Kingdom where he has at some time resided. It must also state that he is a Commonwealth or Irish Republic citizen, whether he has reached the age of 18, and if he has not, his date of birth. It must confirm that it has been made without help and be attested in the prescribed way. Once this is sent to the registration officer, the patient is entitled to be registered as resident at the address *outside* the hospital. Hence if he gives more than one, the declaration is void. The declaration is effective for both national and local elections, but it cannot be made specially for the purpose of local elections unless the patient is a peer (who is only entitled to vote in local elections).

Getting to the polling station is now much less of a problem, as the registration officer may grant an application for an "absent" vote at any particular election if satisfied that the applicant's circumstances are such that he cannot reasonably be expected to vote in person (Representation of the People Act 1985, s. 7(1)). *Home Life* (Centre for Policy an Ageing, 1984) suggests that people living in residential care homes should be encouraged and helped to continue and develop outside interests and activities but particular help with voting is not mentioned.

It is to be hoped that no legally incapable candidate would ever be elected, but a sitting member might later become so. There is a statutory procedure for vacating the seat of any Member of Parliament who has been compulsorily detained because of mental illness for more than six months (Mental Health Act 1983, s. 141; see DHSS, 1987, para. 294).

(b) Serving on juries

Apart from standing and voting in elections, the main badge of citizenship is the right and duty to serve on a jury. But a large number of mentally disordered people are ineligible to do so (Juries Act 1974, s. 1 and Sched. 1, Group D). They fall into three categories. One is any person who is at present under guardianship. Another is any person who has been determined by a judge to be incapable of managing his property and affairs. But the main category is very wide. It covers anyone who suffers or has suffered from mental illness, psychopathic disorder, mental handicap or severe mental handicap and because of that is either resident in a hospital "or other similar institution" or "regularly attends for treatment by a medical practitioner". The definition of ordinary and severe mental handicap for this purpose is the same as the definition of ordinary or severe mental impairment under the Mental Health Act, but without the reference to abnormally aggressive or seriously irresponsible conduct (p. 38, earlier). If a broad view of "mental illness" is taken, an anxious or depressed person who regularly takes medication prescribed by a doctor is ineligible to serve. A psychopath who has been discharged from Broadmoor and is at present receiving no medical treatment is not, unless disqualified on other grounds.

(c) Other disqualifications

An applicant for or holder of a driving licence must disclose any prescribed disability (Road Traffic Act 1988, s. 92). These include severe mental handicap, as a result of which the patient is under guardianship or receiving local authority care, and epilepsy, unless the patient has been free from attacks for two years or has had attacks only while asleep for the past three years (Motor Vehicle (Driving Licence) Regulations 1987, (S.I. 1987 No. 1378) amended (S.I. 1989 No. 373) reg. 24). A licence must then be refused or revoked.

Not surprisingly, the police must refuse a firearms certificate to a person they have reason to believe to be "of unsound mind" (Firearms Act 1968, s. 27(1) proviso).

2. RIGHTS TO FAMILY LIFE

Article 8 of the European Convention on Human Rights (to which our laws must conform) secures for everyone the right to respect for his private and family life, his home and his correspondence. The only exceptions allowed are those which are necessary in a democratic society in the interests of national security, public safety or the economic well-being of the country, for the prevention of disorder or crime, for the protection of health or morals, or for the protection of the rights and freedoms of others. The

United Nations *Standard Rules on the Equalization of Opportunities for Persons with Disabilities* (1994) go further: disabled people must not be denied the opportunity to experience their sexuality, have sexual relationships and experience parenthood, but they need to be fully informed about taking precautions against sexual and other forms of abuse (Rule 9). There are obvious risks of degradation and exploitation, against which some people may need protection. But that need not be given at the cost of denying to people with learning disabilities the opportunity to form warm and satisfying relationships. The recent more liberal approach raises the alternative question of whether providing contraception, abortion or sterilisation is itself a recipe for exploitation or a means of protection.

(a) Having sexual relationships

All the usual offences which punish sexual aggression or the exploitation of youth may protect mentally disordered people. It is rape to have intercourse with a woman who is incapable of understanding the situation and exercising choice in the matter (*R. v. Howard* [1966] 1 W.L.R. 13; see also *R. v. Barratt* (1873) L.R. 2 C.C.R. 81), either knowing that she does not consent or being reckless as to whether or not she does so (Sexual Offences (Amendment) Act 1976, s. 1(1)). There are also specific offences aimed at protecting mentally disordered people from sexual exploitation by people looking after them and severely handicapped people from sexual activity generally.

It is an offence for a man on the staff of, or employed in, or who is one of the managers of a hospital or mental nursing home to have extra-marital sexual intercourse with a woman who is at present receiving treatment for mental disorder in that hospital or home; or to have such intercourse on the premises with a woman who is receiving treatment there as an out-patient; or for a man to have such intercourse with a mentally disordered woman who is under his guardianship, or otherwise in his custody or care under the Mental Health Act, or under arrangements made under the National Health Service Act 1977, Part III of the National Assistance Act 1948, or as a resident in a residential home (Mental Health Act 1959, s. 128(1)). The maximum penalty is two years' imprisonment (s. 128(3)), but it is not an offence if the man did not know and had no reason to suspect the woman to be a mentally disordered patient (s. 128(2)).

These offences apply to people suffering from any form of mental disorder, but it is also an offence for any man to have extra-marital sexual intercourse with any woman who suffers from "a state of arrested or incomplete development of mind which includes severe impairment of intelligence and social functioning", unless he did not know and had no reason to suspect her to be so (Sexual Offences Act 1956, ss. 7 and 45). Nor can she give a valid consent to an indecent assault. The man involved may find it difficult to determine whether the woman is "severely" rather than only "significantly" handicapped. Severity is to be judged by comparison with normal people rather than with other handicapped people (*R. v. Hall (John)* (1987) 86 Cr.App.R. 159). But the definition could include some women who are capable of giving a real consent to intercourse and would not be harmed by it. Ironically, of course, the man himself is also likely to be handicapped. It is wrong that he should run a greater risk of prosecution than does the woman if neither has been in any way exploiting the other. Severely handicapped men are protected against, or denied the benefit of, homosexual acts in the same circumstances as the offences against women described above (Sexual Offences Act 1967, s. 1(3) and (4)).

But is prosecution the answer? Convictions are notoriously difficult to secure in all sex offences, but particularly where the victim's evidence may present problems (see section 6(b) later). The Criminal Law Revision Committee (1980b) thought that a civil procedure to protect a particular woman from a particular man might be better, but this was not pursued. The declaration procedure cannot be used to interfere in what would otherwise be lawful (p. 233, later). The Law Commission (1995) have now proposed a general protective jurisdiction over mentally incapacitated people within which such orders could be made.

(b) Getting married

Logically, it might be thought that if one can have intercourse one can marry, and vice versa, but the tests of capacity are not quite the same. English law takes a relaxed view of the qualifications for matrimony, although it seeks to preserve the idea that it is a voluntary union. There are two grounds on which marriage of a mentally disordered person might be annulled. The first is that he did not give a valid consent to it, because of "unsoundness of mind" (Matrimonial Causes Act 1973, s.12(c)). This only applies if at the time of the ceremony the bride or groom could not understand the nature of the contract being entered and appreciate its basic responsibilities. As marriage is a relatively simple concept, few people who can actually get through the ceremony are likely to be incapable under this test. An elderly and confused person might even be able to get married but unable to make a new will on the same day (*In the Estate of Park; Park v. Park* [1954] P. 112). The second ground is that, although able to give a valid consent, the bride or groom was suffering (whether continuously or intermittently) from mental disorder within the meaning of the Mental Health Act, but this must be "of such a kind or to such an extent as to be unfitted for marriage" (1973 Act, s. 12(d)). In *Bennett v. Bennett* [1969] 1 W.L.R. 430, Ormrod J. decided that it was not enough that the wife was difficult to live with because of her disorder and should probably not have got married. She had to be incapable of living in the married state and carrying out the ordinary duties and obligations of marriage, and this she was not.

In that case, it was the mentally disordered person's spouse who wished to have the marriage annulled. But the mentally disordered person himself might wish to do so, particularly if he has been tricked or exploited in some way. However, although either party may apply to the court, these grounds render the marriage voidable, rather than void. They simply allow the court to annul it, if asked to do so by either party while they are both still alive. Even after a decree, it is treated as if it had existed up till that time (1973 Act, s. 16). This means that any children of the marriage are automatically legitimate, but it also has less desirable effects. Marriage automatically revokes a previous will, unless that will provides that this is not to happen when the testator marries a particular person (Wills Act 1837, s.18). Even if the testator was so disordered as to be incapable of consenting to the marriage, his surviving spouse will be entitled to claim his estate under the rules of intestacy (*Re Roberts, Roberts v. Roberts* [1978] 1 W.L.R. 653).

There must be a danger that "old and lonely people not fully in control of all their mental faculties are particularly susceptible to the attentions of fortune hunters" (Law Commission, 1982). There are two possible solutions. If the person is unable to make a new will for himself, the Court of Protection may make one for him (see section 3(a) later; *Re Davey (Deceased)* [1980] 1 W.L.R. 164 is an example of a will made by the court in just these circumstances). The alternative is to petition for nullity. This will not revive the earlier will, but it will remove the automatic right of the spouse to a share in the intestacy or benefit under any will which was made after the marriage (Wills Act 1837, s. 18A). If the mentally disordered person is unable to petition for himself, the Court of Protection may do it for him (see section 5 below). The normal time limit of three years from the marriage may be extended in such cases if the court thinks it just (1973 Act, s. 13(4) and (5)).

None of this solves the problem of the person who dies before anything is done. It might be thought better to prevent the marriage taking place at all. Anyone can enter a *caveat* with a superintendent registrar against the issue of a certificate or licence for the marriage of a named person (Marriage Act 1949, s. 29). The registrar cannot then issue the certificate or licence until he has looked into the matter and satisfied himself that the *caveat* ought not to obstruct it. If in doubt, he can refer it to the Registrar-General, or if he refuses the certificate or licence, the person named can appeal to the Registrar-General. A frivolous *caveat* can result in costs, and damages for the named person. Even if the Registrar-General refuses the certificate or licence, the matter could be taken to the High Court by way of judicial review.

The purpose of the *caveat* procedure must be to prevent marriages which would otherwise be void. It cannot be intended to obstruct the freedom of adults to marry whom they wish. But marriages which might be voidable on either of the above grounds fall between these two extremes. The general reason for making a marriage voidable rather than void is to allow the parties themselves to decide whether they wish to continue it or not. If they are happy, the State does not interfere. Logically, therefore, the registrar should not deny a certificate for the marriage of a mentally disordered person any more than he should deny one to a person who cannot consummate the marriage. He certainly should not deny one simply because some doctor believes that his patient ought not to get married. But this logic rather breaks down at the point where the person is actually incapable of consenting to the marriage, for to carry out such a ceremony knowing this fact would be contrary to the long-standing tradition of the "voluntary union". With hindsight, it is a great shame that marriages without consent, which were void at common law, became voidable if contracted on or after August 1, 1971.

Indeed, the law goes out of its way to help the marriage of patients who are detained under any of the long-term powers in the Mental Health Act, by allowing them to be married at the hospital (Marriage Act 1983, s. 1 and Sched. 1; see DHSS Circular No. HC(84)12).

(c) Marriage breakdown

An existing marriage may break down because of one spouse's mental disorder. The fact that he is not to blame is no longer an obstacle to divorce or other forms of relief. The sole ground for divorce is that the marriage has irretrievably broken down; there are five ways of proving this (Matrimonial Causes Act 1973, s. 1(1),(2)). One is that they have lived apart for five years, unless the divorce would cause the respondent grave financial or other hardship and it would be wrong to grant it (ss. 1(2)(e) and 5). People living in hospital or long-term care are unlikely to suffer grave hardship simply because they are no longer married. A divorce can also be granted after only two years' separation, provided that the respondent consents (s. 1(2)(d)). In *Mason v. Mason* [1972] Fam. 302, Sir George Baker P. decided that the test of capacity to agree to a divorce was the same as that to agree to a marriage. The respondent must be able to understand its nature, effect and consequences, and to express his consent. He may do this even if he is not otherwise capable of managing his property and affairs and is therefore represented by the Official Solicitor and subject to the jurisdiction of the Court of Protection. However, consent has to be the expression of the state of mind of one of the parties to the marriage, so the Official Solicitor cannot give it on his behalf. The Court of Protection might be able to do so, as part of its power to conduct proceedings, and it does have power to petition on the patient's behalf.

An immediate divorce may be obtained for adultery or if the respondent has behaved in such a way that the petitioner cannot reasonably be expected to live with him (s. 1(2)(a), (b)). The test of the latter is whether a "right-thinking person would come to the conclusion that *this* husband has behaved in such a way that *this* wife cannot reasonably be expected to live with him, taking into account the whole of the circumstances and the characters and personalities of the parties" (*Livingstone-Stallard v. Livingstone-Stallard* [1974] Fam. 47; approved in *O'Neill v. O'Neill* [1975] 1 W.L.R. 1118), not whether the behaviour itself is unreasonable or blameworthy. A spouse may reasonably be expected to be more tolerant of behaviour which is the result of illness than of the deliberate, malicious or merely thoughtless behaviour of a normal person (*Richards v. Richards* [1972] 1 W.L.R. 1073). But conduct which has a serious effect upon the petitioner will certainly be enough (*Williams v. Williams* [1964] A.C. 698; *Katz v. Katz* [1972] 1 W.L.R. 955). It may even be both completely blameless and largely negative in character. In *Thurlow v. Thurlow* [1976] Fam. 32, the wife suffered from a severe neurological disorder leading to a gradual mental and physical deterioration at an early age. She had displayed some temper, thrown things at her mother-in-law, burned things, and had a tendency to wander. She eventually became bedridden, unable to walk or stand unaided, or to feed and dress herself. Her husband coped with her at home for as long as he could, until his own health was affected and she had to go into hospital, where she would require indefinite care. The husband was granted his decree. Rees J. expressly disagreed with the result in *Smith v. Smith* (1973) 118 S.J. 184, where the husband failed to get a decree after caring for his wife for many years while she degenerated into a "cabbage-like" existence as a result of pre-senile dementia. Ironically, he would have been able to do so had he put her into hospital five years earlier instead of looking after her at home for as long as possible.

Finally, a divorce may be granted after two years' desertion (s. 1(2)(a)), which normally requires an intention to desert. But if a person who has deserted his spouse later becomes incapable of retaining the necessary intent, he remains in desertion for this purpose provided that the court thinks that he would have done so had he been capable (s. 2(4)). In practice, desertion is rarely alleged in divorce cases. Defended divorces are themselves extremely rare. Most attention is devoted to sorting out appropriate arrangements for the couple's finances, property and children, in which questions of fault are largely irrelevant.

(d) Having (and not having) children

Undoubtedly, it is the relationships of mentally disordered people with their children which are the most vulnerable to outside intervention by the agencies of the state. This is because the welfare of the child has to be the paramount consideration (Children Act 1989, s. 1(1)). If parents split up, it is usually best for the children to live with their mother, especially if they are young. But should mental disorder affect her capacity to love and care for them properly, she may lose them to the father, other members of the family or to the local authority. A high proportion of parents whose children are looked after by local authorities have mental health problems (Quinton and Rutter, 1984; Isaac, Minty and Morrison, 1986). Local authorities can provide accommodation for a child in need if the person caring for him is prevented for any reason from providing him with suitable accommodation or care (Children Act 1989, s. 20(1)(a)). This is a voluntary service, so a parent can remove the child at any time; but formal parental agreement is not necessary. Where a severely disabled mother does not object, it may be lawful to accommodate her child without legal proceedings, controversial though this may be.

Generally, however, and whenever the parent objects, the authority will seek to acquire parental responsibility for the child by obtaining a care order. The court must first be satisfied of the "threshold criteria": the child must be suffering or likely to suffer significant harm which is attributable to a lack or likely lack of reasonable parental care or being beyond control (1989 Act, s. 31(2); p. 63, earlier). The care expected is that of a reasonable parent, not what can reasonably be expected of this particular parent. The court must then decide what to do about it. The child's welfare is the paramount consideration (s. 1(1)), taking into account a "checklist" of factors relevant to his needs, wishes and feelings and the capacity of others to meet those, as well as the alternative orders available (s. 1(3),(4)); these include a supervision order or an order that the child live with someone else, such as another member of the family (see s. 8). The court can only make an order if to do so would be better for the child than doing nothing (s. 1(5)).

The law is the same whether the child is already being accommodated by the local authority, and the authority wish to prevent the parent removing him, or the authority wish to remove the child from his parents. On the other hand, if there is no harm or likelihood of harm, perhaps because the child is already being accommodated, and the mother is not likely to disrupt this, then no care order can be made. This should not impede the local authority in making plans for the child, because anyone who is actually caring for a child may do what is reasonable in all the circumstances to safeguard and promote his welfare (s. 3(5)).

In the long run, if a permanent substitute home is needed for the child, his existing foster parents may apply either for a residence order or to adopt him, or the child may be placed with another family for adoption. Parental agreement to adoption can be dispensed with if the parent is "incapable" of giving it, or is withholding it "unreasonably" (Adoption Act 1976, s. 16(2)). If the local authority already have a care order, they may apply to have this question resolved before the adoption proceedings, by having the child freed for adoption (1976 Act, s. 18).

Many local authorities try long and hard to help parents with mental illnesses or learning disabilities to bring up their children; but in the end they have to put the children's welfare and safety before the parents' mental health, let alone their wishes and feelings. If the mother is severely disabled, some might think that abortion or sterilisation would have been preferable in her own best interests. *Re F. (Mental Patient: Sterilisation)* [1990] 2 A.C. 1 (p. 137, earlier) established that this is the test to be applied in making such decisions on her behalf. At least in theory it rules out eugenics and the convenience of carers. It is still all too tempting to conclude that the traumas of childbirth and the almost inevitable loss of the child will be worse for her than the loss of her reproductive capacity. It is also tempting to apply the concept of mental or intellectual age to equate her with a child, when by definition it is not childhood capacities and activities we are considering. But if she is thought incapable of making her own decisions about the effects of intercourse, then perhaps she is incapable of giving consent to the intercourse itself? It might then be better for her to be protected from that, unless she actively wants it, particularly if there is a chance that she may develop to want them both in the future. These decisions require the most sensitive, individualised attention. It must be questioned whether the High Court is best equipped for the task, particularly as long as it relies upon any "responsible body of medical opinion", however controversial, as a test of the woman's best interests (see further, *e.g.* Freeman, 1988; Heginbotham, 1989; Lee and Morgan, 1988; Carson, 1989c; Brazier, 1990).

(e) Disputes among families or friends

Family disputes may also arise about where a mentally disabled adult is to live or who may have contact with him. There is no equivalent of the Children Act 1989 and the High Court's inherent or wardship jurisdiction over children, or the Court of Protection's jurisdiction over property and finance (see section 5, later), under which these disputes can be decided. The only possibility is to use the High Court's power (see Rules of the Supreme Court, Ord. 15, r. 16) to make binding declarations of right. This has mainly been used to declare that a proposed medical procedure is lawful because it is necessary in the best interests of the patient (see *Re F. (Mental Patient: Sterilisation)* [1990] 2 A.C. 1, p. 137, earlier). The same principles are now being developed to apply to other questions, but there are serious limitations.

First, the procedure can only deal with the legal position in the light of the facts as they exist at the time. Hence there cannot be an interim declaration to preserve the status quo while the facts are investigated (*Riverside Mental Health NHS Trust v. Fox* [1994] 1 F.L.R. 614). But if there is a risk that something which may be unlawful will be done before the case can be heard, an interim injunction can be granted to prevent it (*Re S. (Hospital Patient: Court's Jurisdiction)* [1995] Fam. 27). Secondly, it can only deal with legal rights and duties of or towards the person concerned.

In *Re C. (Mental Patient: Contact)* [1993] 1 F.L.R. 940, the High Court could decide whether the father of a mentally disabled young woman could lawfully prevent her from seeing her mother, because their right of access to one another was recognised by the law. But in *Cambridgeshire C.C. v. R.* [1995] 1 F.L.R. 50, the court could not decide whether a local authority could lawfully prevent a mentally disabled young woman, who was living in accommodation arranged by them, from seeing the family from whom she had been removed as a child because of serious sexual abuse by her father, because there is no legal right to interfere with another person's freedom of association (although if there had been a threat of some legal wrong towards her from her family, the court could have protected her from it).

Re S.(Hospital Patient: Court's Jurisdiction) [1995] 3 W.L.R. 78 was described in the Court of Appeal as a custody dispute. An elderly foreign millionaire had left his wife and adult son to live with another woman in this country. Six months later he had a massive stroke which deprived him of much of his power of communication and comprehension. He spent a year in a private hospital being visited regularly by his woman friend, who used a power of attorney he had granted over certain Swiss bank accounts to pay the fees. When there was nothing more the hospital could do for him, his wife and son wanted him to go into a nursing home near them, while his friend wanted to look after him at her home. The Court of Appeal held that the declaration procedure could be used to resolve this dispute, which involved his right to bodily integrity, and that as a provider and potential carer the friend could invoke it. It was eventually decided that it would be best for him to return to his home country. One reason for this was that a guardian had been appointed for him there who could continue to look after his best interests, while in this country that cannot be done. His property here, of course, was under the control of the Court of Protection in quite separate proceedings.

One object of the Law Commission's Report on Mental Incapacity (1995) is to provide a more suitable way of deciding what will be best in these cases. One court would be able to decide on issues of personal welfare, health care and protection, as well as on matters of property and finance. It could simply resolve the question at issue or appoint a manager to look after some or all of the life and affairs of the person concerned.

3. MAKING GIFTS OR CONTRACTS

(a) Wills and other gifts

Unlike other transactions, a person's capacity to make a will depends upon his passing, not only a test of his understanding, but also a test of his memory. According to the classic statement;

> "He ought to be capable of making his will with an understanding of the nature of the business in which he is engaged, a recollection of the property he means to dispose of, of the persons who are the objects of his bounty, and the manner in which it is to be distributed between them . . . ,"

but only in simple terms—he does not have to be a lawyer (*Banks v. Goodfellow* (1870) L.R. 5 Q.B. 549). Provided that he has this capacity, the testator does not have to weigh these various factors wisely. He can make whatever dispositions he chooses, however foolish, cruel or improvident (although if he fails to make reasonable financial provision for certain members of his family and dependants, they may apply for the court to order such provision from the estate, under the Inheritance (Provision for Family and Dependants) Act 1975). Despite this, it is often the eccentricity of the will itself which prompts the dispute.

Testators rarely fall into the easy category of the permanently, totally and completely incapable. Even here, it may be possible, although very difficult, to prove that the will was made in a "lucid interval". If the testator has recovered enough, and for long enough, to have the required capacity, he need not have recovered completely and may relapse again quite quickly (*Ex p. Holyland* (1805) 11 Ves.Jun. 10; *Cartwright v. Cartwright* (1793) 1 Phill.Ecc. 90; *Banks v. Goodfellow*, above). Alternatively, a testator may have delusions about some things, but not about others. Thus, "a degree or form of unsoundness which neither disturbs the exercise of the faculties necessary for such an act, nor is capable of influencing the result ought not to take away the power of making a will . . . " (*Banks v. Goodfellow*, above). If so, it will all depend on whether his particular delusional system has influenced the provisions in the will. Above all, however, mere eccentricity, whether in previous lifestyle or in the contents of the will, is not the same as incapacity. But capricious, harsh and unreasonable views could amount to delusions (*Boughton v. Knight* (1873) L.R. 3 P. & D. 64). Similarly, confusion and forgetfulness are not enough, if the testator was able to concentrate at the time when he made the will, but of course they could be if they induced him to make it (*Benyon v. Benyon* (1844) 2 L.T. 477; *Singh v. Armirchand* [1948] A.C. 161).

If the testator does have capacity to make a will, he can do so even if he is otherwise incapable of managing his property and affairs. The Court of Protection has no power to stop him. This is because of the general principle that the court only has jurisdiction over the patient's estate while he is alive (*e.g. Re Bennett* [1913] 2 Ch. 318). However, since 1969, the Court of Protection has been able to make a statutory will where it has reason to believe that the patient is incapable of making a valid will for himself (Mental Health Act 1983, s. 96(i)(e) and (4)(b)). This can do anything that the patient could have done if he were not mentally disordered. It will then have the same effect (at least for property which is governed by the law in England and Wales) as if the patient had made it and was capable of doing so (s. 97).

The court is not expressly required to apply a "substituted judgment" test to determine what the patient himself would have wanted. The only statutory guidance given is in the court's general power to do whatever is "necessary or expedient" for the maintenance or other benefit of the patient or members of his family, for providing for other people or purposes for which the patient might be expected to provide, or otherwise for administering his affairs (s. 95(1)). In *Re D.(J.)* (1982) Ch. 237, however, Megarry V.C. observed that "One is not concerned with the patient on the Clapham omnibus," but with the actual patient "whose views while still of a sound disposing mind might be idiosyncratic and far from impartial." The court should seek to make for him the will that he would have made for himself, within reason and assuming competent legal advice. Where a person has never had capacity, it was held in *Re C. (A Patient)* [1991] 3 All E.R. 866 that the court will assume that he would have been a normal decent person who would have acted in accordance with contemporary standards of morality: a person who had spent almost all her life in hospital might therefore be expected to divide the fortune she had inherited from her family equally between family members and mental health charities.

A good example of the case for making an emergency will occurred in *Re Davey (Deceased)* [1981] 1 W.L.R. 164. An elderly spinster with quite a large estate moved into a nursing home in June. In July, she made a will dividing her property between her relations. In September she was married to a middle-aged employee at the nursing home. This automatically revoked the will. The marriage came to light in December during the process of placing her affairs under the jurisdiction of the Court of Protection. Her receiver immediately applied for a statutory will in the same terms as the one which she herself had made in July. The court granted this without giving notice to her husband or to the proposed beneficiaries. She died six days after it was executed. The husband's appeal was dismissed. In all the circumstances, this had been the best possible way of providing for a full investigation and a just result in the end, because the husband could always apply for reasonable provision under the Inheritance (Provision for Family and Dependants) Act 1975 while the other beneficiaries could not.

Giving away property while alive seems to cause far fewer disputes than do wills, perhaps because the Court of Protection can intervene before it is too late. The first modern case was *Re Beaney* [1978] 1 W.L.R. 770, where it was held that the degree of understanding required depends on the importance of the transaction: so if the gift is trivial in relation to the donor's other assets a low degree of understanding is enough; but if he gives away his only asset of value, effectively disinheriting his heirs, then the degree of understanding required will be as high as that for a will. The same test was applied to gifts made by an eminent forensic scientist after he had developed a brain tumour in *Simpson v. Simpson* [1992] 1 F.L.R. 601. The donee can be obliged to return an invalid gift, but an innocent third party may be in the same position as someone who has made a contract with an incapacitated person (see (b) below).

(b) Making, getting and keeping contracts

A patient's capacity to make contracts (see *Boughton v. Knight* (1873) L.R. 3 P. & D. 64) depends upon whether he was capable of understanding the nature of the contract involved. Even a person who is generally incapable may have contracted in a lucid interval, or the particular transaction may be one which he is quite capable of understanding, or his particular delusional system may have nothing to do with the transaction in question. Hence, the incapacity may affect all transactions at all times, or only some or at some times (Law Commission, 1976). Once again, the test is understanding, not wisdom.

However, the law has had to balance two conflicting policy considerations. One is the need to protect those who cannot protect themselves. But another is that the other party to the contract should not be prejudiced by an incapacity which he had no reason to suspect. The general rule is that a mentally incapable person is bound by a contract he has made, unless he can prove that the other person knew of his incapacity (*Imperial Loan Co. v. Stone* [1892] 1 Q.B. 599). However, the circumstances may be such that any reasonable man would have realised that the patient was incapable (*York Glass Co. v. Jubb* (1925) 134 L.T. 36). This may apply particularly to people with severe disabilities. But apart from very obvious cases, the other person does not seem to have any duty to make inquiries.

The only exception to this general rule relates to "necessaries". Section 3(2) of the Sale of Goods Act 1979 provides that if necessaries are supplied to a mentally incompetent person, he must pay a reasonable price for them. Necessaries means goods which are suitable to his condition in life and to his actual requirements at the time. The object of this rule seems to be that tradesmen should not be deterred from supplying the needs of mentally incapable people by fear of not being paid (Law Commission, 1976). But it also protects the incapable person, who need only pay a reasonable price, rather than the inflated one which may have been agreed. Similar principles apply to the supply of services which are "necessaries", such as accommodation and medical attention (see *Re Rhodes* [1890] 44 Ch.D. 94), and also the money to buy such things (*Re Beavan* (1912) 1 Ch. 196). The Law Commission (1995) have recommended putting all this on a statutory footing, including the right of a person who reasonably spends money for the benefit of an incapacitated person to be reimbursed from that person's assets.

There is another important difference between contracts and wills. Once a person's affairs have been taken over by the Court of Protection, he cannot deal with them in a way which is inconsistent with the court's powers of control (*Re Walker* [1905] 1 Ch. 160; *Re Marshall* [1920] 1 Ch. 284). Even if he has capacity to make the contract in question, it seems that he cannot do so. Indeed, logically, the contract should be quite void, even if the other party did not know of the court's jurisdiction. But the rule about necessaries should remain.

All of these rules assume that the other person is only too happy to deal with the mentally disordered person. But even if there is no risk of incapacity, people may be reluctant to supply services, housing, accommodation, finance, and employment to a mentally disordered person. People are generally free to choose to supply or not to supply such things, whether they are doing so for a good reason or out of pure prejudice. However, the Disability Discrimination Act 1995 will prohibit discrimination against people who have or have had "a physical or mental impairment which has a substantial and long-term adverse effect upon his ability to carry out normal day-to-day activities" (s. 1(1)). "Mental impairment" does not have its restricted Mental Health Act meaning (s. 68(1)), although obviously someone may fall within both. It only includes an impairment resulting from mental illness "if it is a clinically well-recognised illness" (Sched.1, para. 1(1)), which many might think a helpful concept in the 1983 Act as well. Generally the person must be, have been or expect to be impaired for 12 months (para. 2). It will be unlawful for employers (Part II) or providers of goods, facilities and services (Part III) to discriminate against people with such disabilities unless they can show that this is justified; and they will not be able to justify it if it would be reasonable for them to make adjustments to cater for disabled employees or customers. Until there has been some experience with the new Act, it is difficult to say whether it will affect cases such as *O'Brien v. Prudential Assurance Co. Ltd.* [1979] I.R.L.R. 140, where it was held not unfair to dismiss an employee who had failed to disclose a history of mental illness at interview even though it had no effect upon his present capacity to do the job. Unjustified discrimination may be more of a problem for people with mental disorders who are not sufficiently disabled to qualify for the Act's protection.

4. ACTING FOR A PERSON WITHOUT CAPACITY

Most of the people who suffer from mental disorder within the meaning of the Mental Health Act are quite capable of looking after their own affairs, whether or not they are in hospital. The law assumes this until the contrary is proved and there is no category of patient whose affairs are automatically taken out of his hands. Once again, there are conflicting policy considerations. A mentally disordered person must be protected against the risk of exploitation and abuse. There must also be adequate procedural safeguards against the unjustified removal of his right to look after his own affairs. But both of these can lead to procedures which are, "it is said, inevitably cumbersome, time-consuming and expensive" (Law Commission, 1976). This means that there is a great temptation to ignore them. Many children of mentally infirm parents would be horrified to learn that they cannot strictly decide to give up a tenancy or sell the furniture. The protective mechanism should not take a sledgehammer to crack a nut. It should provide essential protection while interfering as little as possible in the person's ordinary rights and freedoms (Gostin, 1983b). At present, once a person becomes incapable of looking after his own affairs, these must be placed under the jurisdiction of the Court of Protection, unless they can be adequately dealt with under the few provisions mentioned below or fall within the limited exceptions which the court is prepared to make. One object of the Law Commission's proposals on Mental Incapacity (1995) is to increase the scope for handling such things in a sensible way without the need to go to court.

(a) Statutory powers

Several types of income can by statute be paid to someone other than the person who is entitled to them, if that person is incapable of managing his property and affairs. The most important of these are social security benefits and income support. The Department of Social Security (DSS) have the power to appoint a suitable person to receive both of these on behalf of a person who is "unable to act" (Social Security (Claims and Payments) Regulations 1987, reg. 33).

Patients living with their families or independently are, of course, entitled to the full rate of benefit appropriate to their circumstances. Patients who have to spend any length of time in hospital or residential accommodation will usually only receive money for their personal expenses, once their accommodation and any dependants have been taken care of. The hospital management have power to pay pocket money to in-patients in hospitals which are wholly or mainly used for the treatment of people suffering from mental disorder, if they would otherwise be without resources for personal expenses (Mental Health Act 1983, s. 122). In fact, the hospitals take responsibility for most patients admitted before November 17, 1975 and the DSS for patients admitted after then. The amount will be the same, but income support is a right whereas hospital pocket money is not. Social security benefits, income support and hospital pocket money can all be reduced if the doctor responsible for the patient's treatment considers that, because of the patient's medical condition, the full amount cannot be used by or on behalf of the patient for his personal comfort or enjoyment.

There are two important points to note. First, the patient is entitled to have and to spend his own money unless he is incapable of doing so. That right can only be taken away if he cannot manage his property and affairs, and his personal allowance is usually all the property and affairs that he has. Many severely disabled patients should be able, with a little help, to decide whether to spend this on sweets, cigarettes or other transient comforts, or to save for new clothes, a radio, cassette player or the like. Secondly, if the patient is indeed incapable, the money must still be spent for his personal benefit. Hence there are practical problems about pooling some of it to buy such things as mini-buses for excursions, because of the difficulty of proving individual benefit in proportion to contributions and of reimbursement should the patient be discharged. Nor should the money be spent on general improvements and amenities inside a hospital or home which it is clearly the responsibility of the management to provide. Hospitals have found it particularly difficult to spend their patients' money within the limits of the law and large balances have accumulated. Hard-pressed staff have little time to consider how best a small sum might be used to enhance each patient's quality of life.

There is a potential conflict of interest where managers are appointed to receive their patients' or residents' benefits. *Home Life* (Centre for Policy on Ageing, 1984) points out that it is "most undesirable that a manager or proprietor should take on this role whatever the pressures" (para. 2.6.5). The DSS do look for an alternative "appointed person" whenever possible. But there are few formal safeguards over appointed persons, other than the ordinary law against theft and fraud. The Law Commission (1993a, 1995) canvassed various possible safeguards but concluded that these were for departmental regulations rather than Parliamentary legislation.

There is a similar power for salaries, pensions and other work-related periodical payments made from funds administered by government departments. The department must have medical evidence of the recipient's incapacity. They can then pay all or part of the money to the institution or person caring for him, to be applied for his benefit. Any remainder may go to or for the benefit of his family or other people for whom he might be expected to provide, or to reimburse people who have helped to pay his debts or to maintain him and his dependants (Mental Health Act 1983, s. 142). There are similar powers over the armed forces' pay and pensions, under the Royal Warrant; and over the pensions of Members of Parliament (regulations under the Parliamentary and Other Pensions Act 1987), Church of England clergymen (Clergy Pensions Measure 1961, s. 36), and some local authority employees (Local Government Act 1972, s. 118), but in the last two the Court of Protection must be informed.

There are a few other statutory provisions allowing for money due to a person without capacity to be paid to some suitable person (see the Industrial and Provident Societies Act 1965, s. 6, and the National Savings Bank Regulations 1972, reg. 7(4)).

(b) Powers under a contract or trust

Some building societies have rules which allow for payments to be made to some other suitable person if the account holder becomes unable to deal with them. These seem to work well in allowing the customer's money to be spent for his benefit without the need for costly proceedings in the Court of Protection. There is nothing to stop such clauses being included in contracts between insurance companies, banks and similar institutions and their customers, but this is far from universal. The Law Commission (1995) have recommended that certain institutions should be protected from liability if they release funds to a person who provides a certificate that the customer lacks capacity and a formal acknowledgement that the money must be applied in the best interests of the customer, that there may be civil and criminal liability if it is not, and that no-one else is entitled to receive it on the customer's behalf.

Pension fund trustees may be given a similar power in their trust deed. Trusts may also be set up for the express purpose of providing for an already incapacitated person, for example a severely disabled child of the settlor. The settlement should be so drawn as to avoid giving the person the right to an income which requires the attentions of the Court of Protection (although the court may still have to ask how the trustees are exercising their discretion). Sometimes property may be left to a charity, in the expectation that they will provide a home for the person concerned.

(c) Enduring Powers of Attorney

But what if a person would like to appoint his own agent to manage his finances in case he becomes incapable of doing so for himself? No doubt many people would like to put their affairs in the hands of a trusted friend or adviser before their faculties fail. They might be surprised to learn that any ordinary agency, even if given by deed in a power of attorney, is automatically revoked when the person giving it becomes incapable of contracting. It is not always easy to know when this has happened, because capacity can vary from time to time and from transaction to transaction. For as long as the agent remains in ignorance of the incapacity, he is safe if he acts under a power of attorney (Powers of Attorney Act 1971, s. 5(1)). The transaction itself will be valid if the third party who deals with an agent who has power of attorney does not know of the incapacity (s. 5(2)). This also applies to any contract which is within the scope of the agent's apparent authority (*Drew v. Nunn* (1879) 4 Q.B.D. 661). Other transactions, however, may be invalid even if the third party did not know of the incapacity. In that case, the agent will be liable to the third party for breach of warranty of authority (*Yonge v. Toynbee* [1910] 1 K.B. 215). This is so even if the agent did not know about the incapacity, although in that case he should be able to claim reimbursement from his principal. The moment that the agent knows of the incapacity, however, he acts at his peril, except where he contracts for "necessaries" for the patient (Law Commission, 1976; but see Farrand, 1989).

Prompted by the legal profession, therefore, the Law Commission (1983) proposed the scheme which was enacted in the Enduring Powers of Attorney Act 1985. This allows donors to execute a special type of power of attorney, which remains valid even after they have lost their capacity to act. It is more elaborate than many enacted elsewhere in the world (see Creyke, 1989). It certainly provides reassurance to the attorney and those who deal with him, but is doubtfully any more effective in protecting the donor than a much simpler system would be (see Farrand, 1989; Cretney *et al.*, 1991; Law Commission, 1993a, 1995). There are three basic safeguards.

First, the power (EPA) must be granted on a prescribed form (s. 2(1); see Enduring Powers of Attorney (Prescribed Form) Regulations 1990 (S.I. 1990 No. 1376)). This contains an explanation of its effect but not of all its consequences. Curiously, neither the Law Commission nor the Act addressed the question of the capacity needed to grant the power. Does the donor have to be capable of managing all his property and affairs at the time, or is it enough that he understands (in the usual "broad terms" way) the nature and effect of EPA itself? It was decided in *Re K.* [1988] Ch. 310 that the latter would do. The donor need only understand that (if it is a general power) the attorney can assume control over all his affairs, can do anything the donor can do, can continue in power even if the donor becomes incapable, and that the power cannot then be revoked without the confirmation of the Court of Protection (see s. 7).

Secondly, once the attorney "has reason to believe" that the donor is or is becoming mentally incapable of managing his property and affairs, the attorney must apply to register the EPA with the Court of Protection (s. 4(1), (2)). The administrative functions of the registration procedures are carried out by the Public Trust Office (see The Court of Protection (Enduring Powers of Attorney) Rules 1994 (S.I. 1994 No. 3047) r. 6). The attorney must notify both the donor and his relatives of this application (s. 4(3)). The list of relatives begins with the donor's spouse, then goes on to his children, his parents, his siblings, his deceased children's widows or widowers, his grandchildren, his nephews and nieces of the whole then of the half blood, his uncles and aunts of the whole blood, and ends with their children; only three relatives need be told, but if this includes one in any category then all in that category must be told; minors and the mentally incapable are excluded, as are those whose name and address cannot reasonably be discovered; the attorney may also apply to the court to dispense with the requirement to notify someone if it would be undesirable or impractical or serve no useful purpose (Sched. 1).

Notifying the relatives was thought to be the best safeguard, but they can only object that the power was not valid, or that it no longer exists, or that the donor is not yet becoming incapable, or that it was induced by fraud or undue pressure, or that in all the circumstances the attorney is unsuitable (s. 6(4)). In practice, by the time the power has to be registered it may be too late to make any of these points. Notification at the time of creation would have been a better safeguard, but it would certainly have made more work. Many more EPAs are granted than ever come to be registered, often as a precaution long before there is any question of incapacity (Cretney *et al.*, 1991). Once granted, an EPA operates like an ordinary power of attorney, so that if the donor becomes incapable, the ordinary law will apply unless the power has been registered; pending registration, the attorney has limited powers, mainly to maintain the donor and protect his estate (see ss. 1(1), (2), 13(1)).

Thirdly, once registered, the court has various supervisory functions. The donor is not deprived of his right to carry out any transaction of which he is capable but he cannot revoke or change the power, even if he is capable of doing so, without the court's approval (ss. 7(1),(2), 8(3)). The court must cancel registration if the donor is and is likely to remain mentally capable; if the EPA is revoked, or expires, or was invalid or obtained by fraud or undue pressure; if the attorney disclaims or is unsuitable; or if the court itself assumes control over the donor's property and affairs (s. 8(4)). The court can also give directions to the attorney, require accounts and information from him, and authorise him to do things he would otherwise need the donor's authority to do (s. 8(2)). But these are primarily to give effect to the power itself: the court cannot direct the attorney as to how he is to dispose of the donor's property, for example by requiring him to make a gift in recognition of the donor's moral obligation to a housekeeper-companion (*Re R. (Enduring Power of Attorney)* [1990] Ch. 647).

Powers can be in general or specific terms, but they are limited to the donor's "property and affairs". This means his financial and business affairs (see *Re F. (Mental Patient: Sterilisation)* [1990] 2 A.C.1); an EPA cannot be used at present to authorise (or forbid) medical treatment or personal care decisions. But the idea of an EPA is extremely attractive. The donor can choose an attorney he trusts, to act as he would have wished, and can give him general or precise instructions as he thinks fit. The Law Commission (1995) have proposed a comprehensive new scheme, with much simpler procedures, which can be used for all kinds of decisions, including personal welfare and (within limits) health care.

5. THE COURT OF PROTECTION

The court has a long history as it stems from the power (and duty) of the monarch to look after the property of lunatics and idiots, which was recognised even before the Statute *De Praerogativa Regis* of Edward II. The King delegated this function to the Lord Chancellor, and later to other judges. Patients had to be found of unsound mind by inquisition, and then their affairs would be managed by a "committ*ee*". It was also possible to appoint a committee of the person but this was rarely done. Legislation modified both the inquisition procedure and the powers of the court, but the basis of the jurisdiction remained the royal prerogative, delegated by warrant under the sign manual, until the Mental Health Act 1959. This established the Court of Protection on a fully statutory basis, but dealing only with the "property and affairs" of a patient. The royal warrant was revoked and no one is quite sure whether it can be reissued and if so how (see Hoggett, 1988).

(a) The court

The court's powers and procedure are governed by Part VII of the Mental Health Act 1983 and the Court of Protection Rules 1994, (S.I. 1994 No. 3046) (see generally Heywood and Massey, 1991; Whitehorn, 1991). Technically, the court is an office of the Supreme Court (Mental Health Act 1983, s. 93(2)). Its judicial functions are carried out by judges nominated by the Lord Chancellor (in practice those in the Chancery Division of the High Court) and by the Master, Deputy Master, and assistant Masters or other officers nominated by the Lord Chancellor (ss. 93(2), (3) and (4)). Its administrative functions are carried out by the Public Trustee (see Court of Protection Rules 1994, r. 6). A person aggrieved (including the patient) by the decision of a Master can appeal to a nominated judge and thereafter to the Court of Appeal.

There are also the Lord Chancellor's Visitors (ss. 102 and 103), who visit patients and investigate either their capacities or any aspect of the court's functions in respect of them. All Visitors may interview patients in private and medical Visitors may examine them and their records. Reports to the court are confidential unless the court allows disclosure. Unless legal or medical expertise is essential, visits are made by general Visitors (in practice the Lord Chancellor's Department welfare officers). The Master may also visit patients for the same purpose and interview them in private (s. 103(7)).

(b) Grounds

The court's jurisdiction only arises "where, after considering the medical evidence (it) is satisfied that a person is incapable, by reason of mental disorder, of managing and administering his property and affairs" (1983 Act, s. 94(2)). It may make interim orders pending the determination of that question, if there is reason to believe that the person may be incapable and it is necessary to act immediately (s. 98). But the fact that some other court has decided that the person is incapable, for example, for the purpose of appointing someone to act as his next friend (p. 250, later) in a nullity suit, does not mean that he is automatically subject to the Court of Protection (*Re S. (F. G.) (Mental Health Patient)* [1973] 1 W.L.R. 178).

The criterion for intervention is both wide and vague. It covers any form of mental disorder, including "arrested or incomplete development of mind" and "any other disorder or disability of mind", which are not sufficient for long-term compulsory admission to hospital. It is not clear what is meant by an incapacity to manage one's property and affairs, but a patient may be unable to do this despite the fact that he is able to carry out many individual transactions. This means that the court's intervention can prevent his doing things that he would otherwise be able to do. There is no specific provision in the procedure for an assessment of his social competence, such as is contemplated by the United Nations *Declaration on the Rights of Mentally Retarded Persons* (p. 225, earlier). It is also unfortunate that the procedure places most of the burden on the patient. Once a medical certificate has been produced, it is up to him to raise doubts about whether he is indeed incapable. However, recent guidance from the BMA and Law Society on Assessment of Mental Capacity (1995) may bring improvements in practice.

(c) Procedure

The initial application will usually be for the appointment of a receiver but it could be for a "short order or direction". This simply directs an officer of the Public Trustee or some other suitable person to deal with the matter in a particular way. It can be done if either (a) the patient's property is worth no more than £5,000 or (b) it is appropriate for some other reason *and* it is not necessary to appoint a receiver. The court can make an order instead of granting an application to appoint receiver and the Public Trustee can make a direction, provided there is no such application (r. 9).

There is a formal application form (Form A) for the appointment of a receiver; but other applications can be made by letter, unless the court or Public Trustee as appropriate directs otherwise; in urgent cases they may proceed without a written application (r. 8). The court and Public Trustee can also act of their own motion without any application at all (r. 7). Usually, the patient's nearest or any relative applies, but a friend or a solicitor, or even a local social services authority or an individual social worker could do so. In the last resort, the court can direct an officer of the Public Trustee or the Official Solicitor to apply (r. 12). If the patient's estate is large or complicated, or something needs to be done which will require a solicitor anyway (such as selling a house), the applicant should instruct a solicitor. But if the estate is small or relatively straightforward, application can be made directly through the court's Enquiries and Applications Branch.

The court supplies the necessary forms. On the first application, either to appoint a receiver or for a short order or direction, there must be a medical certificate from a doctor that the patient is incapable, by reason of mental disorder, of managing and administering his property and affairs (r. 36). Unlike a compulsory admission to hospital, only one certificate is required and the doctor need not have any particular expertise in mental disorder. He will normally be the patient's "medical attendant"; the form expects him to state when he examined the patient in order to ascertain "the state of his mind" and to give grounds for his opinion. Clearly, some will take a much broader view of incapacity than do others. The other document required is a certificate of family and property or, if the court so directs, a sworn affidavit. This sets out particulars of his relatives, property and affairs and of the circumstances giving rise to the application (r. 36).

The patient must normally be notified of the first application, or where the court or Public Trustee proposes to make a short order or direction, but they can dispense with notification if satisfied that the patient is incapable of understanding it, or if it would injure his health, or indeed for any other reason (r. 26(2)). The court is reluctant to dispense with notice to the patient unless satisfied that this is clearly in his interests, because even the most irrational patient may have something to contribute (Whitehorn, 1991). A medical report on the point should therefore be filed. Even so, it cannot be right that the patient may be deprived of his right to administer his own affairs without even being told that this is under consideration. In the *Winterwerp Case* (1979) 2 E.H.R.R. 387, the European Court of Human Rights held that Article 6(1) of the Convention, which requires a person's civil rights to be determined in a "fair and public hearing within a reasonable time by an independent and impartial tribunal established by law", applies to decisions about a person's capacity to deal with his own property.

If the patient is notified, he can write to the court. He may object to the whole proceedings on the ground that he is not incapable and some medical support for this is important. Alternatively, he may simply wish to object to or make comments on what is proposed and to make his own suggestions. The court may try to take his wishes into account. It may invite the Official Solicitor to represent him (r. 15). But the rules do not give the patient, or anyone else, a right to be heard in person if he wants. The court can proceed without a hearing if it considers it proper to do so (r. 10) and is entitled to decide who may attend any hearing (r. 40). Usually the case is dealt with on the papers and attendance is not required.

Apart from the patient, only relatives equal to or closer than the applicant need be notified of an application to appoint or change a receiver, unless the court directs otherwise (r. 27). The receiver must always be told of any application made by anyone else (r. 21(2)). Apart from special rules about certain types of application, other business can be conducted by the receiver without notifying anyone, unless the court requires this. Ten days' notice must be given of the hearing of a first application to appoint a receiver but only two days' notice of other applications (r. 21(5)).

If the court is satisfied that the patient is incapable, it will usually make the order applied for. If it has any doubt, it may ask a medical Visitor to examine the patient and report confidentially on his condition (r. 69). If the Visitor reports that the patient is incapable, a new hearing date will be set for the application to be reconsidered if there are any further objections.

(d) Effects

Once the patient is subject to the court's jurisdiction, it has exclusive control over all his property and all his affairs. Its guidance must be sought whenever anything not provided for in an existing order or direction needs to be done (*Re W. (E.E.M.)* (1971) Ch. 123). Its general function is to "do or secure the doing of all such things as appear necessary or expedient" for the maintenance or other benefit of the patient or his family, for providing for other people or purposes for which he might be expected to provide, or for otherwise administering his affairs (s. 95(1)). "Benefit" is not confined to material benefit and includes whatever may be in the true interests of the patient or his family (*Re E. (Mental Health Patient)* [1985] 1 W.L.R 245). Without prejudice to that general proposition, the court may do a long list of things for that purpose: control and manage any property of the patient; sell, dispose or deal with it; acquire property for him; make settlements or give it away to members of his family or other people or purposes for which he might be expected to provide if he were not mentally disordered; make a will (p. 235, earlier); carry on his profession, trade or business through any suitable person; dissolve a partnership; carry out a contract entered into by the patient; conduct legal proceedings in his name or on his behalf; reimburse those who have paid his debts or supported him or his family or provided for other purposes for which he might be expected to provide; and exercise any power (including a power to consent) vested in him, either for himself or as a trustee or guardian, or otherwise (s. 96(1)). The court's first concern is always for the maintenance and other requirements of the patient, and it has a wide discretion about whether and to what extent to discharge his debts and other obligations, although it must have regard to the interests of creditors, who are no longer entitled to enforce their rights in the normal way (s. 95(2)).

The court has no jurisdiction over the management and care of the patient's person and so is not concerned with his admission to or discharge from hospital, his medical treatment, or other aspects of caring for him. But the dividing line is not always easy to draw, as arrangements for expenditure upon his accommodation (for example, in a private nursing home) are clearly within the court's jurisdiction. And its powers to conduct legal proceedings can be used for purposes such as divorce, with obvious personal consequences. The court will also want to know if the patient is contemplating marriage. One object of this is to enable it to make a statutory will if need be. But it might want to direct the entry of a *caveat* in the hope of stopping the wedding (p. 230, earlier; see Gostin, 1983b). Whether this would succeed is more doubtful, but the possibility illustrates how all-embracing the court's powers can be.

The case may be dealt with by a short order or direction (p. 243, earlier). But unless the patient's property is all disposed of in some way, it remains under the court's control. The capital will be invested and administered by the Public Trust office, which also supervises and advises receivers. A receiver will usually be appointed (s. 99) to enable the income to be spent for the patient's benefit and otherwise to carry out the court's instructions. The receiver will usually, but not inevitably, be the person who applied to the court. The court prefers a close, but not too elderly, relative. If there is no suitable relative, it is not normal practice to appoint a solicitor (because the solicitor dealing with the case is an independent protection for the patient), but a bank manager, accountant or estate agent (in the old sense) may be appropriate. A friend could be appointed, or the local social services authority, if they could be persuaded to take it on. Around 19,000 receivers are relatives, 4,000 are professionals, and 2,400 are local authority officers. Where there is no other suitable person, or there is a dispute within the family, the Public Trustee may be appointed (see Public Trustee and Administration of Funds Act 1986, s. 3(2)), currently in around 2,600 cases (see National Audit Office, 1994).

The order appointing the receiver will usually be in precise terms, setting out what he must and what he may do. He will have to return to court for specific authority to do anything else. The order will probably give him authority to receive the patient's income and direct how it is to be spent for the maintenance of the patient and his family. It may deal with carrying on or closing down a business, the retention or surrender of insurance policies, savings certificates and other investments, the upkeep or surrender of the patient's home, furniture and the like. The sale of a house is normally dealt with in a separate order. A receiver is usually required to give security for the proper performance of his duties, as is the administrator of a dead person's estate (r. 58). This is normally done through an insurance company's fidelity guarantee bond, the premium being allowable out of the patient's estate (r. 59). He will be required to render precise accounts to the Public Trust Office, usually annually at first (r. 63). A professional receiver may be allowed remuneration out of the estate (r. 45). He may of course be removed or replaced by the court if appropriate, or he might ask to be discharged because of ill-health or other commitments.

(f) An endless burden?

The court's functions usually come to an end when the patient dies. If he recovers, a specific finding that he is now capable of managing his own affairs, together with the discharge of any receiver and release of any funds held by the court (r. 76(1)), is required. There is no automatic review of whether the court's intervention is any longer necessary. Each year there are only around 60 applications for discharge of receivership, most of which apparently succeed. The court or Public Trust will not initiate a review unless asked. The receiver is under no obligation even to visit the patient, let alone to report regularly on how he is getting on. Very few private receivership patients are visited each year on behalf of the Public Trust Office and some are not visited at all (National Audit Office, 1994).

A recent survey revealed a reasonable degree of satisfaction among users of the Public Trust Office, but some serious criticisms can be made (National Audit Office, 1994; House of Commons Public Accounts Committee, 1994). Patients and their families still feel that matters are taken out of their hands by a remote and complicated machine which cannot always adapt to changing needs. Everything is done at a distance. This saves costs but reduces the opportunity to object. Comparatively little trouble is taken at the outset to ensure that the person appointed receiver is entirely suitable or that receivership is really necessary. Thereafter the "all or nothing" approach of the present law deprives the patient of the right to do even those things, such as granting an enduring power of attorney, which he still has capacity to do. It also deprives his family or receiver of the right to do things for him. The court takes full control over all his capital and business or financial affairs. In practice, it does not give the receiver powers over capital and only rarely sets up trusts of his property for his benefit. The Public Trust Office has a monopoly of the control of patients' capital. This caution may sometimes be justified but it may also be quite unsuitable for dealing with some types of estate. The Public Trust Office has not been particularly efficient in checking receivers' accounts. It all costs a great deal of money. Fees are charged at the beginning of the proceedings, for many specific transactions, and annually, although there are exemptions from the first and last for patients on low incomes. These all come out of the estate, in addition to any fees charged by the receiver or solicitor. The comprehensive new jurisdiction recommended by the Law

Commission (1995) would preserve the person's right to take for himself those decisions which he is able to take and allow the court either to decide other issues for him or in suitable cases to appoint managers who could take full control over his estate.

6. PATIENTS AS PROSECUTORS, WITNESSES AND LITIGANTS

(a) Criminal liability towards patients

All the ordinary offences against the person can be charged against those who ill-treat mental patients. Sexual exploitation by staff of patients in their care has already been mentioned (p. 228, earlier). Other offences prohibit ill-treatment or wilful neglect of certain patients. These may be committed by anyone on the staff of, or employed in, or who is one of the managers of, a hospital or mental nursing home, towards people who are receiving treatment for mental disorder as in-patients there, or towards people who are receiving treatment there as out-patients but only while on the premises of which the hospital or home forms part (s. 127(1)). Similar offences may be committed by any individual towards a patient in his guardianship under the Act or "otherwise in his custody or care (whether by virtue of any legal or moral obligation or otherwise)" (s. 127(2)) or towards a patient who is currently subject to after-care under supervision (s. 127(2A)). The maximum penalty is imprisonment for two years, or an unlimited fine, or both (s. 127(3)). In *R. v. Newington* (1990) 91 Cr.App.R. 247, the Court of Appeal decided that ill-treatment and wilful neglect are two separate offences. Ill-treatment is any deliberate conduct "which could properly be described" as such, whether or not it had caused or was likely to cause harm. The defendant must either realise that he is inexcusably ill-treating the patient or be reckless as to whether he is doing so.

Other offences relate to falsifying documents. It is an offence wilfully to make a false entry or statement in any document required or authorised to be made for the purposes of the Act, or to use such an entry or statement with intent to deceive knowing it to be false (s. 126(4)). It is also an offence to have any such document in your custody or control without lawful authority or excuse, knowing or believing it to be false (s. 126(1)), or without lawful authority or excuse to make or have in your custody or control any document which so closely resembles one made under the Act as to be calculated to deceive (s. 126(2)). The penalties are the same as for the other offences.

Local social services authorities can prosecute for offences under section 126 and 127 (s. 130), as well as for the offences of helping compulsory patients to escape (s. 128; p. 164, earlier), and of obstructing inspection, visiting, interviewing, examining, or any other function authorised under the Act (s. 129).

(b) Patients as witnesses

Obtaining sufficient reliable evidence can be a major difficulty in prosecuting offences against mentally disordered people. Some victims may be judged incompetent to give evidence at all. There is no provision like that allowing children to give evidence without taking an oath or affirmation (Children and Young Persons Act 1933, s. 38; Children Act 1989, s. 96(1), (2)). It appears that a mentally handicapped person may only give evidence if he understands, not only the duty to tell the truth, but also the extra obligation and sanction involved in the oath or affirmation (*R. v.*

Dunning [1965] Crim. L.R. 372). Yet a person may be quite capable of giving an accurate account of what has happened even if he understands neither of these concepts.

Medical evidence is admissible on the question of whether or not a witness is competent to give evidence at all. Experts cannot usually give evidence of whether they think that a competent witness is telling the truth—that is for the court or jury to decide (*R. v. Turner* [1975] Q.B. 834; *R. v. MacKenny* (1980) 72 Cr.App.R. 78; *R. v. Weightman, The Times,* November 8, 1990). But they may give evidence on whether the witness suffers from some disability or illness which substantially affects his ability to give reliable evidence (*Toohey v. Metropolitan Police Commissioner* [1965] A.C. 595).

Even if the complainant is competent to give evidence, the jury may have to be warned to be very careful about accepting it. In several prosecutions of Rampton staff for abusing patients, culminating in the House of Lords ruling in *R. v. Spencer* [1987] A.C. 128, it was held that juries must be warned in clear terms of the dangers of convicting on the unsupported evidence of special hospital patients, who were of bad character, mentally unstable, and might have a common grudge against the staff. Is this right or a case of old stereotypes dying hard? There is a careful discussion of these issues in the Ashworth Inquiry Report (Blom-Cooper, 1992, Chap. III).

(c) Civil liability to patients

Unless prevented by section 139 of the 1983 Act (see section (d) below), patients may seek damages for false imprisonment, assault or battery, or negligence. If the Act has been properly complied with, their detention will not usually be unlawful. However, in *Furber v. Kratter, The Times,* July 21, 1988, a hospital order patient, who had been secluded for 16 days after attacking a nurse, was allowed to pursue her claim that it was false imprisonment to detain her in conditions which were so seriously prejudicial to health as to make an originally lawful detention unlawful. But such claims by prisoners have since been disallowed by the House of Lords in *Hague v. Deputy Governor of Parkhurst Prison; Weldon v. Home Office* [1992] 1 A.C. 58; patients whose original detention was lawful are unlikely to fare any better.

Claims in negligence are a different matter. A recommending doctor or an approved social worker (ASW) could be liable for the detention if they failed to take the care that a reasonable professional would take in the circumstances (*Harnett v. Fisher* [1927] A.C. 573). For example, in *Winch v. Jones* [1986] Q.B. 296, a patient was given leave to sue the recommending doctors and the responsible medical officer (RMO) for negligence (and the claim was later settled for £27,500); in *Buxton v. Jayne* [1960] 1 W.L.R. 783, leave was given to sue the applicant social worker (but the eventual action was unsuccessful). Hospital and other staff may also be liable for any harm done if they fail to take reasonable care of the patient while he is under their care.

Nor can a claim by a patient for failing to "section" or otherwise control him be ruled out. Hospitals have on occasion been held liable for serious failure to supervise a suicidal patient, even though the injury is self-inflicted (see *Selfe v. Ilford and District Hospital Management Committee* (1970) 114 S.J. 935); but in *Hyde v. Tameside Area Health Authority, The Times,* April 15, 1981, Lord Denning thought that the law should not permit such actions. Obviously, there are problems in seeking to control a patient who is not liable to be detained under the Act. No such problems arise for detained patients and other prisoners. In *Kirkham v. Chief Constable of Greater Manchester* [1990] 2 Q.B. 283, C.A., the police were held liable for the suicide of a man detained in a remand centre because they failed to pass on the information about his suicidal tendencies. And in *Knight v. Home Office* [1990] 3 All E.R. 237 it was held that the appropriate standard of care for mentally ill prisoners in a prison hospital is not as high as that in a psychiatric hospital.

(d) Section 139 of the Mental Health Act 1983

It used to be thought that doctors, hospitals and others required special protection from frivolous and vexatious actions by patients. Section 139(1) of the 1983 Act provides that:

> "No person shall be liable, whether on the ground of want of jurisdiction or on any other ground, to any civil or criminal proceedings to which he would have been liable apart from this section in respect of any act purporting to be done in pursuance of this Act or any regulations or rules made under this Act, or in, or in pursuance of anything done in, the discharge of functions conferred by any other enactment on the authority having jurisdiction under Part VII of this Act, unless the act was done in bad faith or without reasonable care."

The House of Lords held in *Pountney v. Griffiths* [1976] A.C. 314 that the actions of a Broadmoor nurse which he claimed were done to control a detained patient were acts "purporting to be done in pursuance of the Act"; but in *R. v. Moonsami Runighian* [1977] Crim. L.R. 361, a Crown Court judge held that the section did not cover the treatment of an informal patient.

How much extra protection does section 139(1) in fact give? People who are acting without negligence and within their lawful powers will not be liable at all and the section gives no protection against negligence. But it does give protection to people who have made an honest and reasonable mistake, including a mistake about the extent of their powers. If the Act is so clear that even a layman could not have misconstrued it, then he will still be liable, but if it could reasonably be thought to mean what he thought it did, then he will be protected (see *Richardson v. L.C.C.* [1957] 1 W.L.R. 751). This could be particularly useful for staff in their day-to-day dealings with detained patients, where the precise extent of their powers of control and discipline is so difficult to determine.

More important in practice, however, is the requirement in section 139(2) that in order to sue in respect of acts covered by section 139(1) the patient must first have the leave of a High Court judge. The judge no longer has to be satisfied (as he did under the 1959 Act) that there is "substantial ground" for the contention of bad faith or lack of reasonable care. The object of the section is to prevent harassment by "clearly hopeless actions", so leave should be granted if the case deserved further investigation, even if it is unlikely to succeed on the law or the merits (*Winch v. Jones* [1986] Q.B. 296). But leave may be refused, even if there is a conflict of evidence, if it is "virtually unarguable" that there has been a lack of reasonable care, for example by a social worker or doctor making decisions in an obvious emergency (see, *e.g. James v. London Borough of*

Havering (1992) 15 B.M.L.R. 1). On the other hand, the fact that leave has been granted under section 139(2) does not prevent the court stopping the case later if there is no reasonable cause of action (see *X. v. A., B., and C. and the Mental Health Act Commission* (1991) 9 B.M.L.R. 91).

It was held in *Ex p. Waldron* [1986] Q.B. 824 that the section does not cover applications for judicial review to quash allegedly illegal admissions. This must be right, for judicial review itself requires leave, and the release of unlawfully detained patients should not be effectively discretionary. Nor does it cover actions against the Secretary of State or any health authority (s. 139(4)), although it does apply to actions against a local authority. The section does not apply at all to the offences of ill-treatment or neglect under section 127 (s. 139(3)); but otherwise the defence in section 139(1) covers both civil and criminal proceedings. The requirement of leave in section 139(2) now applies only to civil proceedings.

Mental patients are still at some disadvantage compared with other litigants. They have to go first to a High Court judge even if the claim is within the jurisdiction of the county courts (now very wide). They have to persuade the judge that they have a case which should be tried, whereas with other litigants the burden is on the defendant to show that it should not be tried. There is still some risk that the judge will consider the claim so hopeless on the merits that he will refuse leave. In any event, there is no objective justification for the section even in its now attenuated form. Only a minority of patients, even of those compulsorily detained, are suffering from disorders which make it at all likely that they will harass other people with groundless accusations. Rather more of them are suffering from disorders which make it likely that they will not complain at all, even if they have every reason to do so. Protection against frivolous, vexatious or abusive litigation can be granted either in relation to the particular proceedings (Rules of the Supreme Court, Ord. 18, r. 19; County Court Rules, Ord. 13, r. 5) or in relation to a particular individual (Supreme Court Act 1981, s. 42). But there is no necessary connection between vexatiousness and the use of compulsion under the Mental Health Act. There is no evidence that the floodgates would open if section 139 were entirely repealed. There is more evidence, from a series of reports and investigations, that mental patients are in a peculiarly powerless position which merits, if anything, extra safeguards rather than the removal of those available to everyone else.

(e) The conduct of litigation

There is another way in which some mental patients may be denied the usual access to the courts, although this is meant for their benefit rather than their detriment. Actions cannot be brought or defended in the courts by "patients" unless they are represented by a "next friend" (if the patient is the plaintiff, petitioner or applicant) or by a guardian *ad litem* (if he is the defendant or respondent) (Rules of the Supreme Court, Ord. 80; County Court Rules, Ord. 10; Family Proceedings Rules 1991, Part IX). A patient for this purpose is someone who, because of mental disorder within the meaning of the 1983 Act, is incapable of managing or administering his property and affairs. This is a matter for the court in which the litigation is taking place, which will also approve the appointment. The official solicitor often acts for these patients, but any suitable person may do so. Although the criterion is the same, the patient is not necessarily under the jurisdiction of the Court of Protection (*Re S. (F.G.)* [1973] 1 W.L.R. 178).

The guardian's role is to conduct the action in the interests of the patient, and he may be able to secure a benefit for the patient which the patient could not secure for himself. Nevertheless, the patient is denied the right to conduct the action in the way that he would have wished to do. For that reason, appointments should be confined to people who are genuinely unable to act for themselves, even with legal representation.

In others respects, however, the law is kind. There may be no point in making an injunction against a mentally disordered person, for example to protect an elderly wife against the obsessive and violent jealousy of her demented husband, if he cannot understand the nature and requirements of the order; it will have no deterrent effect and he would have a good defence to any enforcement proceedings (*Wookey v. Wookey* [1991] Fam. 131, C.A.).

People under a disability are also exempt from the normal rules requiring that actions be brought within a certain time of the cause of action arising. In general, time only begins to run from when the patient ceases to be under a disability (Limitation Act 1980, s. 28). People under disability include not only those who are incapable of managing their property and affairs, but also those subject to detention or guardianship under the Mental Health Act, and even those informal in-patients whose treatment immediately follows a period of detention (s. 38(2) to (4)). This tenderness contrasts oddly with the barriers placed in their way by section 139 of the 1983 Act (see section (d) above).

7. CONCLUSION

Attention is now shifting, away from the compulsory hospitalisation of mentally ill and behaviour-disordered patients, and towards the care and protection of incapacitated and vulnerable people living in the community. As we have already seen in Chapter 4, the present law does not give local authorities sufficiently clear and coherent powers to investigate and protect vulnerable people from abuse, neglect or exploitation in their own homes. As we have seen in this chapter, it does not provide a comprehensive scheme to enable decisions to be taken on behalf of those who are unable to take them for themselves. The deficiencies of the present system are well illustrated by the three recent cases (p. 233, earlier) about the High Court's powers to decide what will be lawful in that person's best interests.

The Law Commission's proposals on Mental Incapacity (1995) reaffirm the right of anyone to take for himself any decision which he is able to take. Others would be able to take reasonable steps in looking after the health or personal welfare or health care of someone who did not have the capacity to do so for himself. A Code of Practice would give guidance about what was reasonable. And there would be a new and comprehensive scheme for allowing a person to appoint an attorney while he still had capacity, or for the court to resolve disputes or appoint a manager when he did not, which would cover any or all of the decisions which the person was unable to take for himself. Decisions should always be made in his best interests, but his own past and present wishes and feelings, the views of other important people in his life about this, and the need to maximise his own potential and minimise interference would be important factors in deciding what would be best.

The Mental Health Act would continue to provide for the detention, treatment and supervision of patients requiring treatment for psychiatric disorder. But this Act is also beginning to look decidedly old-fashioned. Important voices are calling for its complete revision. Together these developments reflect the transformation of mental health care and the shift in values which have taken place since the 1983 Act: does this mean that the battles of the 1970s are now far behind us?

BIBLIOGRAPHY OF REFERENCES AND FURTHER READING

Aarvold, Sir C. (1972), *Report on the Review of Procedures for the Discharge and Supervision of Psychiatric Patients subject to Special Restrictions*, Cmnd. 5191 (London: HMSO).

Age Concern (1986), *The Law and Vulnerable Elderly People* (London: Age Concern).

Age Concern Institute of Gerontology and Centre For Medical Law and Ethics, King's College, London (1988), *The Living Will: Consent to Treatment at the End of Life* (London: Edward Arnold).

Anderson, E.W. (1962), "The Official Concept of Psychopathic Personality in England" in Krauze, H. (ed.), *Psychopathalogie Heute* (Stuttgart: Georg Thieme Verlag).

Ashworth, A. and Gostin, L., "Mentally Disordered Offenders and the Sentencing Process" [1984] *Crim.L.R.* 195.

Ashworth, A. and Shapland, J., "Psychopaths in the Criminal Process" [1980] *Crim.L.R.* 628.

Ashton, G.R. and Ward, A.D. (1992), *Mental Handicap and the Law* (London: Sweet and Maxwell).

Audit Commission (1986), *Making a Reality of Community Care* (London: HMSO).

Audit Commission (1994), *Finding a Place: A Review of Mental Health Services for Adults* (London: HMSO).

Audit Commission and HMI (1992), *Getting in on the Act. Provision for Pupils with Special Educational Needs: the National Picture* (London: HMSO).

Baker, E., "Dangerousness. The neglected gaoler: disorder and risk under the Mental Health Act 1983" (1992) 3 *J. Forensic Psych.* 31.

Barnes, M., Bowl, R. and Fisher, M. (1990), *Sectioned: Social Services and the 1983 Mental Health Act* (London: Routledge).

Baxter, R., "The mentally disordered offender in hospital: the role of the Home Office", in Herbst and Gunn (1991), *op. cit.*

Bean, P. (1980), *Compulsory Admissions to Mental Hospitals* (Chichester: Wiley).

Bean, P. (1983), *Mental Disorder and Legal Control* (Cambridge: Cambridge University Press).

Bean, P. (ed.) (1986), *Mental Illness: Changes and Trends* (Chichester: Wiley).

Bean, P. *et al.* (1991), *Out of Harm's Way* (London: MIND).

Beardmore, V. (1981), *Conscientious Objectors At Work: Mental Hospital Nurses: A Case Study* (London: Social Audit).

Beebe, M., Ellis, D. and Evans, R., "Research Report on Statutory Work under the Mental Health Act 1959: Experience in the London Borough of Camden" (1973) 5 *The Human Context* 377.

Bell, K. (1969), *Tribunals in the Social Services* (London: Routledge and Kegan Paul).

Bell, K., "Mental Health Review Tribunals: A Question of Balance" (1970) 16 *Case Conference* 385.

Berrios, G.E. and Freeman, H. (eds.) (1991), *150 Years of British Psychiatry 1941–1991* (London: Gaskell).

Bingley, W., "The Mental Health Act Commission: an audit" (1991) 2 J. *Forensic Psych.* 135.

Bingley, W., and Blom-Cooper, L., 'Sharp Eyes: Keen Ears" *Community Care,* October 15, 1990, p. 23.

Blackie, J. and Patrick, H. (1990), *Mental Health: A Guide to the Law in Scotland* (Edinburgh: Butterworths).

Bloch, S., and Chodoff, P. (eds) (1991), *Psychiatric Ethics,* (2nd ed., Oxford: Oxford University Press).

Blom-Cooper, Sir L., "All Change in the Mental Health Field" *Health Service Journal,* June 21, 1990, p. 908.

Blom-Cooper, Sir L. (1992), *Report of the Committee of Inquiry into Complaints about Ashworth Hospital,* Cm. 2028 (London: HMSO).

Blom-Cooper, Sir L., Hally, H. and Murphy, E. (1995), *The Falling Shadow: One patient's mental health care 1978–1993* (London: Duckworth).

Bluglass, R., "Origins of the Mental Health Act 1983: Doctors in the House" (1984) *Bull R.C. Psych.* 127.

Bluglass, R., "The Development of Regional Secure Units", in Gostin, L. (ed.) (1985), *op. cit.*

Bluglass, R. and Bowden, P. (eds) (1990), *Principles and Practice of Forensic Psychiatry* (London: Churchill Livingstone).

Blumenthal, S. and Wessely, S. (1992), *The Extent of Local Arrangements for Diversion of the Mentally Abnormal Offender from Custody.*

Blumenthal, S. and Wessely, S. (1994), *The Pattern of Delays in Mental Health Review Tribunals* (London: HMSO).

Boehringer, G.H. and McCabe, S. (1973), *The Hospital Order in London Magistrates' Courts* (Oxford: Blackwell).

Bott, E. (1971), *Family and Social Network: Roles, Norms and External Relationships in Ordinary Urban Families,* (2nd ed., London: Tavistock).

Bottoms, A.E. and Brownsword, R., "The Dangerousness Debate after the Floud Report" (1982) 22 *Brit J. Criminol.* 229.

Boynton, Sir J. (1980), *Report of the Review of Rampton Hospital,* Cmnd. 8073 (London: HMSO).

Brandon, D. (1981), *Voices of Experience: Consumer Perspectives of Psychiatric Treatment* (London: MIND).

Brazier, M.R. "Prison Doctors and their Involuntary Patients" [1982] *Public Law* 282.

Brazier, M.R., "Sterilisation: Down the Slippery Slope" (1990) *Professional Negligence,* March, p. 25.

Brazier, M.R. (1992), *Medicine, Patients and the Law,* (2nd ed., Harmondsworth: Penguin).

British Association of Social Workers (1977), *Mental Health Crisis Services: A New Philosophy* (Birmingham: British Association of Social Workers).

British Medical Association (1995), *Advance Statements about Medical Treatment* (London: British Medical Journal Publishing Group).

British Medical Association and The Law Society (1995), *Assessment of Mental Capacity: Guidance for Doctors and Lawyers* (London: British Medical Association).

Brown, H. and Craft, A. (1989), *Thinking the Unthinkable: Papers on Sexual Abuse and People with Learning Difficulties* (London: FPA Education Unit).

Buchanan, A.E. and Brooks, D.W. (1990), *Deciding for Others: the Ethics of Surrogate Decision-Making* (Cambridge: Cambridge University Press).

Butler, Lord (1974), *Interim Report of the Committee on Mentally Abnormal Offenders*, Cmnd. 5698 (London: HMSO).

Butler, Lord (1975), *Report of the Committee on Mentally Abnormal Offenders*, Cmnd. 6244 (London: HMSO).

Campbell, T. and Heginbotham, C. (1991), *Mental Illness: Prejudice, Discrimination and the Law* (Aldershot: Dartmouth).

Carson, D. (1982a), "Detention of the Mentally Disordered" (1982) 146 *Loc.Gov.Rev.* 887.

Carson, D. (1982b), "Comment on 'Care in the Community: A Consultative Document on Moving Resources for Care in England' " [1982] *J.S.W.L.* 195.

Carson, D, "Mental Processes: The Mental Health Act 1983" [1983] *J.S.W.L.* 195.

Carson, D., "Registered Homes: Another Fine Mess?" [1985] *J.S.W.L.* 67.

Carson, D. (1989a), "The Meeting of Legal Rights and Therapeutic Discretion" (1989) 2 *Current Opinion in Psychiatry* 737.

Carson, D. (1989b), "Prosecuting People with Mental Handicap" [1989] *Crim.L.R.* 87.

Carson, D. (1989c), "The Sexuality of People with Learning Difficulties" [1989] *J.S.W.L.* 355.

Carson, D. (ed.) (1990), *Risk Taking in Mental Disorder* (Chichester: SLE Publications).

Carson, D., "Holding the patient to account at the gatekeeping stage" (1992) 2 *Criminal Behaviour and Mental Health* 224.

Carson, D., "Disabling Progress: the Law Commission's proposals on mentally incapacitated adults' decision-making" [1993] *J.S.W.F.L.* 304.

Carson, D. and Wexler, D.B., "New Approaches to Mental Health Law: Will the U.K. Follow the U.S. Lead, Again?" [1994] *J.S.W.F.L.* 79.

Cavadino, M. (1988), *Mental Health Law in Context: Doctor's Orders?* (Aldershot: Gower).

Cavadino, M. (1991a), "Mental Illness and Neo-Polonianism" (1991) 2 *J. Forensic Psych.* 294.

Cavadino, M. (1991b), "Community Control?" [1991] *J.S.W.F.L.* 259.

Cavadino, M. , "Commissions and Codes: A Case Study in Law and Public Administration" [1993] *Public Law* 333.

CCETSW (1992), *A Double Challenge: Working with People who have both Learning Difficulties and a Mental Illness*, CCETSW Paper 19.27 (London: Central Council for Education and Training in Social Work).

CCETSW (1993), *Requirements and Guidance for the Training of Social Workers to be considered for Approval in England and Wales under the Mental Health Act 1983*, CCETSW Paper 19.19 (revised ed.) (London: Central Council for Education and Training in Social Work).

Centre for Policy on Ageing (1984), *Home Life: A Code of Practice for Residential Care* (London: Centre for Policy on Ageing).

Centre for Policy on Ageing (1990), *Community Life: A Code of Practice for Community Care* (London: Centre for Policy on Ageing).

Chaffey, B., "Detaining the detained: an injustice" (1991) 2 *J. Forensic Psych.* 331.

Chief Medical Officer (1966), *Annual Report of the Chief Medical Officer—On the State of the Public Health* (London: HMSO).

Clare, A.W., "In Defence of Compulsory Psychiatric Intervention" [1978] 1 *Lancet* 1197.

Clare, A.W., "Therapeutic and Ethical Aspects of Electro-Convulsive Therapy: A British Perspective" (1978) 1 *Int.J.Law and Psych.* 237.

Clare, A.W. (1980), *Psychiatry in Dissent: Controversial Issues in Thought and Practice*, 2nd ed. (London: Tavistock).

Clerk, J.F. and Linsell, W.H.B. (1989), *Torts*, 16th ed. (London: Sweet and Maxwell).

Clinical Standards Advisory Group (1995), *Schizophrenia, Report of a CSAG Committee on Schizophrenia* (London: HMSO).

Cocozza, J.J. and Steadman, H.L., "The Failure of Psychiatric Predictions of Dangerousness: Clear and Convincing Evidence" (1976) 29 *Rutgers L.R.* 1084.

Cohen, D. (1981), *Broadmoor* (London: Psychology News Press).

Committee on Mental Health Review Tribunal Procedures (1978), *The Procedures of Mental Health Review Tribunals: A Discussion Paper* (London: DHSS).

Cooper, D.G. (1967), *Psychiatry and Anti-Psychiatry* (London: Tavistock).

Cope, R., "A survey of forensic psychiatrists' views on psychopathic disorder" (1993) 4 *J. Forensic Psych.* 215.

Council on Tribunals (1989), *Annual Report for 1987–88*, H.C. 102 (London: HMSO).

Council on Tribunals (1990), *Annual Report for 1988–89*, H.C. 114 (London: HMSO).

Council on Tribunals (1994), *Annual Report 1993–94*, H.C. 22 (London: HMSO).

Cox, B. (1994), *Research on Guardianship for Mentally Ill People* (London: Social Services Inspectorate).

Cretney, S.M. (1991), *Enduring Powers of Attorney: A Practitioner's Guide*, 3rd ed. (Bristol: Jordan).

Cretney *et al* (1991), *Enduring Powers of Attorney: A Report to the Lord Chancellor* (London: Lord Chancellor's Department).

Creyke, R., "Guardianship: Protection and Autonomy—Has the Right Balance been Achieved?" in Eekelaar and Pearl (eds.) (1989), *op cit.*

Crichton, J., "A New Look at *Asylum*" (1993) 17 *Psych. Bull* 758.

Crichton, J., "Supervised Discharge" (1994) 34 *Med. Sci. and Law* 319.

Crichton, J., "Psychiatric In-Patient Violence: Issues in English Law and Discipline" (1995) 35 *Med. Sci. and Law* 53.

Crichton, J. (ed.) (1995), *Psychiatric Patient Violence: Risk and Response* (London: Duckworth).

Criminal Law Revision Committee (1980a), 14th Report, *Offences against the Person*, Cmnd. 7844 (London: HMSO).

Criminal Law Revision Committee (1980b), *Working Paper on Sexual Offences* (London: HMSO).

Criminal Law Revision Committee (1984), 15th Report, *Sexual Offences* (London: HMSO).

Crown Prosecution Service (1994), *The Code for Crown Prosecutors* (London: Crown Prosecution Service).

Curran, W.J. and Harding, T.W. (1978), *The Law and Mental Health: Harmonizing Objectives* (Geneva: World Health Organisation).

Davies, Sir M. (1973), *Report of the Committee on Hospital Complaints Procedure* (London: HMSO).

Dell, S., "The Transfer of Special Hospital Patients to the NHS" (1980) 136 *Brit. J. Psych.* 222.

Dell, S., "Diminished Responsibility Reconsidered" [1982] *Crim.L.R.* 809.

Dell, S., and Robertson G. (1988), *Sentenced to Hospital* (Oxford; Oxford University Press).

Dell, S. and Smith, A., "Changes in the Sentencing of Diminished Responsibility Homicides" (1983) 142 *Br. J. Psych.* 20.

Department of Education and Science (1980), *Special Needs in Education*, Cmnd. 7996 (London: HMSO).

Department of Education and Science (1992), *Choice and Diversity. A New Framework for Schools*, Cm. 2021 (London: HMSO).

Department of Health, Circular No. H.C. (90) 21, Approval of Doctors under Section 12 of the Mental Health Act 1983.

Department of Health, Joint Health/Social Services Circular No. HC (90)23, LASSL(90)11, The Care Programme approach for People with a Mental Illness referred to the Specialist Psychiatric Services.

Department of Health, Circular No. HC(91)29, National Health Service and Community Care Act 1990: Consequential Amendments to the Mental Health Act 1993.

Department of Health (1992), *The Health of the Nation* (London: HMSO).

Department of Health (1993), *Legal Powers on the Care of Mentally Ill People in the Community, Report of the Internal Review* (London: Department of Health).

Department of Health, Circular No. LAC(93)10, Approvals and Directions for Arrangements From 1 April 1993 Made Under Schedule 8 of the National Health Service Act 1977 and Sections 21 and 29 of the National Assistance Act 1948.

Department of Health, NHS Management Executive, Health Service Guidelines HSG(93)20, Recall of Mentally Disordered Patients subject to Home Office Restrictions on Discharge.

Department of Health, NHS Management Executive, Health Service Guidelines HSG(94)5, Introduction of supervision registers for mentally ill people from 1 April 1994.

Department of Health, NHS Executive, Health Service Guidelines HSG (94)27, LASSL(94)4, Guidance on the discharge of mentally disordered people and their continuing care in the community.

Department of Health (1994), *The Health of the Nation: Key Area Handbook: Mental Illness*, 2nd ed. (London: HMSO).

Department of Health (1994), *Mental Health Act Guardianship: A Discussion Paper* (London: Department of Health).

Department of Health (1995a), In-Patients Formally Detained under The Mental Health Act 1983 and Other Legislation, England: 1987–88 to 1992–93, Department of Health Statistical Bulletin 1995/4 (London: Department of Health).

Department of Health (1995b), *Acting on Complaints: The Government's proposals in response to "Being Heard", the report of a review committee on NHS complaints procedures* (London: Department of Health).

Department of Health (1995c), *Building Bridges: A guide to arrangements for inter-agency working for the care and protection of severely mentally ill people* (enclosed with HSG(95)56 and LASSL(95)12) (London: Department of Health).

Department of Health, Circular No. LAC(95)12, Regulation of Residential Care Homes.

Department of Health, NHS Executive, Health Service Guidelines HSG (95)41, Regulation of Nursing Homes.

Department of Health et al (1989), *Caring for People: Community Care in the Next Decade and Beyond*, Cm. 89 (London: HMSO).

Department of Health and Welsh Office (1993), *Mental Health Act 1983: Code of Practice, Laid before Parliament pursuant to section 118(4) of the Mental Health Act 1983*, revised ed. (London: HMSO).

DHSS, Circular 19/71, Welfare of the Elderly: Implementation of Section 45 of the Health Services and Public Health Act 1968.

DHSS (1971), *Better Services for the Mentally Handicapped*, Cmnd. 4683 (London: HMSO).

DHSS (1975), *Better Services for the Mentally Ill*, Cmnd. 6233 (London: HMSO).

DHSS (1976), *A Review of the Mental Health Act* 1959 (London: HMSO).

DHSS (1981a), *Care in the Community: A Consultative Document on Moving Resources for Care in England* (London: DHSS).

DHSS (1981b), *Review of Leave Arrangements for Special Hospital Patients* (London:DHSS).

DHSS, Patients' Money: Accumulation of Balances in Long Stay Hospitals, January 29, 1981.

DHSS, Circular No. HC(81)5, Annex Part III, Memorandum of An Agreement for Dealing with Complaints relating to the Exercise of Clinical Judgement by Hospital Medical and Dental Staff.

DHSS, Circular No. HC(81)9, LAC(81)4, Health Service Management: Registration and Inspection of Private Nursing Homes and Mental Nursing Homes (Including Hospitals).

DHSS, Circular No. HC(83)14, Health Service Management, Representation of the People Act 1983, Electoral Representation in Mental Illness and Mental Handicap Hospitals.

DHSS, Circular No. HC(83)19, Health Services Development: Mental Health Act 1983—Keeping of Records and Giving Access to Mental Health Act Commission.

DHSS, Circular No. HC(84)12, LAC(84)9, Marriage Act 1983, Marriage of Housebound Persons and of Patients Detained under the Mental Health Act 1983.

DHSS, Circular No. LAC(86)15, Mental Health Act 1983—Approved Social Workers.

DHSS (1987), *Mental Health Act 1983: Memorandum on Parts I to VI, VIII and X* (London: HMSO).

DHSS, Circular No. HC(88)37, Health Service Management: Hospital Complaints Procedure Act 1985.

DHSS et al (1978), *Review of the Mental Health Act 1959*, Cmnd. 7320 (London: HMSO).

DHSS et al (1981), *Reform of Mental Health Legislation*, Cmnd. 8405 (London: HMSO).

DHSS and Home Office (1986), *Consultation Document: Offenders suffering from Psychopathic Disorder* (London: DHSS).

DHSS and Home Office (1987), Supervision and After-Care of Conditionally Discharged Restricted Patients—Notes for the Guidance of Supervising Psychiatrists.

Dick, D. (1991), *Report of the Panel of Inquiry appointed by West Midlands Regional Health Authority, South Birmingham Health Authority and the Special Hospitals Service Authority to Investigate the Case of Kim Kirkman* (Birmingham: West Midlands Regional Health Authority).

258

Dolan, B. and Coid, J. (1993), *Psychopathic and Antisocial Personality Disorders: Treatment and Research Issues* (London: Gaskell).

Dolan, M. *et al*, "An audit of recalls to a Special Hospital" (1993) 4 *J. Forensic Psych.* 249.

Donnelly, A. (1995), *Court of Protection Handbook*, 10th ed. (London: FT Law & Tax).

Donovan, W.M., and O'Brien, K.P., "Psychiatric Court Reports: Too Many or Too Few?" (1981) 21 *Med. Sci. and Law* 153.

Dunn, J., "Community Treatment Orders: do we need them?" (1991) 2 *J. Forensic Psych.* 153.

Edmunds, R., 'Statutory Wills for Mental Patients" (1992) 3 *J. Forensic Psych.* 350.

Eekelaar, J. and Pearl, D. (eds.) (1989), *An Aging World: Dilemmas and Challenges in Law and Social Policy* (Oxford: Clarendon).

Emerson, E., and Hatton, C. (1994), *Moving Out: The Impact of Relocation from Hospital to Community on the Quality of Life of People with Learning Disabilities* (London: HMSO).

Emery, D. (1961), *Report of the Working Party on the Special Hospitals* (London: HMSO).

Ennis, B.J. (1972), *Prisoners of Psychiatry: Mental Patients, Psychiatry and the Law* (New York, Harcourt, Brace, Jovanovich).

Ennis, B.J. and Emery, R.D. (1978), *The Rights of Mental Patients* (New York: Avon).

Ennis, B.J. and Litwack, T.R., "Psychiatry and the Presumption of Expertise: Flipping Coins in the Courtroom" (1974) 62 *Calif. L.R.* 693.

Exworthy, T. *et al*, "Section 48: an underused provision?" (1992) 16 *Psych. Bull* 97.

Fahy, T.A., "The Police as a Referral Agency for Psychiatric Emergencies—A Review" (1989) 20 *Med. Sci. and Law* 315.

Farrand, J.T., "Enduring Powers of Attorney" in Eekelaar and Pearl (eds.) (1989), *op. cit.*

Farrington, D.P. and Gunn, J. (eds.) (1985), *Aggression and Dangerousness* (Chichester: Wiley).

Faulk, M., "Mentally Disordered Offenders in an Interim Regional Medium Secure Unit" [1979] *Crim.L.R.* 686.

Fennell, P., "The Mental Health Review Tribunal: A Question of Imbalance" (1977) 4 *Brit. J. Law and Soc.* 186.

Fennell, P. (1979), Justice, Discretion and the Therapeutic State, M.Phil. Thesis, University of Kent.

Fennell, P., "Detention and Control of Informal Mentally Disordered Patients" [1984] *J.S.W.L.* 345.

Fennell, P., "Sexual Suppressants and the Mental Health Act" [1988] *Crim.L.R.* 660.

Fennell, P., "The Beverley Lewis Case: was the law to blame?" (1989) 139 *N.L.J.* 559.

Fennell, P., "Inscribing Paternalism in the Law: Consent to Treatment and Mental Disorder" (1990) 17 *J. Law and Soc.* 29.

Fennell, P., "The Mental Health Act Code of Practice" (1990) 53 *M.L.R.* 499.

Fennell, P., (1991a), "Diversion of Mentally Disordered Offenders from Custody" [1991] *Crim.L.R.* 333.

Fennell, P., (1991b), "Double Detention under the Mental Health Act 1983: A Case of Extra-Parliamentary Legislation?" [1991] *J.S.W.F.L.* 194.

Fennell, P., "Balancing Care and Control: Guardianship, Community Treatment Orders and Patient Safeguards" (1992) 15 *Int. J. Law and Psych.* 1.

Fennell, P., "The Criminal Procedure (Insanity and Unfitness to Plead) Act 1991" (1992) 55 *M.L.R.* 547.

Fennell, P., "Informal Compulsion—The Psychiatric Treatment of Juveniles under Common Law" [1992] *J.S.W.F.L.* 311.

Fennell, P., (1993), Treatment without Consent under Part IV of the Mental Health Act 1983.

Fennell, P., "Statutory Authority to Treat, Relatives and Treatment Proxies" (1994) 2 *Med. L.R.* 30.

Fennell, P., (1996), *Treatment Without Consent: Law, psychiatry and the treatment of mentally disordered people since 1845* (London: Routledge).

Fingarette, H. (1972), *The Meaning of Criminal Insanity* (London: University of California Press).

Fisher, Sir H.A.P. (1977), *Report of an Inquiry into the circumstances leading to the trial of three persons on charges arising out of the death of Maxwell Confait and the fire at 27 Doggett Road, London SE6.* Session 1977–78, H.C. 90 (London: HMSO).

Fisher, M., "Guardianship under the Mental Health Legislation: A Review" [1988] *J.S.W.L.* 316.

Flew, *A.G.N.* (1973), *Crime or Disease?* (London: Macmillan).

Floud, J. and Young, W. (1981), *Dangerousness and Criminal Justice* (London: Heinemann).

Foucault, M. (1967), *Madness and Civilisation: A History of Insanity in the Age of Reason*, trs. R. Howard (London: Tavistock).

Freeman, M.D.A., "The Rights of Children in the International Year of the Child" (1980) 33 *Current Legal Problems* 1.

Freeman, M.D.A., "Sterilising the Mentally Handicapped" in Freeman (ed.) (1988), op. cit.

Freeman, M.D.A., (ed.) (1988), *Medicine, Ethics and the Law* (London: Stevens).

Freeman, M.D.A., "Deciding for the Intellectually Impaired" (1994) 2 *Med. L.R.* 77.

Genn, H. and Genn, Y. (1989), *The Effectiveness of Representation at Tribunals*, Report to the Lord Chancellor's Department.

Glancy, J. (1974), *Revised Report of the Working Party on Security in MHS Psychiatric Hospitals* (London: DHSS).

Goffman, E. (1961), *Asylums: Essays on the Social Situation of Mental Patients and other Inmates* (New York: Doubleday).

Goldstein, J., "For Harold Laswell: Some Reflections on Human Dignity, Entrapment, Informed Consent and the Plea Bargain" (1975) 84 *Yale L.J.* 683.

Gordon, R. (1993), *Community Care Assessments: A Practical Legal Framework* (London: Longman).

Gostin, L. (1975), *A Human Condition: The Mental Health Act from 1959 to 1975: Observations, analysis and proposals for reform*, Vol. 1 (London: MIND).

Gostin, L. (1977), *A Human Condition: The law relating to mentally abnormal offenders: Observations, Analysis and proposals for reform*, Vol. 2 (London: MIND).

Gostin, L., "The Merger of Incompetency and Certification: The Illustration of Unauthorised Medical Contact in the Psychiatric Context" (1979) 2 *Int. J. Law and Psych.* 127.

Gostin, L., "Psychosurgery: A Hazardous and Unestablished Treatment? The Case for the Importation of American Legal Safeguards to Great Britain" [1982] *J.S.W.L.* 83.

Gostin, L. (1983a), "The Ideology of Entitlement: The Application of Contemporary Legal Approaches to Psychiatry" in Bean (ed.) (1986), *op. cit.*

Gostin, L. (1983b), *The Court of Protection—a legal and policy analysis of the guardianship of the estate* (London: MIND).

Gostin, L. (ed.) (1985), *Secure Provision: A review of special services for the mentally ill and mentally handicapped in England and Wales* (London: Tavistock).

Gostin, L. (1986), *Institutions Observed: towards a new concept of secure provision* (London: King's Fund).

Gostin, L. (1986), *Mental Health Services: Law and Practice* (London: Shaw).

Gostin, L. and Fennell, P. (1992), *Mental Health: Tribunal Procedure*, 2nd ed. (London: Longman).

Greenland, C. (1970), *Mental Illness and Civil Liberty* (London: Bell).

Grey, M., "Forcing Old People to Leave Their Homes: The Principle", *Community Care*, March 8 1989, p. 19.

Griew, E., "The Future of Diminished Responsibility" [1988] *Crim.L.R.* 544.

Griffiths, Sir R. (1988), *Community Care: Agenda for Action: A Report to the Secretary of State for Social Services* (London: HMSO).

Grounds, A., "Transfers of Sentenced Prisoners to Hospital" [1990] *Crim.L.R.* 544.

Grounds, A., "Risk Assessment and Management in Clinical Context" in Crichton J. (ed.) (1995), *op. cit.*

Grounds, A., *et al* (1991), Mentally Disordered Remanded Prisoners: Report to the Home Office (unpublished).

Grubb, A. (ed.) (1994), *Decision-Making and the Problems of Incompetence* (Chichester: Wiley).

Grubb, A. and Pearl, D., "Sterilisation and the Courts" (1987) 46 *C.L.J.* 439.

Grubb, A. and Pearl, D., "Sterilisation—Courts and Doctors as Decision-Makers" (1989) 48 *C.L.J.* 380.

Grubin, D.H., "Unfit to Plead in England and Wales, 1976–88: A Survey" (1991) 158 *Brit. J. Psych.* 540.

Grubin, D., "What Constitutes Fitness to Plead?" [1993] *Crim.L.R.* 748.

Gunn, J., "The Law and the Mentally Abnormal Offender in England and Wales" (1979) 2 *Int. J. Law and Psych.* 199.

Gunn, J., Maden, T. and Swinton, M. (1991), *Mentally Disordered Prisoners* (London: Home Office).

Gunn, J., Maden, T. and Swinton, M., "How many prisoners should be in hospital?" (1991) 31 *Home Office Research Bulletin* 9.

Gunn, J. and Joseph, P., "Remands to hospital for psychiatric reports: a study of psychiatrists' attitudes to section 35 of the Mental Health Act 1983" 17 *Psych. Bull* 197.

Gunn, M., "Mental Health Act Guardianship: where now?" [1986] *J.S.W.L.* 144.

Gunn, M., "Judicial Review of Hospital Admissions and Treatment in the Community under the Mental Health Act 1983" [1986] *J.S.W.L.* 290.

Gunn, M., "Treatment and Mental Handicap" (1987) 16 *Anglo-American L.R.* 242.

Gunn, M., "*R. v. Secretary of State for the Home Department, ex p Stroud*" (1993) 4 *J. Forensic Psych.* 330.

Gunn, M., "The Meaning of Incapacity" (1994) 2 *Med. L.R.* 8.

Hamilton, J.R., "The Special Hospitals", in Gostin, L. (ed.) (1985), *op. cit.*

Harlow, C., "Self Defence: Public Right or Private Privilege" [1974] *Crim.L.R.* 528.

Harvey, C., "Forcing Old People to Leave Their Homes: The Practice", *Community Care*, March 8 1979, p. 20.

Health Advisory Service (1994), *Comprehensive Mental Health Services* (London: Health Advisory Service).

Health Advisory Service and Social Services Inspectorate (1988), *Report on the Services provided by Broadmoor Hospital.*

Heginbotham, C., "Sterilising people with mental handicaps", in McLean, SAM. (ed.) (1989), *Legal Issues in Human Reproduction* (Aldershot: Gower).

Hepworth, D., "The Influence of the Concept of 'Danger' on the Assessment of 'Danger to Self or Others' " (1982) 22 *Med. Sci. and L.* 245.

Herbst, K. and Gunn, J. (eds.) (1991), *The Mentally Disordered Offender* (London: Butterworth-Heinemann).

Heywood, N.A. and Massey, A. (1991), *Court of Protection Practice, 12th ed.* (London: Stevens).

Hodgins, S. (ed.) (1993), *Mental Disorder and Crime* (London: Sage).

Hodgins, S., "*The Criminality of Mentally Disordered Persons*", in Hodgins S. (ed.) (1993), *op. cit.*

Hoggett, B., "Legal Aspects of Secure Provision", in Gostin (ed.) (1985), *op. cit.*

Hoggett, B., "The Royal Prerogative in Relation to the Mentally Disordered: Resurrection, Resuscitation or Rejection?" in Freeman (1988), *op. cit.*

Home Office (1990), Circular No. 66/90, *Provision for Mentally Disordered Offenders* (London: Home Office).

Home Office (1995a), *Statistics of Mentally Disordered Offenders, England and Wales 1993, Home Office Statistical Bulletin Issue* 1/95 (London: Home Office).

Home Office (1995b), *Police and Criminal Evidence Act 1984* (s. 60(1)(a) and s. 66): *Codes of Practice* (London: HMSO).

Home Office (1995c), *Circular No. 12/95, Mentally Disordered Offenders: Interagency working* (London: Home Office).

Home Office and DHSS (1987), *Report of the Interdepartmental Working Group of Home Office and DHSS Officials on Mentally Disturbed Offenders in the Prison System in England and Wales* (London: Home Office).

House of Commons Health Committee (1993), *Community Supervision Orders, Fifth Report, Session 1992–93,* H.C. 667 (London: HMSO).

House of Commons Health Committee (1994), *Better off in the Community? The Care of People who are seriously mentally ill, First Report, Session 1993–94,* H.C. 102 (London: HMSO).

House of Commons Public Accounts Committee (1994), *Looking After the Financial Affairs of People with Mental Incapacity,* 39th Report, Session 1993–94, H.C. 308 (London: HMSO).

House of Commons Social Services Committee (1985), *Community Care, with special reference to adult mentally ill and mentally handicapped people, Second Report, Session 1985–86*, H.C. 13 (London: HMSO).

House of Lords (1989), *Report of the Select Committee on Murder and Life Imprisonment, Session 1988–89*, H.L. 78 (London: HMSO).

House of Lords (1994), *Report of the Select Committee on Medical Ethics, Session 1993–94*, H.L. 21 (London: HMSO).

Howlett, M.V., "Mental Patients and the Right to Litigate" [1978–79] *J.S.W.L.* 337.

Ingleby, D. (ed.) (1981), *Critical Psychiatry: the Politics of Mental Health* (Harmondsworth: Penguin).

Isaac, B.C., Minty, E.B. and Morrison, R.M., "Children in Care—the Association with Mental Disorder in the Parents" (1986) 16 *Brit. J. Social Work* 325.

Jacob, J., "The Right of the Mental Patient to his Psychosis" (1976) 39 *M.L.R.* 17.

James, A., "The Criminal Procedure (Insanity and Unfitness to Plead) Act 1991" (1993) 4 *J. Forensic Psych.* 285.

James, D.V. and Hamilton, L.W., "The Clerkenwell scheme: assessing the efficacy and cost of a psychiatric liaison service to a magistrates' court" (1991) 303 *B.M.J.* 282.

Jones, K., "The Limitations of the Legal Approach to Mental Health" (1980) 3 *Int. J. Law and Psych.* 1.

Jones, K., "Scull's Dilemma" (1982) 141 *Brit. J. Psych.* 221.

Jones, K. (1993), *Asylums and After. A Revised History of the Mental Health Services from the early 18th Century to the 1990s* (London: Athlone).

Jones, R. (1994), *Mental Health Act Manual*, 4th ed. (London: Sweet & Maxwell).

Jordan, B., Review of Bean (1980), *op. cit.*, in [1981] *J.S.W.L.* 383.

Joseph, P., "Mentally disordered offenders: diversion from the criminal justice system" (1990) 1 *J. Forensic Psych.* 133.

Kennedy, I. and Grubb, A., "The Law Commission's Proposals: An Introduction" (1994) 2 *Med. L.R.* 1.

King, M., "Welfare and Justice" in King, M. (ed.) (1981), *Childhood, Welfare and Justice* (London: Batsford).

King, M. and Trowell, J. (1992), *Children's Welfare and the Law: The Limits of Legal Intervention* (London: Sage).

Kittrie, N.N. (1971), *The Right to be Different* (Baltimore: Johns Hopkins Press).

Laing, R.D. (1959), *The Divided Self* (London: Tavistock).

Laing, R.D. and Esterson, A. (1971), *Sanity, Madness and the Family*, 2nd ed. (London: Tavistock).

Lanham, D., "*Arresting the Insane*" [1974] *Crim.L.R.* 515.

Law Commission (1976), *The Incapacitated Principal, Working Paper* No. 69 (London: HMSO).

Law Commission (1982) *Time Restrictions on the Presentation of Divorce and Nullity Petitions*, Law Com. No. 116 (London: HMSO).

Law Commission (1983), *The Incapacitated Principal*, Law. Com. No. 122, Cmnd. 8977 (London: HMSO).

Law Commission (1989), *A Criminal Code for England and Wales*, Law Com. No. 177 (London: HMSO).

Law Commission (1991), *Mentally Incapacitated Adults and Decision-Making: An Overview*, Consultation Paper No. 119 (London: HMSO).

Law Commission (1993a), *Mentally Incapacitated Adults and Decision-Making: A New Jurisdiction*, Consultation Paper No. 128 (London: HMSO).

Law Commission (1993b), *Mentally Incapacitated Adults and Decision-Making: Medical Treatment and Research*, Consultation Paper No. 129 (London: HMSO).

Law Commission (1993c), *Mentally Incapacitated and Other Vulnerable Adults: Public Law Protection*, Consultation Paper No. 130 (London: HMSO).

Law Commission (1995), *Mental Incapacity*, Law. Com. No. 231 (London: HMSO).

Law Society, Mental Health Sub-Committee (1989), *Decision-Making and Mental Incapacity: A Discussion Document* (London: The Law Society)

Law Society, Mental Health and Disability Sub-Committee in conjunction with MIND (1994), *Being Heard, Response to the Report of the Wilson Committee on NHS Complaints Procedures* (London: The Law Society).

Lawson, A. (1966), *The Recognition of Mental Illness in London: A Study of the Social Processes determining Compulsory Admission to an Observation Unit in a London Hospital* (London: Oxford University Press).

Le Mesurier, A.A., "The Duly Authorised Officer" (1949) 1 *Brit. J. Psych. Soc. Work* 45.

Lee, R. and Morgan, D., "Sterilisation and Mental Handicap: Sapping the Strength of the State?" (1988) 15 *J. Law and Soc.* 229.

Lee, R. and Morgan, D. (1993), *Death Rites: Law and ethics at the end of life* (London: Routledge).

Letts, P. (1990), *Managing Other People's Money* (London: Age Concern).

Lewis, P. (1980), *Psychiatric Probation Orders: Roles and Expectations of Probation Officers and Psychiatrists* (Cambridge: Institute of Criminology).

Littlewood, R. and Lipsedge, M. (1993), *Aliens and Alienists: Ethnic Minorities and Psychiatry*, 2nd ed. (Harmondsworth: Penguin).

Loder, M. (1981), *The Mind Benders: The Use of Drugs in Psychiatry* (London: MIND).

McCreadie, C. (1991), *Elder Abuse: An Exploratory Study* (London: Age Concern Institute of Gerontology).

MacDermott, J. (1981) *Report of the Northern Ireland Review Committee on Mental Health Legislation* (Belfast: HMSO).

Macfarlane, A.B., "Court of Protection" (1991) 33 *L.S. Gaz.* 15.

Mackay, R.D., "Fact and Fiction about the Insanity Defence" [1990] Crim.L.R. 247.

Mackay, R.D., "Dangerous Patients, Third Party Safety and Psychiatrist's Duties—Walking the Tarasoff Tightrope" (1990) 30 *Med. Sci. and Law* 52.

MacMillan, H.P. (1926), *Report of the Royal Commission on Lunacy and Mental Disorders* 1924–1926, Cmd. 2700 (London: HMSO).

Martin, J.P. (1984), *Hospitals in Trouble* (Oxford: Blackwell).

Masson, J., "Adolescent Crises and Parental Power" [1991] *Fam. Law* 528.

MENCAP (1989), *Competency and Consent to Medical Treatment, Report of the Working Party on the Legal, Medical and Ethical Issues of Mental Handicap* (London: MENCAP).

Mental Health Act Commission (1985, 1987, 1989, 1991, 1993, 1995), *First, Second, Third, Fourth, Fifth and Sixth Biennial Reports* (London: HMSO).

Mental Health Act Commission, Practice Note 1, *Guidance on the Administration of Clozapine and other treatments requiring blood tests under the provisions of Part IV of the Mental Health Act (1993)*; *Practice Note 2, Nurses, the Administration of Medicine for Mental Disorder and the Mental Health Act*

(1994); Practice Note 3, Section 5(2) of the 1983 Mental Health Act and Transfers (1994).

Mental Health Review Tribunals for England, Annual Report 1993 (London: Department of Health).

Mental Health Review Tribunals for England and Wales, Annual Report 1994 (London: Department of Health).

Mental Health Foundation (1994), *Creating Community Care, Report of the Mental Health Foundation Inquiry into Community Care for People with Severe Mental Illness* (London: Mental Health Foundation).

Mental Welfare Commission for Scotland (1970), *No Folks of Their Own* (Edinburgh: HMSO).

Mental Welfare Commission for Scotland (1970), *A Duty to Care* (Edinburgh: HMSO).

Mental Welfare Commission for Scotland (1975), *No Place to Go* (Edinburgh: HMSO).

Mental Welfare Commission for Scotland (1981), *Does the patient come first? An account of the work of the Commission between 1975 and 1980* (Edinburgh: HMSO).

Mental Welfare Commission for Scotland (1992), *Guardianship in Scotland*, by Richards, H. and McGregor, C. (Edinburgh: HMSO).

Mental Welfare Commission for Scotland, Annual Reports (Edinburgh: Mental Welfare Commission for Scotland).

Merrison, Sir A. (1979), *Report of the Royal Commission on the National Health Service*, Cmnd. 7615 (London: HMSO).

Mill, J.S. (1859), *On Liberty* (reprinted as Three Essays: *On Liberty, Representative Government, The Subjection of Women*) (London: Oxford University Press).

Miller, D.W., "The Mentally Disordered Patient in Hospital" (1975) 125 *New L.J.* 884.

Milner, N., "Models of Rationality and Mental Health Rights" (1981) 4 *Int. J. Law and Psych.* 35.

MIND (1978), *The Great Debate: MIND's comments on the White Paper on the review of the Mental Health Act* 1959 (London: MIND).

Mittler, P. (1979), *People not Patients: Problems and Policies in Mental Handicap* (London: Methuen).

Mokhtar, A.E., and Hogbin, P., "Police May Underuse Section 136" (1993) 33 *Med. Sci. and Law* 188.

Monahan, J., "John Stuart Mill and the Liberty of the Mentally Ill: A Historical Note" (1977) 134 *American J. of Psych.* 1428.

Monahan, J., "Mental Disorder and Violence: Another Look", in Hodgins (ed.) (1993), *op. cit.*

Morris, G.H. (1978), *The Insanity Defense: A Blueprint for Legislative Reform* (Farnborough: Lexington).

Morris, P. (1969), *Put Away: a Sociological Study of Institutions for the Mentally Retarded* (London: Routledge and Kegan Paul).

NACRO Mental Health Advisory Committee (1994), *Diverting Mentally Disturbed Offenders from Custodial Remands and Sentences* (London: National Association for the Care and Resettlement of Offenders).

National Audit Office (1994), *Report by the Comptroller and Auditor General, Looking After the Financial Affairs of People with Mental Incapacity*, Session 1993–94, H.C. 258 (London: HMSO).

National Schizophrenia Fellowship (1990), *Provision of Community Services for Mentally Ill People and their Carers* (Kingston: National Schizophrenia Fellowship).

NCCL (1973), *The Rights of the Mentally Abnormal Offender: The National Council for Civil Liberties' Evidence to the Butler Committee* (London: National Council for Civil Liberties, now Liberty).

NHS Management Executive, Guide to Con· ·nt for Examination and Treatment (published with Department of Health Circular No. H.C. (90)2).

Nicholls, D., "Legal Arrangements for Managing the Finances of Mentally Disabled Adults in Scotland" [1992] *J.S.W.r.L.* 193.

Norman, A. (1980), *Rights and Risk: A Discussion Document on Civil Liberty in Old Age* (London: National Corporation for the Care of Old People, now Centre for Policy on Ageing).

Norman, A. (1987), *Severe Dementia: the provision of long stay care* (London: Centre for Policy on Ageing).

North, C., Ritchie, J. and Ward, K. (1993), *Factors Influencing the Implementation of the Care Programme Approach* (London: HMSO).

Oram, E.V., "The Case for More Informal Admissions" (1972) 2 (19) *Social Work Today* 21.

Parker, E. and Tennant, G., "The 1959 Mental Health Act and Mentally Abnormal Offenders: A Comparative Study" (1979) 19 *Med. Sci. and Law* 29.

Peay, J., "Mental Health Review Tribunals: just or efficacious safeguards?" (1981) 5 *Law and Human Behaviour* 161.

Peay, J., "Mental Health Review Tribunals and the Mental Health (Amendment) Act" [1982] *Crim.L.R.* 794.

Peay, J., "Offenders suffering from Psychopathic Disorder: The Rise and Demise of a Consultation Document" (1988) 23 *Brit. J. Criminol.* 67.

Peay, J. (1989), *Tribunals on Trial: A Study of Decision-Making under the Mental Health Act 1983* (Oxford: Clarendon Press).

Percy, Lord (1957), *Report of the Royal Commission on the Law relating to Mental Illness and Mental Deficiency 1954–1957*, Cmd. 169 (London: HMSO).

Porter, R. (1987), *Mind-Forg'd Manacles: A History of Madness in England from the Restoration to the Regency* (London: Athlone).

Price, D.P.T., "*Civil commitment of the mentally ill: compelling arguments for reform*" (1992) 2 *Med. L.R.* 321.

Prichard, J.C. (1835), Treatise on Insanity and other Disorders affecting the Mind.

Prins, H., "A Danger to Themselves and Others (Social Workers and Potentially Dangerous Clients)" (1975) 5 *Brit. J. Social Work* 297.

Prins, H. (1986), *Dangerous Behaviour: The Law and Mental Disorder* (London: Tavistock).

Prins, H. (1993), *Report of the Committee of Inquiry into the Death in Broadmoor Hospital of Orville Blackwood and a Review of the Deaths of Two Other Afro-Caribbean Patients. "Big, Black and Dangerous?"* (London: Special Hospitals Service Authority).

Prins, H. (1995), *Offenders, Deviants or Patients? An Introduction to the Study of Socio-Forensic Problems*, 2nd ed. (London: Tavistock).

Prior, P.M., "The Approved Social Worker—Reflections on Origins" (1992) 22 *Brit. J. Social Work* 105.

Quinton, D. and Rutter, M., "Parents with children in care. 1. Current circumstances and parenting" (1984) 25 *Psychology and Psychiatry* 211.

Radnor, Lord (1908), *Report of the Royal Commission on the Care and Control of the Feeble-Minded 1904–1908*, Cd. 4202 (London: HMSO).

Reed, J. (1992), *Review of Health and Social Services for Mentally Disordered Offenders and others requiring similar services: Final Summary Report*, Cm. 2088 (London: HMSO).

Reed, J. (1994a), *Report of the Working Group on High Security and Related Psychiatric Provision* (London: Department of Health).

Reed, J. (1994b), *Report of the Department of Health and Home Office Working Group on Psychopathic Disorder* (London: Department of Health and Home Office).

Richardson, G. (1993), *Law, Process and Custody: Prisoners and Patients* (London: Weidenfeld and Nicholson).

Richardson, G., "Openness, Order and Regulation in a Therapeutic Setting" in Crichton (ed.) (1995), *op. cit.*

Ritchie, J.H. *et al* (1994), *Report of the Inquiry into the Care and treatment of Christopher Clunis* (London: HMSO).

Robb, E. (1967), *Sans Everything: A Case to Answer* (presented on behalf of AEGIS). (London: Nelson).

Robertson, A.H. and Merrills, J.G. (1993), *Human Rights in Europe: A study of the European Convention on Human Rights*, 3rd ed. (Manchester: Manchester University Press).

Robertson, G., "Informed consent to medical treatment" (1981) 97 *L.Q.R.* 102.

Robertson, G., "The Restricted Hospital Order" (1989) 13 *Psych. Bull.* 4.

Rogers, A. and Faulkner, A. (1987), *A Place of Safety: MIND's research into police referrals to the psychiatric services* (London: MIND).

Rollin, H.R. (1969), *The Mentally Abnormal Offender and the Law* (Oxford: Pergamon).

Rosenhan, D.C., "On Being Sane in Insane Places" (1973) 179 *Science* 250.

Rosettenstein, D., "Living Wills in the United States: The Role of the Family" in Eekelaar and Pearl (eds.) (1989), *op. cit.*

Roth, M. and Bluglass, R. (eds.) (1985), *Psychiatry, Human Rights and the Law* (Cambridge: Cambridge University Press).

Roy, R.G., "*A Brief Study of Night Calls*" (1966) 13 *Case Conference* 97.

Roy, R.G., "Problems of Compulsory Admissions" [1968] 1 *Lancet* 83.

Royal College of Psychiatrists (1981), *Mental Health Commissions: The Recommendations of the Royal College of Psychiatrists* (Approved by Council, June 16).

Royal College of Psychiatrists (1987), *Community Treatment Orders—A Discussion Document* (London: Royal College of Psychiatrists).

Royal College of Psychiatrists (1989), *Consent of Non-Volitional Patients and De Facto Detention of Informal Patients*, Council Report CR6.

Royal College of Psychiatrists (1991), *Good Medical Practice in the Aftercare of Potentially Violent or Vulnerable Patients Discharged from In-patient Psychiatric Treatment*, Council Report CR12.

Royal College of Psychiatrists (1993), *Community Supervision Orders* (London: Royal College of Psychiatrists).

Royal College of Psychiatrists *et al* (1980), *Behaviour Modification: Report of a Joint Working Party to Formulate Ethical Guidelines for the Conduct of Programmes of Behaviour Modification in the National Health Service: A Consultative Document with Suggested Guidelines* (London: HMSO).

Ryan, J., with Thomas, F. (1987), *The Politics of Mental Handicap*, revised ed. (London: Free Association Books).

Sandland, R., "Minors and Consent to Treatment" (1993) 4 *J. Forensic Psych.* 138.

Scott, P.D. (1975), *Has Psychiatry Failed in the Treatment of Offenders? Fifth Dennis Carroll Memorial Lecture* (London: ISTD).

Scottish Action on Dementia (1987), *Dementia: Guardianship* (Edinburgh: Scottish Action on Dementia).

Scottish Action on Dementia (1988): *Dementia and the Law: The Challenge Ahead* (Edinburgh: Scottish Action on Dementia).

Scottish Home and Health Department (1990), *Mental Health (Scotland) Act 1984: Code of Practice* (Edinburgh: HMSO).

Scottish Law Commission (1991), *Discussion Paper No. 94, Mentally Disabled Adults: Legal Arrangements for Managing their Welfare and Finances* (Edinburgh: Scottish Law Commission).

Scottish Law Commission (1993), *Discussion Paper No. 96, Mentally Disordered and Vulnerable Adults: Public Authority Powers* (Edinburgh: Scottish Law Commission).

Scottish Law Commission (1995), *Report on Incapable Adults*, Scot. Law. Com. No. 151, Cm. 2962 (Edinburgh: HMSO).

Scott-Moncrieff, L., "Injustice in Forensic Psychiatry" (1993) 4 *J. Forensic Psych.* 97.

Scull, A.T. (1979), Museums of Madness: *The Social Organisation of Insanity in Nineteenth Century England* (London: Allen Lane).

Scull, A.T. (ed.) (1981), *Madhouses, Mad-doctors and Madmen: The Social History of Psychiatry in the Victorian Era* (London: Athlone Press).

Sedgwick, P. (1982), *Psychopolitics* (London: Pluto Press).

Seebohm, F. (1968), *Report of the Committee on the Local Authority and Allied Personal Social Services*, Cmnd. 3703 (London: HMSO).

Sensky, T. *et al*, "Compulsory Treatment in the Community. I. A Controlled study of compulsory community treatment with extended leave under the Mental Health Act: special characteristics of patients treated and impact of treatment. II. A controlled study of patients whom psychiatrists would recommend for compulsory treatment in the community." (1991) 158 *Brit. J. Psych.* 792.

Sheppard, D. (1995), *Learning the Lessons. Mental Health Inquiry Reports published in England and Wales between 1969–1994 and their recommendations for improving practice* (London: The Zito Trust).

Showalter, E. (1987), *The Female Malady: Women, Madness and English Culture 1830–1980* (London: Virago).

Skegg, P.D.G., "A Justification for Medical Procedures Performed without Consent" (1974) 90 *L.Q.R.* 512.

Skegg, P.D.G. (1988), *Law, Ethics and Medicine: Studies in Medical Law* (Oxford: Clarendon).

Smith *et al*, "Transfers from Prison for Urgent Psychiatric Treatment: a study of section 48 admission" (1992) 304 *B.M.J.* 967.

Social Services Inspectorate (1990), *Caring for Quality: Guidelines on Standards for Residential Homes for Elderly People* (London: HMSO).

Social Services Inspectorate (1991), *Approved Social Workers: Developing a Service* (London: Department of Health).

Social Services Inspectorate (1992), *Confronting Elder Abuse* (London: HMSO).

Social Services Inspectorate (1993), *No Longer Afraid: The Safeguard of older people in domestic settings* (London : HMSO).

Social Services Inspectorate (1994), *It Could Never Happen Here! Inter Agency Study Day Report* (London: Social Services Inspectorate).

Social Services Inspectorate (1995), *Social Services Departments and the Care Programme Approach: An Inspection* (London: Department of Health).

Soothill, K.L. *et al*, "Subsequent Dangerousness among Compulsory Hospital Patients" (1980) 20 *Brit. J. Criminol.* 289.

Soothill, K.L. *et al*, "Compulsory Admissions to Mental Hospitals in Six Countries" (1981) 4 *Int. J. Law and Psych.* 327.

Soothill, K.L. *et al*, "Compulsory Hospital Admissions: dangerous decision?" (1990) 30 *Med. Sci. and Law* 17.

Speaker's Conference on Electoral Law (1968), *Final Report of the Conference on Electoral Law*, Cmnd. 3550 (London: HMSO).

Speaker's Conference Electoral Law (1973), *Letter dated 25th October 2973 from Mr Speaker to the Prime Minister*, Cmnd. 5469 (London: HMSO).

Special Hospitals Service Authority (1993), *The Use of Seclusion and the Alternative Management of Disturbed Behaviour within the Special Hospitals* (London: Special Hospitals Service Authority).

Special Hospitals Service Authority (1994), *Complaints in the Special Hospitals, Statement of Policy* (London: Special Hospitals Service Authority).

Spokes, J. (1988), *Report of the Committee of Inquiry into the Care and After-care of Miss Sharon Campbell*, Cm. 440 (London: HMSO).

Steadman, H.J. and Cocozza, J.J. (1974), *Careers of the Criminally Insane: Excessive Social Control of Deviance* (Lexington, Neb: D.C. Heath).

Steadman, H.J., "Attempting to Protect Patients' Rights under a Medical Model" (1979) 2 *Int. J. Law and Psych.* 185.

Stern, K., "Advance Directives" (1994) 2 *Med. L.R.* 57.

Sugarman, P. and Collins, P., "Informal admission to secure units: a paradoxical situation" (1992) 3 *J. Forensic Psych.* 477.

Szasz, T.S. (1961), *The Myth of Mental Illness: Foundations of a Theory of Personal Conduct* (New York: Harper and Row).

Szasz, T.S. (1963), *Law, Liberty and Psychiatry* (New York: Macmillan).

Szasz, T.S. (1970), *Ideology and Insanity: Essays on the Psychiatric Dehumanisation of Man* (New York: Doubleday).

Tomlin, S. (1989), *Abuse of Elderly People: an unnecessary and preventable problem* (London: British Geriatrics Society).

Turk, V. and Brown, H., "The Sexual Abuse of Adults with Learning Disabilities: Results of a Two Year Incidence Survey" (1993) 6 *Mental Handicap Research* 193.

United Nations (1971), *Declaration on the Rights of Mentally Retarded Persons, General Assembly Resolution 2856 (XXVI)*, 20 December 1971 (New York: United Nations).

United Nations (1975), *Declaration on the Rights of Disabled Persons, General Assembly Resolution 3447 (XXX)*, 9 December 1975 (New York: United Nations).

United Nations (1994), *The Standard Rules on the Equalization of Opportunities for Persons with Disabilities, adopted by the United Nations General Assembly at its 48th session on 20 December 1993* (Resolution 48/96) (New York: United Nations).

Unsworth, C. (1987), *The Politics of Mental Health Legislation* (Oxford: Clarendon Press).

Unsworth, C. "Law and Lunacy in Psychiatry's 'Golden Age' " (1993) 13 *O.J.L.S.* 479.

Walker, N.D. (1973), *Crime and Insanity in England. Vol. 1: The Historical Perspective* (Edinburgh: Edinburgh University Press).

Walker, N.D., "Butler v. the CLRC and Others" [1981] *Crim.L.R.* 596.

Walker, N.D. and McCabe, S. (1973), *Crime and Insanity in England. Vol 2: New Solutions and New Problems* (Edinburgh: Edinburgh University Press).

Ward, A.D. (1990), *The Power to Act: the development of Scots Law for Mentally handicapped people* (Glasgow: Scottish Society for the Mentally Handicapped).

Warnock, M. (1978), *Report of the Committee of Enquiry into the Education of Handicapped Children and Young People,* Cmnd. 7212 (London: HMSO).

Webb, D., "Wise after the Event: Some Comments on 'A Danger to Themselves and Others' [Prins, 1975]" (1976) 6 *Brit. J. Social Work* 91.

West, D.J. and Walk, A. (1977) *Daniel McNaughten: His Trial and the Aftermath* (London: Gaskell).

Wexler, D.B. (1990), *Therapeutic Jurisprudence: The Law as a Therapeutic Agent* (Durham, N.C.: Carolina Academic Press).

White, S., "Insanity Defences and Magistrates' Courts" [1991] *Crim.L.R.* 501.

White, S., "The Criminal Procedure (Insanity and Unfitness to Plead) Act 1991" [1992] *Crim.L.R.* 4.

Whitehead, J.A. and Ahmed, M., "Chance, Mental Illness and Crime" [1970] 1 *Lancet* 137.

Wilkinson, P. and Sharpe, M., "What happens to patients discharged by Mental Health Review Tribunals?" (1993) 17 Psych. Bull 337.

Williams, G.L. (1983), *Textbook of Criminal Law, 2nd ed.* (London: Stevens).

Williamson, C. (1991), Hearing patients' appeals against continued compulsory detention, 2nd ed. (National Association of Health Authorities and Trusts).

Wilson, A. (1994), *Being heard: The report of a review committee on NHS complaints procedures* (London: Department of Health).

Wilson, M. (1993), *Mental Health and Britain's Black Communities* (London: King's Fund Centre).

Wing, J.K. (1978), *Reasoning about Madness* (Oxford: Oxford University Press).

Wood, Sir J., "The Impact of Legal Modes of Thought upon the Practice of Psychiatry" (1982) 140 *Brit. J. Psych.* 551.

Wood, Sir J., "Reform of the Mental Health Act 1983: An Effective Tribunal System" (1993) 162 *Brit. J. Psych.* 14.

Wootton, B. (assisted by Seal, V.G. and Chambers, R.) (1959), *Social Science and Social Pathology* (London: Allen and Unwin).

Wootton, B., "Diminished Responsibility—A Layman's view" (1960) 76 *L.Q.R.* 224.

Wootton, B., "Psychiatry, Ethics and the Criminal Law" (1980) 136 *Brit. J.Psych.* 525.

World Health Organisation (1990), *International Classification of impairments, disabilities and handicaps* (Geneva: World Health Organisation).

World Health Organisation (1992), *The ICD–10 Classification of Mental and Behavioural Disorders: Clinical descriptions and diagnostic guidelines* (Geneva: World Health Organisation).

Younghusband, E.L. (1959), *Report of the Working Party on Social Workers in the Local Authority Health and Welfare Services* (London: HMSO).

270

INDEX

ABORTION,
mothers with mental disorders, and, 233
necessity of treatment, and, 136
referral to High Court, 137

ABSCONDERS AND ESCAPERS,
escaping from,
England and Wales, 166
legal custody, 164–5
going absent without leave, 165–6
hospital remands, 166
interim hospital orders, 166
related offences, 164
Section 2, and, 83

ABUSE. See also CIVIL LIABILITY; HARM;
OFFENCES
protection from, 217–18, 223, 227

ABWOR. See ASSISTANCE BY WAY OF
REPRESENTATION

ACCESS,
patients, to. See ENTRY (right of)

ACCUSED PERSONS,
Crown Court's power to find,
not guilty due to insanity, 15, 110–13
unfit to plead due to mental disorder,
15, 108–10
remand to hospital for treatment by
Crown Court, 15, 106–8

ADMISSION,
assessment, for. See ASSESSMENTS
(admission for)
compulsory. See COMPULSORY ADMISSION
confessions. See CONFESSIONS
documents. See DOCUMENTS
emergency treatment, for. See EMERGENCY
TREATMENT (admission for (Section
4))
informal, to hospitals. See INFORMAL
PATIENTS
NHS hospitals, to, 18–21
private mental nursing home, to, 23–4
regional secure units, to, 21
special hospitals, to, 22–3
treatment, for. See TREATMENT (admission
for)

ADOPTION,
children with mentally disordered
parents, of, 232

AFFAIRS, RIGHT TO LOOK AFTER OWN,
armed forces pay and pensions, right to,
239
assumption in favour, 237
benefits, entitlement to, 238–9
Court of Protection taking over once
patient incapable, 238. See also
COURT OF PROTECTION
enduring powers of attorney, 240–2
funds administered by government
departments, right to, 239

AFFAIRS, RIGHT TO LOOK AFTER OWN—cont.
pensions of MPs, clergymen and some
local authority employees, rights
over, 239
powers under contract or trust, 239–40
Royal Warrant, under, 239
statutory powers, 238–9

AFFIDAVIT,
sworn, regarding Court of Protection,
243–4

AFTER-CARE UNDER SUPERVISION,
application for, 14, 67, 70, 169–70
community responsible medical officer,
169–71
consultation, 170–71
discharge by mental health review
tribunal, 200
duration of, 170
judicial review used to support duty to
provide, 160, 209
leave of absence, 161
review by mental health review tribunals,
178. See also MENTAL HEALTH REVIEW
TRIBUNALS
use of, 200
written recommendations, 169

ALCOHOL ABUSE,
psychopathic disorders, and, 35
social services duty to provide,
residential care, 210
services, 213

AMBULANCE SERVICES, 83

APPLICATIONS,
admission to special hospital, for, 22
after-care for, 169–70
compulsory admission, for,
related to in-patients, 10
under Part II of 1983 Act, 12–14
Court of Protection, and, 243–4
enduring power of attorney, to register,
240–1
guardianship, for, 219–20
habeas corpus, for, 174–5
mental health review tribunals, to,
177–81
supervision, after-care, for, 14, 169–71

APPROVED SOCIAL WORKERS,
applications for,
compulsory admission, 12
guardianship, 219–22
supervision of detained person after
departure from hospital, 14,
169–71
appointment as nearest relative, 62
definition, 53
detention in place of safety, and, 98
inter-disciplinary co-operation, 74

271

273

287

288